RAYFORD W. LOGAN

*and the Dilemma of the
African-American
Intellectual*

๕

RAYFORD W. LOGAN

and the Dilemma of the African-American Intellectual

Kenneth Robert Janken

THE UNIVERSITY OF MASSACHUSETTS PRESS
Amherst

To the memory of my grandmother,
Rose Morhar (1907–1975)

Library of Congress Cataloging-in-Publication Data

Janken, Kenneth Robert, 1956–
Rayford W. Logan and the dilemma of the African-American
intellectual / Kenneth Robert Janken.
p.   cm.
Includes bibliographical references and index.
ISBN 0–87023–858–2 (alk. paper)
1. Logan, Rayford Whittingham, 1897–   . 2. Historians—United
States—Biography.   3. Afro-American historians—Biography.
I. Title.
E175.5.L64J36   1993
973'.07202—dc20
[B]   92–43282
                                  CIP

British Library Cataloguing in Publication data are available.

Chapter 6, *What the Negro Wants* and the "Silent South," appeared first in
North Carolina Historical Review 70 (April 1993).

TABLE OF CONTENTS

PREFACE

This book grew out of a 1989 suggestion by my dissertation adviser, David Levering Lewis, that I might find an interesting story in Rayford Logan's diaries, which are deposited in the Library of Congress. At the time, I knew what most historians of the black American experience did about the now dimly remembered Logan: that he had written a useful book called *The Betrayal of the Negro* and that he minted the phrase "the nadir" to describe the position of African Americans between Reconstruction and World War I. The diaries convinced me that there was more to Logan than a few books or acute turns of phrase. As Logan was a distinguished African-American intellectual and scholar; a Pan-Africanist and civil rights activist; an associate of better-known black leaders like W. E. B. Du Bois, A. Philip Randolph, Walter White, Carter G. Woodson, and Mary McLeod Bethune; and an inveterate politicker and socializer among the black bourgeoisie, his life is an excellent perch from which to observe and analyze the intellectual and social history of the African-American elite—what Du Bois called the Talented Tenth—during more than half of the twentieth century. This swath of black history and Logan's role in it as both participant and griot is one major theme of this work.

Logan kept a diary for more than four decades, from 1940 until just before his death in 1982. The eleven years, to 1951, that are, in 1992, open to scholars are remarkable both for their regularity—he wrote something several times a week—and candor. Reading through it, one is transported to an era that is both long past and close by. The struggle, often futile, of one talented black scholar for recognition from the white world is narrated in excruciating detail; it is a story that has been played out countless times, and the politics of race in the academy is a second major theme.

The diary, though, yields keen observations on an array of African-American life, and especially the activities of the Talented Tenth. A frequent traveler, Logan was careful to enter into the record dozens of examples of the hazards, humiliations, inconveniences and paradoxes that awaited African Americans on the Jim Crow trains of the 1940s. Here, too, are firsthand accounts of the civil rights movement during its "forgotten years" of the 1940s. Logan also recollected in these pages his disagreements and spats with such luminaries as Walter White, Ralph Bunche, President Mordecai Johnson of Howard University, and E. Franklin Frazier, and he reconstructed the intellectual vigor of Howard during its "golden years." He allowed a peek, too, at the social lives and peccadilloes of his rather large circle of friends and acquaintances—mostly men, it should be noted, for he had only limited dealings with women.

Logan's evident discipline as a diarist (and hints in other manuscript collections that he had written an autobiography) raised the question of whether other unpublished materials existed as well, which was affirmatively answered after much detective work and some good fortune. The Rayford W. Logan papers, an unprocessed (and previously unused) manuscript collection squirreled away at Howard University's Moorland-Spingarn Research Center, is a historian's dream: an enormous cache of personal, professional, and business correspondence, drafts of speeches and articles, photographs and other memorabilia, and a two-volume autobiography in typescript.

Asides in his diary to future readers, an autobiography, fugitive statements in his papers directed at posterity—all indicate that Rayford Logan had a healthy estimate of his place in history. He was, after all, as the *Chicago Defender* dubbed him, a "bad Negro with a Ph.D.," a phenotype with enough daring, scope, and skills to lead his people to an equal place in America. If he at times inflated his role or unjustly faulted others for his apparent failure to rise to the top, this by no means invalidates his viewpoint. Logan fought many battles in his life, and like the young Count Rostov in *War and Peace,* he occasionally evaluated his role not as it occurred but as he would have liked it to have occurred. He measured himself and his life worth not only against the Talented Tenth in general, nor even the smaller cohort of African-American holders of doctorates, but against the legend of his alma mater. The District of Columbia's M

Members of the Howard University faculty, November 1940: (*left to right*) James Nabrit, Charles Drew, Sterling Brown, E. Franklin Frazier, Rayford W. Logan, Alain Locke. Courtesy *Our Word* magazine.

Street High School was renowned for graduating future race leaders like Charles Hamilton Houston and William Hastie, who were "bad Negroes" in their own right. But even when one sifts through his boasting, Logan compares favorably.

The diary and the autobiography are invaluable on another count in addition to providing insight into Logan's persona. His chronicle and documentation of events in which he was a participant was thorough, scrupulous, accurate, and in accord with materials in other archival collections. Of the many roles he assumed, Logan was above all a historian. He had, as his friend John Hope Franklin said, a high regard for the truth; he knew the power of evidence and strived to uncover it. "The standard of excellence that early became the Logan hallmark was reflected in everything that he did," said Franklin. So although he flattered himself and often wrote harshly about perceived and actual rivals among the Talented Tenth, Logan was faithful to the raw data of the historical record.

But hubris is an inadequate explanation for why Logan labored so long and diligently and in many settings for the rights of African Americans; it is hard to imagine that overweening pride could sustain him and keep him from becoming thoroughly bitter during the countless times that he felt he was denied his place in the African-American pantheon. What emerges from his diaries and autobiographical manuscript and from the testimony of friends, colleagues, and former students is a man who, for all his foibles and vanities, was driven to contribute to the cause of racial advancement. He was present, often at the epicenter, at many of the defining moments in African-American history, from the First World War to the dawn of the decolonization of Africa. He implemented his multisided attack on racial discrimination in both activist and scholarly modes, and he did it at a furious and unrelenting pace.

By the time he had breathed his last in November 1982, he had written a dozen books, edited several others, written hundreds of scholarly articles and newspaper columns, and had spoken to countless audiences. To be sure, Logan enjoyed other aspects of life. He was an avid baseball fan; on at least one occasion, when he had a few hours between trains in Chicago, he headed out to the old Comiskey Park to catch the White Sox. He had a fine art collection, principally works of New Negro artists. In his later years he had a reserved table at a restaurant near his northwest Washington, D.C., home, at which he sipped the finest gin martinis and received the best service. But he was most comfortable when he was speaking, teaching, researching, writing.

What provoked Logan (and, by extension, many other members of the Talented Tenth) to take such a rugged and protracted—some might say punishing—path in life is a third major theme of this work. In one way or another, Rayford Logan pledged his entire life to the cause of racial equality, and it was here that his special talents shone. John Hope Franklin once wrote that it was the American Negro scholar's dilemma to be obligated constantly to challenge the notion of black inferiority. Proving the worth of one's race to an audience, the white part of which was indifferent and at times hostile, must have been a uniquely frustrating job; no matter how much talent he possessed, and no matter how finely honed were his skills, in the eyes of society he would always be at most a Negro scholar, a label which, like "Negro" and other less polite terms, denoted a second-class status.

At the same time, scholarship was an arena in which Logan could exercise some control and express his innermost desires. Restricted in possibilities, he focused his creative energies on illuminating America's racial past and correcting its racial present. In a different, but still applicable context, the writer Alice Walker divined the source and legacy of this type of creativity. Her mother, she wrote in an essay called "In Search of Our Mothers' Gardens" (*In Search of Our Mothers' Gardens: Womanist Prose* [New York: Harcourt Brace Jovanovich, 1983], 241–42; I thank Mary Kemp Davis of the English department at the University of North Carolina for bringing this essay to my attention) lived the confined and oppressed life of a Georgia sharecropper. But whatever mind-numbing, spirit-robbing work had to be done, her mother always managed to raise an ambitious flower garden and bring some beauty into the family's life. "Whatever she planted grew as if by magic, and her fame as a grower of flowers spread over three counties," Walker remembered.

> I notice that it is only when my mother is working in her flowers that she is radiant, almost to the point of being invisible—except as Creator: hand and eye. She is involved in work her soul must have. Ordering the universe in the image of her personal conception of Beauty.
>
> Her face, as she prepares the Art that is her gift, is a legacy of respect she leaves to me, for all that illuminates and cherishes life. She has handed down respect for the possibilities—and the will to grasp them.

Walker's mother created in relative anonymity. But she gave a gift to her daughter and helped her to define her voice, which reaches millions. It is similar with Rayford Logan. He did not labor in obscurity, as did Walker's mother, but much of his life's work has been hidden. Still, he planted an expansive perennial garden, which can be profitably harvested by scholars, African-American activists, and all people with a vision of equality and justice.

Chapel Hill, N.C.
July 1992

ACKNOWLEDGMENTS

When I began this project in 1989, I thought that it would be a straightforward proposition: First I would do the research and then I would write the story. Thankfully, the logistical problems were not apparent then, else I likely would not have started in the first place. The first—and chronic—obstacle was financial. Paul G. E. Clemens, who was at the time the vice-chair for graduate education in the Department of History, Rutgers University, scrounged two years of fellowships and some travel grants, which was welcome assistance, especially during dismal times for graduate student funding. A Junior Faculty Development Grant for summer 1992 from the University of North Carolina at Chapel Hill provided the means for the final preparation of the manuscript. The major funding, however, was graciously and generously provided by my wife, Patricia Puglisi, who, upon the completion of her graduate education, supported us both, which allowed me to labor full-time to finish the Ph.D.

A second barrier to the swift completion of this book was accommodations: Where to stay when rooting through out-of-town archives? Neil and Claudia and Johanna Prose provided fun company, a comfortable bed, and delicious meals during a trip to the Southern Historical Collection at the University of North Carolina at Chapel Hill; happily, we are now neighbors and I can repay their hospitality. For the one or two weeks per month—stretched out over an extended period—that I conducted research in Washington, D.C., the Blom family of Baltimore—John and Brenda and Joe, Ruth and Jacob—became my family. We are friends of long standing, but the warmth and camaraderie that they gave in full measure exceeded anything I could have imagined.

Michael R. Winston, Rayford Logan's literary executor, gave me access to Logan's personal papers, which are deposited at Howard University's Moorland-Spingarn Research Center; the finished product would have rested on a far thinner research base had Dr. Winston not made this collection available. At the Moorland-Spingarn is Esme Bhan, and one would be hard-pressed to find a more competent and conscientious research associate anywhere. More than once she suggested fruitful avenues for investigation and brought to my attention documents from other collections that I would have overlooked; in our many conversations, she shared unstintingly her knowledge of Rayford Logan's Washington, D.C., and Howard University. The staff of the Manuscript Division of the Library of Congress, too, was extraordinarily helpful, especially in helping me to negotiate the voluminous NAACP Papers. Dean Carroll Miller of Howard University was conducting research at the Moorland-Spingarn at the same time I was, and he gave freely of his encyclopedic knowledge of Howardiana: his recollections of Mordecai Johnson were particularly enlightening.

The scholars whom I encountered in the course of writing this book have without exception been generous with their time and expertise. Colleagues and friends of Rayford Logan whom I interviewed are listed in the bibliography; they patiently answered my questions and in turn caused me to think about Logan and the African-American intelligentsia in new ways. David Levering Lewis saw this book through all its phases from conceptualization to dissertation. Those who know his work know the premium he places on quality; I also received regular and frequent phone calls, especially in the early stages, demanding to know what progress I had made. His critical judgment—and his insistence that I write the dissertation in publishable prose—helped me to avoid the most egregious lapses of form and substance. Working with him was a marvelous education in the historian's craft.

Virginia Yans-McLaughlin first got me interested in pursuing biography in a graduate colloquium. I was delighted when she agreed to help shepherd the dissertation to completion; she put to me hard questions about writing life histories and added texture to sometimes flat interpretation. Arnold Rampersad and David Oshinsky offered early encouragement and read the completed dissertation; as skilled biographers, they each raised questions that altered and improved my line of investigation. August Meier closely scrutinized the entire manuscript, returning to me lots of encouragement and a bundle of comments. He led me to rethink several questions concerning the history of race relations and the NAACP and urged me to excise my most unjudicious polemics and replace them with scholarship. Esme Bhan, too, read the entire manuscript and substantially improved the final product. I had to travel to Paris to meet Walter Jackson, though he teaches just down the road at North Carolina State University; his close read of Chapter 6 fine-tuned this particularly nettlesome part. Needless to say, none are implicated in any of this book's shortcomings; they are mine alone.

Plenty of other people offered support and encouragement. My parents, Isabel and Harold Janken, and my aunt and uncle, Nadine and Harold Hankin, were four of my biggest boosters during this undertaking, as they have been throughout my life. My brother Glen Janken listened to me complain—and then promptly told me to shut up because at least I liked what I was doing. None of these five ever asked the dreaded question: "So when are you going to be done?" On the other hand, my parents-in-law, Joe and Anita Puglisi, did query several times about deadlines and thus gave added impetus to finish at the quickest possible pace.

Patricia Puglisi has been a constant source of joy, both during the course of this book and as we go through life together.

RAYFORD W. LOGAN

and the Dilemma of the African-American Intellectual

❧

chapter one

GROWING UP IN THE NADIR

ૐ

(1897–1917)

To MOST PEOPLE who knew him well, Rayford Logan will forever be remembered as the man who rejected the appellation "black." Long after the lexicons had been revised in the wake of the civil rights movement, Logan still insisted upon referring to himself and his race as "Negro." "Black" was the term of racial chauvinists who denied that the American Negro also had European roots. "Black" was the term of the "prophets of doom" who preached that Negroes could not succeed in America. "Black" homogenized the Negro race, masking color differences. Many African Americans of Logan's generation favored "Negro" over "black," but they chose to adopt the new terminology so long as the content of their demands for equality was not compromised. Not so Logan; so insistent was he that he would terminate a conversation, break an engagement, even resign from an organization he had spent decades building if, in his presence, the term "black" was used to describe anything other than the color of formal evening wear.[1]

Far more than a matter of personal quirkiness, these anecdotes highlight Logan's militant integrationism, even assimilationism. He was, he once wrote, "forty-sixty-fourths or ten-sixteenths white, eight-sixty-fourths or two-sixteenths Indian, and sixteen-sixty-fourths or four-sixteenths Negro. Legal legerdemain classifies me as a Negro, but I have occasionally had difficulty in convincing some persons that I am."[2] The young mulatto boy who became Rayford W. Logan, distinguished historian and veteran civil rights activist and Pan-Africanist and, later, a severe critic of the black pride movement of the 1960s and 1970s, was born on January 7, 1897, to Arthur C. Logan, Sr., a butler to a prominent white family, and Martha Wittingham Logan, a laundress. The turn of the century was a time in American history he later called the nadir in the condition of African Americans. He had, however, the good fortune to be born in Washington, D.C., "a consequence primarily of my mother's moving to the city in 1883."[3] Washington had a mature African-American community with an excellent, although segregated, school system and was less adversely affected than other parts of the country by the racial intolerance that swept the country during and after the Redemption. Many of Logan's ideological and cultural traits—his racial ambivalence, his striving for excellence, his dedication to the cause of civil rights, his craving for recognition from both African-American and white society, his elitism— he inherited from his mother and from the geographical circumstances of his birth.

His mother, Martha Ann Logan (née Wittingham), was the third of thirteen children born to Marshall Wittingham, a freeborn Negro, and his wife, on September 6, 1866, in Farquier County, Virginia. Nestled in the foothills of the Blue Ridge Mountains about fifty miles west of the nation's capital, Farquier was a center of free Negroes in the years before the Civil War. Free Negro labor was an important feature of the northern Virginia economy, because the slave trade created a shortage of slave labor. The area's produce, mainly wheat, was frequently harvested by free blacks. But their social position was hardly different from that of their slave cousins, and their economic position—they worked for low wages on contract— also differed little. In Farquier County, as in some other areas of the state, free Negro land ownership was quite limited and land tenantry was high, for the white community remained hostile to the idea of a viable and independent black community.[4]

Logan's maternal grandfather, Marshall Wittingham, was born on March 20, 1829. Little hard evidence of his early life survives, and most of what is known about him is a mixture of family tradition and hearsay. He insisted he was the son of Margaret Wittingham, a white woman whose family migrated from Bucks County, Pennsylvania, to Farquier in the late eighteenth century, and Rice Paine, a freeborn black man; the two were probably not married. Sometime after Marshall's birth, Paine moved to Ohio, because of the intensification in the county of proslavery and anti– free Negro sentiments.

The white Wittinghams were a distinguished lot, family lore had it. Young Logan frequently heard that Grandfather Wittingham's white half-brother was a bishop in the Methodist Church.[5] He also heard the story of Grandfather Wittingham's large inheritance. Marshall once received a letter from an English solicitor advising him that if he was indeed a Wittingham then "he could share in a rather large estate." He did not respond because he neither believed that an African American would be recognized as an heir nor was anxious to parade his "illegitimacy." Logan speculated, tongue in cheek, that he might have been "an illegitimate descendant of the ancestors of Arthur James Balfour, Viscount Traprain of Whittingehame, Prime Minister of Great Britain."[6]

Young Logan remembered his grandfather as a Virginia gentleman, with "courtly, almost aristocratic manners." The pastor of the Mount Morris Baptist Church, Marshall Wittingham could read and write, and Logan was quite proud of the fact that his grandfather did not falter when it came to grammar and diction. As refined in his appearance as in his manner, Marshall Wittingham dressed for church in a silk hat and Prince Albert suit, walking there in erect form and with a compact gait. He was also a man in command of his emotions. Powell Gibson, a church member and former boarder with the Wittinghams, recalled that Marshall never lost control of his voice during his preaching and that his warnings from the pulpit were sound. A proud man, he rarely reacted to the insults and slights that he must have suffered. Only once, recalled Gibson, did Marshall lose his temper. The white pastor of the neighboring Leeds Episcopal Church spoke curtly to him as Marshall tried to lead some stray horses off the road. He took umbrage at the treatment he received and complained to Gibson that "I am quite as sincere in my ministry as he is and it is plain that I have better manners."[7]

Little, too, is known about Martha's early years, except that she completed a fourth-grade education in a one-room schoolhouse in Hume, Virginia, and that she moved to Washington, D.C., in 1883 at the age of seventeen. She met her future husband, Arthur C. Logan, there and married him in 1893. It is certain, however, that her personality was molded by the influence of her father. She inherited the family traditions and stories, learned the important lessons of good manners, and absorbed pride in both her free Negro and white ancestry. She repeated these same lessons to young Logan. That these stories cannot be verified—in 1978, Logan, an elderly man, traveled to Great Britain in an unsuccessful search for his family roots—makes them no less powerful. For Logan, hearing them on a regular basis since childhood, they took on the force of reality.

If the imprint of the Wittinghams on his personality is clear and abundant, the Logan side of his family seems to have provided little but the genes. Facts about Arthur Logan and his family are vague. He was born in Greenwood, South Carolina, in 1866, the son of a freedwoman, Eliza Croft, and a white man. The identity of Arthur's father is a mystery, but Logan heard stories as a child that he was a surgeon in the Confederate army and a mayor of Columbia, South Carolina. Arthur ran away from home at an early age, and practically nothing more is known of him until he married Martha Wittingham in 1893.

One explanation for the haziness of Logan's paternal ancestry is the legacy of slavery. "What is the point in all this speculation, this mixing of fact and tradition?" he reflected in 1948.

> First, hundreds of thousands of Negroes in the United States, Latin America and the colonial West Indies would be compelled to be equally vague in tracing their ancestry. . . . [My grandmother] was the bed-companion, apparently, of whatever white man chose her. In brief, like many mulattoes today, I am a second generation bastard, a relict of the foul slave system that was one of the worst disgraces of American history.[8]

Another reason is that the paternal side of Logan's family apparently lacked the family traditions of the Wittingham side. While young Logan was regaled with stories of the white and Negro Wittinghams, his father spoke little about his family. Yet Rayford was not very curious about that side of his family. He was not outwardly embarrassed by his father's slave heritage or the fact that he was not the issue of a legal marriage, but Arthur exercised precious little influence over his son. In his autobiography Logan made his mother, Martha, and Grandfather Wittingham the moral anchors of his youth; his father was never even mentioned by name. It must have been made clear to him in whose family footsteps he was to follow, and Logan must have grown up thinking that his free Negro heritage was more important, more distinguished, more worthy of emulation than his slave background. It was the Wittingham traditions that sustained the Logan family in its life in Washington.

The District of Columbia was a segregated town by the end of the nineteenth century. The hopes that were raised for harmonious race relations in the 1870s had vanished within three decades. The year that

Martha Wittingham moved to Washington, the Supreme Court overturned the Civil Rights Act of 1875. At issue in this decision was an interpretation of the Fourteenth Amendment; the high court ruled that that amendment prevented only the states, and not individuals, from engaging in racial discrimination in public accommodations, transportation, and entertainment facilities. Congress could not pass general laws concerning civil rights, the Court ruled, and unless the states passed such laws, African Americans had little legal recourse. Over the next thirteen years, the Supreme Court further restricted the public life of African Americans. It made it easier for states to exclude African Americans from juries and established such levels of evidence for proving racial discrimination by government as to eliminate any chance of achieving racial justice. Finally, in 1896, the high court issued its opinion in the case of *Plessy* v. *Ferguson,* legalizing "separate but equal" accommodations and institutionalizing racial classification and discrimination in all spheres of public life.[9]

Racial subordination did not mean, however, that the African-American community was a homogeneous one. Washington was a center for the nation's African-American elite, and it was also a magnet for African Americans of lesser means who sought the protection of the federal government. African-American society in the District of Columbia was well developed despite segregation, and it was divided along class, but also color, lines. At the top were the "upper tens," the Syphaxes, Wormleys, Bruces, Pinchbacks, Terrells, and no more than one hundred other families in an African-American population of about seventy-five thousand in 1900. Most of the families were wealthy by community standards, some even by the standards of white society. Langston Hughes, who, by virtue of his uncle John Mercer Langston, a visible "aristocrat of color," gained entrée into Washington's elite society, recorded that although the African-American upper crust enjoyed living like aristocrats, they were in fact only middle class.[10] The "upper tens" and their children occupied the highest and most distinguished positions African Americans could hope to attain in federal and city government, they dominated the city's segregated school system, and they favored the legal, medical, and teaching professions.

What surely distinguished the elite from the rest of African-American Washington was family pedigree, light complexion, and education. The Wormleys traced their free Negro heritage back to the eighteenth century;

most aristocratic families traced their free Negro ancestry back at least a generation before the Civil War. The Syphaxes were descendants of Martha Washington; several others, like Blanche K. Bruce, were offspring of prominent whites, and most knew and celebrated their European ancestry. Most, but not all were quite light complexioned.

The one characteristic that virtually all of the aristocrats of color shared was the possession of a liberal arts education, often from a prestigious northern college. Like members of the Wormley clan, they may have been intimately involved with the affairs of Howard University, but they preferred their children to receive Harvard educations. When Langston Hughes planned his return to college in the mid-1920s, he was pressured to choose Harvard over Lincoln, the oldest black college in the nation, for "You'd get just the mere formal 'book-larnin' and no contacts to speak of."[11] Robert H. Terrell was graduated from Harvard, while his wife, the former Mary Church, was an Oberlin alumna. Francis Grimké was a graduate of Princeton Theological Seminary, while his brother Archibald took a law degree from Harvard Law School. An African American without a distinguished ancestry or quantities of European blood could move in the refined circles provided he or she had a sheepskin from a prestigious northern college.

Nothing would have been more preposterous to the African-American elite than the proposition that all African Americans were the same. The aristocrats of color were refined and cultured—acculturated, really—and they hoped eventually to be assimilated into white upper-class society. Sensitive to Jim Crow, they at times opposed separate facilities for blacks and whites on the grounds that this would force them to associate with the lower class of their race, which "would be an unmerited rebuke upon the colored man of finer sensibilities."[12] Carrie Hughes suffered constant slights and insults from the elite because her son Langston got a job in a laundry. His status improved somewhat when he left the laundry and went to work for Carter Woodson at the Association for the Study of Negro Life and History—even though his job there included stoking the fire, dusting furniture, sorting mail, and wrapping and mailing packages. Langston found the black bourgeoisie obsessed with money and position.[13]

Although they involved themselves in some community self-help efforts, these were generally not expansive,[14] and the bourgeoisie sought to distance themselves from the masses both socially and spatially. Generally unable to buy homes in white neighborhoods that were commensurate with their life-styles, the aristocrats of color established separate enclaves within the African-American neighborhoods. Langston Hughes's street in the Le Droit Park area of the city included a Methodist bishop, a judge, the U.S. recorder of deeds, a high official at Howard University, and a half-dozen doctors and lawyers.[15] The author and poet Jean Toomer, who grew up in the house of his grandfather P. B. S. Pinchback and was a high school classmate of Rayford Logan, wrote of the gulf between the aristocracy and the rest of Washington's African Americans. The world of the aristocrats was "mid-way between the white and negro worlds. . . . They had a personal refinement, a certain inward culture and beauty, a warmth of feeling such as I have seldom encountered elsewhere or again."[16]

When Arthur and Martha Logan began married life on November 8, 1893, they could only dream of sharing the comfortable material circumstances of the African-American bourgeoisie. Arthur butlered for the household of two wealthy Washington sisters, Mary and Annie Guthrie, and continued in that capacity after Mary Guthrie married Frederic C. Walcott, a prominent Connecticut Republican and later a senator from that state. He earned thirty dollars a month plus board and that amount plus bed and board when he accompanied his employers to their Bar Harbor, Maine, summer vacation home. His income was supplemented by that of Martha, who took in laundry.[17]

Arthur's occupation was far removed from the professional status of honorific politician, professor, doctor, lawyer, or even teacher, occupations that were filled by the city's elite and upper middle class. It even lacked the respectability of the few jobs in the federal government that were open to African Americans—typist, messenger, and custodian—which, despite the restrictiveness of the federal service, placed an African-American family firmly within the community's middle class.[18] On the other hand, his job did have the status that went with being a domestic in a wealthy white home. Further, Arthur's was a steady job, and unemployment and underemployment among the city's African Americans was a severe problem. A fifth of the black population lived in the District's alley dwellings. Three quarters of the alley-dwelling families earned less than eight hundred dollars a year; the average worker experienced 6.6 weeks a year of unemployment, while for 45 percent of the alley residents that figure jumped to 13.4 weeks lost for reasons other than illness.[19]

The Logan family's living arrangements were typical of many of the

District's African-American residents. From 1897 until 1916, and then again from the early 1920s until 1926, the Logan family—Arthur, Martha, Arthur junior, who was born in 1895, and Rayford—shared a house with Martha's sister Elizabeth Simms, her husband Robert, and their son Robert junior. Housing in the District was dear and in short supply for those of modest means. Among the city's nonprofessional adult African Americans, over 40 percent lived with boarders or lodgers. Over a third of the nonprofessional African-American family households consisted of extended families, two or more related nuclear families, or a family or families with boarders or lodgers. The city's African-American professionals were not immune to such pressures. More than a quarter either were boarders or lodgers or maintained boarders or lodgers in their homes. Over a third of the professional households were consanguineous in nature, with either one parent and children or with unmarried siblings.[20]

If their material circumstances were indistinguishable from the thousands of other lower-middle-class African-American families in Washington, D.C., the Logans capitalized on the Wittingham traditions to identify themselves with the city's aristocrats of color. Respectability started with a church life for the family. Soon after her move to Washington, Martha had joined the Nineteenth Street Baptist Church, and Arthur and Martha were married in the home of the first president of the church's Missionary Society. The church was composed of "colored families with a cult of respectability, thrift, and ambition."[21] Martha, the preacher's daughter, felt so strongly about her religion and the Nineteenth Street Church that she converted her husband to her faith. She also tried to ensure that her children were brought up in the church's fold, but she was unable to pass along to them her spiritual devotion. Even as a boy Logan lacked religious enthusiasm. He went to Sunday school, but he never got religion. Not until high school did he get the call—and not from the Lord so much as from his mother:

> It was her worry more than deep conviction that led me to say to her one Sunday: "Mama, I've got religion." She embraced me, though I suspect that she must have known that I was no zealot. She coached me in the answers to the questions I would be asked by the Deacons who would determine whether I was a true convert. I passed this examination with flying colors, for my memory was very good, and was duly baptized in the pool on the second floor behind the choir.[22]

While he was unconcerned with the fate of his soul, Logan was not indifferent to the Nineteenth Street Baptist Church, and he gravitated to its social gospel and temperance activity. Besides his mother and his school, the Reverend Walter H. Brooks, pastor of the Nineteenth Street Baptist Church, appears to have been the most important force that shaped his character and education.[23] While it was by no means in the same category as the Fifteenth Street Presbyterian Church, presided over by Francis J. Grimké and attended by aristocrats like the Pinchbacks, Terrells, and Langstons, the Nineteenth Street Baptist Church was active in the city's moral life.

Brooks, who took the pulpit around the same time Martha joined the flock, had previously made a name for himself in Richmond, Virginia. From 1877 to 1880 he was the pastor of the Second Baptist Church there. Since the end of the Civil War, Virginia's white Baptist Convention had refused to recognize its African-American coreligionists; in 1879, however, Brooks was the first black Baptist to address the Convention. He not only succeeded in establishing relationships between the two Baptist wings, but he also garnered a reputation as a courageous, articulate leader. He enhanced his reputation in 1880 by leading a campaign in Richmond to get African-American teachers installed in the segregated school system. Although the city had a surfeit of African-American educators, Richmond was the only sizable community in the state to employ whites in the black schools. Brooks campaigned against this practice by pointing out that the one school that employed black teachers was also the one with the highest attendance rates. And, borrowing a page from the segregationist handbook, he argued that white teachers in black schools violated the principal of racial separation.[24]

During his time in Washington, Brooks was the chaplain of the Anti-Saloon League of the District of Columbia; Francis Grimké declared that he knew no one who had "spoken more strongly or fearlessly in favor of temperance and against the liquor traffic." During his pastorate the church also became a meeting place for groups and individuals seeking social justice; it sponsored speakers such as Carter Woodson, the founder of the Association for the Study of Negro Life and History; Garnet Wilkinson, the first assistant superintendent of the Washington public schools; and Robert Daniel of Shaw University. The National Association of Colored Women was founded at a meeting in the church. Brooks served as a first vice-president of the Bethel Literary and Historical Association, which was a center for those concerned with social justice; he was also a trustee of the National Training School for Women and Girls, which was founded by Nannie H. Burrough.[25]

Another attempt by the Logan family to distance itself from the African-American lower classes was its determination to live in integrated neighborhoods. Turn-of-the-century Washington had no ghetto, but was more a checkerboard of racial neighborhoods. Although blacks and whites might live on neighboring streets, they rarely crossed over, except for the African-American domestic servants and a minuscule number of black professionals who worked on white blocks.[26] The block of Twentieth Street, between K and H streets, where the Logans moved in 1900, was integrated, as was the surrounding neighborhood in the northwest section of Washington. About a third of the families were African-American, and their homes were interspersed with those of the white families. Residents for the most part coexisted peacefully, and some African-American and white children played together. For a few years after their arrival, Logan's favorite playmate was white. G. R. F. Key, an African-American friend of Logan's who lived nearby on Twenty-second Street, also played with white children. The children got along despite their parents, for as a young adult, Key remembered the mother of a white playmate of his youngest sister keeping her son from the Keys' home because the parent did not want her son to be around the "niggers." The young playmate retorted that his friends were not "niggers" because Harriet Key was among them.[27]

The arrival of the Logans, simultaneously with six other African-American families, on Twentieth Street caused some ripples in the normally calm racial waters, and was also the occasion for racial confusion. Some of the block's white residents considered seven African-American families to be an invasion of sorts. The Logans hoped to avoid any sticky situations in their new neighborhood. Martha, a church-going woman and stern disciplinarian, made sure that her children stayed in line and out of trouble. The Logans hoped their light complexion would help them avoid the hostility that would be visited upon a darker family. But fair-skinned as they were, the Logans and Simmses were, except for Rayford's brother, Arthur junior, of a slightly browner shade than the Prices and the Grays, two of the block's established African-American families, and, apparently, the darkest shade tolerable to the white residents. Soon after they moved in, a gang of white children began throwing rocks at the Logan residence. Another time, Logan, Arthur junior, Robert Simms, Jr., and some friends fought a group of white boys their age after "they called us 'niggers' and we retaliated by calling them 'poor white trash.' "[28]

More serious incidents occurred throughout the city in 1906 and 1908 when Joe Gans, an African-American prizefighter, met Danish-born Battling Nelson in a lightweight boxing match. Gans beat Nelson in 1906 to become champion, and white Washingtonians took their revenge by attacking black residents. Two years later, when Nelson beat Gans and won the crown, blacks defended their racial honor by beating up white residents. While Logan was involved in some of these scrapes, it was his brother Arthur who took the worst hits. Arthur was even fairer than his brother, with wavy red hair and blue eyes. In later years he would utilize his light complexion for business and pleasure. He acted as Logan's "spy" to gain information on the discriminatory employment practices in New Deal programs and in the private sector, and "passed" to gain entrance into whites-only entertainment. But in these childhood fights it was all pain and no gain. In 1906 Arthur was assaulted by white hooligans, and in 1908 he was attacked by African Americans who did not know him.[29]

It is not clear how frequently such color misidentification occurred, but it must have caused confusion in young Logan's mind. He grew up with colliding racial attitudes. The beatings inflicted at the hands of white children nurtured within him "as bitter a prejudice against the disinherited whites as many whites had against most Negroes."[30] As a child he heard stories about the horror of lynching.[31] But he also drew the color line within the African-American community. Logan was the son of two of the "older inhabitants" of Washington. While certainly not part of the colored aristocracy, his parents had arrived in town before the large influx of African Americans in the late nineteenth early twentieth centuries. These later waves of African Americans were pushed out of the South by the depression of the 1890s and by deteriorating race relations. They were generally straight from the farm, unskilled—and darker. While he and his family were, like the rest of the lighter, longer-resident Washingtonians, "respectable, church-going people who were 'ladies and gentlemen,' at home and in public," those with pigment were raucous and presented discipline problems in school.[32]

Invidious color distinctions and their practice by African Americans were the heritage of a racist, segregated society that placed a premium on whiteness.[33] An African-American physician from Chicago reported in the 1940s that

When we are little children we use story books in which all the characters have long blond hair. When we go to church we're taught that God is a white man. The Virgin Mary is white. What can you expect? All our early concepts of desirable physical attributes come from the white man. . . . People in America don't black their faces and make their hair kinky. They would be laughed at; it would be too different from the American standard.[34]

In their study of African-American life in Chicago, *Black Metropolis,* St. Clair Drake and Horace R. Cayton documented the operation of color distinctions. African Americans of light complexion were often "color-struck"; that is, they preferred to associate with those of the same or lighter hue and discouraged their children from playing with those who were of darker complexion. In choosing their mates, African Americans of all shades were "partial to color," wanting to "marry light." Drake and Cayton could find only a few social organizations specifically organized as the "blue-vein" societies, but social cliques based upon skin color existed nevertheless.[35]

The distinctions had an economic as well as an aesthetic basis. In the antebellum South mulattoes, often offspring of the slave master, had been a favored group of slaves, receiving jobs in the Big House. In more recent times, light-complexioned African Americans received marginally more employment opportunities in the clerical and personal service positions. Waitresses were likely to be light-skinned, as were clerks, stenographers, and typists, the latter three being sources of prestige in the African-American community.[36] Among the complaints of dark-complexioned African Americans were not only the superior airs of their light-complexioned brethren, but also limited employment opportunities and the spitefulness of the light-skinned African American employed in a low-status job.[37]

The last point suggests that color distinctions and prejudices were compounded by class status. W. Lloyd Warner, in his study *Color and Human Nature,* concluded, for example, that light-complexioned men who were in the upper classes were apt to be quite well adjusted, for the status accorded their color was matched by their material position. On the other hand, light-complexioned African Americans who, like Rayford Logan, came from the lower-middle or lower class had a difficult time reconciling their economic and social circumstances with their light skin color. Warner found two broad categories of behavior for light-skinned men. If they were social climbers, they often became "race men" and were vocal in their opposition to whites; on the other hand, if they preferred to associate with whites and distance themselves from those of a darker color, they generally developed retiring personalities.[38]

Logan developed both modes of behavior. His family was definitely striving to climb the social ladder; his readiness to indict whites, especially poor whites, for blocking his advancement was compounded by the fact that Washington was essentially a southern city. When white southerners had to come into contact with African Americans, they preferred to deal with darker women and men; mulattoes made white southerners uncomfortable.[39] Thus Logan, who had drawn the color line against darker African Americans, was not accepted in the white world either, and he learned to lash out at it, too.

But the Logan family's successful climb up the ladder also depended upon contact with whites.[40] More important than the marginal status of Arthur senior's position per se was the patronage of specific whites: the Guthries and, later, the Walcotts. The association with Arthur senior's employers was a source of pride, for it simultaneously helped the family distance itself from the dark-skinned element in the community and close the gap between it and the light-skinned African-American elite.

The awe with which Logan regarded the culture and status of his father's employer shaped that side of him that was in chronic conflict with the side shaped by his experiences with poor whites: his combative nature would often give way to suppliant, even sycophantic, behavior in the presence of powerful whites. The roots of this aspect of his personality are not hard to detect. While Arthur butlered for the Guthries and later the Walcotts, Robert Simms, his brother-in-law, worked as a butler for U.S. Supreme Court Justice Melvin W. Fuller, at the same modest salary Arthur received. These reasonably powerful white employers were looked up to in the Logan-Simms household, and the relationship between the Logans and the Guthries stretched beyond the usual cash nexus. Arthur, who had little formal education as a child, "spoke and wrote as if he had some considerable schooling" as a result of working for his employer.[41] The Guthrie sisters paid attention to young Logan's education, giving him occasional gifts of books. Senator Walcott and his wife helped Arthur and Martha purchase a house. "I am sending you the regular $30 [monthly salary] with an extra $100 to go toward paying for the house," Mary Guthrie Walcott wrote to Arthur senior. "You can let me know, sometime, how much you owe toward paying for it and from time to time I will send a little extra till it is all paid off."[42] As an adult, Logan maintained a correspondence with Senator Walcott, frequently thanking him for the kindnesses he had shown to him and his family, sharing with the senator his views on national and international affairs, and asking Walcott to use his good offices for various projects. Walcott in turn had procured a political job for Arthur junior, after he had temporarily moved to Connecticut to take charge of getting out the Negro vote in the senator's 1928 election campaign. Looking back from the perspective of middle age, Logan wrote to the senator that "the investment of Mrs. Walcott and you in me was not in vain."[43]

The Logans had hitched their wagon to a powerful white family, absorbing in the process its formality, refinement, and status consciousness. Identification with the values and habits of whites was not an uncommon occurrence among domestic servants. James Edward Ellington, a contemporary of Arthur senior, was the butler to Dr. M. F. Cuthburt, a physician whose patients reputedly included the Du Ponts and the Morgenthaus. Ellington "knew what a gentleman was, and he was determined to be one." Like Arthur senior, Ellington received little formal education during his childhood in North Carolina, but he improved on his already florid speech and acquired his Victorian manners—and gifts of the odd piece of silver and china—from his employer. Like Arthur senior and Martha, who passed these manners and the Wittingham family traditions to their children, so J. E. and his wife, Daisy, passed his acquired manners and his wife's family gentility on to their son—Duke Ellington.[44]

Such a relationship, of course, was not free of conflict. No matter how close the relationship, the Logans and the Ellingtons were never allowed to forget their caste status. Duke Ellington was raised to be proud of his heritage, but he preferred to ignore racial problems and avoid dicey situations. Racial tensions found a creative outlet in his music, which he insisted was not jazz but "Negro music."[45]

Logan diffused the tensions that the meeting of the races generated by establishing an aloof, distant posture. Throughout his adult years he never lost the formality, even stiffness, that he absorbed from the Wittinghams and the Walcotts. But this bearing and his family's church activities jarred against the Logans' actual relatively low position in the African-American community's class structure. As a youth, Logan was particularly affronted by the fact that his mother had to take in laundry to supplement the family budget. "I was also keenly sensitive about my parents' lowly status. My mother had to add to my father's monthly wages of thirty-five dollars a month by doing a day's work and by 'taking in washing.' It galled me to have to deliver the washing."[46]

Logan also received contradictory signals on race relations during the summers he spent as a child on his grandfather's farm in Farquier County. White neighbors of Grandfather Wittingham addressed one of his daughters as "Aunt Bert," but they tipped their hats as they passed by her. Grandfather Wittingham occupied a high position in local society, though, and apparently succeeded in garnering for himself the respect he thought he deserved. As he was a leader of his church, his white neighbors called him "Elder Wittingham," and never addressed him simply as "elder."[47]

In his childhood and teen years, though, Logan's caste and color torments were muted in part by the peculiar nature of segregation in Washington. Segregation in public accommodations was rigidly enforced, of course. He could buy licorice or peppermint sticks at the candy store at Twentieth and M streets because one did not sit in the store and eat sweets. At the drugstore soda fountain at Nineteenth Street and Pennsylvania Avenue, he could not get counter service, but he could get a cone to go. At one neighborhood establishment, after the rare African American was served, the owner smashed the dishes from which he ate.[48] But for Logan, his family, and thousands in similar material straits, it was the laws of economics more than the laws of segregation that kept them out of the places they were not allowed to enter. The only restaurant in town that served both whites and African Americans was at Union Station, but prices there were prohibitive.

Several areas of public life were not regulated by Jim Crow laws or customs, however. The streetcars were not segregated. Neither was the zoo nor the ballpark, so Logan and his friends could buy some inexpensive amusement *and* go there without experiencing the petty indignities of segregation that saturated the African-American experience in other southern towns. Probably more important from the view of his lifetime was the fact that neither the public library nor the Library of Congress was segregated, and this arrangement probably helped nudge Logan toward a career in academia.[49]

His inner tensions were also muted by two other conditions. Logan's youth was a time of "progressive disintegration of Washington's Negro world," owing principally to restriction of economic opportunity. Only the "strongest individual able to draw upon deep inner resources" was capable of avoiding a prevailing sense of despair within African-American Washington.[50] Logan had such fortitude. His mother had always taught him that he was special by virtue of his Wittingham blood, and his father's employer had made an investment in him. With this constant reinforcement, Logan was able to keep doubts about his future under check and strive to distinguish himself from the rest of the community.

The second condition was the superior education available to the brightest youths of colored Washington. Possession of a light complexion was no guarantee of advancement to the upper reaches of African-American society—"Nameless mulatto nobodies," as Roi Ottley called them, tried in vain to gain entrance. But possession of an education, especially if it was coupled with refined manners, could get even one of humble origins admitted to the elite. Because of restricted occupational opportunity, education was both a mark of status in society as a whole and a way to "mark off social divisions *within* the same general occupational level."[51] In 1909 Rayford Logan applied for and was admitted to the M Street High School, the most prestigious public school for African Americans and one of the best high schools in the country, period. This education put him on a level plane with the aristocrats of color and opened opportunities to him that were available to few young people of any race.

At various times in its past Washington had flirted with the idea of an integrated school system, but the attempts to establish a unitary system were short-lived. They provoked anger among many whites, who chafed at the prospect of their children having intimate social contacts with black children. But the proposals also distressed African Americans. An integrated system would shortchange them, they felt. Washington, with Miner Teachers College, Howard University, and a relatively prosperous and less restricted African-American community, had attracted a large number of teachers and others qualified to teach in the public schools; they feared loss of their jobs to white teachers should the classrooms be integrated.

The efforts of the city's African-American elite resulted in the establishment in 1870 of the Preparatory High School for Colored Youth, known during the time of Logan's attendance as M Street High School, and, beginning in 1916, as Dunbar High School, in honor of Paul Laurence Dunbar.[52] At first supported by private philanthropic funds, it became a tax-supported institution within a few years and actually preceded the establishment of the public high school for whites. From the beginning it functioned, as its name implies, as a preparatory school for the "Talented Tenth."

M Street High School was an anomaly of segregation. A few African-American communities in the country were mature and self-conscious enough to produce and support a first-rate center of learning; the mulatto leadership in Charleston, South Carolina, developed the Avery Institute, a preparatory school that graduated more than a generation of that city's African-American business, political, civic, and civil rights leadership.[53] New Orleans and Kansas City also produced excellent academies. But Washington's M Street enjoyed a nationwide reputation. Parents moved families to the city from Maryland, Virginia, and points south so their children could soak up the advantages of an M Street education. Some students walked the four-and-one-half miles to school from the Anacostia section of the city, or took the streetcars from Alexandria, Virginia. Commensurate with this reputation, M Street produced a cadre of leaders of Afro-America whose prestige and sheer numbers have not been equaled by any other institution: Benjamin O. Davis, Sr., was the country's first African-American general; Francis F. Rivers was appointed a New York City court judge, was later elected New York State assemblyman from Manhattan, and took an active role in that city's political life; Eugene Davidson, who went on to receive a Harvard education, returned to Washington to head the New Negro Alliance in the 1930s and remained a permanent fixture in the city's civil rights and labor establishment into the 1940s and 1950s; Charles Hamilton Houston and William Hastie distinguished themselves as the developers of the legal strategy for civil rights that culminated in the 1954 decision in *Brown* v. *Board of Education*. In the field of business, M Street graduated Hilyard Robinson, one of the most successful African-American architects of his time, and John R. Pinkett, a successful businessman in real estate and insurance. Charles Drew, the discoverer of blood plasma, was a product of M Street, as was Montague Cobb, the professor of medicine at Howard University and former president of the NAACP. The school also nurtured outstanding figures from the arts, including the poets Sterling Brown and Jean Toomer, a classmate of Logan's who was a Harlem Renaissance figure and grandson of P. B. S. Pinchback. The school's history and tradition weighed heavily upon its students. Attending M Street was not only the way to get one's ticket punched; it was also an obligation to serve the African-American community.

The school's first principal was a white woman, Emma J. Hutchins, from a New England Quaker background, but succeeding principals were African Americans who exemplified the Talented Tenth's traditions of hard work and struggle exemplified in the M Street motto, *Viam reperiam an faciam*—"I will find a way or make one." Mary J. Patterson was the school's second principal; the daughter of a fugitive slave, Patterson was the first African-American woman to receive a college education, graduating from Oberlin College in 1862. Richard T. Greener, the first African American to graduate from Harvard University, also served briefly in M Street's early years. Also among the first principals were Francis L. Cardozo, Sr., who served from 1884 to 1896; Winfield Scott Montgomery (1896–1899); and Robert H. Terrell (1899–1902), the second African American to receive a Harvard A.B. degree.

M Street also attracted a faculty that would have been the envy of any white high school, and many colleges. Among the better-known faculty members were Mary Church Terrell; Jessie Fauset, later the literary editor of the *Crisis;* Ida A. Gibbs, who later married William Henry Hunt, the U.S. consul to Africa and France, and who became a leader in the Pan-African movement after World War One; Angelina Grimké; and Carter G. Woodson. Twenty of the thirty faculty members at the school between 1902 and 1906 had degrees from prestigious northern colleges, including Harvard, Yale, Oberlin, Amherst, Dartmouth, and Bowdoin. Five others had degrees from Howard University, the premier African-American school. The faculty was as committed to excellence among the students as it was distinguished. Students were admitted based on their academic promise, and they were not promoted unless they continued to display that promise. One student reportedly took seven years to graduate. The faculty and administration was not about to promote him just to push him through the system, and as long as he adhered to the school's values of discipline and good behavior, he was allowed to stay until he could legitimately pass.[54]

The African-American elite of Washington resisted the introduction of trade and industrial education courses into the M Street curriculum, fearing they would impinge upon the college-preparatory nature of the school. They did support, however, the founding of the Booker T. Washington–inspired Armstrong Technical High School in 1902. Mary Church Terrell rebuked those who opposed industrial education, for the founding of Armstrong allowed the separation of the college-bound student from the masses and allowed the M Street School to concentrate on the elite students.[55]

By all accounts, the school did just that. The rigorous academic curriculum required first-year students to take English, history, algebra, Latin, and physics or chemistry. English and Latin were the only required subjects for third- and fourth-year students. Logan took a typical academic load, including two years of Greek, three of French, four of Latin, two of English and geometry, trigonometry and higher algebra. But there were other options as well, including courses in German, Spanish, and political economy.[56] The typical route to a prestigious northern college for gifted African-American graduates of segregated schools included a stop after high school graduation at a New England prep school. E. E. Just, the gifted marine biologist, for example, graduated from the Classical Preparatory Department of South Carolina State College in 1899, and then attended Kimball Union Academy in New Hampshire before entering Dartmouth College in 1903.[57] But students who graduated from M Street were spared the extra time and expense of attending another prep school. The M Street faculty prepared special tutorials to assist students in their studies for college entrance examinations, and Brown, Harvard, Yale, and Oberlin agreed to admit students on the basis of the test results, without requiring further preparation.[58]

Logan was an eager student, but he was by no means sold on history. In fact, during his four years at M Street he took only one history class, taught by Neval Thomas. Although Logan said he did not care much for Thomas's teaching style, he could not have helped but to have been struck by his forthright denunciation of segregation. In later years Thomas became the vice-principal of the high school, president of the Washington branch of the NAACP, and an NAACP executive board member. Segregation in Washington and in the civil service was beginning to spread as a consequence of Woodrow Wilson's presidential victory in 1912, the year before Logan graduated from high school. Neval Thomas took up the challenge and, in his various capacities at M Street and in the NAACP, made the fight against segregation a central part of his political and educational activities.[59] Logan later said that he recalled a certain bitterness in Thomas's demeanor;[60] indeed, the spread of Jim Crow in the District under Wilson and after was enough to embitter any of the Talented Tenth teachers at M Street. But as a teenager the humiliation of Jim Crow rarely touched Logan directly; he was more infected by the optimism inherent in an M Street education.

Contrary to what the heavy academic load might indicate, student life in high school was not all drudgery. Logan had wanted to go out for football, but as his nickname "Weenie" implies, he was too slight to stand up to the punishment meted out by hefty opponents. He was not an especially skilled athlete, but he was an avid participant, going out for soccer and cross-country and even earning a letter in track. Participation in athletics may have taught him something of good sportsmanship, but in at least one instance, he learned that the sports arena was also a political arena, and that school spirit also contained a partisan spirit. "We were proud and arrogant followers of Du Bois, superior in every respect to the students at Armstrong," he wrote. In his senior year, Logan represented M Street in a half-mile race during a dual meet with Armstrong. As he entered the backstretch on the final lap, the other team's leading half-miler passed him, taunting, "You needn't worry Ray, you'll come in second." The jeer so infuriated Logan that he lit the afterburner and beat his opponent to the tape. "I did not beat him: M Street beat Armstrong; Du Bois defeated Booker T. Washington."[61]

Logan also found time for the Cadet Corps, a high school ROTC-type program founded in 1891. Cadets took courses in military science, wore their dress uniforms to school, and engaged in competitive drilling, both among the school's cadet companies and between the school's champion company and the champion of Armstrong High School. Since 1897 the cadets had marched in every president's inaugural parade and participated in special events on the White House lawn.

Participation in the Cadet Corps was more than a casual activity. The program taught discipline, stressed comportment, and rewarded scholastic achievement. A request from the faculty adviser was in actuality a command to be obeyed, and a cadet treated it as he would one from his mother. A cadet began his career as a private, and promotions were based strictly upon performance.[62] The cadets were highly competitive and determined to safeguard their school's honor. Logan was a cadet throughout high school, rising through the ranks as "A" Company won three successive titles both within M Street and against Armstrong. No company, at either school, had ever won more than two consecutive titles. In 1913, his senior year, Logan was awarded the singular honor of being made captain of A Company, the commanding officer of the unit, succeeding his brother Arthur, who had commanded the same company the previous year. During his senior year Logan had decided to resign from the Corps as a protest against his friend Campbell C. Johnson being denied a promotion in rank. The faculty sponsors of the Cadet Corps refused to promote Johnson, but accused the two cohorts of being afraid of losing in the city-wide competition. Their integrity was impugned, and they abandoned their plans to resign. The A Company beat Armstrong for an unprecedented fourth time; Johnson, who remained Logan's lifelong best friend, in adult life embarked on a distinguished career in the military and in social work, achieving the rank of colonel and serving as assistant to the director of the Selective Service under Franklin Roosevelt and as assistant director of the Selective Service under Lyndon Johnson.[63]

The high regard in which the teachers and students of M Street held Logan was evident in his being chosen class valedictorian. Over four years he had acquitted himself admirably in the classroom; he was a disciplined student, ready to tackle college-level courses. But his selection as valedictorian was equally an estimate of the leadership abilities he had begun to cultivate. He may have sniffed at the Armstrong student body, for although he was closer in class origins to them than he was to the children of the aristocrats of color, he was poised to abandon the one for the other. But he had learned the imperative to lead, and that one must strive to lead not just the M Streeters of Afro-America, but the Armstrongers as well. His valedictory address expressed both his sense of superiority and his sense of responsibility.

While much of the speech was similar to countless other valedictories before and since that express sadness at leaving the security of the familiar or at the breakup or postponement of friendships, and the anticipation of embarking on a new journey, the speech does carry Logan's distinct imprint. Evident is the impression of the social gospel of the Reverend Walter H. Brooks: the principal value taught at school was "to love the things that the Father loveth, equality, justice, truth and liberty."[64] Also inscribed in embryo in Logan's oratory were his visions of service to the race and the struggle for equality and human dignity.

He acknowledged that it was his perseverance that had won the day in his campaign to join the Talented Tenth, because "application, untiring energy and ceaseless perseverance have raised many men from the humblest ranks to the positions of usefulness and influence." He dared his classmates, too, to match his commitment to sacrifice. The struggle, though, would not only be an intellectual struggle, a battle of ideas. Adversity came in all shapes, and response to obstacles must entail action, not merely talk. Like Frederick Douglass and W. E. B. Du Bois, he was convinced that the overcoming of prejudice and the advancement of the race would exact a human toll, and he called upon his classmates to concentrate their energies and make the sacrifices necessary to contribute to the struggle. Certainly he and his classmates were talented, yet "it is not eminent talent that is required to insure success . . . but the will to labor energetically and perseveringly."

Even allowing for the extra rhetorical flourish demanded by the occasion of graduation, it was apparent that Logan had developed a habit of using bold, blunt language to motivate his listeners into action and impress upon them his own commitment and radicalism. At a ceremony usually reserved for syrupy sentiment he focused on images of carnage and destruction—the Greek wars and the Civil War. After World War I he would call for another world war, if that is what it took to achieve the liberation of the race. In the wake of World War II, he would invoke the specter of an African country possessing the atom bomb and threatening its use to force decolonization. Logan projected himself as a radical conscience of the race, speaking things that others thought but feared to say. The invocation in his valedictory of Lincoln and Grant was mild compared to his later utterances, of course, but then Logan was only graduating from high school. He still lived in the rather insular world of Washington's secret city, had not yet felt the full sting of Jim Crow, and still firmly believed his school motto: "I shall find a way or make one."

After a summer of working at jobs to raise the cash for college, Logan made his way to the University of Pittsburgh, in what turned out to be merely a two-semester detour on his way to Williams College. The year before, Arthur junior had graduated from M Street, and, his latest passion being engineering, he set out to study at the University of Colorado.[65] Logan looked up to his older brother, and he, too, decided to pursue an engineering education. It was a poor choice. He could not draw, was not particularly sharp when it came to spatial relations, and lacked manual dexterity. After a year at Pittsburgh he decided to pursue a degree in the humanities. An African-American physician in Pittsburgh, Dr. Harrison M. Brown, was a graduate of Williams College, and he helped Logan secure a scholarship there. In the fall of 1914, Logan moved to Williamstown, Massachusetts.

In his later years, Logan spoke quite fondly of his time at Williams College. He contributed regularly to the Class of 1917 Alumni Fund and willed half of his estate to the college. But this fondness was strictly retrospective, a result of friendly relations with a handful of his classmates that developed only after the class's ten-year reunion.[66] He received a superior academic education, but in his first extended sojourn from the relative security of Washington colored society, he began to learn firsthand the social isolation of racial discrimination.

Williams College had manifested some degree of concern with the conditions of African Americans since 1823, when Chester Dewey, a professor of mathematics and natural philosophy, formed the Anti-Slavery Society of Williams College.[67] The society drew upon two traditions. Despite its deserved reputation as an elite school for the rich, "At the outset [in 1793], and long after, Williams was emphatically a poor man's college. The founders of it proposed to establish that sort of institution," and it had a strong concern for the underdog.[68] The second tradition the society drew upon was New England antislavery sentiment. At the time of the society's founding, more than 75 percent of the college's student body hailed from Massachusetts, and there were no students from the South to blunt the antislavery message among the student population.

By the time Logan arrived in 1914, Williams had already graduated eleven African Americans, and enrolled two others: John Freeman, class of 1915, and John Rector, class of 1917. African Americans were no longer considered in the fashion of Abe the Bunter, a local, late-nineteenth-century African American, best known to the Williams community for crushing all manner of objects with his head.[69] But neither were they judged fully equal either. In the classroom and official school activities there appears to have been a policy of strict formal equality. Classrooms were not segregated, and the African-American students participated in extracurricular activities. George Chadwell, class of 1900, was an all-star end on the varsity football team and president of his sophomore class. As a junior, he participated in the annual Moonlight Oratorical Contest, winning second prize in his class. His classmate and roommate was Harrison Brown, the man who introduced Logan to Williams. Brown was a native of Winchester, Virginia, who arrived at Williams via

Phillips Andover Academy. Taking a premed course of study, Brown took part in student activities by being active in the Chemical Society, the Lyceum of Natural History, and the Press and Andover clubs.[70] Logan ran track and cross-country; when the team traveled to Boston, he stayed in a white hotel and had a white roommate. African-American students were welcomed to functions in the president's house.[71] For most of the African-American students, the years at Williams were probably more idyllic than they could expect to have in their future relations with white America. Their sentiments were expressed best by George Chadwell, who addressed his classmates at a banquet the evening of his commencement. Explaining how much his four years at Williams meant to him, he concluded his speech by saying "tomorrow I become a nigger."[72]

While formal equality was a considerable part of the college experience for African Americans at northern colleges—especially those from the South—it was often neutralized by the strict segregation in the dining and living facilities and the pervasive social isolation. At Williams, with one exception, African American students, until the 1920s, were discouraged from living on campus and had to live off campus. When Logan arrived, he roomed with John Freeman and John Rector at the home of Mr. and Mrs. Amos Tucker, the coachman for Williams's President Garfield. When the poet Sterling Brown arrived at Williams on scholarship in 1918, he was allowed into the dormitory, but he had to room with a Jewish student, Victor Jacobson; Jews and African Americans at Williams shared a similar situation. In his sophomore year, Brown was not allowed accommodations in the dormitory and lived with the other African Americans at a boarding home run by a Mrs. Hogan near campus.[73] The fraternities excluded African Americans, as did the boarding houses where white students who had yet to pledge a fraternity lived.

For Logan, the humiliation of being denied admission to the fraternities and dining clubs was compounded by his poverty and his light complexion. In addition to race discrimination, he had to put up with the snobbishness of rich college boys every day, for he worked his way through Williams by waiting tables and washing dishes at the fraternities and a whites-only boarding house, which was run by a southern woman. Although he was, in the last semester of his senior year, occasionally invited by a member to dine in one or another fraternity, he was never admitted, and this pained him. The disappointment was even more pointed because he was often mistaken for white.[74] He set straight those in error, although he clearly felt himself superior to Howard Lewis, a dark-complexioned student from Stamford, Connecticut, who was not especially popular with the student body. Lewis had difficulties in some of his courses—a result, Logan insisted, of the fact that, as a dark-skinned African American, Lewis had a disorganized family life and was thus unprepared to take on the rigors of a superior New England college education.

Logan's reaction to being misidentified betrayed once again his racial ambivalence. In a part of the country unaccustomed to entertaining black people, Logan could pass for white, yet he insisted on identifying himself as Negro. But even then he had rejected the notion of racial homogeneity; like the aristocrats of color with whom he identified, Logan believed he had more in common with fellow fair-skinned mulattoes and middle- and upper-class whites than with African Americans of a darker hue. While he acquiesced in his exclusion from the fraternities, he never fully accepted it, feeling he ought to be admitted, whereas someone like Lewis ought not. The Williams experience led Logan to believe that "equal rights for deserving American men were achievable within the framework of our existing society and government." But he also knew that no matter how deserving he was, this equality included only "non-personal relationships" and specifically excluded "social equality."[75]

While African-American students at Williams were welcomed at football games and formal Williams events, they still led a social life isolated from the rest of the student body. They were unwelcome at social events like proms where females were in attendance. "It was an unwritten understanding that colored students did not attend proms. I made no effort to find out since I did not have money to invite to Williamstown the kind of girl whom I should have liked to take there," Logan remembered.[76] The African Americans in Williamstown and nearby North Adams comprised a small community, consisting mainly of waiters, bellmen, and domestic servants. Logan and John Freeman sought their entertainment in North Adams, where they went to dances and other community socials. Sterling Brown, who encountered an occasional racial epithet and once got into a fight over it—"I was not a fighter, but I had my race to defend," he said—led an equally segregated social life. His close friends were the few African Americans on campus, including fellow M Streeter Allison Davis, who was two years behind him and later became a distinguished professor of social psychology at the University of Chicago. Brown's and Davis's principal recreation in Williamstown was going for long walks, on which they

discussed the solution to the race problem. For other forms of excite-
ment—and to meet women—Brown traveled across Massachusetts to
Boston.[77]

For many African-American students who attended predominantly
white northern colleges, the college experience was a relatively painless
one; while they were never allowed fully to shed the disabilities of racism,
they were generally spared the rudeness and brutality that lay beyond the
college gates. But for those students who, like Rayford Logan, were raised
in a segregated—but mostly insulated—environment, there were likely to
be one or two incidents that crystallized for them what it meant to be
African-American in the United States. For some students it might have
been receiving a grade lower than they thought they deserved, or not being
allowed to play a sport.[78]

Logan had his moment during the second semester of his sophomore
year. Although he had grudgingly accepted exclusion in the intimate and
personal spheres of life, he had expected to be treated fairly and accorded
the respect commensurate with his intellect. In fact, during his year at
Pittsburgh and his first semester at Williams he compelled this respect by
tutoring slower students; if he could not be an intimate of his white
classmates, he could at least divest them of some of their cash. He had also
learned that he could compete successfully with whites. Yet the value of all
that respect evaporated in Rhetoric 4, taught by a southerner named
Albert Licklider. One day the class discussion turned on the character
development in Rudyard Kipling's "Barrack Room Ballads." The class
was unresponsive, and to make his point, Licklider asked the class, "Suppose that he made him talk like a nigger?" Logan was stunned and
protested Licklider's language. It was to no avail, though, and Licklider
heaped on more insult by giving him a final grade of C. Some of his
classmates came to his defense and protested to Licklider, but none could
understand the horror and discomfort Logan felt, and they concluded that
he was too thin-skinned.[79] To be sure, Licklider did not define the character of Williams College. There were many fine, sympathetic teachers there,
and one who even introduced his students for the first time to Frederick
Douglass. But Logan learned in his sophomore year that he would never
be allowed to forget his race and that he would have a most difficult time
shedding the disabilities imposed by racism.

Stung by these reminders, Logan set himself off from the majority in
quiet rebellion. He became the prophet without respect in his home, rail-

ing against the racial and class injustice of the system and predicting disaster unless corrective measures were taken. The rebellion started mildly enough in his junior year, when he quietly resisted the "pro-capitalist principles warmly advocated" by his Harvard-trained economics professor. He remained tight-lipped in the course and received the only other C in his college career, a better grade sacrificed at the altar of principle.[80]

During his junior and senior years, in 1916 and 1917, Logan began to think more deeply about matters of social justice and their relationship to American foreign policy. He developed a social critique that placed the needs and interests of African Americans and disinherited whites above the interests of the Rockefellers and war profits. The evolution of his opinion is most clearly seen in two speeches relating World War I to domestic issues. The first speech, "Profits and Preparedness," was delivered in June 1916 and was the junior class entry in the Moonlight Oratorical Contest; the second speech, "The Consent of the Governed," was delivered a year later, and was one of three commencement speeches.[81]

"Profits and Preparedness" displays a temperament and logic influenced heavily, but not exclusively, by progressivism. Logan was neither a pacifist nor an isolationist; he believed in preparedness. As his high school commencement speech indicated, force was often a necessary component in the triumph of justice over injustice. But the biggest enemies of preparedness were not the pacifists—they were merely mistaken—but the Rockefellers and other financiers and industrialists. "While the U.S. is simply rolling in prosperity, the greatest nations of Europe are staggering under a burden comparable only to that of the Son of Man in the Garden of Gethsemane. The U.S. actually is growing rich on the agony and misfortune of the belligerent nations," selling them defective munitions and raking in fat profits from the interest on war loans. "If we must commercialize the agony and folly of Europe, at least give her value received!!! Let it not be said that the Yankee drives a shrewd bargain even in the presence of the most awful calamity that modern civilization has seen."

The industrialists were enemies of preparedness because they believed that the only measure of preparation was the size of the army and the quantity of armaments, the provisioning and production of which would lead to more profit. In fact, the essential ingredient of preparedness was having the support of the civilian population. This was impossible so long as there was no social justice. In the first place, the military policy of racial discrimination demoralized African Americans. "Preparedness places a soldier's fitness above race or religion," he intoned. In the second place, big business's labor policies ensured organized labor's boycott of the preparedness movement. Class antagonisms were poised to erupt into strikes that were sure to hobble preparedness. Rather, big business must be compelled to bend before demands for racial and social justice. "Let the businessman take the lead by abolishing sweat shops and child labor. . . . Let us endeavor to secure the good will of the Eur[opean]. nations instead of trying to filch every cent possible out of them. Let us lay aside prejudices & selfish interest & submerge all in the general good of the nation," he perorated.

A year after this declamation on social justice, he delivered a strident commencement address on racial injustices before an audience of graduating seniors and their families. From a mainstream progressive indictment of the robber barons, Logan demanded full equality, the vote, and the right of self-government for African Americans. With the Russian Revolution the Allied Powers in Europe could legitimately claim that they were becoming champions of democracy. But the United States possessed many of the undemocratic defects of its allies, and this qualified its image as a democratic country: it "has the problem of woman suffrage just as England has, has labor questions almost as menacing as those in Germany and Russia, and finally has the problem of a subject people, a race governed without its consent."

He lambasted the racial status quo in the South, black leaders who accommodated themselves to it, and especially the racial stereotype of the "black man [who is] indifferent, illiterate, and of criminal mind." He did not deny that there were "too many" like this, but he rejected the classification of the entire race on the basis of one segment, and noted that the race's shortcomings during and since Reconstruction were products of slavery. And he ridiculed the notion "that the art of governing is the Anglo-Saxon's peculiar attribute," for whites had lived in freedom for a far longer time than African Americans, yet white-run government was full of corruption.

Despite the degraded condition of African Americans in the South, Logan did not consider the white South the greatest enemy. Certainly the white South used an unlimited supply of tricks like grandfather clauses and literacy tests to keep African Americans disfranchised. But in a passage that calls to mind assertions made by Marcus Garvey five years later, he rather welcomed its forthright statements that " 'this is a white man's country and the white man is going to rule.' We must give these gentlemen of the South credit for their frankness. They are not afraid to say that by forcible persuasion and gentle coercion they are holding the black man down." Of greater danger to the liberty and freedom of African Americans was the "enervating attitude of laissez-faire [that] has developed in the North," and a pervasive feeling among white northerners that the South alone knows the solution to the race problem.[82] He did not directly accuse his classmates of neglect, but he did poke at the smug Williams milieu.

Logan exhorted his classmates to be better than this. The Williams tradition, he said, was the tradition of service in the cause of liberty and freedom, of service to the freed slaves. Without abandoning their legitimate and numerous grievances, African Americans would continue to fight in the war for democracy, "an anomaly of disfranchised thousands fighting that others might be free." The questions facing Williams men was whether they would stand by and watch this happen, or struggle to include African Americans in full measure in American society. It was their answer to this question that determined whether Williams men—indeed, white America—were themselves fit to enjoy democracy, he preached, concluding his speech with the following quatrain:

> If you do not feel the chain
> When it works another's pain
> Are you not base slaves indeed
> Slaves unworthy to be freed?

There is no record of the reception his speeches received. It is hard to imagine that more than a few remained unmoved by his eloquent commencement appeal. His classmates no doubt appreciated his efforts at advancement—his choice as commencement speaker was likely based as much on his diligence as on his *B* average[83]—but they also found him rather obtuse. He placed sixth in the class poll for most studious and fifth for brightest, but classmates thought tenacity was also his downfall. "His very earnestness leads him into his greatest fault," his classmates wrote in the 1917 Class Book, "for when his ire is aroused he will stick to his premises, right or wrong, from sheer determination not to be beaten."[84]

His classmates may have failed to grasp that Logan's plea reflected a new insistence by African Americans on civil rights that was occasioned by President Wilson's declaration of war against Germany in April 1917.

Virtually all African-American spokespersons supported the U.S. entry into the war. Accepting at face value Wilson's insistence that it was now a war to save democracy, they thought that the honorable discharge of military obligations would lead to the conferring of equal rights on African Americans.

A distasteful personal incident helps to account for the searing indictment of American race relations contained in Logan's commencement speech. Upon the declaration of war, Williams, like many colleges around the country, established a Student Army Training Corps. Logan enlisted. Owing to his four years as a leader of the M Street High School Cadet Corps, he assumed he would become a commissioned officer in the Williams College Battalion. Instead, he received a foretaste of what awaited him in his postcollegiate life: he was passed over for commission and only attained the rank of corporal. Once again, race frustrated his efforts to achieve personal equality.[85]

Sheepskin in hand, Logan could look back on the previous four years with a great deal of pride and sense of accomplishment. Although he had not decided on a career—he had decided to enlist in the army, and a career would have to await the end of the war—he had received a superior education, one to which few whites, and far fewer African Americans, had access. But the Williams years were also a "reality check." During his childhood in Washington he had been shielded from the fallout of racial discrimination and the petty indignities of segregation. When he left Washington, it is likely he thought as did his friend Eugene Davidson, that racial discrimination could be overcome purely by the efforts of individual Negroes to "measure up."

After three years at Williams College Logan was less certain about the immediate prospects for overcoming racial discrimination and achieving acceptance in white society. If his fellow classmates could not really understand him and continued to remind him that race was the essential difference between them, how could he expect to reach accord with the rest of white America? By his own reckoning, his intellect, leadership capabilities, and lightness of color should have gotten him through the door.[86] It was all the more painful when these qualities got him part of the way in and then could not prevent the door from being slammed on him; certainly it hurt more than if the door had never been opened at all. This troubling situation produced within Logan desires alternately to belong to that society even while it rejected others of his race and to stand off to the side and be the conscience, the critic, the prophet.

But if his time at Williams produced within him some measure of doubt, he still had a youthful optimism about the prospects for equality. He would get his due through military service. The day after commencement, Logan began his trip back to Washington to enlist in the First Separate Battalion of the District of Columbia National Guards.

chapter two

MR. WILSON'S WAR AND MR. LOGAN'S WAR

ॐ

(1917–1924)

M R. WILSON'S WAR, for African Americans, was not only a war to bolster European democracy or a war to end all wars. When hostilities first shattered peace on the European continent, many African Americans were quick to grasp the imperialist racial bases of the conflict. W. E. B. Du Bois, writing on "The African Roots of War" in the May 1915 issue of the *Atlantic Monthly,* forcefully argued that the underlying cause of the war was the European scramble for African colonies. The European bourgeoisie had welded successful national alliances with portions of their respective working classes for the purpose of raiding their neighbors' African colonies. While there was certainly a class dimension to this struggle—only the labor aristocracy, a small portion of the working classes, was to benefit from the national alliance—the conflict was chiefly national and racial in character, and the exploitation of Africa was justified with theories of racial inferiority. "We speak of the Balkans as the storm-centre of Europe and the cause of war, but this is mere habit," Du Bois wrote. "The Balkans are convenient for occasions, but the ownership of materials and men in the darker world is the real prize that is setting the nations of Europe at each other's throats to-day." He did not define an active role for African Americans in the war, for both sides were equally distasteful. He did insist, however, that the only way to prevent war in the future was to remove Africa from the spoils of war. Africans must be given back their land, "train[ed] . . . in modern civilization," and extended home rule. Du Bois envisioned African Americans in the world conflict not in the role of warriors but as mentors for the African people.[1]

As the United States became more entangled in the war and war preparedness became a national concern, Du Bois and the National Association for the Advancement of Colored People (NAACP) began to modify their positions. They no longer considered both Allied and Central Powers equally responsible for the exploitation of Africa. When President Wilson declared war against Germany in April 1917, Du Bois and the NAACP declared their allegiance to the U.S. and the Allied cause. Belgium and England were still stained with African blood, and the United States' record on race questions was also blemished, but they were the best hope for the attainment of democracy for Africans in Africa and in the diaspora. This support was at first qualified, though. Participation in the war effort was the route to civil rights. African Americans legitimately demanded full civil rights, including the right to vote, and an end to lynch law and segregation. War or no, these demands had to be met. "Let us, however, never forget that this country belongs to us even more than to those who lynch, disfranchise, and segregate," Du Bois wrote.[2]

African Americans rushed to join the military, but they bristled at their restriction to the ranks of enlisted personnel. They wanted not only to serve but also to officer. Soon after the war declaration, the NAACP requested Secretary of War Newton Baker to enroll African Americans in the newly established Officer Training Camps. Baker refused, and the NAACP countered by proposing a segregated training program; while this proposal went against the NAACP's integrationist program, its end result, argued Joel Spingarn, the association's chairman, would be an opportunity for African Americans to prove to the American public their proficiency as well as their loyalty. Baker acquiesced after more than a month of intense lobbying, especially by African-American college students at Fisk, Howard, and Atlanta universities and the Tuskegee Institute. The Officer Training Camp for African Americans was opened in Des Moines, Iowa, in July 1917.

Logan had wanted to attend this camp, and when he returned to Washington, D.C., at the end of June, he joined with some old high school friends and Howard University students to lobby the War Department for admittance.[3] Logan and his friends were rejected out of hand, because the army established a minimum age of twenty-five years for admittance to

Officer Training Camp. The age qualification was instituted as a way to exclude college students and recent college graduates, who were likely to be independent and possess initiative. Instead of choosing those candidates with the most potential, the War Department chose less competent and more pliant African Americans—especially career soldiers—for Officer Training Camp. Army hostility was based on a combination of deep-seated beliefs in the inferiority of African Americans, fear that African-American officers might be put in positions of command over white officers and soldiers, and anxiety that African Americans would gain a new self-confidence and pride from having their own officers. Further, the white southerners in the army and government who set racial policies thought it bad enough that blacks could be soldiers, for they were haunted by the specter of armed African Americans pursuing their rights. They were determined that the officer training program for African Americans would not succeed.[4] Disappointed but not yet bitter at his inability to enter Officer Training Camp, Logan enlisted in the National Guard on July 10, 1917, as a private. An ambitious young man, Logan was determined to rise through the ranks and earn a commission one way or another. Before the end of his military career, an officer shortage would enable him to rise to the rank of first lieutenant.

The First Separate Battalion of National Guards of the District of Columbia had been mustered into federal service just before Wilson declared war on Germany. Its mission was to guard the White House, the U.S. Capitol, and strategic areas like bridges and water supply in the Washington area. For the African-American community this assignment was a badge of honor, a reward for its unwavering loyalty to the United States. For the army command, however, the assignment was one of convenience: no German agent could possibly go undetected in the unit.[5] The battalion continued this detail until Christmas Eve 1917, when it was shipped south, to Camp Stuart in Newport News, Virginia. It was merged on New Year's Day with other African-American units to form the 372d Infantry Regiment of the 93d Division.[6] Logan, who by this time had been serving as battalion clerk and had won a promotion to corporal, headed to the South for the first time since he spent childhood summers at his grandfather's.

The quality of army life in the South for African Americans was dominated by one circumstance. The War Department, adhering to the prevailing view, believed that southern whites best knew how to "handle"

African Americans; further, it believed that African-American soldiers would not respond to officers of their own race. Segregated units were permitted to have African-American line officers (below the rank of major), but all regimental officers (major and above) were southern whites. As in civilian life, the southern white soldiers and officers made life miserable for African Americans, and they reserved a special hostility for those African Americans who displayed any measure of initiative, independence, or desire to lead.

Echoing the dominant sentiment in the South, the army made it clear that whether or not African Americans wore military uniforms, the United States was still a white man's country. The southern white civilian population demonstrated this most clearly by beefing up Jim Crow restrictions in the cities and towns surrounding the army bases; the military brass ordered African-American soldiers to respect segregation in the South and in other regions as well, even when Jim Crow was only the custom and not the law.[7] When the soldiers, many of whom were from the North, defied segregation, civilian and military authorities were quick to resort to force to quell the challenge.[8]

Nothing Logan had learned during his first twenty years prepared him for the racial belligerence he faced in the army. There is no doubt that army life not only soured him on America, but was also the catalyst of his career as an organizer against racial discrimination and for civil rights. Some of the harassment amounted to chronic disrespect of the kind that African Americans had come to expect in civilian life. Logan arrived at Camp Stuart with the rank of battalion sergeant-major, the senior noncommissioned officer. Yet when he took his place at the head of the chow line, which is traditionally reserved for the senior noncom, the white cook would root through the food and pick out the worst portions for Logan.[9]

Another incident was far more serious, however. Logan's commanding officer was Colonel Glendie Young, who never reconciled himself to the idea and reality of African-American officers; Young tried several means to undermine the effectiveness of these officers and to get rid of them. He once appointed Logan, who had attained the rank of first lieutenant in January 1918, officer of the day and assigned him the impossible job of guarding prisoners without also assigning him a complement of guards. When some of the prisoners escaped for a few hours, Young had Logan arrested on charges of negligence; he spent a week in the stockade, but was released when Young refused to formally charge him.[10]

If any African-American soldier or officer thought his misery would end when the 372d sailed for France on March 30, 1918, his hopes were soon dashed. On the way over, white officers were assigned the best ship cabins regardless of rank. Segregation was strictly enforced during both meals and entertainment, leading Logan to organize a boycott of all shipboard festivities unless Jim Crow was eliminated; he attended no social activities during the two-week transatlantic crossing. Upon arriving in France, the 372d's officers were separated by race, or when they shared the same barracks, African-American officers were placed behind hastily erected curtains. The African-American soldiers' social needs were also neglected by the military on French soil; the YMCA, which was the main provider of recreation, was rigidly segregated, and the facilities for African Americans were definitely inferior, when they existed at all.[11]

The military waged a protracted war against African-American participation in the Allied struggle. With few exceptions African Americans were confined to the role of militarized labor force; these troops were not only detailed to the most arduous, physically demanding work, they were also assigned the most repulsive tasks. At war's end, the black Pioneer Infantry was given graves registration duty—they were assigned to comb battlefields and disinter decayed U.S. soldiers for reburial in the Argonne National Cemetery.[12] African-American troops were also the objects of physical violence at the hands of white MPs. An officer in the security forces reported that "our 'Niggers' were feeling their oats a bit and that instructions had been given to 'take it out of them' quickly, . . . so as not to have any trouble later on." African-American soldiers were also the targets of firing squads and lynch mobs.[13]

The war against African Americans in the military was not only physical—it was ideological and psychological as well. The army tried to erase any memory of African-American participation in the war effort. African-American soldiers were excluded from the victory parade in Paris following the war, although African troops from the British and French colonies were permitted to march; of the parades in the United States, only the one in New York contained troops from the African-American units. In *Le Panthéon de la Guerre,* a frieze depicting the troops who had contributed to the final victory over Germany, black troops from all the Allied countries were represented—except those from the United States.[14]

In the summer of 1918, Colonel Young of the 372d removed virtually all of that regiment's African-American officers for incompetence or inefficiency and had them shipped to other units. The real reason for his action was contained in a memo he wrote: "The racial distinctions which are recognized in civilian life naturally continue to be recognized in the military life and present a formidable barrier to the existence of that feeling of comradeship which is essential to mutual confidence and *esprit de corp.*"[15]

Following the last campaign of the war, in which the poorly trained, meagerly equipped African-American 92d Division achieved mixed results, the High Command labeled the troops cowards and court-martialed many of the African-American officers. The military brass constantly tried to remove African-American officers from combat positions, and it manufactured charges of incompetence and inefficiency against them.[16] They were not shown the respect their rank demanded by either white officers or soldiers. Often their basic necessities, like an officers' mess when they were excluded from the white officers' facility, were not provided by the military; at the same time, they were punished by military discipline if they sought to be fed with the African-American enlisted men. Logan once recalled how he was "unmercifully bawled out for violating army regulations by eating with enlisted men. The rank injustice of it all overwhelmed me. . . . It is perhaps fortunate that I was not wearing my sidearms."[17]

The rage that was building within Logan was symptomatic of the fact that he was in fact fighting two wars: one against the Germans and another against American whites. His enthusiasm for combat against the Germans was dampened by his exposure to the horrors of war: the funerals for soldiers, visits to the trenches, exposure to live fire. One incident during his participation in the Argonne Forest campaign during the summer of 1918 both effectively ended his participation in Mr. Wilson's War and was the opening shot in Mr. Logan's War.

In June 1918 the 372d assumed command of the Argonne-Ouest sector of the Argonne-Meuse front and moved into the trenches. Logan had been on the front lines for several days when, on June 13, the German army unleashed an artillery barrage whose force flattened him. Although he got up under his own power, that evening

> my orderly told Captain Dunghill that I was raving like a mad man. . . . [A] white major came to visit me and I drove him out of the dugout by threatening to fire at him. I had no particular grudge against him . . . ; it sufficed that the major was white.[18]

Something inside Logan had snapped—he momentarily lost his usual composed demeanor. One military doctor diagnosed Logan as suffering from "Paranoid States . . . brought on by overexhaustion and by being caught in a bombardment." Another diagnosed his affliction as "war neurosis."[19]

Had they probed more deeply for the cause, they would have found that Logan was probably not paranoid—the military was indeed waging a fight against African Americans in uniform. The cause of his outburst, while ostensibly a bombardment, was in fact the accumulation of racial insults and harassment Logan had to bear. The artillery barrage had triggered one incident, but the fallout could not be contained. Somewhat paradoxically, the injury Logan suffered also had a cathartic effect: he released his rage and he would no longer suffer insults and harassment in silence. But as punishment for his threats against the white officer and his continuing opposition to Col. Glendie Young, Logan was declared unfit for service at the front and transferred to the 840th Transport Company, a stevedore outfit at Camp Bassens, in Ancona, near Bordeaux. Logan thus became a casualty in the army's war against African-American soldiers.

His appetite for the shooting war evaporated, but Logan relished his war against racism in the army. After his injury, he went out of his way to prick the racist military establishment. In one instance, Logan was with a group of African-American officers when a white colonel who had a reputation for refusing to salute African-American officers passed nearby. "I told the officers with whom I had been talking to watch me. I walked right in his direction and passed him without saluting him."[20] No racist remark went unanswered, either. While he was recuperating in hospital, a group of white officers on the ward were telling their share of racist jokes and stories. "I stood their stories as long as I could, and then went out into their ward and threatened to kill any of them who repeated their anecdotes."[21]

One of the most fiercely contested battle terrains in the war was the relationship between African-American soldiers and the French. The U.S. Army tried to prevent cordial and intimate interaction between the two. When, as was the case with the 93d Division, African Americans served with the French under French command, the U.S. Army discouraged fraternization between the two groups. On American insistence, the French military authorities issued orders forbidding a variety of behaviors that would offend white Americans:

> We must prevent the rise of any pronounced degree of intimacy between French officers and black officers. We may be courteous and amiable with

these last, but we cannot deal with them on the same plane as with the white American officers without deeply wounding the latter. We must not eat with them, must not shake hands, or seek to talk or meet with them outside of the requirements of military service.

French officers were instructed not to compliment "too highly" African-American troops, "particularly in the presence of [white] Americans." The rationale for the instructions was that the French did not understand "the position occupied by Negroes in the United States" and that white Americans considered the "familiarity" with which French treated black people "an affront to their national policy."[22]

The army also tried to prevent the formation of bonds between African-Americans and French people. In the same order issued by the French military command, the French army was encouraged to keep the "native cantonment population from 'spoiling' the Negroes."[23] Despite the orders, the civilian population displayed remarkably little animosity toward African Americans. The *Crisis,* magazine of the NAACP, reported a French newspaper account of an ordinary encounter between soldiers and civilians. The population of a rural village awaited the arrival of American troops, only to find that "they are *black* soldiers! Black soldiers? Great astonishment, a little fear." Fear was soon dispelled, and within a short time, "we see the little children in the arms of the huge Negroes, confidently pressing their rosy cheeks to the cheeks of ebony, with their mothers looking on in approbation." Families invited the troops into their homes for dinner, and the single female villagers developed crushes on them.[24]

In one instance, Logan's race saved him from receiving a thorough thrashing at the hands of some French sailors. Initially mistaking him for a white American soldier, four seamen proceeded to punch him and curse the "*sale Américain.*" As one was about to punch him once more, Logan grabbed the assailant's hand and rubbed it over his own hair. Upon feeling "*les cheveux frisés,*" he realized that Logan was indeed African-American; the sailors then all apologized, mumbling that they thought he was white.[25]

Particularly offensive to the American army command was romance between French women and African-American soldiers. But Logan did not care. He was young, away from home, rebellious—and spoke French. He circumvented military orders in two ways. His linguistic facility commended him to the post of regimental interpreter. Among his assignments during the week that the 372d was in St. Nazaire was "bistro patrol," on which he was to spy on the African-American troops, keep them away from French women, and report back to Colonel Young. Logan instead let the troops have a good time and warned them who the spies were. Not content merely to warn others, he soon became friendly with a young French woman, Suzanne Lemercier. Only the watchful eye of her mother prevented their friendship from blossoming into romance. In other towns Logan had other girlfriends, and he delighted in twitting the sensibilities of the southern white soldiers and officers by escorting these women around town after hours.[26]

Logan's rebellion went beyond circumventing the rules; he also took an affirmative stand against the harassment of African-American officers and enlisted men. He once criticized a white officer in front of enlisted personnel because that officer had berated a black soldier for making a mistake. For this action Logan received a job demotion (but not a demotion in rank). He brought charges against white soldiers who refused to salute African-American officers. He served as defense counsel for African-American soldiers court-martialed for various trumped-up charges. African-American soldiers who asserted their rights paid a price, and Logan took it upon himself to make sure the price was either lowered or eliminated.

In April 1919 Logan was appointed to an official Board of Inquiry to investigate tension between white and African-American troops in Bordeaux. After a white marine stumbled into a barroom reserved for African-American troops and started a fight, the military police arrived to arrest the "usual suspects," and an African-American soldier was taken into custody. But the black troops resisted and succeeded in freeing the prisoner. The African-American soldiers knew too much of military life to expect justice from an official inquiry. They armed themselves and marched into town to take revenge on the white soldiers. With a strenuous effort, Logan convinced the troops that white soldiers were lying in wait along the road to Bordeaux with orders to shoot any black on his way to town; he persuaded them to lay down their arms and prevented any African American from being court-martialed.[27]

Soon after these incidents Logan received notice that he would be demobilized, and he headed for Brest to prepare to sail back to the United States. The war had taken a lot out of him. He had had to face more malevolence than he had known existed. While he could proudly say that he had resisted and had not compromised himself, he was bitter. America had made it clear that it would not welcome the returning African-American soldiers, nor would it accommodate African Americans who thought that their patriotism during the war entitled them to full citizenship. That whites feared the new self-confidence of returning African-American soldiers is evident in the fact that most of the seventy-six victims of lynchings that took place in 1919 were veterans of World War I. The summer of 1919, known as the "red summer," saw the worst racial violence the country had seen. Riots swept through Chicago; Elaine, Arkansas; Longview, Texas; and Washington, D.C.[28]

Logan must have considered the racial climate at home as he considered his future. Having tasted the relative freedom of French society, he was not sure he wanted to return to America and second-class status. While he contemplated his next move, a friendly American officer (whom he did not identify by name or race) explained to Logan the prospects of making a tidy sum in Europe by speculating in currency. The possibility of earning a comfortable living tipped the scales in favor of abandoning America. He sought a discharge in France, and on August 21, 1919, his request was granted. "My experience in the army left me so bitter against white Americans that I remained an expatriate in Europe," he wrote. "The hostility toward me of some colored soldiers and officers probably rendered me all the more susceptible to bitterness but did not influence my decision not to return home in 1919. I forgave my colored comrades in arms; I *hated* white Americans."[29]

France was the perfect place for him to exorcise the devil of white America. Although France had African colonies, it appeared to treat Africans and African Americans with a semblance of dignity and equality when they were on French soil. The French just did not, immediately after the war, discriminate on the basis of race. Many African-American soldiers, returning to a homeland full of race hatred and violence, chose to head back to Paris. They were stunned to see French Catholics praying before images of a black Virgin Mary; only her skin was black, and her other facial features were European, but it was enough to capture the attention and sympathy of African-American visitors.[30] James Weldon Johnson wrote that his visit to Paris in 1905 was the first time since childhood that he experienced "the sense of being just a human being." Joel A. Rogers described African-American expatriates in the 1920s as canaries released from cages. "No more bars to beat against," he wrote, "they have disappeared as if by magic."[31]

France was also a magnet for African-American writers and musicians.

To be sure, not everyone intended to stay permanently. Many stayed only a summer, or a few months. Langston Hughes, throwing his old self overboard as he crossed the ocean in January 1924, spent eight months in Paris acquiring new meanings for his life. After James Reese Europe popularized jazz in France during the war, many musicians jumped at the chance to escape segregation and tour Europe with Will Marion Cook's Southern Syncopated Orchestra in 1919. Josephine Baker went because Paris offered her a chance to expand her performance roles; in the United States she would always be a comic dancer and a "Negro performer."[32]

Rayford Logan was neither a musician nor a writer, but he was closely connected with the African Americans in Paris, and he played the role of greeter for newcomers. When Langston Hughes arrived in Paris, he knew no one, but he did have Logan's address, supplied to him by Jessie Fauset, the *Crisis* literary editor and former high school teacher of Logan's. Logan got Hughes a job as *sous-chef* at Le Grand Duc, a nightclub partially owned and managed by Eugene Bullard, an African American who had moved to France in 1915. The clientele at Le Grand Duc was upper crust, but the place really came alive after 3:00 A.M., when the musicians from the other clubs around the city would arrive to play until dawn. Among the regulars sitting in was the jazz violinist Louis Jones; Logan was especially close to Jones, who later was professor of violin at Howard University. But the star attraction at the club was Florence Jones, who after a while left to work at Louis Mitchell's new club, which he named Chez Florence. Mitchell was a drummer who, like Bullard, had arrived in France before the war; his connection to Logan was that he was married to the former Antoinette Brooks, the eldest daughter of Rev. Walter H. Brooks, the pastor of the Logan family church.[33]

Not even the tight-knit character of the expatriate community could shield African Americans from racism, however, for Europe was crowded with white American tourists. Little by little, French proprietors gave in to the Americans, who controlled the power of the purse. The Folies-Bergere was forced to cancel a dance number that featured close dancing by a Senegalese man and a scantily clad white woman. Restaurants began to refuse service to African Americans and hotels commenced barring them from staying there. The discrimination took root despite its condemnation in the French Chamber of Deputies.[34]

Logan had an unusual vantage point on the mechanics of racial discrimination in France and the rest of Europe. Because African Americans and other persons of color were not on the Continent in inordinately large

numbers, Europe was not especially color conscious, nor did it discriminate on the basis of color. Certainly most Europeans did not expect to find
African Americans in the speculation business, Logan's choice of occupation. This circumstance, combined with Logan's very light complexion
and his command of the French language, allowed him to pass in European society; more accurately, white society decidedly declared him not
African-American. He was thus privy to the candid thoughts of American
whites who were on holiday or living in Europe. On a trip to Vienna, an
American woman eyed Logan's Phi Beta Kappa key and struck up a
conversation with him. Mistaking him for a white American, she confided
in him her revulsion for the African Americans in Europe. "We ought to
form a society here to teach the 'darkies' that they have no more rights
than in America," she offered.[35]

In April 1920, Logan sustained sizable losses in the currency market.
The stress was such that his doctor ordered him to Dax, France, to take a
rest. His losses were not so great, however, that they prevented him from
going first class. Nor did they prevent him from playing bridge and
billiards, enjoying the theater and dressing in a tuxedo for dinner each
evening. He was kept informed of his financial affairs by his bank, which
telephoned him daily with stock quotes. One evening he was approached
by an American woman speaking French who was most curious about his
background:

> "Pardon me, but is the gentleman Polish?"
> "Why, no, Madame, I am an American."
> "You American? Whoever saw an American who looked like you? Be-
> sides," she changed suddenly to English, "you can't fool me. You may be
> able to fool these Europeans, but we Americans can recognize one another
> anywhere. Come now, there is no use in continuing your incognito. We all
> know that you are a Polish prince."
> When I had recovered, I blurted:—
> "Since you are an American, you will certainly recognize an American
> Negro."
> She nearly screamed with delight.
> "You a 'nigger'! A 'nigger' here in Dax, staying at this hotel, speaking
> French better than I can, eating in the first class dining room while I eat in
> the second! That is the cleverest disguise I have ever heard in my life. A
> Polish prince passing for a 'nigger.' That is *too* funny."[36]

Americans were not the only ones to misidentify Logan. His position as
a speculator took him all over the Continent. Inflation and the market's
volatility often eroded the value of, say, the German or Austrian mark or

the Polish zloty relative to the French franc, just at the time Logan was long on those other currencies. His choice was to either take a bath in the market or pack up his inflated marks or zlotys and travel to those countries, where the money had greater purchasing power. Nationals of various European countries targeted Logan for abuse as a member of whatever nationality was despised in whatever country he happened to be visiting. In 1921 and 1923, business and pleasure took Logan to Spain, Italy, Belgium, Switzerland, England, Germany, Austria, and Poland.[37] In Germany, his French accent and French clothes caused the Germans to mistake Logan for French. His consumption of red wine in a Berlin beer garden was sufficient reason for disgruntled imbibers to mumble threats against his life; a cab driver in Munich pretended to take Logan to his destination and then dropped him several miles away, forcing the hated "Frenchman" to walk the rest of the way. On trains and in the streets, Logan was the subject of torrents of verbal abuse. In Austria, he was taken for an Italian and harassed by the police. In Warsaw he was denied hotel accommodations because he was an American Jew. While a Polish Jewish family took him in, he was "harshly criticized by a Parisian Jew for trying to 'pass for a Negro.' "[38]

Whatever hopes Logan had entertained of assimilating into the white world were scotched with these incidents. He had abandoned the United States in order to escape life as a second-class citizen. This he had done, but as the "unwilling Nordic" he found that, in another context, it was hardly to his benefit to be white. If he could not be white in America, and if in Europe he would be taken for a member of a despised white minority, then he would insist on being African-American. Logan's ambivalent racial self-identification took another turn. During his years at Williams College his exclusion from the most intimate spheres of white society was a deep source of humiliation. Now, having experienced discrimination in many languages, he decidedly (at least for the time being) threw his lot with his race. "If Heflin or Blease succeeded in having passed a law requiring all anomalous Negroes to wear on their exterior garments and on the windshield of their automobile a sign, 'colored,' I should comply most willingly," he now declared in a 1927 article that he titled "Confessions of an Unwilling Nordic."[39]

Logan saw the pervasiveness of national, ethnic, religious and racial antagonisms, and he began to grasp the nature of American race relations in an international context. "The *wanderjahre* in Europe, 1919–1924, taught me . . . that differences in nationality, language, religion, and traditions created as many intra-racial problems as did Negro-white relationships in the United States," he wrote. He now understood race and nationality to be the driving forces of politics and history. Between 1917 and 1919 he had fought a private war for equality against the U.S. Army, and he searched for direction in this fight. He had almost certainly, during his college days and in postwar France, been exposed to Marxism and other radical class-based theories of social change. Whatever affinity he may have had for them was dashed by his new understanding. Any successful strategy for liberation must emphasize the primacy of race and nationality. He was undoubtedly an African American, he concluded, and in the wake of the world war, he embraced Pan-Africanism.

The word "Pan-African" was put "in the dictionaries for the first time" in 1900, according to W. E. B. Du Bois. In July of that year Du Bois attended the first Pan-African Conference, called by Henry Sylvester Williams, a Trinidadian lawyer who lived in England.[40] Of the thirty delegates, African Americans and Afro–West Indians contributed eleven each. The African continent contributed four delegates, products of Western educations. The Pan-African Conference of 1900 had in fact only tenuous ties to Africa. The three-day meeting petitioned Queen Victoria about the colonial abuses in southern Africa, and the participants received vague assurances from Her Majesty's Government that the queen would not overlook injuries to the African's welfare. Although the conference failed in its attempt to establish a permanent organization, it left an enduring legacy in the appeal written by Du Bois, "To the Nations of the World":

> The problem of the twentieth century is the problem of the color line, the question as to how far differences of race, which show themselves chiefly in the color of the skin and the texture of the hair, are going to be made, hereafter, the basis of denying to over half the world the right of sharing to the utmost ability the opportunities and privileges of modern mankind.[41]

Du Bois injected into the meaning of Pan-Africanism the idea of self-determination; by that he meant the training of Africans and West Indians in the rights and responsibilities of government and the granting of self-rule within the framework of imperialism.[42] At the turn of the century and for nearly five decades after, the Pan-African movement (with the exception of the trend initiated by Marcus Garvey) did not advocate independence for Africa; rather it called for more or less extensive periods of tutelage under European supervision with the objective of training Africans for autonomy.

It should not be surprising that Pan-Africanism in the first half of the twentieth century did not advocate African independence. Pan-Africanism was, Imanuel Geiss wrote in his thorough account of the movement's history,

> predominantly a modern movement. It is the reaction of the most advanced, most intensively Europeanized Africans and Afro-Americans to contact with the modern world. Its representatives have been Africans or Afro-Americans who in many cases had an academic education in Europe, America or West Africa, or who were exposed for a long time to modern influence in their own country. They embraced the European and North American principles of equality and democracy and on this basis elaborated their own ideology of emancipation from White supremacy. . . . [T]hey protested against racial discrimination and European colonialism, turning against their White masters the very political and intellectual principles they had learned from them.[43]

Pan-Africanism waxed and waned in popularity among African Americans in proportion to racial discrimination and its effect on the African-American intelligentsia. The turn of the century was the low-water mark of African-American life. Political disfranchisement and racial segregation were on the increase, while during and after the world war, racial violence increased exponentially. By the 1920s, it seemed as if integration into American society was a distant dream. "Thus the appearance of Pan-Africanism among Afro-Americans in the USA was a by-product of the permanent tension between assimilation and segregation; this became particularly acute at the turn of the century with the emergence of a modern Afro-American intelligentsia which had less scope than ever for social and political activity," wrote Geiss.[44]

The surrender of Germany in 1918 created an opportunity for the resurrection of organized Pan-Africanism on the North American, European, and African continents. W. E. B. Du Bois, backed by the NAACP, traveled to Paris in December of that year to investigate complaints of discrimination and mistreatment of African-American troops and to look after African interests at the impending Versailles peace conference. Stopping off in London, Du Bois made contact with Africans and with well-meaning whites. Moving on to Paris, he met Blaise Diagne, the Senegalese politician who served in the French Parliament and who during the war was in charge of organizing France's African troops. The two planned to hold the First Pan-African Congress (as opposed to merely a conference) February 19–21, 1919. Their plan was opposed by the American government, which refused to issue passports to Americans who wished to attend the meeting and which pressured the French government to cancel the Congress. The American government had proclaimed its war aim of a peace without annexations, but it had no intentions of honoring this principle and a companion one supporting self-determination when non-European peoples were involved.

Through the good offices of Blaise Diagne, however, the French government was persuaded to allow the meeting. Among the resolutions of the Congress were ones calling for full international recognition of Haiti, Abyssinia, and Liberia, the only independent black countries in the world; for Germany's former African colonies to be turned over to a League of Nations mandates committee which would be responsible for their development in the interests of the native Africans; and for Africans to

> have the right to participate in the government as fast as their development permits, in conformity with the principle that the government exists for the natives, and not the natives for the government. . . . [T]his participation shall gradually extend, as education and experience proceed, to the higher offices of State; to the end that, in time, Africa be ruled by consent of the Africans.[45]

Du Bois had a grand vision of the mission of the Pan-African Congress activity. It was to form a permanent Pan-African Association and issue the *Black Review* first in English and French, and later in Spanish and Portuguese. It was to monitor conditions in Africa and vigorously protest colonial violations of the Africans' welfare to the League of Nations. But, owing to unfavorable conditions and the fact that the meeting was called on such short notice, the First Pan-African Congress was able to do little more than meet and issue a declaration. A Pan-African Association was scaled down to a permanent committee presided over by Du Bois and Diagne. The *Black Review* never appeared. One resolution the gathering successfully implemented was the promise to hold another Congress in two years.[46]

Logan did not attend the First Pan-African Congress—he was still on active duty. It is possible that he did not even know that the Congress was held. But whether or not he was aware of its convening, it is certain that the First Pan-African Congress was aware of Rayford Logan (probably through Jessie Fauset), for it elected Logan *in absentia* to its permanent bureau.[47]

Logan became a Pan-African activist during the interval between the first and second congresses. This was a time of growing political friction between English- and French-speaking blacks that at times threatened the unity of the movement. The divergence between the anglophones, who were led by Du Bois, and the francophones, who were led by Diagne, turned on what attitude the movement ought to assume toward imperialism in Africa. The First Congress succeeded in papering over the differences with the resolution that called only for native participation in colonial government; it skirted the question of whether Africa should be governed by Africans. In the time between the two congresses Du Bois began to lean toward preparation of Africa for self-government; Diagne favored the continued control of francophone Africa by the French and full citizenship rights for Africans. While it is true that Diagne made his peace with the French empire in 1923 and ultimately became its quisling, the division between the two men in 1920–22 appears not so much as a proimperialist against an anti-imperialist; rather, the two were responding to different sorts of obstacles put in the way of their struggles for full equality within a Western context.

Du Bois was responding to a rapidly deteriorating racial climate of escalating violence and more rigid segregation. During the war he and the NAACP had put their demands for racial equality on hold in the hope—chimerical, as it turned out—that that would gain African Americans admittance to civil life. Disfranchised and despised in the United States, African Americans, and the African-American intelligentsia in particular, were increasingly cut off from public life with ever fewer avenues for protest. For Du Bois and others, the only way forward was vigorous protest, and a fight against colonial abuse in Africa was an indirect way of fighting for full rights in the United States.

Blaise Diagne faced a different set of barriers. During his rise in Senegalese politics during the fifteen years before World War I, the French practiced a policy of assimilation, which was a product of the age of European democratic revolutions.[48] Colonial subjects were granted certain citizenship rights in theory and were represented in Parliament. While local colonial government was headed by a white governor, some authority devolved to the *evolués*, who were the most westernized Africans. The

French assumed that their colonial subjects labored under an inferior culture, but they did not conclude from this assumption that the colonials were racially inferior. Blind to indigenous cultures and civilizations, assimilation was supposed to "civilize" the colonial subjects and grant them progressively more rights until they were "Frenchmen." The French were on a *mission civilatrice*. When Diagne served in Parliament during the war, he won the right for Africans to join the French army, in which they fought with distinction. Like Du Bois, Diagne had to overcome white opposition to win this right. But the Senegalese already had a greater measure of citizenship rights than did African Americans.[49]

Logan stepped into the breach between Du Bois and Diagne in the summer of 1920 with the intention of being both a champion of Du Bois and a referee. As one who ardently believed in his own personal equality with white Americans and who was then subjected to the indignities of army life, Logan embraced Du Bois's perspective; Logan's belief in protest was all the stronger for his initial belief in assimilation.[50]

In the months leading up to the Second Congress, Logan took on the delicate job of reconciling Du Bois and Diagne. As early as June 1920, Logan was conducting talks with Diagne, probably at the behest of Du Bois. Diagne was certain that the state of African Americans would be the most important item on the agenda of the Second Congress, but he worried that African Americans were disunited.[51] What was behind this worry was fear of Marcus Garvey's separatist movement under the slogan "Africa for the Africans." Diagne despised Garvey's movement, he shuddered at the possibility that the Pan-African Congress movement would be labeled Garveyite, and he took even the mildest criticism of the legitimacy of colonial rule to be a sign of Garveyism. He complained that there were divisive elements among African Americans who were intent on destroying the unity of the Pan-African Congress and preventing it from influencing the Western powers. He insisted that Du Bois police the American delegation to the upcoming Second Congress.[52]

Actually Marcus Garvey was both Diagne's and Du Bois's bugbear. Garvey's Universal Negro Improvement Association was the largest black organization in the world. As it called for an independent Africa and rejected the idea of African tutelage, it threatened the stability of colonial rule. Diagne opposed Garveyism because it threatened his relationship with the French colonial authorities. Du Bois equally feared Garveyism because the hard edge of nationalism, which had popular appeal in Harlem and other African-American communities, threatened to cut through Du Bois's integrationist program.[53]

The Congress was scheduled to be held in three cities: London on August 28 and 29, Brussels from August 31 to September 3, and Paris on September 4 and 5. As the opening date approached, Diagne began to drag his feet, and it looked as if the movement might self-destruct. Ida Gibbs Hunt, the former teacher at M Street High School and the wife of William Henry Hunt, a black American chargé d'affaires in France, was particularly upset by the turmoil in Pan-African circles; she sought solace in the fact that the future had to be brighter: "Things look discouraging often, but one never knows what may happen. The Big Three or Four can't always run the world, justly or unjustly," she wrote to Du Bois.[54] Logan reported that Diagne was holding up Congress preparations. He wanted to postpone the Paris sessions from the beginning of September to the end; the American Legion, he explained, was spreading rumors about the Garveyite influence in the Pan-African Congress movement, and it would thus receive unfavorable coverage in the French press. He may himself have believed it, for the radicalism of the American delegation led him to disparage the incipient gathering as "a Congress of colored American men passing through Europe." Logan speculated that Diagne's procrastination was related to displeasure within the French government over the Congress.[55] The task fell to Logan to fashion a compromise between Du Bois and Diagne.

The agreement, which Logan concluded on August 26, just two days before the London session was to convene, emerged partly out of a meeting of Du Bois and Diagne, which was held sometime between August 23 and August 26; as Du Bois spoke French badly, and Diagne spoke English not at all, Logan acted as translator. The two exchanged harsh words, but Logan softened them in his translation and thus calmed both men.[56] In a separate meeting with Diagne at his summer home on August 26, Logan closed the deal on what Diagne termed *une formule transactionnelle:* the Congress would condemn Garveyism (a goal approved equally by Diagne and Du Bois), it would call for self-government, and it would petition the League of Nations to put an end to racial discrimination; Diagne would preside over the Brussels and Paris sessions but would later resign from the Pan-African Association, the organization that was created by the Second Congress.[57]

The London session opened on the appointed day, August 28, 1921, in Central Hall, near Westminster Abbey. Anglophone blacks, principally from the United States and British West Indies, numerically dominated the sessions, and W. E. B. Du Bois was firmly in command. As African Americans, anglophone Africans, and Afro–West Indians faced similar problems of racial discrimination and disfranchisement, there were few political differences. Jessie Fauset, a participant and chronicler of all Congress sessions, wrote, "We were all one family in London. What small divergences of opinion, slight suspicions, doubtful glances there may have been at first were all quickly dissipated. We felt our common blood with almost unbelievable unanimity."[58] The manifesto of this session, written by Du Bois, condemned British colonial abuses and pilloried the United States for its treatment of African Americans; it took a critical, but markedly more measured, account of Belgian, Spanish, Portuguese, and French imperial policies. It called for world recognition of the independent nations of Liberia, Abyssinia, Haiti, and the Dominican Republic, and for increasing local self-government for "backward groups." The manifesto was a stirring plea for racial equality—"The recognition of civilized men as civilized despite their race or color." But the form of this equality was left open—either Africa would be assimilated into Europe (Diagne's preference) or it would achieve independence.[59]

Despite the inclusion of Diagne's option for assimilation, the London resolutions did not travel well across the English Channel. When the Brussels sessions opened in the Palais Mondial, the francophone Pan-Africanists were well represented. With Diagne in the chair, Du Bois introduced for a vote the resolutions that were passed in London. Diagne refused to consider them, "for without doubt M. Diagne on account of his high position in the French Government felt called on to assure the Belgian Government that no radical step would be taken by the Congress."[60] Another observer, writing in the London newspaper *African World,* reported that Diagne opposed the London resolutions because he feared that they were riddled with communist theories. Logan gave credence to this interpretation. According to him, the phrase "local self-government" was translated into French as *commun;* Diagne, who was sensitive to charges that Pan-Africanism was dominated by Garveyism and Bolshevism, became alarmed and refused to allow the Brussels gathering to consider Du Bois's manifesto. In its stead, and after much protest from the anglophone delegates, Diagne exacted—as the price for unity—a mild resolution calling for education for Africans and leaving out any mention whatsoever of the imperial powers.[61]

The fragile agreement that Logan brokered before the Congress still held when the Paris session opened in the Salle Ingenieurs Civils, rue Blanche, but the debate continued to be fierce. Diagne continued his denunciation of Garveyism and his praise of France; he concluded with a defense of the race: it served loyally during the war and so had the right to demand equality in peace. Another delegate, Gratien Candace, the delegate to the French Chamber of Deputies from Guadeloupe, continued in much the same vein. Behind this criticism of Garveyism and its linkage with communism was a strong antipathy for the African-American delegates by the francophone delegates. Despite the fact that Diagne had wanted the racial situation in the United States to dominate the Congress agenda, most of the French-speaking participants felt that the Americans were trying to control the movement and dictate policy to the French blacks; in particular they felt that the Americans "had come to France to settle the problems of France and her coloured citizens."[62] Du Bois addressed these undercurrents of suspicion in one of his addresses to the Congress and was able to allay the fears of the French—at least temporarily—and he was thus able to get the Paris session to pass his London resolution.[63]

The Second Congress was the high-water mark of the Pan-African movement during the interwar years. It not only issued a ringing condemnation of race discrimination and an insistence on absolute equality; its demand for eventual self-government was an advance over the First Congress's demand for an Africa ruled with the consent of Africans. The sessions also reached out to Africa, despite Diagne's fears that it would be nothing more than a meeting of African Americans in Paris. Of the 113 people who participated in sessions in London, Brussels, and Paris, over one third came from Africa. Twenty-four participants were Africans or African Americans living in Europe, while forty-one people came from the United States and seven from the British West Indies. E. Franklin Frazier, the sociologist and later a colleague of Logan's at Howard University, attended the Paris sessions. So did William Stuart Nelson, an ex-officer in the U.S. Army, the future head of the Howard School of Religion, and a close friend of Logan's. (According to Logan, Nelson participated in some of the negotiations with Diagne). The Congress was a gathering of some of the most talented black people the world over. Jessie Fauset described it in the *Crisis:*

> On the platform was, I suppose, the intellectual efflorescence of the Negro race. To American eyes and, according to the papers, to many others, Dr. Du

Bois loomed first, for he had first envisaged this movement and many of us knew how gigantically he had toiled. Then there was M. Bellegarde, the Haitian minister to France and Haitian delegate to the assembly of the League of Nations. Beside him sat the grave and dignified delegate from the *Liga Africana* of Lisbon, Portugal, and on the other side the presiding officer, M. Diagne and his colleague, M. Candace, French deputy from Guadeloupe. A little to one side sat the American Rayford Logan, assistant secretary of the Pan-African Congress at Paris and our interpreter. His translations, made off-hand without a moment's preparation, were a remarkable exhibition.[64]

The lustrous quality of the event could not compensate for the fact that the organizers' vision ran far ahead of their ability to achieve it. The permanent organization established by the Congress was the Pan-African Association. Du Bois was the premier figure in the association, but the office of president fell to Gratien Candace, the parliamentary representative for Guadeloupe; Isaac Beton, an educator from Martinique who resided in Paris, was elected general secretary. Logan was a member of the permanent bureau based in Paris. The Second Congress charged the Pan-African Association with the goal of "the improvement of the position of negroes [*sic*] all over the world by developing their economic, political, intellectual and moral faculties through co-operation and organization." Chapters, authorized by the bureau, would be represented at future Pan-African Congresses at an established rate of one delegate for chapters of at least 250 members, an additional delegate for chapters with up to 5,000 members, and a third for chapters with up to 10,000 members.[65] The vision was not within grasp; as Beton reported soon after the Congress, the Pan-African Association had only twenty-five dues-paying members, and had neither an office nor means of printing the organization's constitution.[66] After the final session adjourned, the Congress leaders reconvened for a celebratory dinner. "In retrospect," Logan wrote, "it seems to me that a *haute cuisine* dinner at La Rue's, a famous restaurant, Place de la Madeleine, was almost a wake, though at the time it was a jovial occasion."[67]

One of the principal reasons for the inability of the Pan-African movement to flourish after the successful Second Congress was the lingering effects of the dispute between francophone and anglophone blacks. The French-speaking delegates felt their struggle for equality far more advanced, and they did not hesitate to make known their feelings during the Congress sessions. "[E]very one of the American delegates," Du Bois wrote to Beton, "returned to the United States with the idea that the French Negroes, with one or two exceptions like yourself, had no appreciation or deep interest in what the American Negroes were seeking to do."[68]

While this harsh treatment made it difficult to generate and sustain interest among African Americans for the Pan-African cause, it made it even more difficult to raise money, and the Pan-African Association operated in chronic penury. The NAACP, which had contributed four thousand dollars to the organization of the first two congresses, refused to be the sole supporter of the Pan-African endeavor; it would still contribute to the operation of the association, but only as a member organization and only in conjunction with other member organizations. This refusal was apparently an affront to the French Pan-Africanists, who viewed the NAACP and African Americans as their cash cow. Beton pleaded with Du Bois to raise money for the survival of the Pan-African Association. Logan, Beton wrote, had previously contributed significant amounts of money when he was a successful speculator; but he had made a series of bad investments, was approaching financial insolvency, "and indeed is toiling like an honest working man to make both ends meet. Just now he is in Poland for commercial reasons." If Logan could not contribute financially, other African Americans would have to pick up the slack. "It is the responsibility of each to serve the Race according to his means," Beton wrote to Du Bois, and African Americans had more means than any other group in the struggle.[69]

Money worries plagued the Pan-African Association throughout the next two years, and the recrimination that usually accompanies financial difficulty nearly grounded the movement. Gratien Candace had left the association, and Isaac Beton took over responsibility for running the organization. Beton once again complained to Du Bois that African Americans were not supporting the organization—only one American, probably Logan, had paid dues—and in August 1923 he canceled the Third Congress, planned for September in Lisbon. Furious, Du Bois insisted that a biennial meeting was obligatory and not optional under the Association statutes. He unilaterally announced that the Congress was on, with sessions in London and Lisbon in November, and he tried to enlist Logan once again to fight for his views.[70]

Logan found it difficult, however, to completely endorse Du Bois's position. He agreed with Du Bois that a Congress needed to be held "in order to prove to the world that the Negro race is capable of continuing what it has undertaken."[71] But the members of the Association Bureau— and not just the French members—considered Du Bois's actions to be high-handed. Several of the Americans resident in Paris suspected that Du Bois did not like Beton's leadership and that he was withholding money he had raised for the association until Beton was ousted.[72] Logan accused Du Bois of not giving full support to Beton. Beton had given a full measure of work toward the Pan-African cause, and had been "met with indifference and hostility on all sides." Logan had worked closely with Beton and was "in a better position than any one else to have a sane and valid opinion. I must therefore say that M. Beton deserves unlimited praise rather than the blame implied in your letter." Logan conceived of his role on the Bureau as "a buffer between the French and American delegations." In this latest disagreement he felt that the French, not Du Bois, were right. He would not assist Du Bois to make an end run around Beton, but he would facilitate a reconciliation.[73]

Nevertheless, when it became clear that Du Bois would go ahead with his plans for the Third Congress, Logan did take up his cause. He joined forces with Ida Gibbs Hunt, and the two persuaded Beton and the other French blacks to join in the drive for the Third Congress. "Mrs. Hunt and I succeeded Sunday," Logan wrote to Jessie Fauset, "in convincing the Frenchmen that, inasmuch as Dr. Du Bois is going ahead with the Congress in spite of all difficulties, we might as well do all in our power to make it a success. I am not going to say anything more about the controversy between Dr. Du Bois and M. Beton."[74] On September 20, 1923, Logan sailed for Lisbon to arrange the Congress session. Logan was mollified—but only temporarily.

When Du Bois had first asked Logan for assistance, he implied that he would compensate Logan for his time and expense.[75] Although Logan had raised money from the African-American musicians, and Hunt contributed three hundred francs, he needed more money and was glad to receive Du Bois's offer. As he was about to depart for Lisbon, he wrote Jessie Fauset that "it is a pity that lack of funds prevent me from doing something worth while. I am short of money myself as the result of an unfortunate investment and really should be looking around for work." He arrived in Lisbon short of funds. Upon securing agreement from the Portuguese *Liga Africana* to host the Congress in November, he wrote to Du Bois that "In view of the urgency of the situation, I left [Paris] before I had a sufficient sum of money. I am therefore obliged to borrow three hundred and fifty escudos from Dr. de Magalhaes in order to return to Paris. I am sure that you will be only too glad to forward him this sum as soon as possible because the results obtained fully justify this small expense."[76]

Back in Paris on October 4, Logan wrote a fuller account of the Pan-African situation for Du Bois. Logan was laboring diligently to head off a move by Isaac Beton to denounce Du Bois in the press. There was to be a meeting the following night of the Permanent Bureau, and Logan was to be the only American there, "but I am going to make a fight to try to stop M. Beton from executing his plan." Logan seemed to be enthusiastic about Congress preparations, and he looked forward to meeting Du Bois in London. "I venture to hope that your funds will allow you to pay me one hundred dollars and my expenses in second class. For two months' work, that is certainly not asking too much," he wrote Du Bois.[77]

It was, apparently, too much. During the first two weeks of October, Du Bois sent Logan three letters telling him that he had no money with which to compensate Logan for his efforts in Lisbon. He wrote that he could neither reimburse the Portuguese Pan-Africanists for the loan they extended Logan, nor pay Logan's expenses to the London sessions of the Congress. Nevertheless, Logan traveled to the London sessions (courtesy of Mrs. Hunt), and he was a most active participant in it, cosigning the final declaration with Hunt and Du Bois.

As the French-speaking delegates were not in London in large numbers, the final declaration was similar to the one passed at the Second Congress sessions in that city. But the absence of francophones also took up a considerable amount of attention, perhaps because Du Bois was sensitive to charges that the Congress movement was not representative of all Pan-Africa. Du Bois renewed the debate between anglophone and francophone blacks by once again charging that the principal problem was that the leaders of the francophones considered themselves, in Diagne's words at the Second Congress, "as Frenchmen first and as Negroes second." Du Bois then proposed practical measures to ensure that the French delegates did not control the administration of the Pan-African Association. The Permanent Bureau would become simply a committee for France and its colonies, while other committees would be formed in Europe, the Americas, and Africa; together they would be responsible for calling the next Congress. Responding to claims that Americans had not financially supported the Association, Du Bois proposed an audit of the Permanent Bureau's books and reimbursement for legitimate expenses.[78]

Although he was an enthusiastic participant in the London proceedings, Logan took umbrage at what he considered shabby treatment by Du Bois. He had, he felt, not only worked diligently for the Pan-African cause, but had also put aside his differences with Du Bois for the health of the movement. He must have thought that Du Bois's inability to pay was symptomatic of the movement's inability to grow. Logan now soured on Du Bois, and he wondered whether the Pan-African Congress movement, despite Du Bois's astute political analysis and formulation of demands, would advance and become a vital political movement (as distinct from a trend of political thought).

Logan was so disillusioned with Du Bois that he "switched" sides. Logan approached his old political enemy Blaise Diagne about touring the United States with the object of dramatizing black political power in France and the absence of such power among African Americans. He no longer believed Du Bois had the ability to head the Pan-African movement. Although he suspected that Diagne created many of the obstacles he and Du Bois encountered in the organizing of the Third Congress,[79] he turned to someone who he believed had power to effect change. Logan even set up a committee of prominent Harlemites headed by the Reverend Frederic Cullen to promote the tour.[80] When Du Bois heard of Logan's defection, he tried to dissuade Diagne from crossing the Atlantic; Logan blasted Du Bois for his meddling: "Allow me to advise you, that unless you wish to become involved in legal difficulties, you had better refrain from your insidious activities that are due only to your personal jealousy." And he continued to rail against Du Bois for withholding money due him.[81]

The degeneration of the relationship between two of the primary protagonists of Pan-Africanism into a squabble over money is pertinent to an estimate of the Pan-African Congress movement. The movement, and principally Du Bois, bequeathed to Africans in Africa and in the diaspora a rich intellectual tradition, upon which they drew in the post–World War II era. The congresses drew together some of the most brilliant minds of the black race and proved—to whites, but more so to blacks—that they could organize on their own behalf and struggle for their own solutions to their own problems. For African-American intellectuals, Pan-Africanism was an entrée to a lifetime of civil rights activity. But the movement's principal weakness during the 1920s was that it *did* nothing much of practical consequence. Du Bois was unable to realize any of his grand plans for the movement. No journal was published, no significant protest was made, no lasting cooperation among blacks of different nationalities was effected. In short, the movement was unable to amplify the individual creative genius that Du Bois put into it. And, as happens in such situations, the "efflorescence of the Negro race" commenced to bicker.

This weakness was precisely what disturbed Logan. He was attracted to Pan-Africanism by its powerful intellectual content; but he was also anxious to make a difference in his actions, something he increasingly came to realize could not happen within the context of the Pan-African Congress movement. His disappointment was compounded by an incident that occurred a few weeks after the London session of the Third Congress. As he prepared to board a bus on the Avenue de la Grande Armée in Paris, Logan was hit by a car and fractured his leg. Throughout the fall of 1923, Logan was either in hospital, confined to bed, or restricted in his ability to get around the city. He used his enforced idleness to rethink the course of his life. Expatriate life had been most exciting, but he had "extracted as much fun out of life as a healthy, unmarried male in his early twenties could do in France."[82] It had also been rewarding. He had worked intimately with a score of the brightest and most influential black people from Africa, Europe, and the Americas, and he had gained a detailed knowledge of the League of Nations and its supervision of colonial mandates; he was, in fact, something of an expert in this field.

For all the benefits of expatriation, though, there were considerable drawbacks. His prolonged absence caused his parents a great deal of anguish. Then, too, he felt that he was letting down his high school teachers (with the possible exception of Jessie Fauset). "I was not carving the niche that my teachers had expected of me," he wrote. He also came to realize that although expatriation had solved his problem of freedom, his choice of an individual solution did not benefit all African Americans. "I decided that while I had solved my own personal problem as far as freedom from segregation was concerned, I was hardly living up to what had been expected of me when I had finished college." If guilt was not enough of a motivator, he was also homesick—a condition likely aggravated by an encounter with Langston Hughes—and had diluted his hatred of white Americans. "I had stopped hating white Americans, partly because I saw so few of them. It is probable that my meeting Langston Hughes was the catalytic agent that brought my yearning to return home to fruition."[83]

Logan sued the driver who hit him, and the suit was settled in November 1924. He received the sum of two thousand dollars, which he used to book third-class passage to New York in December. His anxieties about rejoining life in America doubled as he boarded the U.S. steamer *George Washington*.

> Just as I stepped on deck, my first time on American "soil" in six years, over the strains of the band playing the Star Spangled Banner, I heard a steward say: "Look at that damned nigger." For a moment I felt like getting off the ship and returning to France, but my decision had been firmly made.

His decision was made somewhat easier to execute when Logan met a jovial traveling companion, who was constantly drunk and who in his insobriety denounced "various bigots, especially the Ku Klux Klan and Catholics." The two men—Logan did not name his companion—were inseparable on the voyage across the Atlantic; as they cruised into New York Harbor, they especially delighted in "pointing out that the Statue of Liberty had its back to the United States, clear evidence that the immortal words inscribed on it had little meaning for the people of the Nation it was supposed to honor."[84]

Logan, a jumble of mixed emotions, was repatriated. From the ship he went to the annual meeting of the Alpha Phi Alpha fraternity, which was meeting in New York December 27–31, 1924. Most of his fraternity brothers treated him as a returning hero, but Jesse Moorland, the YMCA official in charge of work among African Americans, treated him more as the prodigal son returned. Moorland "publicly congratulated me on leaving the flesh pots of Paris to attend the Convention." After a few days in New York, Logan returned to Washington, D.C. He would continue the fight for civil rights (he could never abandon that), but he would have to do it in a respectable way. He was determined to make a professional—as well as political—name for himself. On the train south, though, the political experience and personal knowledge he had gained over the last six years counted for very little, and Logan, the *bon vivant* from Paris, felt chastened, almost overwhelmed.

> I felt no great sense of joy on returning to the land of my birth. . . . Above all, I recall almost a sense of shame during the ride to Washington—so much had been expected of me when I was graduated from Williams; . . . I returned to Washington, an impecunious dismal failure.[85]

chapter three

PROFESSOR AND POLITICIAN

৯৯

(1925–1932)

UPON HIS RETURN to the States, Logan decided to pursue a career in education. Teaching was, of course, a respectable (and respected) profession. Although, like other African-American intellectuals before him, he would be restricted to working in segregated schools and colleges, at least the Library of Congress did not exclude blacks, so Logan could plan to spend summers in Washington, D.C., absorbed in research. Furthermore, as his role model, W. E. B. Du Bois, had proven during his time at Atlanta University at the turn of the century, academia could provide an institutional base for political activism, and Logan was a young firebrand. His command of French and Spanish—and his facility with languages, generally—and his experience abroad made Logan an attractive candidate for a faculty position at a black college. In the summer of 1925 Virginia Union University in Richmond offered him a job teaching French and Spanish; Logan grabbed the opportunity, and he once again moved south.

When he arrived in Richmond, Virginia's African Americans were in a state of political somnolence. In 1920, they had found a way around their constitutional disfranchisement by hitching their wagon to female suffrage.[1] Once the Nineteenth Amendment became law, civil rights activists had enthusiastically gone about the business of registering African-American women to vote. Their energy was met with an equal zeal on the part of Virginia's white politicians to deny them any say, and election officials resorted to delaying tactics. During the September 1920 registration period in Richmond, officials registered more than three times as many white women as black, while turning away as many African-American women as they allowed to register.[2]

Although the tangible results were meager, the state's African Americans would not be ignored as a political force. When the Republican party, which was controlled by lily-whites, refused to put up a senatorial candidate against the Democrats, the party's African-American faction fielded its own. Richard Pollard, an attorney and chair of Richmond's segregated Republican faction, received just seventeen thousand votes, but this total amounted to 20 percent of the vote for Republican presidential candidate Warren Harding. The lily-whites were not impressed; they once again moved to exclude African Americans from their party. In 1921, African-American Republicans broke with the party to form a "lily-black" faction and nominated John Mitchell, Jr., the publisher of the *Richmond Planet* and a militant civil rights advocate, to run for governor. This time, though, the movement was disabled in its fight against the Democrats and Republicans by internal bickering. Mitchell could barely muster five thousand votes. Following this rout, African-American participation in Virginia's politics went into a decade-long decline.[3]

A resurgence of racist organizations and the extension of segregation laws accompanied this political decline. In the years following the "red summer" of 1919, the Ku Klux Klan experienced sustained growth throughout Virginia and especially in industrial towns. The Klan controlled Richmond's Business Men's Club and frequently paraded down Broad Street, the city's main commercial strip. Among the KKK's membership were the chiefs of police and other officials of Norfolk and Newport News.[4] The Anglo-Saxon Club was founded in Richmond in 1922, and within a year had spread throughout the state and eleven others. Devoted to the "preservation and maintenance of Anglo Saxon ideals in America," this organization's roster included at least one high state official and an editor of the *Newport News Daily Press*. Lynchings and other incidents of racial violence and intimidation during this period were especially horrific.[5]

In the mid-1920s the Virginia legislature passed a new round of rigid segregation laws, including one banning interracial marriages. In 1926 the legislature passed the Massenberg Bill, which for the first time required segregation in all places of public assembly, including theaters and auditoriums. Before this law was enacted, African Americans were separated by custom in such public places. But when whites attended programs at the Hampton Institute and other black spaces, they were not guaranteed separate seating. "Reportedly," explained the historian Charles Wynes, "in 1925 a white couple from nearby Newport News found themselves seated next to Negro students at a dance recital, after which the husband 'launched a crusade for "better" segregation ordinances.' "[6]

At the time Logan took up residence in Richmond in mid-1925, the city's African Americans were badly demoralized and economically battered. A shortage of housing and jobs (African Americans were also excluded from city employment) coalesced with fossilized race relations and led to an exodus of black Richmonders during the 1920s; Richmond was the only southern city to experience such a population decline.[7] Those who stayed responded by forsaking militant leaders in favor of those of a more conservative stripe. Logan cut his political teeth in America as a radical among African Americans who for the time being had no fight left in them, and had the dubious honor of being crowned "the best Negroes in the world."

His best-known foray into Richmond politics concerned the employment of African-American principals in the segregated schools. Education for African Americans in Richmond was symptomatic of the raw deal they received. According to a report written by a biracial group of Richmonders under the auspices of the Richmond Council of Social Agencies, African-American children had no access to wholesome recreational facilities, kindergartens, and day-care centers. While the city spent annually more than $50 per white student, it spent less than half that sum on instruction for each African-American student. White teachers were paid between $550 and $800 more than their African-American counterparts. No special classes existed in the Jim Crow schools for mentally and physically disabled students.[8] The African-American schools had shorter terms, and attendance was poor partly because there was no compulsory-attendance law.[9]

Logan, who had received his public school education in a system that was controlled by African Americans, was appalled at the situation in Richmond, and he was determined to alter the status quo. Logan organized a petition drive to demand that the school board change its policy and appoint African-American principals. It was, one newspaper reminisced, "a lusty vitriolic campaign. . . . The fight was bitter, no quarter asked or given."[10]

Despite the fact that the petitions contained thousands of signatures, the campaign stalled, as black conservatives, apparently led by some teachers, opposed the drive.[11] There are a variety of explanations for why Richmond's black establishment opposed the initiative. It is possible that the teachers were coerced into accepting the status quo; they might have been told that their jobs were at stake. This explanation would have brought little comfort to radicals like Logan, who believed that principle ought to take first place. Militant observers of the Richmond scene believed that the teachers received some tangible benefits from the school system the way it was. They feared retaliation from white administrators should they become identified as race leaders. As frequently happens when social movements implode, the participants assign blame, and in this case Richmond's black teachers were accused of excessive cowardice and venality.[12]

Whether or not the radicals correctly divined the reasons for them, the community establishment's actions discouraged protest. After the defeat in 1921, the middle-class leadership of black Richmond eschewed participation in politics. One survey found that of the city's 150 active ministers, only nine were registered to vote. It was the same in other professions; the middle class could qualify to vote, but just did not take the time to register.[13] Not all of the conservative leadership was indifferent, of course; Gordon Blaine Hancock of Virginia Union, and P. B. Young, publisher of the *Norfolk Guide,* were quite active in the cause of social betterment. But the radicals believed that the conservative philosophy of self-help became an excuse for the middle class to "help yourself." The opposition Logan met from the African-American teachers and established leadership illustrates the obstacles that he and other militants encountered in the battle against segregation. They had to fight not only legal segregation, but also the dead weight of Jim Crow customs which had been internalized by a respected section of the African-American community.

The conservatism of Richmond's African-American leadership spilled over to Virginia Union University, and on campus, too, Logan's militant politics and brash manner earned him the prominent spot of premier opponent of the school's administration and much of its faculty. "Those old-timers in Richmond, of course, did not appreciate my statement that they were naive in accepting the definition by the white newspapers that they were 'the best Negroes in the world,' " he said.[14]

Virginia Union was a contradictory academy. It was controlled by paternalistic whites, but it insisted on educating African Americans for full citizenship. It professed the importance of a liberal university education as the only way to develop race leaders with sufficient broadmindedness and culture, and was at the time one of the nation's best black colleges; but it often was more interested in "building character" than in promoting excellent scholarship. Founded by the American Baptist Home Mission Society, VUU had a racially mixed board of trustees, but the school had had a series of white presidents. The university was controlled by racial meliorists who often capitulated to hard-line segregationists, but there was simultaneously an atmosphere that was congenial to—and even encouraged—discussion of strategy and tactics for racial equality. Although Rayford Logan ultimately was fired from VUU for his radicalism and left the institution with harsh, unambivalent memories, he in fact had an extremely productive five years there and matured as a "race man" and a scholar.

Union possessed milder versions of the maladies that plagued other institutions of higher education for African Americans, especially the land-grant colleges. Although the presidents and faculties of the public colleges were almost always African Americans, decision-making was controlled by whites who were generally hostile to a liberal arts education for African Americans. Appointed for their trustworthiness, the presidents were the "black power brokers who could transform themselves from sycophantic Uncle Toms—when in the presence of whites—to dictatorial Emperor Joneses—when dealing with blacks."[15] One of Logan's peers described for him the atmosphere that the president of the college at which she taught promoted:

> The thing that stuns me most is the complacency of the Negroes at Alabama A&M. They truly feel that they have reached the pinnacle of success. Even the President told me that he "loves it here in Alabama and would not change it for the world." He said that he is not interested in any Negro problem—integration or anything else: that his objective is to build a good school and let the legislature in Montgomery decide who will attend it.[16]

J. Saunders Redding's *Stranger and Alone* is a fictionalized account of one black college, the Arcadia State College for Negroes.[17] The president ran his school like a plantation, making sure that students and faculty were appropriately servile; he frowned upon students' carrying too many books about, for this might give visitors the wrong idea. He squashed independent thinking among his teachers and promptly fired anyone who acted or even thought in a remotely radical fashion; his spies kept him abreast of all developments at the school. His chosen heir also displayed remarkable disdain for higher education and the fight for racial equality: "He did not want to think about the race problem nor live on two levels nor make life more difficult by trying to analyze everything. All he wanted was to get what he could out of life."[18]

Virginia Union escaped the more blatant deformities of so-called Negro education—it tolerated and even encouraged limited debate on the issues of importance to black America—but as an institution dependent upon the coffers of white philanthropies, it could hardly avoid the foundations' one-dimensional notions of black higher education. Most philanthropies considered a wide array of projects inappropriate for African-American higher education. Big science, for example, was out. Ernest E. Just discovered this when the Julius Rosenwald Fund and the General Education Board (GEB) for many years would not fund his basic research activities.[19] The philanthropic organizations decided that the most prudent course of action was to encourage the formation of only a few centers of African-American higher education—notably at Fisk University and the Atlanta University Center—while refusing requests for large amounts of aid to other schools. Because of this policy, Virginia Union did not share in foundation largesse to the extent that other black colleges did. But the pressure to conform was nevertheless ever present.[20] In 1931, for example, a sizable gift to Virginia Union (with promise of further support) for a race relations institute was canceled soon after it was given. The donor, a widow of a wealthy northern capitalist, wanted a program that emphasized racial accommodationism in the Booker T. Washington mold; when the donor heard criticisms of this orientation from some Union faculty, she withdrew her offer of aid.[21]

In 1929 school officials were offered a substantial contribution to its building fund for a science hall by Confederate veterans. The only condition was that the new building contain within it a plaque memorializing "their love for their 'old black mammies' . . . [and] bearing the names of these faithful servants." The director of the fund-raising campaign accepted the offer and the university president William J. Clark, a white Baptist preacher whom Logan described as a "broken-down minister," was ready to accede when Logan raised a storm of protest. Organizing students and teachers who were offended by the offer, Logan ridiculed the project, proposing to name the new building "Mammy Hall"; the school then chose not to accept the contribution "of the Bourbons who could neither learn nor forget."[22]

Logan was shocked at the effects of racial meliorism he found at Virginia Union. White professors were habitually paid more than African-American ones. Logan was paid $1,800 annually and provided with room and board, but when he discovered that the evening meal often consisted of a half of a canned peach and a glass of iced tea, he declared that the faculty meal plan insulted the dignity of his position; one time he took a particularly bad meal straight to President Clark's house. His protests went unanswered, but he was more dismayed by his colleagues' silence and their failure to follow his lead.[23]

Logan expressed even more alarm at the prestige enjoyed by the conservative ideas of Gordon Blaine Hancock, a professor of sociology, among the faculty and administration. Despite the paternalism of President Clark's administration, Logan helped initiate among the university community a vigorous debate on a wide range of topics, including the purpose of a university education and the obligation of African-American students to contribute to race advancement, the future of African Americans, the prospects for African-American art and literature, and the course of the Harlem Renaissance.[24]

The sharpest debates occurred over the appropriate strategy and tactics to achieve racial equality. In addition to articles in the *Virginia Union Bulletin,* an irregular publication, the debate was carried out in the community setting of the weekly chapel services. Unlike many other church-supported schools, Union's devotionals, while mandatory for students and faculty, were neither perfunctory nor mechanical. The atmosphere was informal yet serious, as services included not only prayer but also regular speakers to discuss current events; speakers were frequently grilled by the audience and "a student might arise in the audience and with a bow of recognition from the president launch a drive."[25] Coburn Chapel was the site of many exchanges between Logan and Gordon B. Hancock.

Logan and Hancock dueled over the relative merits of political action and self-help in the search for race advancement. Each man saw the drastic decline in the standard of living of African Americans. Hancock, in particular, struggled to come to grips with acute job shortages and the exclusion of African-Americans from jobs that they had traditionally held. Too much attention, he felt, was paid to the advancement of a relative few in the business and professional worlds; there were far too many professionals of all kinds, he felt, and far too few semiskilled and unskilled workers to support the professionals.[26] Hancock's prescription for Afro-America's dire straits was a "Hold-Your-Job" campaign.[27] Because community survival depended upon jobs, it was incumbent upon those who had jobs to keep them at any cost. If this meant silently taking abuse, then take it. If it meant avoiding union drives, then avoid them. The alternative to a return to industrial education was a return to slavery, he said.[28] Hancock castigated those who complained about their working conditions or their wages; "Many a longwinded talker is a short-winded worker," he wrote.[29]

Political agitation, for Hancock, was not only decidedly secondary; in most cases it was downright detrimental. He expressed pleasure that African Americans were disfranchised in the situation prevailing in the 1920s because he believed that that ought to eliminate race-baiting from electoral politics. African Americans who persisted in political agitation were guilty of "aggravating race prejudice." Taunting Logan and other radicals, he claimed they played to the "grandstand" and then abandoned the community to the mercy of wrathful whites.[30] Although he was more evenhanded in his tone regarding the NAACP, he felt that with such pressing problems as jobs and the economy, that organization spent its resources unwisely when it chose to fight the nomination to the Supreme Court of John J. Parker, the racist North Carolina jurist.[31] To Hancock, the outcome of political agitation was like manna from heaven: it was unpredictable and not under control of human beings. His constant query to radicals was: "What if the manna faileth?"[32]

"Then we shall all die!" declared Logan in one of his rejoinders to Hancock in Coburn Chapel.[33] Improvements in the political climate were not gifts from God, but the lifeblood of liberation; without agitation and political struggle, Logan felt, the race was doomed. Borrowing a page from Frederick Douglass, he insisted that those who wanted to be free must strike the first blow. Writing on the one hundredth anniversary of Nat Turner's execution, Logan castigated those like Hancock who considered Turner a fiend rather than a martyr, and he called on them to unshackle their minds. Unless whites assented to the demands for substantial equality, "who will dare predict that there will never be another Nat Turner?"[34]

In Logan's scheme of things, politics ruled economics; he was intensely interested in the economic welfare of Afro-America. The key to economic advancement—and political vitality and equality—was a solid middle class. Logan lauded the achievements of exceptional people like E. E. Just in science and James Weldon Johnson in international politics, but they were not the stuff of which racial advancement was made. Using the metaphor of a tree to describe Afro-America, Logan wrote that Just and Johnson represented the outermost limbs of a tree. The problem was that they were connected to the root system—the masses—only by a slender cord; the race met the greatest obstacles not in the development of the high branches but in the growing of a strong trunk, the middle class.[35]

Whereas Hancock counseled the African-American lower classes to hold on to their jobs at any cost, Logan encouraged them to build and strengthen the middle class of professionals—not by merely patronizing them, but through collective struggle to open up the doors of opportunity. There were not too many professionals, as Hancock claimed, but too few—too few doctors, lawyers, qualified teachers, and trained ministers (the latter being a slap at Hancock, who was a minister). The middle class must be built by raising the educational level and increasing the access to education of the lower class. African Americans must simply fight exclusion. Logan's was an aggressive, not a defensive, approach to improving the standing of African Americans.[36] He wanted to start his program for empowerment on the campus of Virginia Union University and demanded that President Clark be replaced by an African American; for that matter, there were enough talented African Americans to replace every white president of a predominantly black college in the country.[37]

Knowledge is power, and Logan was also a strong believer in instilling in his students an appreciation of their heritage. Before he arrived at VUU, the school offered only ancient Greek, Roman, and Bible history; although he was initially hired to teach French and Spanish, Logan established the first courses in Negro history, African history, and the history of imperialism.[38] He not only brought to the students a storehouse of knowledge concerning Africa and colonialism; he was also a creative and engaging instructor. For Negro History Week he had his class research the speeches given by the African-American delegates to Virginia's Constitutional Convention of 1867–68; these twenty-four delegates held the balance of power and were responsible for establishing a tax-supported public school system for all Virginians. Because there were still some nonbelievers in his class about the crucial role played by these delegates, Logan had the class research the entire convention and recreate portions of the meeting, with students acting "as a real historical Unionist, as a scalawag, as a carpet-bagger or as one of the Negroes." This convinced the students of the centrality of black participation.[39] Logan struggled to open students' minds, to get them to think for themselves. He demanded much from his students, and in return he gave a great deal; in 1928 he was voted Favorite Teacher by the student body.[40]

Popularity aside, the university administration was fed up with Logan's radicalism. In 1930 Logan went on leave; he had been admitted to the Ph.D. program in history at Harvard University. In late 1931, VUU President Clark sacked him. According to the *Baltimore Afro-American,* the administration had accumulated a variety of complaints against Logan: he demanded an African-American president for Union; he "urged students in classroom and assembly to do their own thinking and not to accept old stereotyped notions and forms" (one student said that Logan did not flunk those who disagreed with him); he criticized Gordon Hancock in the local white newspaper for being a reactionary; he was radicalizing the students.[41]

Logan's firing caused a brief uproar on campus, and some students threatened a strike, although nothing came of such talk. His firing was a blow to the militant community in Richmond. One radical educator, Thomas Dabney, wrote of Logan that

> He is no white man's "nigger," and that means a great deal to me. The Negro has long suffered from an over crop of me-too-boss Negro leaders. . . . the Negro needs some manly, intelligent and courageous leaders. . . . The others are a positive liability to our educational system both public and private.[42]

Despite the protests, Logan did not return to Virginia Union University. He felt—for the first of many times in his adult life—unappreciated. He had fought hard but had not been adequately backed up, he felt; he perhaps even consoled himself with the thought that he was ahead of his time. In later years Logan looked at his five years at Union as a sentence of sorts, or more accurately, a punishing initiation into the academic world. He did not like living in the South, of course, but more important, he formed an essentially negative impression of so-called Negro education.

In addition to his campus and political activities, Logan's years at Virginia Union were also ones of personal growth. In August 1927, after more than a year of dating, Logan married Ruth Robinson in Richmond. Ruth was born on April 12, 1900, on the same plantation in Manchester, Virginia, where her grandparents had labored as slaves. Her parents were "average" people—sharecroppers, said her cousin, Elizabeth Daly—who later moved to Richmond, where her father had lined up a job on the railroad.[43] The two met in 1926, when Ruth was a student at nearby Virginia State College, in Ettrick, and Logan came to campus to speak. One quality that helped attract Logan to Ruth was her glorious voice; at Virginia State she directed the choir, and later, at Virginia Union, she established a music curriculum.[44] Another quality that encouraged Logan's attraction was Ruth's light skin. Their courtship apparently disappointed many women, for as a young and handsome college professor, Logan was a very eligible bachelor, and mothers of several of the female students at both Virginia Union and Virginia State tried to arrange a marriage for their daughters.[45]

As a radical in politics, Logan consistently stood for women's rights; he believed not only in women's civil equality but also that the improvement of their material conditions and their inclusion in the political process were fundamental to the success of African decolonization and independence. Yet his political positions did not transfer to his relations with women, for he had uneasy professional dealings with women. In his personal relations, he held fast to traditional gender roles, and he nearly completely dominated Ruth. Much of their romance was conducted through the mail, and they saw each other only on weekends. Ruth was by nature a warm, outgoing woman, but once she met Logan, she drastically curtailed visits and outings with her friends, and she sought (at his insistence) his permission to go places without him. Because he usually withheld his approval, she stopped going to college basketball and football games and attending other functions to which students went. Further, although he was reluctant early in their relationship to make a monogamous commitment, he frowned upon her seeing other male college students, even if it was in the context of a "group date"; that, he felt, constituted infidelity, at least in spirit.[46] After Logan proposed marriage, Ruth gradually abandoned her gregarious, young adult persona to conform to his image of what she ought to be:

> Won't it be just too sweet for words when I can address you "my dear husband"? . . . I have a different view of life. Instead of seeing myself

amongst a bunch of admirers and pleasure seekers, planning my parties or outings, I picture myself sitting above with you exchanging ideas, planning for our future and enjoying just the you I want, the *you* in whom I feel safe in confiding and trusting.[47]

The irony is that Logan rarely exchanged ideas with his wife; he separated his professional and personal lives in such a way as to exclude her from the former. He restricted her intellectual and cultural growth to the ways he defined. For example, when she wanted to pursue a professional singing career, Logan told her that the penalty for such a choice would be the end of their marriage; he would not stand for his wife to have a career, and that settled the matter, although he did not object to her singing at university functions (where she would be auxiliary to him).[48] Little wonder that acquaintances remembered her in flat, gray tones: she always wore the same blue dress, one noted, while another commented that she was among the "mousiest" of women.[49]

A second event in 1927 also had fortuitous consequences for Logan's life. He received a letter from a former classmate at Williams College inviting him to the tenth anniversary reunion and offering to pay his way. The classmate was Roger William Riis—Bill, to his friends—the son of Jacob Riis, the social reformer, and the letter came at an important juncture in Logan's life. The two years he had spent back in America were something of a shock to his system. He still chafed at segregation, of course; more than that, though, his militancy earned him the distrust of even the liberal whites in Virginia, and he was forming strong opinions about the inherent evil of whites. Riis's invitation turned Logan around: "That event, perhaps more than anything else, led me to believe that there was a possibility for Negroes to fight it out here," Logan recalled.[50]

Their subsequent fast friendship provided Logan significant access to Riis's upper-crust world and gave him life experiences he would have otherwise been denied on account of his race. For example, when Logan developed a political (and soon-to-be scholarly) interest in the American occupation of Haiti in the late 1920s, Riis's mother wrote enthusiastic letters to well-placed Republican officials recommending him for a position on the Haitian Commission.[51] Riis facilitated Logan's social relationships with influential Williams graduates like Hugh Bennett, whose family owned the Toledo Scale Company. In the mid-1930s Logan and Riis successfully fought an incipient trend of racial exclusion at their alma mater imposed by President Tyler Dennett. Dennett had wanted a "diversified" student body and excluded African Americans in the hope of attracting southern whites to Williams. He was forced out of office.[52] Riis also opened up doors for Logan to press the civil rights case directly to President Franklin Roosevelt by introducing him to Lowell Mellett, the president's secretary.[53] For his part, Logan gave his friend a much deeper understanding of the meaning of civil rights; Riis, a civil liberties activist, respected Logan's commitment to the struggle for equality and sought Logan's counsel on all questions of civil liberties.[54]

Logan learned at his class reunion that he could earn a master's degree from Williams without having to spend any time in residence. Enrolling in September 1927, Logan breezed through a two-year, densely packed course of study under the direction of his old professor Arthur Buffinton. Taking the major subject of American history and the minor in government, Logan concentrated on the United States' Caribbean policy; in June 1929 he submitted his master's thesis on the history of education in Haiti, which was subsequently published in the *Journal of Negro History.*[55]

Logan initially came by his interest in the Caribbean during his Pan-African days in Paris. There he met Dantes Bellegarde, the Haitian minister to France and his government's delegate to the League of Nations; Bellegarde, the elder statesman, became Logan's mentor in Caribbean affairs. On Bellegarde's invitation, Logan paid his way third-class to Haiti to investigate the U.S. occupation of his country. His 1926 excursion to Haiti resulted in a spate of articles on the U.S. occupation; when these articles are read alongside several other articles Logan penned on Africa during the late 1920s and early 1930s, a portrait of Logan emerges as both an effective polemicist and propagandist for Pan-Africa and a maturing scholar.

Three themes dominate Logan's views on Haiti and Africa: the indigenous opposition to American or European imperialism is grounded in severe colonial abuses; the Western powers have an obligation to correct the injustices they have perpetrated, principally by training the various indigenous peoples in self-government; and power in Africa and the diaspora ought to be exercised by an appropriately civilized (westernized) indigenous middle class.

Logan wrote two reports on his trip to Haiti to investigate the marine occupation: "The Haze in Haiti" appeared in *The Nation* and "The New Haiti" ran in *Opportunity.*[56] Acid dripped from his pen as he scored the American occupation for its complacency, its racism, and its hypocrisy.[57]

The American occupation, which took over Haiti's finances and assumed responsibility for customs collection, public works, public health, and the gendarmerie, boasted of gains in the fight against corruption and in education, the economy, infrastructure development, and the spread of democratic values.

The actual picture, according to Logan, was far different. The Haitian constabulary, trained and officered by U.S. Marines, lorded it over the population and was rife with graft and bribery, with Americans and Haitians sharing the booty. Racism, too, honeycombed the gendarmerie, for Haitians stood little chance of rising above the rank of lieutenant. As for the claim of the spread of education, in the eleven years of occupation, the United States built only eleven schools, although it claimed it would construct over three hundred by the time the United States was scheduled to leave Haiti in 1936. The occupation's financial adviser, who controlled Haiti's budget, out of which large portions of the occupation were funded, veritably squandered Haitian money on schools that were administered by the occupation and staffed with American experts; those schools that were still under Haitian auspices starved for money, and the teachers were paid a pittance. Infrastructure improvements were a joke, as paved roads were nonexistent and graded roads were passable only in dry weather. Burros were the principal vehicle on Haitian roads, and their presence—and that of Haitians on foot—so choked the roads that they rendered the use of automobile and bus even more impractical.

Logan held out special scorn for the occupation's claim of democratization. Haitian small farmers who had worked ancestral land for generations suddenly found themselves disinherited unless they could prove ownership; so fleeced, they were then forced to abandon traditional crops in favor of sugar cane and rubber for the sole benefit of the U.S. consumers' sweet tooth and love affair with the automobile. The peasants, normally hostile to them, made common cause with the aristocracy and the middle class, which were excluded from politics; while a substantial portion of the latter two classes were corrupt and had no source of income apart from graft, there were many who were patriotic and refused to have any dealings with a government imposed by force from Washington.[58]

Finally, the U.S. high commissioner refused to abide by the Haitian Constitution—which Franklin D. Roosevelt boasted that he had authored in 1917 when he was acting secretary of the navy—which stipulated regular elections "on January 10th of an even-numbered year." But the commissioner refused to say *which* even-numbered year and thus postponed elections indefinitely. To Logan, the height of hypocrisy was this lesson in self-government, which was the putative purpose of the occupation.[59]

Logan extended similar criticisms in "The Operation of the Mandate System in Africa," which appeared in the *Journal of Negro History* in 1928.[60] Established by the League of Nations following World War I, the Permanent Mandates Commission (PMC) had authority over Germany's and the other Central Powers' former colonies. While some colonies, like Armenia and other European elements of the former Turkish Empire, were declared nearly ready for independence, Germany's African colonies were deemed to be not ready for independence and were for an indefinite time to be under the control of a mandatory power. At the time the mandate system was established, no one on the international scene thought in terms of an independent Africa, or even of designing a system with the advice of Africans, much less their consent.[61]

Logan's study then drew out the deficiencies and abuses in mandatory administration: In several areas, the indigenous peoples were stripped of their land; in other areas, they were forced into labor with little or no pay; in all areas, education was sorely neglected—in 1924, Belgium spent only one tenth of a cent per capita in Ruanda-Urundi. In most of the mandated areas, the indigenous peoples had almost no input into their government. Certainly Africans were clerks and other titular functionaries; the British exercised their mandatory powers indirectly and had the putative support of the tribal governments. But not one African held an administrative position for the whole territory, and none sat on the territory's administrative council or participated in elections.

As many people recognized at the time, Logan's critique of American and European imperialism was influenced by the left-liberal school of foreign policy analysis whose foremost proponent was Raymond Leslie Buell, a leading member of the Foreign Policy Association (and its president between 1933 and 1939). Buell, a champion of African-American rights, emphatically opposed the colonial exploitation of and aggression against Africa. He was, for example, an ardent partisan of Ethiopia's struggle against Italy. He also raised his voice against the concessions that the Firestone Tire and Rubber Company had wrung out of Liberia with the assistance of American banks and the consent of the U.S. government in 1927. While he acknowledged the increased revenue that would flow into Liberia's coffers as a result of the agreement, he criticized the overall plan because it virtually placed Firestone in charge of Liberia's finances and otherwise infringed on that country's sovereignty.[62]

Like Buell, Logan studied imperialism from an "externalist" point of view; he pored over colonial policy and catalogued colonial abuses, but did not study Africa from the standpoint of the indigenous societies, cultures, and traditions. He stated at various times that he believed Africa would one day achieve its independence;[63] he also hailed Ras Tafari, the emperor of Abyssinia, as one who was truly "worthy to wear the mantle of the 'Lion of Judah, the Elect of God.' "[64] But he believed that the main forces shaping Africa and the diaspora were not the masses but the Western powers and the westernized middle classes.

Imperialism was a fact of life, Logan thought. It was useless to ask counterfactual questions like "What if imperialism were banished from Africa and the diaspora?"

> Certainly it is an important question whether the loss of some of the fine qualities of African [spiritual] life is more than compensated for by the improvements of European civilization. The fact remains that this loss is proceeding apace. We should rather, then, inquire whether Africa has advanced, materially, under European rule.[65]

Consequently, while he issued searing critiques of the position of black people around the globe, he was surprisingly moderate in his solutions to their plight. Rather than call for an end to the U.S. occupation of Haiti in 1930, Logan insisted that the U.S. stay and prepare Haitians for self-government. When, in 1929, the British government released its Hilton Young Report on the future of British East Africa, Logan applauded its recommendation that the colonial administration make at least minimal effort to protect African rights in the areas of land and labor. He noted with special pleasure a proposed provision for the eventual granting of the franchise to Africans on a level equal to British settlers; in Logan's mind, the only alternative to this policy was rule in East Africa based on the South African model. Having lived under apartheid in the American South, Logan opposed the introduction of white minority rule to any of the colonies, but his alternative was not independence. Rather, he supported a system of indirect rule by the imperialist powers through the traditional African chiefs; he especially hailed the establishment by the British of a school for sons of chiefs to train them in modern methods of rule.[66]

Logan believed in the superiority of European and American civilization over African, and he insisted that Africans be allowed to share in it on an equal level. He was impressed that France granted some of its African subjects French citizenship; he admired the French for not forgetting the heroism of African troops during the war. Undoubtedly, Logan wished that white Americans displayed the civility that the French showed to Africans on French soil and allowed Americans of African descent to assimilate into civil society. Logan continued to be partial to the French attitude toward its colonies even after the idea of assimilation came under attack by scholars and politicians. These critics charged the French advocates of assimilation with cultural chauvinism; assimilationists, they believed, wanted to rid Africans of an inferior culture and civilization by insisting that the indigenous peoples adopt French values, customs, and forms of government, thus completely merging with a superior culture.[67]

On the other hand, if Africans themselves were not capable of exercising self-determination, African Americans were certainly in a position to determine Africa's destiny for them. Africans were progressing in large measure, he noted, because schools modeled on the Hampton and Tuskegee idea were spreading across Africa. In fact, many Africans championed these models; they critically absorbed the emphasis on self-reliance and the fundamentals of nation-building and discarded the compromising aspects (like emphasis on training people to perform semiskilled jobs under white domination) that coresided in the Bookerite model.[68]

The militancy with which Logan insisted upon the rights of African Americans turned to a paternalism of sorts when the subject changed to rights of Africans. While he seethed at the treatment of Africans and other blacks at the hands of whites, he never felt a bond with them, and probably did look upon them as more foreign than kin.[69] Logan lacked the romantic notions of Africa that other Pan-Africanists of his day, noticeably W. E. B. Du Bois, held.[70] But his paternalistic view of Africa was consistent with Du Bois's at that time, and there was a continuity between Logan's strident rhetoric on the situation of African Americans and his condescending tone on Africa.

His demand for social equality for African Americans was based upon his estimate that their best representatives were, in fact, equal to whites. Logan was, in the words Wilson Jeremiah Moses used to describe Du Bois, "caught up in the old Victorian civilization myths—the Negro improvement rhetoric that sought to make the black masses more assimilable by emphasizing their acculturation to the moral values of the Anglo-American bourgeoisie."[71] African Americans, or at least their leadership, had *earned* their equality, and behind this statement was something of a threat: if African Americans were not granted equality, they would explode in rage and would replace their up-to-now responsible leadership with something far more radical. On the other hand, Africans had not yet earned their equality nor their right to govern themselves. But with hard work—and sympathetic stewardship from African Americans—they one day would. "It is particularly gratifying," Logan wrote of Britain's plan to eventually extend a franchise to its African colonial subjects, "to note that the American Negro was cited to justify the unusually optimistic view that the Committee [that produced the Hilton Young report] takes of the African Negro." At various times Logan reserved the final word on the fate of Africa for African Americans.[72]

Logan's work on Africa in the late 1920s won him recognition among scholars and intellectuals. In August 1928 Logan read his piece on the mandate system to the Williamstown Institute of Politics. The institute, which was sponsored by Williams College, was an annual summer gathering during the 1920s and early 1930s of an impressive array of academicians, journalists, and representatives of the United States and foreign governments; internationalist in orientation, the institute cut through the isolationist thinking that dominated contemporary American foreign policy. Logan was the first African American to address the gatherings. His work on the mandates brought him to the attention of Paul Kellog, a founder of the Foreign Policy Association and the editor of the *Survey Graphic* magazine, and Raymond Leslie Buell; in 1929–30 Logan was a speaker for the Foreign Policy Association. An enthusiastic Alain Locke, professor of philosophy at Howard University and an inspirer of the Harlem Renaissance, approached Logan about coming to Howard for the purpose of establishing an African Studies center. Locke's specific plan never materialized—an African research center was not established at Howard until the 1950s—and Logan did not go to Howard until 1938.[73]

Logan had garnered a reputation, then, both as a budding scholar and as a militant activist for civil rights, when he decided to enroll in Harvard University's Ph.D. program in history in 1930. During his two years' residence in Boston he enhanced it. Logan approached historical scholarship in the fashion of Carter G. Woodson, namely with the assumption that the goal of African-American history was the glorification of the race's past in order to improve the race's present and future position.[74] A course that he taught on Negro history at Boston's progressive Ford Hall Forum during his second year contained a lecture titled "The Ballot or the Bullet."[75] A term paper for a course in German History, "German Acquisition of Southwest Africa," made its way into the *Journal of Negro History* and had a presentist edge to it.

Harvard broadened Logan's interests beyond recent history and helped him to bring both his passion for racial justice and an exacting historical method to his research. Initially he had wanted to do his dissertation on the U.S. occupation of Haiti, but his adviser, James Phinney Baxter III, and Arthur M. Schlesinger, Sr., convinced Logan to undertake a topic less charged with contemporary passions. Historical scholarship, they impressed upon him, required detached study; Logan instead produced a major study on U.S.-Haitian relations during the nineteenth century.[76] Completed as a dissertation in 1936 and published in 1941 as *The Diplomatic Relations of the United States with Haiti, 1776–1891,* Logan's studied work was both respectful of the norms of historical scholarship and politically astute.[77] Logan advanced the thesis that America's often hostile posture toward Haiti was colored by the fact that Haiti was the first independent black republic in the world (and the second republic in the Western Hemisphere); his thesis made an impression not only on diplomatic history and Latin American history, but also on the general history of Africans in the New World.[78]

Logan also honed his polemical skills during his two years at Harvard. From the time he had been discharged from the army, Logan had spoken and otherwise concerned himself with African-American communities and organizations. He now began accepting invitations from around Boston and the Northeast to speak on race relations.[79] In addition to supplementing his meager income, these speeches further buttressed his reputation as a combative, articulate spokesperson for civil rights. On one occasion he was asked to be the inaugural speaker at a Methodist church's current events forum. Logan chose as his topic the complicity of organized religion in the slave trade and the ruination of indigenous cultures in Africa and Latin America. When he heard that some congregationists anticipated his remarks with either fear or dissatisfaction, he came out swinging:

We should do well to understand each other from the beginning. May I gently remind you that this is a forum which is supposed to be open to expression of all shades of opinion. Unless you wish to adhere to this ideal, I strongly recommend that you change your name. If you wish to have persons [who] come here say to you only those things which you already believe, do not continue under false pretenses. I purposely selected a subject that would cause dismay to some.[80]

His confrontational, polemical style was designed to jolt whites' sensibilities about race relations, but it clearly was not unfriendly. Logan in fact was popular among whites of good will, and he formed some exceptional friendships with them during his years in Boston. On the suggestion of his teacher Arthur Schlesinger, Logan became involved with Boston's Ford Hall Forum. Massachusetts in the 1920s had restrictive laws concerning freedom of speech in public places, and the Ford Hall Forum was established by a heterogeneous group of liberal Bostonians to promote an unimpeded exchange of ideas. Schlesinger was prominent in it, as were the socialists and labor activists Florence Luscomb and Mary Sanger, and David Niles, who later became an assistant to President Roosevelt.

Logan became particularly attached to Luscomb. The daughter of a single mother of comfortable circumstances and socialist convictions, Luscomb from an early age was involved in feminist, socialist, and labor causes; she was an activist and leader in the Women's International League for Peace and Freedom (for which she recruited African-American women into leadership positions), the NAACP, the American Civil Liberties Union, the International Ladies' Garment Workers Union, and many other organizations.[81] She was a "fearless crusader for equal rights," Logan wrote. She also practiced her beliefs. For all the liberal milieu of Boston, Logan was a guest in only two white people's houses—Luscomb's was one (Arthur Schlesinger's was the other). There was nothing contrived about Logan's and Luscomb's relationship, either. She entertained many other African Americans both in her home and at her summer home in New Hampshire, and Logan felt that his relationship with her was typical of friendships she had with other African Americans.[82]

Luscomb added another dimension to Logan's view of American society. Logan had never become involved in the socialist or communist left. Early in his Harvard career he decided that that segment of the left was undemocratic. Luscomb, however, punctured this view for Logan, and eventually he decided that although he would not embrace communist convictions, he would work with communists in the fight for civil rights. In correspondence and in conversation, and by introducing him to her friends and coworkers, Luscomb unselfishly shared her involvement in issues of social justice with Logan. This window on progressive movements led primarily by whites enriched Logan's appreciation for the struggles of all downtrodden people. Their friendship also blossomed at a time when Logan was again beginning to hate whites "as the result of humiliating experiences in Richmond." Like Bill Riis, Luscomb was "one of the few persons who have convinced me that not all white people are devils or 'radical chics.' "[83]

Lewis Hanke, a Harvard classmate of Logan's, was another white to whom Logan was attracted in Boston. Almost ten years Logan's junior, Hanke had a universalist, humanistic outlook on life that cut through the dominant American racism. Hanke and his wife spent the last three years of the 1920s in Beirut, where he had an appointment at the American University. Their two sons were born there, and they lived in the midst of a multiethnic, multireligious society that taught Hanke about both tolerance and the centrality of respecting human rights.

Logan and Hanke shared an intellectual discipline in Latin American history, a common historical outlook, and a closeness that Logan shared with few others. Just as Logan sought to put black people and their struggle for justice at the center of African, Caribbean, and United States history, Hanke saw the protracted fight for justice as the warp and woof of Latin American history—and the course of contemporary events.[84] "I feel as much at home with him and his family as I do with any of my colored friends because he feels as much at home with me," Logan wrote. Normally reserved and formal—he insisted on addressing (and being addressed by) contemporaries as "Mister"—Logan shielded his personal life and thoughts from others. Yet he occasionally let Hanke peek behind his veil. Hanke's wife related that "once Ray asked Lewis his recipe for having children, remarking quietly that he and Ruth had not found it."[85]

Despite these warm encounters, neither Luscomb nor Hanke nor his contacts with the influential members of the Ford Hall Forum could shield Logan from the reality that, Harvard Ph.D. notwithstanding, he faced limited opportunity in the academic job market. First of all, the Great Depression slowed the pace of hiring as colleges struggled against financial chaos. Logan suffered two additional liabilities: he was African-American, which guaranteed that no white college or university would hire him, and he was a radical, which made the predominantly black colleges wary of bringing him abroad. He certainly expected to be excluded from white institutions of learning, but this did nothing to lessen the sting.

Logan's close friend William H. Dean—Logan was the godfather of Dean's son—was a graduate student at Harvard in economics, and he captured the humiliation in a letter to Logan. Because he was African-American, Harvard would neither place him on their faculty nor recommend him for a position at Queens College of the City University of New York.

> Really, Harvard disgusts me more and more. I have been strongly advised here to go into government service. An institution which will have nothing of me expects me to get a better break from whites elsewhere. Frankly, I don't see what keeps a colored man's courage up. I feel more beat and licked every day.[86]

Dean, the son-in-law of Channing Tobias, who was the head of the YMCA's work among Negroes and a significant African-American power broker, later went on to a distinguished career at Atlanta University and UNESCO. But he never recovered from the pain Harvard inflicted upon him, and in 1952 he committed suicide.[87]

African-American institutions were less than thrilled about hiring a radical scholar and politician, and this was cause for some friction between Logan and his wife, Ruth. In late 1931, as Logan wound down his residency at Harvard, Howard University was considering him for a permanent position beginning in summer 1932, even though Howard administrators were aware of Logan's run-ins in Richmond and on the Union campus.[88] But then his parting with Union—along with Logan's parting shots at the school's president—was made public.

Logan's rancorous comments on his firing and the rumors of student protest made Howard think twice. The university stalled on giving Logan an answer to his application and eventually balked at hiring him.[89] Ruth, who continued to live in Richmond during most of Logan's time at Harvard, was furious. "It was surprising to read [in your letter] that you might have trouble getting on at Howard. I really think you did the wrong thing by telling the students [about your firing] in such a way so that they would cause the rumpus." She then accused him of enjoying the commotion he had stirred up, even if it risked their livelihood and their future.

Logan accused Ruth of trying to back out of her commitment to him and questioned whether she loved him anymore. This further enraged Ruth, who shot back, "Whether I am in love with you or not, I am doing all that I can for you and everything to keep us together."[90]

No consensus between the two emerged out of this quarrel, but impoverishment was postponed when Carter G. Woodson offered Logan a position as his assistant at the *Journal of Negro History* and the Association for the Study of Negro Life and History. This was not Logan's first choice; he had preferred an appointment in a college history department. On the other hand, he owed a great deal to Woodson: he had been the principal outlet for Logan's scholarly production, and it was difficult to refuse Woodson's offer. Besides, Woodson was the founder of the discipline of African-American history, and Logan deeply believed in his mission of popularizing the centrality of black people in the history of the world. He accepted Woodson's offer, and in June 1932, Logan and his wife moved to Washington, D.C., where he became one of "Carter Woodson's boys."

chapter four

"BAD NEGRO WITH A PH.D."

ই‍ৡ

(1932–1940)

OR RAYFORD LOGAN, becoming Carter G. Woodson's assistant at the Association for the Study of Negro Life and History (ASNLH) was a natural extension of both his political inclinations and his graduate training in history. With both men, the politics of race and scholarship were always intimately intertwined. Woodson had founded the Association in 1915, during the high tide of scientific racism; the specific impetus for the formation of the ASNLH was the appearance of D. W. Griffith's racist epic, *Birth of a Nation*. Woodson decided, according to his biographer, Patricia W. Romero, to "form an organization which would offset the attacks made by whites upon blacks and that this organization set forth the true nature of their past through specialization in Negro history." Woodson demanded adherence to high standards of historical inquiry; the ASNLH's research mission was to reinterpret the role of black people in history, to showcase their contributions to world civilization, and to rescue them from oblivion.[1]

When Logan joined the staff in 1932, the ASNLH had been conducting a successful business for almost twenty years. In those years Woodson had gathered around him a group of young scholars, including Logan, Charles H. Wesley, Luther Porter Jackson, Lorenzo Greene, Alrutheus A. Taylor, and W. Sherman Savage; this core of historians became the leading promoters of the cause of African-American history.[2] The *Journal of Negro History* regularly published the researches of Woodson's band of scholars. John Hope Franklin summarized the impact of Woodson and the association on the field of history.

Monographs on labor, education, Reconstruction, art, music, and other aspects of Afro-American life appeared in steady succession, calling to the attention of the larger community the role of Afro-Americans, . . . The articles and monographs reflected prodigious research and zeal in pursuing the truth that had *not* been the hallmark of much of the so-called scientific historical writing produced in university seminars in this country some years earlier.[3]

During Logan's employment at the association headquarters between June 1932 and September 1933, he became, in his words, Woodson's "alter ego." In addition to the routine chores like cleaning the office, answering correspondence, and shipping books, he directed the association's work during Woodson's stays in Paris in the summers of 1932 and 1933; among his more important jobs was organizing programs for Negro History Week, which was started by Woodson in 1926. Logan often pinch-hit for his boss at speaking engagements.[4]

Woodson left a profound impression on Logan. Personally, he found Woodson's singleminded dedication to the cause of African-American history hard to match. Professionally, Woodson's scholarly agenda and his conception of the purpose of African-American history influenced Logan throughout the 1930s and 1940s. Logan had learned to write detached history at Harvard, and produced such thorough, dispassionate monographs as *The Diplomatic Relations of the United States with Haiti, The Senate and the Versailles Mandate System,* and *Howard University: The First Hundred Years.* But he never completely abandoned the Woodson tradition—although he did later modify it in important ways by writing about the collective experience of the race as well as individual African Americans. Like his mentor, Logan wanted to popularize black history and achievement, and Woodson's presence revealed itself in two biographical sketches that Logan authored in the 1940s.[5]

The first article, which appeared in *Opportunity,* the magazine of the Urban League, was on the life of Magloire Pélage, the turn-of-the-nineteenth-century mulatto leader of strife-torn Guadeloupe. He was not of the same calibre as Dessalines, his contemporary who led Haiti to independence from France; in fact, he proclaimed fealty to France, helped to keep his island a part of the French empire, and prolonged the life of the slave system. For all this, though, the white elite he helped maintain in power did not trust him; he was arrested, deported to France, and died in obscurity. While the lesson of his death carried a warning—one risked ignominy by acting as an agent against his or her race—Logan would not pass a final judgment on Magloire Pélage. Indeed, it was not right that a pivotal figure in black history should be ignored, and, as Logan wrote, "he surely needs to be resurrected from oblivion."[6]

In the second biographical piece Logan came up with a unique inter-pretation of the life of Esteban the Moor, the sixteenth-century Spanish explorer of the New World. In 1528, he was part of an expedition through what is now Florida, Texas, and Louisiana, while in 1539 he led the advanced detachment of Coronado's expedition from northern Mexico into what is now New Mexico; he was killed by Zuni Indians who resisted Spanish aggression and who accused him of coveting their womenfolk. Upon studying all the primary sources, Logan concluded that Esteban, also known as Estevanico, was actually of black African descent.[7]

While Estevanico's racial identity was plain from reading the record, nineteenth- and twentieth-century white scholars denied this fact, labeling him instead a Moor or an Arab. To Logan, this was a plain instance of bad faith on the part of scholars who refused to believe that blacks were capable of accomplishing something as momentous as "discovering" the New World. In addition to setting the historical record straight, Logan took the opportunity to critique the present. He questioned how knowl-edge of Estevanico's true identity would change the way white Americans saw African Americans, and he concluded that, unfortunately, it probably would not. For even if they thought "Estevanico a Moor rather than a Negro, he might have suffered in Texas in 1940 the fate that he met in New Mexico in 1539."

Logan did virtually all the research and writing for Woodson's *The African Background Outlined, or Handbook for the Study of the Negro,* a digest of modern scholarship on Africa, complete with a 250-page bibli-ography that covered black history both topically and chronologically from antiquity to the New World through the 1930s.[8] The work extolled Africa's greatness, pointing out its people's contributions, for example, to the concept of monotheism that was later refined by the Jews, and to democratic traditions, in that Africans were the first to institute trial by jury. Logan and Woodson scorned scholars who designated some charac-teristic "African" only if it could not be found elsewhere or who attempted to prove that advanced ideas were brought to Africa by whites.[9]

At the same time that Africa was praised, *The African Background Outlined* rejected the idea of the homogeneity of the people, and ridiculed the American "one-drop theory," whereby anyone with one drop of African blood was classified as black. The first half of the book is devoted to the African civilizations and empires that existed prior to European colonization. The discussion of Abyssinia, for example, notes that that ancient civilization drew people from Asia and the Arab countries; "They are, therefore, one people but of various bloods—Berber, Negro, Peul, Arabic, and the like, the type varying with the regions but after all a fusion of races which Americans would segregate for being black Negroes."[10]

Reinterpreting African and African-American history for the public at large was an enormous undertaking, and Woodson's ambitious research agenda could not be willed to completion, even with the assistance of a hardworking Logan and others in the coterie of committed young scholars. This task begged for financial backing in addition to intellectual muscle, and for the first fifteen years of its existence, Carter Woodson oriented the Association in a way that would attract the much-needed funds from prominent white philanthropies. The executive committee was interracial and included such powerful (and wealthy) whites as Julius Rosenwald, George Foster Peabody, James Hardy Dillard, and Thomas Jesse Jones, who was not rich but who had influence among the philanthropists. Interestingly, Woodson excluded from the early executive committees prominent African Americans who might try to direct the ASNLH's policy. "Woodson was at this stage of development courting any and all whites who could and would aid him," wrote his biographer, Patricia Romero.[11]

For a while this strategy paid off. Between 1920 and 1922, Woodson had solicited $25,000 each from the Carnegie Corporation and the Laura Spelman Rockefeller Memorial (LSRM), which John D. Rockefeller, Jr., established in honor of his wife; throughout the decade he received smaller grants from these organizations and from the Rockefeller-controlled General Education Board (GEB). It could be that Woodson thought that whoever had the milk must be the mother, for he was careful consistently to praise in print the work of the philanthropies, and when he ventured overtly into race politics he aligned himself with the more conservative leaders like Robert Russa Moton of Tuskegee.[12] But at the same time Woodson could not abide whites dictating to African Americans what their program for advancement ought to be. Woodson fought with Thomas Jesse Jones, a white official of the Phelps-Stokes Fund, when Jones tried to arrogate to himself the job of choosing the African-American leadership. He removed Jones from the ASNLH board, an action that cost the association future support from the Stokes Fund.[13]

Far more injurious to Woodson's relations with the white philanthropies was his insistence on full control over the work of the ASNLH and the *Journal of Negro History.* The philanthropic organizations, particularly the GEB and the LSRM, supported research into African-American life and history, but they viewed with suspicion projects conceived and led by blacks. The LSRM eschewed Woodson's emphasis on collecting and documenting the history of African Americans in favor of training sociologists and social workers who would adhere to accommodation to solve the race's problems.[14]

By the time that Logan had come to work for Woodson, most of the foundation support had evaporated, and a bitter Woodson reoriented the ASNLH to the African-American grass roots. Although Woodson was able to snag small amounts of money from the foundations—his procurement of a five-hundred-dollar grant from the GEB enabled Logan to complete his second year of graduate study at Harvard[15]—he turned his principal fund-raising attention to small contributions from individuals in the African-American community. In particular, Woodson spent more time on popularizing African-American history in segregated secondary schools and church organizations. Although Logan absorbed a great deal at the ASNLH, his purpose for attending Harvard was not to spread knowledge of his race's past to high-schoolers and churchgoers. Accordingly, when President John Hope of Atlanta University offered him a position in that institution's history department beginning in the fall of 1933, Logan did not hesitate; the month of September found Logan once again down South. This was not simply another job for Logan; it was a strategic career move to a prestigious black college. Whereas Woodson feared that association with a university would compromise the autonomy of the ASNLH, Logan had no such independent base of operations to protect. He looked to the academy to provide him with the resources and credentials necessary to establish himself as a historian of distinction. Within a year he began collaborating with W. E. B. Du Bois on the latter's "Encyclopedia of the Negro" project;[16] his participation on the Encyclopedia led to a complete separation from Woodson, who both scorned the project and viewed it as a rival to his own work.

The divestment of the philanthropies in the ASNLH's stock formed the background to the dispute between Carter Woodson and W. E. B. Du Bois, who was soliciting foundation support for his "Encyclopedia of the Negro" project, and Logan. In November 1931, just at the time of the philanthropic rejection of Woodson's enterprise, the Phelps-Stokes Fund convened a meeting of prominent white and black experts on Afro-America preliminary to the establishment of an effort to publish an Encyclopedia of the Negro. The session included African Americans like John Hope, President Mordecai Johnson of Howard University, and Walter White and James Weldon Johnson of the NAACP, who were not prone to accommodationism; but the meeting was dominated by whites like Thomas Jesse Jones, Anson Phelps Stokes (who chaired the meeting), and a representative of the Carnegie Corporation who insisted upon supervising any work by and about African Americans. Conspicuously absent were Du Bois and Woodson, although both were later added to the list of invitees at the insistence of White and Johnson.[17]

Du Bois was flabbergasted at his exclusion. "I could not for a moment contemplate a Negro encyclopedia dominated and controlled by Thomas Jesse Jones, . . ." Du Bois wrote to James Hardy Dillard, the head of the Slater Fund and a man whom Du Bois trusted. "[A] Negro encyclopedia that was not in the main edited and written by Negroes would be as inconceivable as a Catholic encyclopedia projected by Protestants." He conveyed his astonishment and annoyance at his exclusion to Anson Phelps Stokes:

> Frankly, when I heard of this movement and realized that I had not been invited to participate, I was surprised. I may be wrong but I doubt if any of the persons originally invited have not based at least a part of their knowledge of the American Negro on my work, and I felt with all modesty that my omission was a personal affront. As I look over the original list, there are others, like Dr. Woodson, whose omission also seems to me inexplicable.[18]

Still, after consultation with philanthropic agents whom he trusted, including Dillard and Edwin Embree of the Rockefeller foundations, he agreed to participate in the project despite the tardy invitation.

From the beginning the philanthropies had an understanding that their underwriting the Encyclopedia project was contingent upon Du Bois moderating his radical politics. Du Bois apparently was amenable to accommodate them because of his intense desire to edit a monumental work such as the Encyclopedia promised to be; he also understood the philanthropies' willingness to underwrite the project as a concession to him. Both Stokes and Jackson Davis, a senior official in the GEB, were pleasantly surprised at Du Bois's readiness to compromise. In a letter written soon after the first meeting of the project attended by Du Bois, Stokes, who sought GEB funding for the project he headed, commented to Davis that

> ten years ago, or even five years ago, it would not have been possible to consider Dr. Du Bois for this position in spite of the fact that he is recognized as the outstanding Negro scholar. He had become such an aggressive protagonist that his name created a lack of sympathy in various conservative circles. This is, of course, still partially true but all who have met him in the last year have been amazed at how much he has mellowed.[19]

Davis replied that he, too, had heard "of the remarkable change in Dr. Bubois' [*sic*] attitude." He hoped that Du Bois would continue to restrain himself—he characterized his previous work for racial equality as "exaggeration and overstatement"—because the white South would respond favorably only to mild requests by African Americans for better treatment.[20]

Woodson was less sanguine about participating. He, too, was stung by his exclusion. But unlike Du Bois, he declined the invitation to join the project. He wrote to one of the original African-American encyclopedists, Benjamin Brawley, that his decision was "for the reason that the persons who called the meeting evidently did not desire my participation." Besides, he wrote, he was in the process of producing his own ten-volume encyclopedia, and he suspected the Phelps-Stokes Fund of supporting a rival effort for the purpose of suppressing his own.[21]

No one, including ASNLH executive board members, was aware of Woodson's plans for an encyclopedia.[22] Whether Woodson had in fact begun work on an encyclopedia is a matter of conjecture.[23] It is also in many respects beside the point, for the altercation between Woodson and Du Bois was not a war over turf. The nub of the disagreement was the proper role for philanthropy in the production of African-American scholarship. Du Bois, writing to Woodson to get him to join his Encyclopedia project, acknowledged the adversarial relationship between the two of them and the pernicious influence of Thomas Jesse Jones. "The enemy has the money and they are going to use it," Du Bois wrote. "Our choice then is not how that money could be used best from our point of view, but how far without great sacrifice of principle, we can keep it from being misused." Woodson saw it differently: "I never accept the gifts of Greeks," he tartly responded to Du Bois. Woodson did not accurately characterize the attitude of Du Bois and Logan, but he did capture the flavor of the philanthropies' disposition toward the project with his peppery comment that "The 'Encyclopedia of the Negro' is now being worked on by traducing whites and hired Negroes."[24]

Woodson's dart, while acerbic, was close to the mark. From its inception, the Encyclopedia project was suffused with politics. Stokes chose the directors for the project not primarily based upon their credentials in the field of Negro scholarship; if he had wanted a board of that composition, he would have in the first instance called upon Du Bois and Woodson and scholars like Logan and Charles Wesley. Stokes constituted a board of directors whose principal skill was in the fields of paternalism and racial meliorism.[25]

Even when Du Bois, a radical voice and fairly consistent critic of white philanthropy, was added to the project and made its editor in chief, Stokes insisted upon retaining oversight. Du Bois's desire for an all-African-American editorial board was rejected in favor of an interracial one. Stokes, who knew of the GEB's jaundiced view of any project touched by radical African Americans, also wrung from Du Bois a concession "in principle to the idea that some representative Southern white scholar should be identified with the project." The new assistant editor was Robert E. Park, a University of Chicago sociologist. A pioneer in the sociology of race relations, Park had previously served as Booker T. Washington's press agent and ghostwriter; while he was at Tuskegee, he had articulated a philosophy of gradualism and accommodationism that influenced white sociologists throughout the 1920s and 1930.[26] Although Du Bois continued to object to Stokes's condition—"Some are liberal because it pays; . . ." he wrote to Stokes, while "so many are apt to regard their liberality as calling for praise and reward when as a matter of fact it ought to be simply human."[27]—he was forced to acquiesce. Further, an advisory board was established, composed of the American Council of Learned Societies, the American Council on Education, the Social Science Research Council, and the National Research Council; these organizations, almost exclusively white, had research agendas on African Americans which they tried to impose upon African-American scholars. In the philanthropies' view, an all-African-American effort was political and not scholarly, while white paternalist oversight made for good scholarship— and good politics.[28]

Despite this oversight, one of the chief features of the Encyclopedia of the Negro project that attracted Logan was the prospect of funding by influential white philanthropy. For one, Logan would be paid for his contributions. He was appointed secretary of the Encyclopedia's board of directors, and his remuneration of fifty dollars monthly plus stenographic and typographic assistance in exchange for ten to fifteen hours of work a week, while hardly extravagant, certainly supplemented his professorial salary at Atlanta.[29] Among his most substantial and sustained contributions to the project was the development of lists of topics and subjects for the Encyclopedia and the preparation of bibliographies, especially on Latin America. He used the project's auspices to develop a network of some of the leading Latin Americanists from throughout the Western Hemisphere. Logan served in effect as Du Bois's principal assistant and collaborator on the project.[30]

The philanthropic blessing legitimized the scholarship in Logan's eyes. He had no direct contact with the project's funders, but in his capacity as secretary he was something of a point man for the project with some of the best-known white academics. His correspondence with such white experts on Africa and Afro-America as Raymond Leslie Buell, Melville J. Herskovits, and W. T. Couch made Logan a known quantity in the white academic world.[31]

This recognition was, to Logan, apparently worth the price he paid in the currency of other personal and professional relationships. When word got back to Carter Woodson about his collaboration on Du Bois's project, he tried to erase Logan's imprint on the ASNLH. First, he removed Logan from a supervisory position in the association's 1936 "One Dollar Sustaining Membership Drive"; Logan had accepted the post of Georgia state chairman of the campaign, which was created as a grass-roots alternative to philanthropic support, at the behest of John Hope, who was an ASNLH board member and a friend of Woodson. Then he fired Logan from his titular position of assistant editor to the *Journal of Negro History*. Finally, Woodson began a campaign among African-American scholars and college presidents accusing Logan of being disloyal to the ASNLH and questioning his competence and integrity as a scholar.[32] Logan gave as good as he got, writing other Woodson protégés and criticizing the master's dictatorial methods.[33]

Logan also had to endure opposition from scholars—Ralph Bunche and Melville Herskovits chief among them—who disagreed with the political thrust of the project. In the 1930s and early 1940s Bunche, then a professor of political science at Howard University, was a radical. In his view, race advancement would come only as a result of an alliance between African-American and white workers. In the sphere of politics, he scorned both leaders who predicted the emancipation of the race through the vitalization of a separate economy—including Du Bois, who now championed a plan for voluntary segregation—and the NAACP, which advocated interracial cooperation and legal challenges to eradicate segregation. The NAACP's reliance upon the good will of liberal whites inevitably led them to compromise and water down demands for equality, Bunche believed.

> Such organizations, if they remain constant in their faith, are forced into a policy of conciliation with the enlightened, i.e., the ruling interests, in the dominant group. . . . They can be militant, but only politely so; they can attack, but not too harshly; they must entreat, bargain, compromise and capitulate in order to win even petty gains.[34]

In the realm of scholarship, Bunche thought that the Encyclopedia project was tainted both by foundation oversight and the impurity of the contributors. Because of the project's encyclopedic scope, there were inevitably conflicting views on many subjects; since many of the expressed views ran counter to Bunche's own, he decided not to cooperate with the project. (In this regard—and in regard to the race advancement organizations—Bunche reflected the views of the sociologist E. Franklin Frazier, his colleague at Howard.)[35] As Logan reported to Du Bois:

> More and more I am becoming convinced that not the least important of the elements of your genius is your patience. As you say, the principal job is reconciling the opposing points of view. Ralph Bunche told me categorically that he would not write an article for the Encyclopaedia because Westermann, Labouret, et al. were not authorities. He (Ralph) and *the* authorities would then sit back and laugh at us. An appeal even to his racial pride seemed unavailing. This sort of talk makes me more desirous than ever to help do a job that will permit us to sit back and laugh at them.[36]

Melville Herskovits's criticisms of the project ran in a different direction. During the 1930s he played a major role in the debunking of scientific racism.[37] Perhaps because of his prominence, Herskovits felt that his ought to be a determining voice in deciding the direction of scholarship on Africa and Afro-America; he served on the project's advisory council as the representative of the National Research Council, one of the organizations trying to dictate policy on African-American scholarship. Yet from the beginning of his association with the encyclopedia, he believed that it ought to be aborted and that Du Bois was unfit—both for reasons of age and political involvement—to edit the undertaking; he also encouraged others on the advisory board to resign.[38] Between 1936 and 1938, Stokes approached the GEB and the Carnegie Corporation for upwards of $200,000 for the completion of the Encyclopedia. Herskovits, according to Logan, was invited by these foundations to pass judgment on the venture's merits. Logan related a subsequent conversation he had with Herskovits:

> He explained that, when the GEB had asked his opinion, he stated that Dr. Du Bois was not a "scholar"; he was a "radical" and a "Negrophile."[39]

Accordingly, Herskovits boasted, "I was the hatchet man," and the GEB denied the grant request, thus effectively scuttling the project.[40] In fact, Herskovits's was not the deciding voice on this matter; that voice came from the executive offices of the GEB and the Carnegie Corporation. Certainly Jackson Davis would have been astonished to hear Herskovits's boasts; just as he felt that African Americans ought not pursue their rights in an aggressive manner, so, too, did he feel that Jews had entirely too high a profile in the United States.[41] Nevertheless, the decision to deny the funding of the Encyclopedia, which was made at the top of the philanthropic ladder, borrowed something from the tone of Herskovits's crowing.

While the foundations had in 1931 and 1932 been captivated with the idea of scholarly work on African Americans, by 1936 and 1937 they were concerned that a project headed by Du Bois—even one with white oversight—would be politically unpredictable. In April 1937, Jackson Davis wrote Stokes with the reasons his organization had been chary of funding the project over the past few years. The GEB was not certain that accomplishments of African Americans should be isolated from those of other Americans, Davis reported. Nor was the philanthropy at all sure that the time was right for scholarly research on African Americans or that such scholarship would have lasting value. Finally, wrote Davis, the GEB was concerned such race scholarship would inexorably lead to race consciousness and be closely followed by race agitation and propaganda.[42] Despite Stokes's attempts to tighten control of the project to meet these objections, the GEB a year later finally denied the Encyclopedia project the grants necessary to keep it alive.[43]

The Carnegie Corporation followed suit just a few months later.[44] John

Dollard of that philanthropy had counseled the GEB to have nothing to do with the Encyclopedia project, principally because of Du Bois's radical politics. But he also turned thumbs down on the Encyclopedia for the additional reason that his foundation was getting ready to launch Gunnar Myrdal's landmark study, *An American Dilemma*. As one historian of philanthropy, John Stanfield, concluded, "Given Dollard's antagonism toward Du Bois, one might speculate that the Carnegie Study [Myrdal's study] represented, at least in part, an effort to prevent Du Bois from making a comparable contribution to race-relations research."[45]

According to Logan, the rejection was entirely unexpected. In fact, he had anticipated that the GEB would appropriate monies for the project. Thirty years later he described how he and Du Bois waited for the formal notification of approval:

> Dr. Du Bois ordered a bottle of champagne and a bucket of ice so that we could celebrate in his office in the Atlanta University Administration Build-ing the confidently expected approval by the full Board of the GEB. The hours passed, the ice melted, and we grew apprehensive. Finally, word came that the full Board had not approved the project. Dr. Du Bois had suffered so many disappointments that he appeared hardly ruffled.[46]

But if Du Bois was not outwardly affected, Logan was. He was soon after informed that the grant was denied because of Du Bois's presence on the project, and he was outraged that whites should have so much influence over the destiny of Afro-America.[47] The rejection was a wake-up call of sorts; Logan was once again alerted to the duplicity of the powerful whites from whom he was trying to gain acceptance.

The culmination of the Encyclopedia episode was not the only disap-pointing encounter that Logan had with influential whites during the 1930s, only the most severe one. The others involved Logan's scholarly and political involvement with Haiti. Logan was the outstanding African-American scholar and observer of Haiti in the 1930s, and one of the most talented of any race. While he had been trained as an educator, he also had other aspirations and felt that a diplomatic posting to Haiti would fulfill his ambitions; there was precedent, of course, for appointing an African American to this position, as both Frederick Douglass and John Mercer Langston had spent time in Port-au-Prince. In 1930 he prevailed upon Frederic C. Walcott, his benefactor and father's employer who was now a Republican senator from Connecticut, to nominate him for a position on the Haitian Commission, the body that oversaw the U.S. occupation; he persuaded his closest white friend, Bill Riis, to procure an endorsement for the job from his mother, Mrs. Jacob Riis. Despite recommendations from rock-ribbed—and highly placed—Republicans, nothing materialized. Although the paper trail peters out after the letters of nomination, it is not too wild to suppose that Logan experienced a great letdown.[48]

In July 1934, Logan, who had continued his agitation against the U.S. occupation, traveled to Haiti with two items on his agenda: to complete the primary research on his dissertation in the Haitian State Archives and to witness and report on the final withdrawal of the marines from that country for the readers of the *Baltimore Afro-American.* The trip got off to an inauspicious beginning. The six-week excursion was to have elements of a vacation, and because his wife, Ruth, was to accompany him, Logan determined he could not travel second class. When he went to board the American-registered liner *Columbia,* he was told that the first-class accommodations he had expected were not available. What he discovered was that the steamship line had a Jim Crow policy: no African Americans in first class, no whites in second class, white stewards and waiters served whites, while black workers were confined to second class. After viewing the accommodations, Logan and his wife walked off the ship just before it set sail. He soon found passage on a Dutch-registered ship, but his protest, which got the NAACP national office involved, caused ripples in the black press.[49]

Logan's scholarship received a boost in Haiti, mainly due to the official courtesies of Norman Armour, the U.S. consul. Armour, at the request of Logan's well-placed white friends, prevailed upon the Haitian government to open its archives. As Haiti had no national library, Armour also provided him with entrée to the Catholic schools, elite society, and the private papers of individuals.[50]

The summer of 1934 was a time for celebration, and Logan was in a celebratory mood: the long-awaited end of the occupation was at hand. At a public forum in 1930 he could not say with any certainty that the marines would ever leave; he said he could only quote the French proverb, *"Il ne faut jamais dire jamais"*—never say never. With the end of the occupation, he was heartened. "I like to recall this incident," he wrote in one of his articles, "because it shows that no cause is ever hopeless."[51] He took due note of some of the improvements in Haiti that resulted from the nineteen-year occupation. President Roosevelt had done an about-face since his time as assistant secretary of the navy when he was in charge of Haiti. In the time since he became president, the occupation had improved morale in the Haitian Garde, turned it into a professional outfit, and— Logan hoped—rid it of political ambition. Medical care had been introduced into the countryside, and public health was greatly improved. Some roads had also been improved.[52]

Logan's tone was mild compared to his articles of the 1920s on the occupation, and his comments were a far cry from the fire-eating essay that his friend Langston Hughes penned on his 1931 visit to Haiti, which emphasized the class divisions in the country and which was being discussed by Haitians when Logan was visiting.[53] But he duly criticized the occupation's shortcomings: the road system was still primitive at best; there was still no higher education, or much of any education, for that matter; Haiti's finances were still controlled by U.S. bankers, who were determined to bleed the country dry; the country was still riven by disparities of class; and most Haitians were desperately poor.[54] On balance, then, one would have to say that not much had changed.

Logan's upbeat timbre in the face of the adversities that Haiti faced was occasioned not only by the end of the occupation. He also felt that there was much that African Americans could do to help Haiti in its time of need. One of the darts that Langston Hughes threw at Haitian society was that too many citizens were unable to afford shoes; Logan agreed, saying that any index of progress must include elimination of poverty. "Of course, all true friends of Haiti will want to see a great decrease in the number of bare feet. Colored Americans must not stand aside and permit white Americans, some of whom are genuinely interested in Haiti, alone to ameliorate this condition." They needed to press for the establishment of a Haitian national university. They ought to give serious thought to buying Haitian products and to spending their vacations there, and in this way "help to raise the standard of living of the one colored republic in the Western Hemisphere."[55]

A better-conceived proposal for helping Haiti (and black people in the Caribbean and Latin America generally) was in the field of scholarship. Just as Logan was convinced that the Encyclopedia of the Negro had to be controlled by African Americans, so too did he think that they had to influence U.S.–Latin American relations. One of his unrealized dreams at Atlanta University was the establishment of a Latin American institute. Black colleges were ignoring this important field and vacating it to white southerners. He complained that "already their special views on the race question have begun to creep in their writings about the countries of Latin America." They were poisoning the cultural relations between the United States and Latin America by promoting discrimination against Afro-Latins in the United States and devaluing the contributions of blacks to Latin American civilization.[56]

Another reason Logan may have modulated his tone in his series on Haiti was that he still had not given up on serving in the diplomatic corps. In early April 1935, Raymond Leslie Buell, Logan's old friend from his days with the Foreign Policy Association, informed him that Norman Armour, the U.S. minister to Haiti, was retiring. Buell apparently wanted to nominate Logan for the post. Although he thought Logan an outstanding candidate, he wondered whether the U.S. government would approve of sending an African American to Haiti. He soon found out. While in Washington on business, Buell raised the idea of appointing an African-American minister to Haiti with "some liberal friends." Without exception they shot down the idea; they were certain that such a person would have no influence in the State Department and thus be unable to direct U.S. policy.[57] The news must have jarred Logan, if it did not completely surprise him. Nevertheless it was bitter medicine for him, and it was a reminder not to surrender the strategy of a direct assault against discrimination against African Americans.

The main vehicle for Logan's militancy became the Alpha Phi Alpha fraternity, the oldest African-American college fraternity. Alpha Phi Alpha was organized in 1906 by seven students at Cornell University who were looking for fellowship and solidarity in an academic world in which they faced isolation because of their race.[58] Over the first four decades of its existence, AΦA earned a reputation as the most prestigious organization for college-educated African Americans. By the 1940s, its ranks included W. E. B. Du Bois; Thurgood Marshall; Charles Hamilton Houston; Paul Robeson; Charles H. Wesley, the historian who became president of Wilberforce University; President H. Councill Trenholm of Alabama State Teachers College; Belford Lawson, the civil rights lawyer; and Walter White.

When Logan joined the University of Pittsburgh chapter during his year there in 1913, the fraternity's focus was servicing its undergraduate members; partying and socializing were the orders of the day. Members who had graduated from college were incidental to the organization. As the number of graduate members increased, AΦA also became a business and professional network. But by the 1930s graduate members who were committed to the cause of civil rights and social justice—men like Wesley, who served several terms as fraternity president, and Howard Long of Washington, D.C.—came to be more prominent in the fraternity.[59] Logan was attracted to this blend of fellowship and politics and became active in AΦA with the aim of shaping it into a self-conscious network for race leaders.

At AΦA's annual convention in December 1933 Logan was elected director of education, and he proposed a program that would change the fraternity's direction and make it far more responsive to the demands of all of Afro-America rather than only to college students and graduates. The first element was the fight for economic equality. The Great Depression had indelibly altered the course of Afro-America. Massive economic distress had stimulated the political interest of African Americans both North and South. Their exclusion from some New Deal programs—and the fact that administration of others was left up to local and state government—helped put blacks in a militant frame of mind. The task at hand was to direct this new militancy toward achieving lasting change.

Forcing Franklin Roosevelt to open up the New Deal to African Americans was the equivalent of the Fourth American Revolution, Logan declared. (The other three were the War of Independence, the extension of democratic rights to the mass of whites in the Jacksonian Era, and the Civil War.) This struggle had many facets, including procuring federal protection for small farmers and domestics, occupations in which African Americans predominated. Logan featured, too, the attainment by African Americans of a fair share of government jobs at all levels and the elimination of the wage differential; he calculated that African Americans had a better chance to achieve these under federal auspices than under state or local authority or in an unregulated economy.[60]

The 1933 AΦA convention authorized the new director of education to form a Committee on Public Policy, which was charged with the responsibility of determining as precisely as possible the "status of the black population, both as to employees in the [New Deal] agencies and as to the services rendered which were affecting its place in American life." The exhaustive study, nearly eighteen months in preparation, canvassed all the major New Deal agencies. Written by Logan and based upon the research conducted by his brother Arthur, the report, which was published in three parts between 1935 and 1937 in the *Sphinx,* the fraternity's magazine, showed just how thoroughly African Americans, and especially African-American women, were locked out of the New Deal.[61] Charles H. Wesley summarized the report with this observation:

> Vast funds were seen pouring into industry and agriculture while the black worker stands apart and the college man studies the plans of the projects. An illuminating part of the report showed that of more than 58,000 un-classified appointments under the new Federal Agencies, blacks received appointments to approximately 294 of these and nearly all of them were in the lower messenger grades.[62]

The activities of Alpha Phi Alpha in the sphere of economic and social policy were part of a larger effort by race advancement organizations carried out under the auspices of the Joint Committee on National Recovery (JCNR). Formed in the summer of 1933 by Robert Weaver and John P. Davis, the JCNR was a coalition of more than twenty black religious, fraternal, sororal, and professional organizations; its initial funding came from the Rosenwald Fund, but when that source dried up, the NAACP became the principal sponsor. Charles Wesley, at that time the president of AΦA, was an official of the Joint Committee. Although the JCNR aspired to be an organization that could mobilize the grass roots for protest, it was primarily an information clearinghouse.[63]

The response of the traditional black associations to the Depression was not as coordinated as John P. Davis would have liked. Despite the titular presence of most of the major national African-American organizations, the Urban League refused to come on board and formed its own agency to deal with the economic crisis. The NAACP, the largest and most influential organization in the JCNR, was ambivalent about the existence of a super-coalition to press for relief; Walter White wanted an organization that the NAACP could control and that would not detract from its focus on traditional legal integrationist struggles.[64]

Finally, it appears as if the relief efforts were hobbled by lower-order rivalries and perceptions by some that certain blacks in leading positions were selling out. Certainly these were Rayford Logan's and his investigator's predispositions. The background materials that informed the AΦA report were critical of some of the black New Dealers. The report's investigator conceded that many of the black appointees were hamstrung in their work by virtue of the fact that they were tokens. Nevertheless, he continued, alluding to Robert Weaver, "THE NEGRO NEW DEALERS WERE NOT INTERESTED IN THE NEW DEAL PROGRAM FROM AN ECONOMIC STAND-POINT, BUT RATHER FROM A POLITICAL STANDPOINT AND EVEN THEN THEY DID NOT ACCOMPLISH MUCH. . . ." The typical black New Dealer was

> not sufficiently militant. . . . [He was] just the type of Negro that the white people wanted—one who knew what to say and what not to say; one who gladly accepted what the white officials gave the Negroes and never made any further inquiry or complaint.[65]

The study met with mixed reaction, both in and out of AΦA. The *Memphis World* credited the report with bringing about remedial changes in the position of African Americans in the New Deal, including more benefits from relief agencies; the report, it stated, was widely circulated in government circles.[66] This bit of friendly reporting is probably exaggerated; no single piece of investigation could have possibly moved the New Deal toward racial equality, especially given the division among the advancement organizations. Other reactions illustrated the difficulty that Logan had in transforming AΦA. Some fraternity members had landed prestigious jobs in the New Deal, like Joseph H. B. Evans, the fraternity's executive secretary, who occupied an important position in the National Youth Administration. These and other black New Dealers had a stake in portraying the New Deal in a favorable light, despite the fact that African Americans were quite marginal to the programs; they were not eager to cooperate in the survey.[67]

Other fraternity members welcomed the program, but not for the reasons that Logan would have hoped. Robert Fairchild was an associate editor of the *Sphinx* and the campaign manager for Oklahoma State Senator Josh Lee; as he wanted to land a federal job, he looked upon the Logan brothers' report as a kind of want ad.[68] While Logan intended this study and subsequent studies to form a basis for intelligent protest, he often had to do battle with fraternity brothers whose pecuniary interests exceeded their social consciences; a 1939 fraternity survey on the economic conditions of Afro-America met with strong resistance from fraternity members who felt that the study had no value and that the focus should have been lining up federal jobs for them.[69]

Logan's second programmatic element for the transformation of AΦA was the establishment of an "Education for Citizenship" campaign to replace the decade-old "Go-to-High School, Go-to-College" drive, whose appeal was limited to the more privileged sections of the African-American community.[70] Citizenship was a broad concept, but Logan specifically planned to challenge the disfranchisement of African Americans by preparing them to vote. While the federal government might open up the New Deal to African Americans, he insisted that the determining factor in their struggle for civil rights was their level of organization and their ability to participate "in the political affairs of the community."[71]

A campaign for citizenship rights potentially had appeal across class lines. Logan was acutely aware of a gulf "separating the well-paid, economically secure, cultured and educated Negroes . . . and the unemployed, underpaid, unschooled masses." The "so-called respectable Negroes" had an obligation to pay attention to the daily life of the majority of African Americans and fight for the rights of the entire community.[72]

> Such a program has an appeal not only to college men and women, but also to all other classes of our population. It is flexible enough to meet the needs of every community. In the South we would tackle squarely the problem of the Democratic white primary and of the Lily White Republican caucus. In the North we would emphasize taking advantage of the opportunities for voting and strive to form the nucleus of an intelligent electorate.

Even among segments of the population like those affiliated with the black land-grant colleges, which, because of their connections to the white power structure, could not see their way to supporting suffrage rights, the campaign concept was sufficiently broad that they could emphasize some other aspect of citizenship.[73] A voting rights campaign would challenge one of the pillars of Jim Crow rule in the South and help forge African-American electoral power in the urban North. Furthermore, thought Logan, it would be a perfect way for ΑΦΑ to place itself in the vanguard of the civil rights movement and blaze new trails.

The main form of the "Education for Citizenship" campaign was to be the citizenship school, and Logan, who had had experience in registering African Americans to vote when he lived in Richmond in the late 1920s, had already experimented with this model in Atlanta. In February 1933, the Atlanta branch of the NAACP approved a recommendation by its president, the conservative attorney A. T. Walden, that a School of Citizenship "be established and conducted by the branch for the purpose of training Negroes relative to . . . the effective use of ballot." A committee to oversee the school was established, with Lugenia Burns Hope, the wife of

President John Hope of Atlanta University, as chairwoman. A succession of six-week sessions began in mid-April 1933 at the Butler Street YMCA. The school attracted the attention of black Atlanta: the first sessions had over 150 students, while subsequent sessions had upwards of 290 participants.[74]

At the request of Lugenia Hope, Logan took over the directorship of the school at the end of the first session and guided it until he left Atlanta for Howard University in 1938. Students passed the course by participating in a mock voter registration and standing their ground when grilled by a surrogate registrar; if they allowed themselves to become entangled in the host of subterfuges that registrars used to keep African Americans off the voter rolls, they failed. Learning to vote was crucial, of course, but perhaps of greater importance was the training of African Americans, who for more than two generations had been taught to stay clear of politics, to stand up for their rights. Years later, Logan remembered that some of the most satisfying moments in his long career came with "the certificates I gave to them, mostly domestic servants by the way, who attended these citizenship schools and who passed their examination."[75]

Word of the success of the Atlanta schools spread throughout the South. Atlanta University had backed the program, and in early 1934, Le Moyne College in Memphis had asked Logan to establish a similar curriculum. Alpha Phi Alpha chapters in other cities established their programs, and the 1934 NAACP National Convention backed Logan's plans for citizenship schools. Walter White expressed interest in cooperating with and learning from AΦA in the area of voting rights.[76] In many areas of the South, especially the Upper South, black activists, either under NAACP auspices or collaborating with its membership, instituted voter registration drives similar to Logan's.

For Logan, winning the franchise was the key to revolutionizing life in the South for African Americans. While some southern African-American leaders wanted to use the citizenship schools and the voter registration campaigns as means to buttress the prospects of the Republican party, Logan fought to guarantee their independence from any politician or party.[77] In a debate with Benjamin Davis, Sr., the Georgia state Republican leader, Logan maintained that there was little difference between the two parties so far as their attitude toward African Americans; each wanted to exclude them from politics in the South.[78] The South was a fascist dictatorship, Logan believed, as fascist as Italy or Germany. It would continue to be one, as long as black disfranchisement and the white primary remained the law of the land. If exclusion from the polls continued, Logan promised that African Americans would take democracy through the force of arms.[79]

Like the research project on African Americans and the New Deal, "Education for Citizenship" received general, but not unanimous, approval within the fraternity. Because African Americans were excluded from the national political life, their organizations—especially churches and fraternal organizations—became arenas in which they struggled for leadership and status. The politicking within Alpha Phi Alpha was ubiquitous and the evidence suggests that there was a core of fraternity brothers for whom the organization fulfilled primarily these needs. These were the "black bourgeoisie" about whom E. Franklin Frazier wrote so disparagingly.[80]

The principal form of fraternity politics in which these brothers wanted to engage was a struggle to see which region of the country would predominate in the national office or which chapter would host the national convention. It was among this grouping that such backward practices as hazing flourished. And it was this grouping that consistently opposed Alpha Phi Alpha's entry into the struggle for civil rights. As director of education (and later, between 1941 and 1945, when he served as general president), Logan regularly faced challenges within the ranks from Alphas who refused to promote "Education for Citizenship." Others felt that the treasury was being bled dry for political action, and that the funds should have been spent to finance chapter houses. These fraternity members had built a respectable organization that imitated its white counterparts. They resented the intrusion of political activists like Logan into their domain.[81]

Logan, however, was adept at politicking, and he was able to beat back challenges to his fraternal authority. After five years of the "Education for Citizenship" campaign, Logan claimed that AΦA had reached over one hundred thousand African Americans with its views. As the director of education, he received impressive reports on voting rights activity from chapters in Nashville, Memphis, Louisville, and Jacksonville, among other places; all had extensive programs that included work in coalition with local ministers and chapters of the NAACP and Urban League.[82] Logan also discussed the fraternity's involvement in the pre-*Brown* legal suits for equality in education, noting the fraternal affiliation of several of the complainants and lawyers like Thurgood Marshall, Charles Hamilton

Houston, and Belford Lawson, and the fraternity's pledge of financial and legal assistance.[83]

It is difficult, however, to gauge accurately the significance and impact of these claims. Did AΦA initiate and lead them, or were its members merely individually involved in them? The fraternity was capable of bold action, as indicated by the citizenship schools and other voting rights activity. In 1935 in Norfolk, the Virginia State College chapter initiated a picket line that demanded the right to vote and proclaimed that "A Voteless People Is a Defenseless People." That same year, the Knoxville chapter initiated a coalition that orchestrated the election defeat of a racist municipal official and fought to ensure that African Americans were not excluded from grand jury service.[84]

Yet there is also evidence that most of the fraternity's high-profile civic activity (especially its rallies and other forms of agitation) can be directly traced back to Logan's initiative. "A legitimate criticism of my administration," Logan wrote in 1945 of his time as AΦA president, "has been lack of adequate publicity. You will appreciate why—most of what we have done, I have done, and I can't send articles to the newspapers about myself."[85] This, too, may be a bit of an exaggeration: AΦA chapters became more active in the early 1940s, when African Americans pressed to be included in the armed forces and defense industries.[86] Clearly, though, Logan was the innovator in AΦA, experimenting in not only new civil rights tactics like citizenship campaigns, but new roles for fraternities; to the extent that AΦA approached an active role in the civil rights movement in the 1930s, Logan was the principal motivator. But it was also a signal of the strength of the black bourgeoisie that once Logan left fraternal office, AΦA gradually reverted to its old spirit.[87]

If Logan had some difficulties swinging his fraternity behind his visionary program, serious obstacles precluded his developing a close connection with the local NAACP. Although Logan's first citizenship school was under the auspices of the Atlanta branch of the NAACP, and despite the fact that he served on the branch executive committee, Logan soon developed the view that the organization did little in the way of advancing civil rights.[88] Except for sponsoring the citizenship schools, the Atlanta NAACP was, during the early 1930s, practically moribund.

Between 1930 and 1932, African Americans in Atlanta and surrounding areas were subjected to a reign of terror as white society sought to control the black population through physical violence. In May 1931, six African-American males were arrested on a charge of raping a white woman near Elberton, Georgia. Six days after the arrests, in an atmosphere saturated with lynch threats, John Downer, one of the defendants, was indicted, tried, convicted, and sentenced to death; his court-appointed attorney was selected only one hour before the trial. Downer was granted a new trial on appeal; but the second trial also ended in a conviction, and Downer was executed in 1934. A. T. Walden, an attorney and president of the NAACP in Atlanta, conducted some legal work on the trial, but his organization stayed noticeably in the background.[89]

The NAACP's deafening silence continued during a wave of murders of African Americans by police in the Atlanta area during 1932. A particularly vicious murder occurred in October of that year, when a court bailiff shot Mrs. Dinah Strickland and her daughter Oneta in nearby Newman; he became enraged when he could not find Mrs. Strickland's son, whom he had come to arrest. While the normally quiescent *Atlanta Daily World*, the South's only daily newspaper for African Americans, railed against the murder, the Atlanta NAACP was most reluctant to protest. Shocked and outraged local civil rights activists pleaded with the NAACP national office to prod the Atlanta branch to act. But even a letter from Assistant Secretary Roy Wilkins to A. T. Walden failed to elicit action.[90]

In some respects this timidity was typical of southern NAACP branches, but the unusually sad state of the association in Atlanta was due largely to the retrograde leadership of Walden. The chapter did nothing and did not even hold regular meetings. Although it had issued some mild protests against one or two cases of police brutality, it had refused vigorously to defend African Americans from the indignities of Jim Crow justice.[91] Walden had lost the respect of the NAACP membership. Known by blacks and whites alike as "Captain" or "Colonel"—monikers bestowed upon adult male African Americans by whites who refused to use "Mister" when referring to black men—Walden was inclined to join various organizations primarily to garner the prestige and business connections that were by-products of his networking. Walden wanted the credit for the citizenship schools even though the work was largely conducted by Lugenia Burns Hope and Logan; Walden's claims in particular upset Logan. By 1936 working relations had become so strained in the branch that the

Women's Auxiliary broke away rather than work with Walden. Auxiliary members were particularly incensed that "the Organization in Atlanta never undertook anything of benefit to the general public."[92]

Logan's differences with the NAACP went beyond issues peculiar to the Atlanta branch, however, and could not be resolved by Walden's retirement as chapter president in 1936. They diverged on the issue of how to build coalitions to fight for civil rights. As a militant, Logan was prepared to unite and work with anyone who supported his goal. The NAACP, on the other hand, weighed its participation in any issue not only against the righteousness of the cause but against whether it might be tainted with the charge of being radical, or worse, communist.

Nowhere is the divergence between Logan and the NAACP clearer than in their attitudes toward the Angelo Herndon case, one of the most important symbols of southern Jim Crow justice in the 1930s. A nineteen-year-old African-American Communist, Angelo Herndon was arrested in Atlanta in 1932 for leading a biracial demonstration for unemployment relief at the Fulton County Courthouse. Both city officials and a resurgent Ku Klux Klan feared not only increased Communist activity, but specifically the Communist party's agitation for African-American legal equality, and especially the prospect of a labor movement that united white and black workers. Herndon's arrest and conviction on charges of inciting an insurrection (a violation of the antebellum slave code) were part of a pattern of harassment against Atlanta's African-American and leftist communities that included killings of blacks by police and the arrests of local labor militants.

The Communist party and the International Labor Defense (ILD), an organization of Communist and sympathetic non-Communist lawyers, mounted a comprehensive defense of Herndon reminiscent of the contemporaneous Scottsboro Boys campaign. The legal defense was only one facet of an integral campaign of rallies, pickets, meetings, and petition drives in Atlanta and across the country designed to call attention to the barbarity of southern justice. In Atlanta, the Provisional Committee for the Defense of Angelo Herndon effectively united the African-American churches and community organizations and white liberals like C. Vann Woodward, who at the time was a young teacher at Georgia Tech.

The NAACP remained on the sidelines. It was reluctant to associate itself with Angelo Herndon for fear of being tarred with the communist brush. Whereas Jesse O. Thomas, the southern director of the Urban

League, told an audience at the Wheat Street Baptist Church on Angelo Herndon Day that the controversy over communism that had been stirred up by whites in Atlanta had distracted African Americans from the true issues of the case, the Atlanta branch of the NAACP refused to get involved in any meaningful way.[93] The national office was only slightly less paralyzed; six days after Herndon's conviction, Walter White wrote A. T. Walden to request that he contact Herndon's lawyers about the appeal. White wanted Walden to inquire about the possibilities of the NAACP taking sole charge of the legal process so as not to have "it distorted by injection of the Communist angle." Not long after this communication, Daisy Lampkin, the NAACP's field secretary, voiced the optimistic hope that black Atlantans would come over to "the saner program of the NAACP" because they would realize that the Herndon case had caused too much racial friction.[94]

The NAACP objected to working with the Communist party for two overarching reasons. As a practical matter, the association wanted to control whatever issues it chose to champion. The Communist party also desired hegemonic control, and in the cases of Angelo Herndon and the Scottsboro Boys, the Party successfully outflanked the association, preventing it from taking the leading role. But ideological reasons also prevented the NAACP from cooperating with the Communists. The association practiced gradualism and conciliation; in its efforts to win short-term gains, it even muted its opposition to racial proscription. Although it was founded on the ideas of the New Abolitionism and agitation for civil rights, when the NAACP engaged in a legal battle it preferred to keep a low profile—cases were won in the courts, not the newspapers, said the conventional wisdom. Communist activity and publicity, with their emphasis on class struggle, inflamed racial tension and caused the "better class" of white southerners to abandon blacks. In the Scottsboro Boys case, the NAACP claimed, a fair trial was the only way to keep "outsiders" from interfering in southern race relations; the last time this happened, said the association's William Pickens, was Reconstruction.[95]

As an individual, Logan had initially decided that he would not become active in the Herndon campaign. It was his considered opinion that political campaigns built around particularly egregious violations of the rights of African Americans were not the most efficient way to advance racial equality. As far back as the Scottsboro Boys case, he concluded that a strategy built around mass actions was inadequate:

> An emotional, blatant, strident radicalism can hardly exist over a period of years unless new fuel is constantly added to the flames. We cannot, however, make a Scottsboro to order every year. . . . I seriously doubt whether it will be possible to create every year the sustained, national interest that has resulted from the Scottsboro case.[96]

But when it came to speaking out for racial and economic justice, Logan was just as strident as the Communist party. He did not fear being associated with it, and when the fallout from the Herndon case became generalized, he joined with the Communists to fight the repression. In the fall of 1934, as the Herndon case wound its way through the legal system and continued to generate controversy in Atlanta, city officials were panicked by a wave of labor unrest in nearby textile mills and agitation in the African-American community against a new outbreak of murders of blacks by police officers. While the *Atlanta Constitution* and the *Macon Telegraph* conducted their own agitation against the labor movement, the police in Atlanta and the suburban city of Decatur raided houses inhabited by suspected Communists; in one night, they arrested eleven suspects—five whites and six African Americans—and charged them with attempting to incite insurrection. A few days later, Atlanta police raided the headquarters of the Urban League; the Butler Street YMCA, which had been a site for Logan's citizenship classes, was also raided around this time.[97]

Logan and a few of his colleagues at Atlanta University struggled to respond to the repressive atmosphere. He was in contact with Alexander Racholin, a New York City attorney and member of the ILD who was in town to work on the Herndon case. At Racholin's request, Logan had called a meeting of "the more militant faculty members and administrators to meet in our home." The night before the meeting, though, Racholin was arrested in one of the raids in Decatur. The meeting went on as scheduled, but Logan was outvoted in his attempt to organize a protest. He himself barely escaped arrest, Logan later told Florence Luscomb, his old Boston friend.[98]

The red scare continued into 1935. The Ku Klux Klan and the American Legion hunted for Communists everywhere. In one instance, the Legion hounded the Southern Institute of International Relations, a conference sponsored by the American Friends Service Committee and other liberal organizations. The scare campaign worked, as the institute was poorly attended.[99] Logan had planned to address the participants, probably on the Italian invasion of Ethiopia and its consequences for African Americans; he in fact did give this speech later in June to the New England Institute of Politics at Wellesley College. But Logan did not speak at the Southern Institute; President John Hope of Atlanta University, acting on some information concerning the disruption of the affair, prevailed upon Logan not to attend. "Professor Logan," Hope told Logan when the two met as they walked across campus, "my ideal is a faculty with very little turnover. I wish you would pull in your horns."[100]

Logan relented—this once.[101] Nevertheless, during his five years in Atlanta, as a scholar and an activist, and as an official in the Alpha Phi Alpha fraternity, Logan developed a reputation as an intelligent and innovative fighter for civil rights. Nannie Burroughs, the veteran Washington, D.C., educator and women's and civil rights advocate, regarded the Rayford Logan of the 1930s "as one of the finest young radicals I ever knew and above all, one of the most sincere."[102] The *Chicago Defender* praised Logan in sociological terms:

> Experts in the sociology of the Negro describe a type—the "Bad Negro" who "despite his unfavorable status with whites and his lack of support from Negroes," is secretly admired by Negroes and scrupulously respected by whites.
> [Rayford Logan is] a "bad Negro with a Ph.D."[103]

The "bad Negroes with Ph.D.'s" were a cohort of young radical intellectuals in the 1930s who sought alternatives to what they considered the tired, inadequate program and tactics of the NAACP. The Great Depression not only had disrupted the lives of millions of African Americans, it also visited a severe disorientation on the association's senior leaders. Joel Spingarn, the longtime president of the NAACP, complained that the organization had no program, only a succession of pending legal cases on discrimination. Nevertheless, the association leadership, which was middle-class, resisted changing its traditional program of fighting for formal equality. They viewed with alarm any attempt to indict the economic system as the principal cause of the plight of African Americans and to shade the association toward fighting for the economic uplift of the black working class.[104]

For some of the young radicals, the alternative was to wage a more forceful class struggle. Abram L. Harris, a Howard University economics professor, sought to get the NAACP to adopt a class-based strategy.

Beginning with the Amenia Conference (which was called by Du Bois), and throughout 1933–34, Harris pushed—unsuccessfully—for the association to become actively involved in building a new working-class movement for economic, social, and racial justice.[105] Ralph Bunche, who in the 1930s had a reputation as a Marxist-influenced radical, was one of the founders of the National Negro Congress (NNC) in 1935. Predicated on the assumption that there would be no racial justice without class justice, the NNC, whose driving force was the Communist party, became a home for young radicals, especially the "black intellectuals and professionals who viewed trade unionism and mass protest as keys to black advancement. . . ."[106]

For others, the ideas of class unity held less allure. Logan's proposed program for AΦA and the one adopted by the NNC overlapped at many points: both emphasized voting rights; both fought discrimination in higher education; and each struggled in its own way to expand the Social Security and Fair Labor Standards acts to include agricultural and domestic workers.[107] Where he parted ways with the NNC was on the issue of an alliance between black and white workers. Although Logan specifically advocated this alignment, he did not hold out much hope for its success, given the dismal track record of the American Federation of Labor.[108] Consequently, he opted for a nationalist strategy.

Of the "bad Negroes with Ph.D.'s," Logan was probably least enamored with class strategies and the Communist party, but he was more than willing to give them credit for agitating African Americans. He was even attracted to some of communism's ideals, like economic parity, an end to the profit system, and the elimination of discrimination. But ultimately he concluded that revolution was not a practical alternative for African Americans: "That revolution may come later," he said in 1933, "but our problem is to obtain for the Negro *now* as many advantages as possible and to avoid as many pitfalls as possible."[109] The young radicals were themselves divided even as they opposed the NAACP. But what united them was a shared desire to articulate a militant strategy for political and economic equality. Unlike the conservative African-American leaders like Walter White, the radicals were not driven to hysterics by the prospect of Communist participation in the civil rights movement.

As the 1930s drew to a close and the world moved steadily toward war, the world of African Americans was about to change permanently. The war would present African Americans with the opportunities to partici-

pate ever more fully in the national life; there would also be fierce resistance to this trend from many quarters of white society. In the 1930s,
Rayford Logan had shown the ability to swim against two tides: racial
discrimination and conservatism within the civil rights movement. The
challenge of the next decade would be whether he and others of like mind
could continue to break new ground in the struggle for racial equality.

chapter five

"THE WHITE MAN'S DISTRESS IS THE BLACK MAN'S GAIN"

❧

(1940–1945)

A S RAYFORD LOGAN peered into the new decade, he had every reason to believe that he would become one of its most effective civil rights leaders. In 1938 he had left Atlanta University to accept a position at Howard University in Washington, D.C.[1] His voter registration activity of the 1930s was pioneering, but it took place in relatively cramped quarters and its results, while significant, were mostly symbolic. In Atlanta and one or two other southern cities, Logan's and AΦA's citizenship campaigns alarmed local white officials, but they did not cause a shake-up of the system of segregation. Besides adding to the civil rights movement's strategic reserves, Logan's tactics earned him a reputation as a distinguished civil rights advocate. The next sequential step was to get a national hearing for civil rights. The creation of such an opportunity was helped along in the 1930s by the beginning of a profound demographic change among African Americans, who, with the start of their second great migration of the twentieth century, were transforming themselves into an urban, northern people. The workings of these two processes secured a wider arena in which African Americans could pursue their rights.[2] By 1940, when the United States was lurching toward joining the war against fascism that engulfed Europe and northern Africa, African Americans were pressing their case before a national audience as never before.

Mussolini's invasion of Ethiopia in 1935 had startled whites and blacks alike in the United States, and many African Americans began to link the worldwide resistance against fascism with the struggle to end discrimination against American blacks. A. Philip Randolph united these two issues in his plea to the American Federation of Labor to initiate a boycott of Italy. The NAACP formed a prestigious delegation to lobby the White House not to aid Italy; the delegation included Logan, U.S. Representative Arthur Mitchell, spokesmen from the major fraternal organizations, publishers of the prominent black newspapers, and the presidents of the Tuskegee Institute and Atlanta and Howard Universities. As John Hope Franklin pointed out, "The interest of the Negro in world affairs lagged very little after Italy invaded Ethiopia in 1935."[3]

Logan had been preparing for the new situation and the new opportunities of the 1940s since the mid-1930s. Despite their interest in the plight of Emperor Haile Selassie, most Americans remained isolationist; African Americans in particular looked askance at fighting a war to excise fascism from Europe when they lived under it in the South. But just as Logan defied convention in his cavalier response to being linked with Communists, he voiced the opinion that the chaos in Europe that would soon break out in war was bound to benefit the cause of freedom for black people worldwide. His June 1935 article, "The Negro Studies War Some More," was widely reprinted in the black press.[4]

"Since war is now imminent, a very pertinent question needs to be brought out into the open," he wrote. "What should be the attitude of black men toward another World War? I, for one, am convinced that it is the best thing that can happen for 200,000,000 black men." Reviewing the status of black people in Africa and the Americas, Logan stated that the inferior position of Africans had been permanently enshrined in the Covenant of the League of Nations; Article XXII, which had established the mandate system, decreed that the mandated African territories would never be independent. In the European colonies and in South Africa, which Logan called the "Hell Hole of Creation," Africans were dispossessed and suppressed at an astounding pace. Drawing an analogy between the situation in Africa and the better-known, but still ignored, plight of the Jews, Logan declared, "If Palestine were given to Adolph Hitler's Germany, a greater crime would not be committed." He repeated the long list of injustices and indignities that African Americans faced, "even under the New Deal and even under a President whose personal attitude on the race question is loftier than that of most of his predecessors."

Logan welcomed the coming war because it would breach the united front of the white race that in practice continually pushed black people into a subordinate position. He had no sympathy for pacifism. "Nothing short of a considerable weakening of the white races by war will, I am afraid, bring any appreciable improvement of the Negro's status." The odds of eliminating Article XXII increased with a war. African Americans could conceivably exact their claim to human rights under law and scrap their status as "recipient[s] of small favors" as the price for their participation in the war effort. The most important ingredient in Logan's vision was the organization of African Americans. Drawing upon his previous experience after World War I, he called upon African Americans to secure their rights in the future postwar order by establishing a movement similar to the Pan-African Congress that would make coherent their diverse demands and pressure the world powers "to adopt a long-range policy looking to the elevation of black men to the status of other human beings."

Logan's prescient voice remained a lone one for more than three years. In 1938, the *Pittsburgh Courier,* the largest and one of the most influential African-American newspapers, translated Logan's polemic into a program. African Americans deserved the opportunity to participate in the defense of their country—and to share in the rights and responsibilities of citizenship on the same basis as other Americans. The *Courier,* angered by the failure of the War Department to execute the mandate given it by Congress in 1939 to provide training for African-American pilots, asked its readers to send letters and telegrams to the president and their congressmen asking them to state their opinion on dramatically increasing the number of African Americans in the armed forces. In 1939 the *Courier* formed the Committee for the Participation of Negroes in the National Defense Program (CPNNDP), which was composed of representatives of the Alpha Phi Alpha, Omega Psi Phi, and Kappa Alpha Psi fraternities; the Alpha Kappa Alpha sorority; the Elks; the Association for the Study of Negro Life and History; the Washington Chamber of Commerce and various black American Legion posts; and the African-American legal, dental, and medical associations. In 1940, Logan was named its chairman.[5]

The CPNNDP developed a two-part program covering military and civil affairs. The military objectives aimed to reverse the attrition of African Americans in the army and to ensure that they would be represented in all phases of military life. Key demands included: the return to combat status of African-American units that had been downgraded in the 1920s; a "fair share of the increased strength authorized for the Regular Army" and the commissioning of African-American officers to command these troops; the activation of black reserve units and officers; the appointment of African-American doctors, dentists, and nurses to the regular army; a "fair share of the flying cadets and aviation mechanics in the Army Air Corps and the Naval Flying Corps"; elimination of the color bar in the navy, which confined African Americans to mess units; and the desegregation of the Marine Corps. "Fair share" was defined as 10 percent, the proportion of African Americans in the national population. The civil program was designed to ensure that African Americans received a proportional share of all federal funds for education and vocational training for jobs in defense industries. The CPNNDP demanded: the appointment of African-American representatives on all advisory committees dealing with education and vocational training; the hiring of African-American staff members on these committees; regulations forbidding any state agency that discriminates against African Americans in defense-related educational or vocational training from receiving federal funds; legislation precluding labor unions from excluding African Americans from training or apprenticeship programs.[6]

The CPNNDP had organized chapters in twenty-five states and the District of Columbia and had managed to develop working relations with a wide array of middle-class organizations, including local fraternity and sorority chapters, businessmen's clubs, and educators' associations. In Louisville, Charles Anderson, an active member of AΦA and the only African-American member of the Kentucky state legislature, anchored the local Allied Councils for Defense, which was composed of twenty-four member organizations. The Norfolk, Virginia, Negro Council for National Defense was able to develop six active committees; according to B. T. Holmes, the council's director and also a leading member of the city's AΦA graduate chapter, the effort was supported by the local branch of the NAACP, women's organizations, churches, the Chemical Workers Union, and the African-American auxiliaries to the Democratic party and the letter carrier's union.[7]

During its first year of existence, the CPNNDP scored two impressive victories in its military program. In the spring of 1940, both houses of Congress began debate on the Military Appropriations Bill of 1941, also known as the Burke-Wadsworth bill. African Americans feared that they would again be excluded from the military, except in the most menial capacities. Despite the fact that Congress passed Public Law 18 in 1939, part of which authorized the establishment of facilities for training African Americans to be pilots, because of War Department resistance none was being trained. In May Logan and Charles Houston represented the CPNNDP at Senate hearings on Burke-Wadsworth.

Logan testified to the several ways in which African Americans were being excluded from the military, including the fact that only two black colleges had senior ROTC programs, whereas virtually all white colleges had them. Participation by African Americans was fundamental to the American system, "especially at a time when we are holding out against totalitarian ideologies the moral force of the principles of American democracy." He called for the earmarking of 10 percent of the military training budget for African Americans. In making this request, Logan denounced the existence of segregated units "which are forced upon us." The CPNNDP, he said, "protests the continuation of separate Negro units. We deplore segregation in any form, especially when it is practiced by the Federal Government." The only reason the committee was prepared to accept these units was the hope that they would be officered by African Americans.[8]

Logan offered similar testimony before the House of Representatives committee that was debating provisions on the draft. Logan supported the draft, he told the House Committee on Military Affairs, but only if it was truly nondiscriminatory. He proposed specific language to the bill that stated that "in the selection and training of men as well as in the interpretation and execution of the provisions of this act there shall be no discrimination against any person on account of race, creed, or color."[9]

As Burke-Wadsworth wound its way through Congress, Robert Wagner, Democratic senator from New York, offered an amendment that would have prohibited discrimination in the case of volunteers, but did not address the issues of discrimination in conscription and training. Logan claimed that this amendment was "virtually meaningless" because of its silence on these key issues. Initially, the NAACP had steered clear of the military issue, for the question had been framed in terms of separate equality. The *Pittsburgh Courier* reported on April 27, 1940, that "it is understood that Mr. [Walter] White does not want his organization introduced into the fight at the present time because of that organization's 'idealism of no segregation' as against The Courier's policy of 'practicality of separate division.'" But now the NAACP, which had done little to influence Burke-Wadsworth and had not even testified at congressional hearings, supported the Wagner amendment; the most likely explanation is that the association had a cordial political relationship with Senator Wagner and feared jeopardizing it if it did not back him. The NAACP tried to pressure Logan and the CPNNDP into supporting it. According to Logan, Charles Houston, on the advice of Roy Wilkins, the NAACP assistant secretary, "called to urge that we not 'squawk' against the Wagner amendment; that, instead, we should urge every Congressman to support it."[10]

After extensive discussion, the CPNNDP decided to oppose the Wagner amendment. With the help of Emmett J. Scott, who had been Booker T. Washington's personal secretary and now was in charge of publicity among African Americans for the Republican party, Logan prevailed upon Hamilton Fish, Republican representative from New York, to sponsor an amendment. The Fish amendment, which was passed in September as part of the bill, was written by Logan and outlawed all racial discrimination in the selection and training of military personnel.[11]

The Fish amendment was an important victory, but it was not a decisive one; because African Americans were still to be assigned to separate units, the total number of African Americans drafted and activated from reserve units depended upon President Roosevelt's decision either to keep the number of separate units constant or to increase them. Quickly following the passage of the Fish amendment, the NAACP sought a presidential clarification. Walter White asked T. Arnold Hill, of the National Urban League, and A. Philip Randolph to join him in a meeting with Roosevelt on September 27 to discuss the implementation of the Fish amendment as well as a number of other items relating to discrimination in the national defense program. Logan was pointedly excluded from this conference, although Hill, "probably at the suggestion of Walter White," called on Logan to propose agenda items for the meeting. Hill promised to inform Logan of the meeting's results, but he never did.[12]

As White later recalled, he, Randolph, and Hill "most emphatically urged upon the President . . . the immediate and total abolition in the armed forces of segregation based on race or color."[13] Roosevelt was predictably vague and avoided promising any changes in military policy or measures to ensure that defense contractors did not discriminate against African Americans in hiring. Two weeks after the meeting, the White

House issued a unilateral statement that implied, falsely, that White, Hill, and Randolph endorsed the principle of a segregated military and the officering of black troops by whites.[14] "This policy," the *Courier* quoted the statement as reading, "has been proven satisfactory over a long period of years, and to make changes would produce situations destructive to morale and detrimental to the preparation for national defense."[15]

The bedrock of Logan's dispute with Walter White was the thorny issue of segregation. White (and to a lesser degree the NAACP) insisted that the demand of the civil rights movement for the national defense program should be the complete abolition of segregation and the integration of the armed forces and defense industries. Any demand short of this was a poor compromise. As a keen politician, White may have thought that the tide of events was on his side: as the country drifted toward war, and as the government took stock of wartime manpower needs, both would realize the efficacy of dismantling the color bar. Logan, however, was not so sanguine. While he, too, was an implacable foe of segregation, he thought that strategic considerations made it more important for African Americans to win the right to serve at all levels in the military, even a segregated one. African Americans would be in a favorable position to demand full equality once they could show that they were discharging their responsibilities as citizens; conversely, they could demand nothing if there was even an aroma of their evading their military obligations in a time of war.[16]

The NAACP was caught in a bind. The public discourse assumed a Jim Crow military and focused upon the seemingly less volatile issue of fairness within the confines of segregation. Because Logan accepted, however reluctantly, these terms, he was able to influence the public debate and secure legal promises for greater African-American participation within the military. The NAACP, however, found it most difficult to take any action to promote African-American participation in the armed service when it seemed as if most of the progressive forces accepted the premise that the only immediate alternative to a segregation in the military was the far less appealing prospect of exclusion from it.

Walter White's insistence on the moral high ground on this issue, though, was offset by certain political realities. The NAACP's friends in Congress did not challenge the military's right to enforce segregation. Despite its integrationist perspective, the NAACP could not risk embarrassing Senator Wagner by opposing his efforts to amend the selective service law by branding them short of the mark. Struggling mightily to accommodate the conflicting pressures, the association determined a tactical line that resembled more closely political paralysis than action. Eschewing both public agitation for a desegregated military and public embrace of the Wagner amendment, the NAACP instead chose to lobby Congress out of public view with the intent of supporting Senator Wagner's efforts.

Within the NAACP Roy Wilkins, the assistant executive director, was the voice for engaging the national debate as it was presently framed. In a frank memorandum to Walter White, Wilkins summed up the price the NAACP paid for its public silence and backroom dealings. He told White that he detected among association members and supporters "a fairly clear implication that the association . . . was not doing anything tangible and effective." When he tried to explain to them what the NAACP had been doing around the Burke-Wadsworth bill, he was "greeted either with a polite silence or with assertions that the Wagner amendment, which we claim as our own, is not very effective." The NAACP was not out in front on this issue, Wilkins wrote; it had been expending all of its energy "on individual lobbying in Washington with politicians rather than on beating the tom tom of public opinion over the country."[17]

When it appeared that the NAACP had failed again in its national defense efforts, Logan, who was piqued at being snubbed by White, tried to secure a meeting with the president. Bill Riis, his Williams classmate and closest white friend, wrote to the president's aide, Lowell Mellett, to set it up, praising Logan lavishly in the process:

> Ray has been very active lately in connection with insuring Negroes an equal right with white men to be shot on the field of battle. . . . He is not going to ask you for jobs or anything of that sort, and I think that a smart guy like yourself will be glad to have Ray as a source of knowledge.[18]

The meeting, held on October 25, was an AΦA affair, for the other two members of the delegation, President F. D. Patterson of Tuskegee and Howard Long, were fraternity brothers. "Today I had one of the greatest experiences of my life," Logan wrote. He was overawed by the president's manner, wit, and folksy charm. But he was also able to wrangle out of Roosevelt a promise that the army would increase the number of African-American units and opportunities for blacks to officer them. He wrote to Bill Riis that "I dictated (ahem!) the order that the president wrote on his pad and said that he was going to send over to the War Department today." A few weeks after the meeting Logan received written confirmation from Roosevelt to that effect.[19] With two victories in the national defense program in just over a month's time, Logan was positioned to be a major player in the gathering protest movement against discrimination.

To Logan, Walter White and the NAACP were parvenus who were meddling in his bailiwick of the national defense struggle. The logical course for the NAACP, in Logan's mind, would have been for it to unite with the CPNNDP, especially since the majority of NAACP members did not support White's position on desegregation of the military and instead supported Logan's concept of parity.[20] African-American leaders like Mary McLeod Bethune and Lester Granger of the Urban League also supported a united effort. The forum for these opinions was two meetings: the Hampton Conference on the Participation of Negroes in National Defense, which was sponsored by that institution in November 1940 on the occasion of the installation of Malcolm MacLean as president, and a follow-up gathering the next week in Washington, D.C. The Hampton Conference was the first national gathering of African Americans on this issue; it brought together two thousand participants in the public sessions and more than two hundred persons, including representatives of the major civil rights organizations, for workshops. The Washington conference called for the CPNNDP, the Urban League, the NAACP, the National Council of Colored Women, the National Association of Colored Women's Clubs, and the various fraternal and sororal orders to unite on a national and local level.[21]

The expressed desire for unity could not by itself effect a reconciliation between the NAACP and the CPNNDP. In early 1941 the Senate had empowered a special committee headed by Harry Truman to investigate irregularities in the defense industry. The Senate was responding to concerns that a relatively small number of companies were receiving the largest portion of contracts, that these companies were having chronic difficulties meeting deadlines, and that they were not coping effectively with manpower shortages. Logan wanted the Truman committee also to investigate racial discrimination in employment by government, management, and organized labor; his plan was not only to testify himself, but to subpoena also national defense program officials like William Knudsen, the former chairman of General Motors who now headed the Office of Production Management, and his assistant in charge of labor, Sidney Hillman of the American Federation of Labor.[22]

Concurrent with Logan's labors to bring racial discrimination before the Truman committee, the NAACP lobbied hard for Senate Resolution 75 (SR 75), which was introduced by Robert Wagner and called for a separate investigation of discrimination in the military and in defense industries. Logan's and Walter White's proposed agendas for Senate investigations were remarkably similar, right down to the prospective witnesses.[23] But White insisted that according to Harry Truman himself, the Truman committee would be unable to plumb effectively charges of discrimination, owing to its already heavy schedule.[24] Logan, however, had heard no such statement from Truman or his staff. In any event, Walter White opposed Logan's efforts, claiming that any hearings before the Truman committee would not only be inadequate—and inadequately publicized—but would also be used by senators opposed to a full-scale hearing on discrimination to claim that SR 75 was now unnecessary. White's reading of the Truman committee's ability effectively to hear the grievances of African Americans was likely accurate, but he had not convinced the prominent witnesses on Logan's list of this. Where Logan doubted the prospects for the passage of SR 75 and thought that African Americans should take whatever hearing they could get, Walter White was uncompromising in his position. He would accept no half-loaf in the form of the Truman committee; it was SR 75 or nothing. In the summer of 1941 White prevailed upon the Truman committee to postpone indefinitely the hearings it had scheduled at Logan's request.[25] But he could not succeed in getting SR 75 passed.

The bickering and infighting between Logan and White and the NAACP ran so high that at times it appeared as if the principals were merely jockeying for position. "It's a damned shame that the whole Negro race must revolve around Walter and the NAACP," a disgusted Logan wrote in his diary after White pulled the plug on Logan's Truman committee hearings.[26] The *Courier* printed, undoubtedly with Logan's approval, an ad hominem attack on White, accusing him of a " 'vicious double-cross' of the entire Negro race," and printing letters assailing White for weak and selfish leadership.[27]

The *Courier*'s antipathy for Water White's and the NAACP's work on the issue of Negroes in the national defense—and A. Philip Randolph's March on Washington Movement, which the NAACP endorsed in spring 1941—had as much to do with personal rivalries as with principled politics. Robert L. Vann, the *Courier*'s publisher, had a longstanding feud with the NAACP, dating back to 1926, when he had accused James

Weldon Johnson and W. E. B. Du Bois of financial impropriety and race betrayal; when Walter White stepped in to defend the association of these serious charges, he too felt Vann's ire. The *Courier* had been a singular voice of support among the black newspapers for Randolph's organizing efforts with the Brotherhood of Sleeping Car Porters during its first years of existence; the paper and the union had a symbiotic relationship: Vann offered publicity and encouragement, and the Pullman porters spread the word about the paper, boosting its circulation. But in 1928, just as the BSCP faced its first major test, the *Courier* turned on the union and its head. What unites both instances is a suspicion—articulated by Vann's biographer—that the publisher's actions were motivated by a strong desire to boost circulation. Simply put, charges of fiscal opportunism and sensational articles about the largest black labor organization made good copy and sold papers.[28] Logan did not share Vann's hostility for either Johnson and Du Bois or Randolph, but their mutual distaste for Walter White was enough for him to weigh in with the *Courier,* even as he remained politically beholden to no one.

While Logan was accusing White of megalomania, White was sticking his own darts into Logan. The entire dispute between the two men could be reduced to the fact that Logan had "a limelight complex," White wrote to Stephen Spingarn, the son of the late Joel Spingarn. Spingarn, who was of the same mind as White, wrote back, saying that Logan's proposed hearings before the Truman committee would satisfy only "publicity seekers" with "stump speeches."[29] The feud continued into December, more than four months after the cancellation of the hearings, when the NAACP approached a meeting of the Greek Letter Societies to ask for a contribution to support a national lobby for civil rights. Logan, who still smarted from the collapse of the Truman committee hearings, told the meeting that "Alpha [Phi Alpha] would contribute $2,000 to a national lobby over my dead body," to which the NAACP staff member present replied that the association would " 'squelch' any other movement which it deemed unwise."[30]

In the field of direct action Walter White similarly refused to recognize the CPNNDP. Ted Berry, a rising and well-connected figure in black Cincinnati—he would later be elected to the city council in 1950 and serve as mayor between 1972 and 1975—had been the NAACP's branch president from 1932 to 1938.[31] In 1940 he became a leader of the CPNNDP, and it was in that capacity that Berry informed White of the formation of local chapters of the committee and asked White to urge NAACP branches to affiliate. Some CPNNDP state directors were NAACP members, Berry told White, and the local committees were designed to "avoid duplication of effort and to unite Negroes in every community to press for fuller integration into the industrial and military defense program." But White would not cooperate with the CPNNDP. He claimed that NAACP branches had already united with other organizations and it would be confusing to work with anyone else.[32]

Of course, it was not only Walter White's doings that kept Logan from reaching the highest plateau of the civil rights leadership. Logan resented those in the movement's top echelons, for he felt that he was more qualified intellectually to fill their positions than they were. He was most bellicose toward those African Americans who received presidential appointments. He thought William Hastie unfit for the position of civilian aide to the secretary of war and concluded that Hastie received the appointment only because he was friends with Robert Weaver, the veteran Black Cabinet member who helped to shape New Deal policy on housing and employment for blacks; going back to the early 1930s, Logan considered Weaver to be uncooperative and even indifferent to the African-American struggle to share in the New Deal.[33] He unfairly tweaked Hastie for making strong statements against segregation in the military before his appointment and then maintaining silence on this matter when in office.[34] He publicly criticized Hastie; Weaver, who had recently been appointed to the Office of Production Management; and even his childhood friend Campbell Johnson, who had been named to the Selective Service Board. Before a crowd of 1,500 in Philadelphia's Union Baptist Church in February 1941, he declared that the three were "appointed only to serve as 'barriers' against Negro 'pressure groups.'" Although he took pains to say that he was not impugning the integrity of the three men, his comments nevertheless had a certain meanness. He offered no constructive comments to the three; nor did he explain how he might do their jobs in such a way as to avoid being a political buffer.[35] When one measures his comments against his later actions, it becomes apparent that Logan often leveled unprincipled criticism at his colleagues as a way of boosting himself.

"Ruth is very much disappointed that I am not offered one of these positions—but my job is to stay out and talk and write," Logan wrote in his diary after he heard of Campbell Johnson's Selective Service appointment.[36] Logan tried to console himself with the thought that he was not considered for government positions because he was too militant and that his acceptance of a post would cramp his polemical style. Yet he likely would have jumped at an offer had one been made, even if acceptance would have hindered his ability to criticize government policy.

In August 1942 it came to Logan's attention that the War Department wanted to establish under its auspices a Civilian Protection School for African Americans at Tuskegee. The department floated the idea of appointing Logan the commander of that school with the rank of captain. He would have been responsible for a faculty of seven. Logan "consulted" with several of his friends and colleagues: Campbell Johnson; Frank Snowden, a professor of classics at Howard, and Snowden's wife Elaine; his wife, Ruth; Charles Thompson, the well-respected educator at Howard and founder of the *Journal of Negro Education;* Charles Wesley, his colleague in Howard's history department; President Mordecai Johnson of Howard University; and Crystal Bird Fauset. From Logan's description, however, it appears as if the consultations were more akin to occasions for Logan to boast of his proposed nomination. Mordecai Johnson and Charles Thompson warned Logan that the appointment had substantially the same intent as those offered to Campbell Johnson and William Hastie. "It may be part of a scheme to shut up outspoken critics." But Campbell Johnson counseled Logan not to accept anything less than the rank of lieutenant-colonel.[37]

Logan eventually decided not to accept the position. In his letter declining the position, he wrote that the school was in the South, and he didn't "get along well with most Southerners. When I left the South in 1938, after five years in Atlanta, I swore that I would never live in the South again." Then, too, he might not be able to get leave from Howard University; he was being considered to replace Charles Wesley as head of the Department of History and dean of the Graduate School. Howard might be willing to grant him leave if the appointment was important enough, but the rank offered, Logan wrote, was not sufficiently high to indicate importance or command the respect of others. Nowhere in the letter did Logan criticize the fact that the school was a segregated institution, and nowhere did he express his opposition to segregation. His letter of refusal lacked any principled reasons for declining the appointment and smacked of the same self-promotion in which he engaged when he told his friends of the job.[38]

In only very few instances did Logan not begrudge his colleagues' success. One person for whom Logan had almost pure admiration was A. Philip Randolph: "Phil is very able, honest, cooperative, willing to divide the glory." Although this private assessment was accompanied by a criticism of Randolph's habit of interrupting people and lecturing them, Logan's praise is most remarkable for its contrast with the vituperation he usually reserved for the major civil rights leaders.[39]

A clue to Logan's generosity is that Randolph sought to include Logan in his plans for the 1941 March on Washington. Logan had achieved much for African Americans in the national defense movement. He had successfully lobbied Congress and the president, and the local committees of the CPNNDP were positioned to mobilize important sectors of African-American opinion. "I followed with great interest and profit your work on this question," Randolph wrote Logan. "I want to offer my commendation to you upon it."[40] But the traditional civil rights methods of petitioning, lobbying, and local mass meetings of well-to-do community members would win at best only limited gains for African Americans in the national defense program.

In January 1941, Randolph, the head of the Brotherhood of Sleeping Car Porters, issued a manifesto for a march on Washington of ten thousand African Americans.[41] The march was scheduled for July 1. Of all the non-Communist civil rights leaders, only Randolph had the audacity of vision to conclude that African Americans could secure their rightful place in the national defense program only if they made a radical break with their past tactics.[42] Trying to enlist the NAACP's support, Randolph wrote to Walter White that "something dramatic has got to be done to shake official Washington and the white industrialists and labor forces of America to the realization of the fact that Negroes mean business about getting their rights as American citizens under national defense."[43] The NAACP, whose own considerably more timid campaign was sputtering, readily agreed to enlist in the March on Washington Movement (MOWM). Randolph also requested the presence in the MOWM of Frank Crosswaith, his close ally and the Harlem organizer of the International Ladies Garment Workers Union, and legitimized the effort with the inclusion of Channing Tobias and Lester Granger of the National Urban League. This group held its first meetings in early April, and in late April Logan was asked to join this select group.[44]

Most of the top leadership welcomed him into the fold, despite the fact that the *Pittsburgh Courier,* which had been the main force behind the formation of the CPNNDP but whose influence waned as Logan's increased, opposed the MOWM.[45] At one of the MOWM's first meetings, Lester Granger proposed

> the possibility of having the Committee on the Participation of Negroes in National Defense act as the official sponsor of this march, with an executive committee of the march itself being organized to be composed of members named by the Rayford Logan–Courier group, and members named by ourselves.[46]

Randolph and White, who were not at this meeting and who were represented by Crosswaith and Roy Wilkins, respectively, would never have allowed control of the march slip out of their hands. Randolph saw this as his project, while Walter White, who never attached his name to anything that he could not demonstrably influence, if not control, was too unfamiliar (and perhaps even uncomfortable) with the idea of massive protest to turn the march over to someone as unpredictable as Logan. But while Randolph thought enough of Logan to ask him to chair the Washington, D.C., MOWM committee—he declined on account of a heavy schedule—White continued to try to exclude Logan from the protest picture. In the winter and spring of 1941, White lobbied without success to hold a White House conference on discrimination in the national defense program; among his chosen participants were himself and Randolph, with Logan pointedly excluded.[47]

The March on Washington caught the imagination of African Americans across the country—so much so that President Roosevelt tried to get the organizers to cancel it. During negotiations between the MOWM and President Roosevelt and his representatives, march organizers agreed to call off the protest in exchange for an executive order banning discrimination in defense industries. On June 18, after a particularly hard bargaining session with march organizers, President Roosevelt appointed his adviser, New York Mayor Fiorello La Guardia, "to work out ways and means of doing something concrete about the problem" of discrimination.[48]

A final meeting to work out the specifics was held on June 23, attended by Randolph; Eugene Davidson, the national MOWM assistant director; Thurman Dodson, the Washington MOWM chairman; and Logan. Aubrey Williams of the National Youth Administration and La Guardia represented the president. La Guardia read a draft of the executive order that Roosevelt was prepared to sign that banned race discrimination in defense industries; Davidson, Logan's friend from high school days, wanted to include a ban against discrimination in government service. As there could be no immediate agreement on this last issue, both sides agreed to a recess so that each could consult with others not present. Randolph telephoned Walter White, who was at the NAACP convention in Houston; White concurred with Davidson, but agreed to the order even if it did not include Davidson's provision. The meeting reconvened, with La Guardia saying that a ban on discrimination in government would delay the issuing of the executive order. Davidson then proposed a compromise: mention at the beginning of the order that it is against government policy to discriminate, and omit reference to government in the section of the order that defined the scope of the ban. This seemed to satisfy all present, except Logan—who kept his opinion to himself—because "it seemed to me to be foolish to recognize the discrimination and then do nothing about it." Late that afternoon, the president agreed to sign Executive Order 8802, which banned discrimination in defense industries and established the Fair Employment Practices Commission. In exchange, Randolph canceled the March on Washington.[49]

Except for his participation in the final negotiations, Logan had little to do with the planning of the march. An important reason for this was his increasing doubt on the efficacy of the protest-march tactic. He doubted the organizers' ability to bring ten thousand African Americans to Washington. He was not alone in this, of course; others were relieved that Roosevelt did not call the MOWM's bluff.[50] But he began to disagree with Randolph that protests like the March on Washington ought to be the movement's staple tactic.

Logan believed that the march's success depended not only upon the agitation and mobilization of African Americans, but upon the circumstances in which the country found itself. He noted, for example, that his October 1940 victory that secured from Roosevelt a statement on black army units and officers was preceded by public opinion polls showing Wendell Willkie gaining in popularity and by CIO President John L. Lewis's endorsement of Willkie for president. Similarly, two days before Roosevelt issued Executive Order 8802, Hitler invaded the Soviet Union; the possibility of a collapse of the Allies caused Roosevelt to speed up the national defense program. This decision dovetailed with the demands of the MOWM to include African Americans in the program. "When he [the president] leans in one direction at any given time," Logan analyzed the reasons for the MOWM's victory, "he does so because that particular group's arguments are buttressed by other factors that transcend the interests of any one group and involve the very safety of the nation itself."[51]

According to Logan, neither Walter White nor Lester Granger of the National Urban League understood the historical movement of forces underlying the ebb and flow of the civil rights movement. Their putative ignorance of the larger picture was one reason that they—and particularly Walter White—scrambled to take credit for every civil rights victory. "Any one of . . . [the major civil rights organizations] that refuses to cooperate with the others in order that its own individual program may be realized has no real concept of the best interests of thirteen millions of American Negroes," he told a summer 1941 gathering of the American Teachers Association. "And so, let's give the credit to Mr. Hitler and stop quarreling among ourselves," he let loose in a burst of polemic.[52]

Logan, as the head of the CPNNDP, had brought the national defense program to the attention of the major civil rights organizations, which then tried to isolate him; Logan was weary of this treatment, and the CPNNDP went out of business soon after the success of the March on Washington Movement. "We felt that we had done as much as we could," he wrote. "We had in fact become a threat to the vested interests of older, recognized pressure groups."[53] He genuinely had lost the fortitude for the close-quarters infighting that he felt characterized much of the civil rights movement's establishment. Yet there is in his comments more than a little hint of the carping that often characterizes the loser of a bruising political campaign. The NAACP and Walter White were undoubtedly guilty of the transgressions Logan ascribed to them, especially the charge of seeking hegemony. But in his own public comments, he often obscured the principled political differences he had with White, preferring instead to render the disagreements in terms of personality.

Logan's disenchantment with this maneuvering was accompanied by a growing conviction that what the movement needed was a large dose of historical and political perspective. For the fight that it was waging was not only for an executive order or a few more jobs, but also to ensure that African Americans would have a say over their position in the post–World War II social order. Beginning in the spring of 1941 Logan wrote pamphlets and articles and accepted speaking engagements throughout the

East, Midwest, and South to promote his position that "the white man's distress is the black man's gain." For example, between March 7 and March 16, Logan spoke on behalf of CPNNDP and AΦA in Cincinnati, Louisville, Nashville, Montgomery, and Atlanta. Over a long weekend in May, he propagated his views at meetings in New York City; Bordentown, New Jersey; and Philadelphia. In February 1942, he spoke in New York City, Boston, Washington, D.C., Buffalo, and again in Washington.[54]

Although his proposition shocked the sensibilities of many people in his audiences, he was so convinced of its correctness that "I am willing to have my whole life judged on the basis of its validity," he said in one speech to two thousand people in Cincinnati. The thrust of his argument was an extension of the one he had presented in his 1935 article "The Negro Studies War Some More." Evidence of the black man's gain could be seen in Ethiopia, according to Logan. In 1936 Britain abandoned Ethiopia to Italy. But with Britain at war against Mussolini, Ethiopia stood a fighting chance, especially with Britain fighting to expel Italy from Africa.[55] The only hope for an Allied victory in the war lay in the inclusion of African Americans and other black people in the West's democratic vision. The Allies faced a threat not only from Nazism, but also from the

> half-democratic (notice carefully the hyphen, please) condition of the Western Hemisphere. Unless the American people believe sincerely that they are fighting for real democracy instead of merely against authoritarian principles, the half-democratic nations of the Western world may be doomed to a defeat which they would well deserve.[56]

The corollary to "the white man's distress is the black man's gain" was "Hitler has provided more jobs for Negroes than all our pressure groups put together." The turmoil in Europe had opened up better jobs paying higher wages for African Americans. Still, the question of equity remained to be settled. The American worker had historically benefited from distress on the European continent. "Your job and mine is to see to it that some of the gains percolate down to the Negro."[57] But Logan was dismayed by what he perceived as the inability of the major civil rights organizations to understand that their opponents' weaknesses—and especially the fear of a quick victory by Hitler—were one of the principal reasons for the gains African Americans made in the national defense program. This blindness impaired their ability further to exploit those soft spots.[58]

Three formidable powers blocked the advancement of African Americans: government, employers, and organized labor, principally the American Federation of Labor (AFL). The National Association of Manufacturers and the U.S. Chamber of Commerce refused to admit that their members discriminated on the basis of race; at the same time they refused to pledge themselves not to discriminate. Before Executive Order 8802 the federal government claimed it had no power to prohibit discrimination; it was still, in Logan's mind, an open question whether the government would force compliance.

Central to Logan's thesis about the "white man's distress" was an assault on the racist policies of organized labor, and Logan, like Walter White, A. Philip Randolph, and other black critics, directed his most acidic comments at the American Federation of Labor. He preferred that African Americans and the labor movement work together for mutual gain. But a Jim Crow labor movement was unacceptable, and African Americans should not support any labor organizations that practiced exclusion. Logan expected a raw deal from government and the employers of the country, and he was prepared to battle that alliance. Yet organized labor, which claimed to favor freedom and democracy, prevented African Americans from reaping the benefits of the war, and he made clear that he would not shy away from opening up a second front. His indictment of the AFL was searing, as he directly chastised union representatives in the audience at one of his appearances:

> I want to say to organized Labor in general that by your own creed and standard, democracy is not a living faith and is not a living reality as far as Negroes are concerned because you, organized Labor, have not permitted Negro workers to be free men. I want to say to organized Labor that you, in a large measure, have built up within this country the very totalitarianism that you denounce. For you have organized in a very large measure an *industrial* totalitarianism of white skilled workers. . . .
>
> Without hesitation I say that the American Federation of Labor is in general one of the worst germs of this disease that has resulted in the wholesale discrimination against Negroes in the defense industries.[59]

Logan was far more impressed with the Congress of Industrial Organizations (CIO). That organization had unhesitatingly declared itself against racial discrimination, and he counted upon its continued goodwill. But as a whole, organized labor was not doing enough to combat discrimination in employment. It was not enough to win concessions from the government and from employers; even if discrimination in hiring was outlawed, it would mean little so long as unions could practice exclusion. Logan therefore proposed that the National Labor Relations Act be amended to include racial discrimination in the definition of unfair labor practice and to exclude from the definition of labor organization any union that prohibited minorities from becoming members.[60] Though this rattled labor and its supporters, Logan placed great store in an alliance with organized labor, calling it "the best hope for a fuller life for Negroes in independent nations and in dependent areas."[61]

The other idea that Logan carried forward from his article "The Negro Studies War Some More" was the necessity for African Americans to join hands with black people in Africa, Latin America, and the Caribbean to articulate their demands for the postwar order. The last peace failed, he said, "Because it was largely a white, victorious, capitalistic, nationalistic peace."[62] One of the failures of blacks after World War I, Logan told an October 1941 meeting of the National Council of Negro Women, was that they lacked the foresight and the organization to demand to be included at the Versailles peace conference; it was left to a minority led by Du Bois to hold a separate conference, which tried mightily, but unsuccessfully, to be heard at Versailles. There would be no world peace without justice, Logan declared. Even if the perfect peace-keeping machinery was discovered, "the causes of war would remain. And those causes are going to remain until the profit motive is abolished and there is established here on earth the brotherhood of man."[63]

Logan expended a great deal of effort trying to get a hearing before liberal white organizations. Virtually all of them, like the Post-War Committee of the National Conference of Protestants, Catholics and Jews, attempted to exclude discussion of race issues from their meetings.[64] The American Council of Learned Societies (ACLS), which was the umbrella organization for United States organizations devoted to the humanities and the social sciences, also established its committees on the postwar order. Yet only one of its proposals, for a "Conference on Education and Post-War Reconstruction," even mentioned the elimination of racial prejudice as a goal.[65] Raymond Leslie Buell, who now was an editor at *Fortune* magazine, had agreed to help Logan draw the attention of the white establishment.[66] But his help was the exception.

When Logan participated in panel discussions and conferences on the postwar order sponsored by liberal organizations, he was almost always the only African-American speaker (and often the only African American present), and he was generally the only one to address the issue of race. Of a gathering in Washington, D.C., Logan complained that "Most of the speakers evaded any reference to the Negro. Even after I had referred to the Negro in the American Democracy in 1940, none of the other speakers followed the cue."[67]

He was especially appalled, though, at the liberal opinion makers' ignorance of—or hypocrisy about—race. In 1944, the journalist Max Lerner addressed a Howard University Forum on "The Coming World Revolution," which dealt with the postwar order. But when Logan asked Lerner about his program "that will enable the peoples of the dependent areas, especially of Africa, eventually to govern themselves," he admitted that he had not thought about it. "Thus even one of the keenest minds in America can think about a world revolution and not include Africa," Logan lamented.[68] In another instance he commented on an unnamed Harvard classmate who was publicly praised for his great liberalism and hatred of fascism: "He never spoke to me even when we passed each other on narrow Dunster Street. Miss Dodd [the classmate's sister] was greatly shocked by the poverty in Russia and the treatment of Jews in Germany. She must have been blind when living here in the United States."[69]

Throughout the war years, Logan worked closely with the American Friends Service Committee, a Quaker organization, because he believed that it was the most progressive and open-minded organization of whites in the United States. But even with the Friends, many of their most urgent questions about the position of black people in the postwar world revolved around their fears of "social equality." When he spoke at the Quakers' Race Street Forum in Philadelphia in January 1941, one of the audience asked Logan for his views on intermarriage; he replied that it was a red herring designed to discredit the need for racial equality. His speech in Wellesley, Massachusetts, on decolonization in the postwar world was largely ignored by the audience, which was more interested in his opinion on interracial liaisons. Following another roundtable discussion, Logan recorded in exasperation that "it was clear that the bugaboo was 'racial equality.' . . . All in all, they are fundamentally as opposed to mixing of the races as is Hitler."[70]

Logan, on the strength of his scholarly credentials, also received a hearing from the highest echelons of American society when, in August 1941, he was asked to join the Advisory Committee of the Office of the Coordinator of Inter-American Affairs (OCIAA). This government agency, which was also known as the Rockefeller Commission because Nelson Rockefeller was the coordinator, was established in the summer of 1940, a time when the United States was alarmed at the Nazi penetration of Latin America. Under Roosevelt's Good Neighbor Policy, the United States had come to realize that hemispheric solidarity had to be based at least nominally upon the principle of respect for the sovereignty and equality of Latin American states. This solidarity was an urgent matter at the outset of World War II. During the 1930s, Germany had geometrically increased its trade with the other American republics, which supplied raw materials in exchange for currency that could be spent only in Germany. Up to a third of the Latin American economy was thus tied to the Axis. With the disruption of the world economy because of the war, Latin America found itself in a severe bind; it was unable to trade with Germany and too impoverished to trade freely with the United States. The economic problems were aggravated by German, Italian, and Spanish fascist migration to South America. The United States feared a hemispheric fifth column in a region that was already susceptible to Nazi propaganda about *Yanqui* imperialism.[71]

The initial focus of the OCIAA, which was based upon a memorandum written for the president by Rockefeller, was to ensure the economic integrity of the United States and its hegemony over Latin America—no matter who won the war. (The United States had yet to enter it.) The memorandum called for new investments in the region and the buying up of excess raw materials that could no longer be sold to Germany. It also envisioned such programs as encouraging rubber production in Haiti to substitute for Liberia's, to which the United States, on account of the war, lacked reliable access. The OCIAA, designed to work closely with other government agencies, included on its staff the president of the Export-Import Bank and representatives of the Departments of State, Agriculture, Treasury, and Commerce.[72]

But Rockefeller was steeped in his family's philanthropic tradition, and he knew that economic domination was all the more stable when it was buttressed by cultural influence and reinforced by social stability. Once the OCIAA initiated its fiscal activities, it turned its attention to social and cultural issues. The OCIAA coordinated its work in these areas with the State Department, which had its own Cultural Relations Division, and the intellectual community, which was represented by Waldo G. Leland of the American Council of Learned Societies (ACLS). The cultural work involved the field of education, art, music, and literature and included activities like fostering exchanges of scholars among the American republics and helping libraries in Latin America to acquire collections on North America. The OCIAA's cultural division also produced movies and radio broadcasts, cartoons and books for Latin consumption.

The idea to include an African American on the OCIAA advisory committee originated with Mary McLeod Bethune and the National Council of Negro Women. The committee's mandate was to advise the coordinator on matters of social policy, and its members included longtime Rockefeller associates like Beardsley Ruml and Anna Rosenberg as well as representatives of various segments of public opinion. Bethune observed that labor and religious groups were represented on the advisory committee and that similar recognition ought to be accorded to racial issues.[73] Mrs. Bethune, who was the Negro affairs advisor in the National Youth Administration, had her own candidate in mind for the analog position in the OCIAA, a Mrs. Pearl Vincent Morton of New York. But after an extensive search that included consultations with administrators and faculty at Howard University, Logan and E. Franklin Frazier emerged as the only two serious candidates. It is not known why the OCIAA decided against Frazier, who had wide knowledge of both African-American and Afro-Latin issues.[74] But Rockefeller gave Logan a ringing endorsement:

> The selection of Dr. Logan is the result of much study. . . . It seems to be generally agreed that he would make the greatest contribution to our work as he is a man of wide experience who commands respect and confidence generally throughout the country.[75]

When Rockefeller first asked him to join the advisory committee, Logan hesitated, for he suspected that Rockefeller was trying to contain the discussion of race and "find some separate place for us." But he quickly became convinced of the genuineness of the offer and of Rockefeller's determination to face squarely the issue of racial discrimination in Latin America. What convinced him was Rockefeller's agreement with the spirit of Logan's proposed program for cooperation between the OCIAA and various African-American scholars and organizations. At the top of the eleven-point proposal was a conception of the position of Negro affairs advisor that was designed to prevent the marginalization of issues of race. The appointee "should be designated not as an advisor on Negro affairs but as another member of the Committee. He should participate in all the meetings of this Committee for the purpose of assuring adequate and equitable consideration of all phases of the Negro problem." Other elements called for the compilation of a history of blacks in Latin America; an increase in the number of black students, teachers, and artists involved in exchanges with Latin American countries; and an investigation into discrimination by common carriers in inter-American travel.[76] Logan considered the OCIAA an ideal forum to develop and publicize a program for postwar racial equality.

Having recently suffered slights at the hands of Walter White, Logan was overwhelmed by Nelson Rockefeller's demeanor. After their initial conversation Logan commented, "My interview with Mr. R. confirms my belief that the really big persons are very modest."[77] The first meeting of the advisory committee that Logan attended was held at Rockefeller's home on Foxhall Road in Washington, D.C. When it came time to break, Rockefeller, mindful of the exclusionary policy of practically every restaurant that catered to a white clientele in Washington, took Logan out to lunch to "avoid any possible embarrassment." Logan was impressed with the ease with which Rockefeller operated:

> As the sun came up over the hills [the meeting was held outdoors on the porch], Mr. R. took off his coat. He is one of the most likable men I have met; naturally democratic, . . .[78]

This impression was reinforced during another meeting two months later when Logan noticed "that R. was wearing the same suit and tie that he had on at meeting at his house."[79] His limited exposure to the Rockefeller family convinced him that what he witnessed was no act. In October 1943 Logan and his wife attended a luncheon given by Rockefeller in honor of Haitian President Elie Lescot. Logan's reflections on the proceedings most closely resemble celebrity-watching:

> Nelson Rockefeller waved to us. . . . [He] then introduced us to his wife who was most gracious and as democratic as he is. . . . Oh yes, the four Rockefeller children came in while we were having cocktails. It was most interesting to see that they had no idea of color. They had to be bounced up and down indiscriminately by all of us.[80]

In September 1941 Logan submitted a proposal for a fifteen-month study of the history of the Negro in Latin America, which included a six-month leave of absence from Harvard, to be spent in Latin America. Perhaps thinking that Rockefeller's earlier approval of the thrust of his program meant automatic approval of all of his specific plans no matter how elaborate, Logan was certain that Wallace Harrison, a longtime Rockefeller aide and head of cultural relations for the OCIAA, would approve his application. He was wrong. For six weeks Logan anxiously awaited an answer. On October 18, an official on the Rockefeller Commission whittled his proposal down to a five-month study and coupled it with the ACLS's proposal for an Inter-American Conference on Negro Studies planned for Havana in late 1941 or early 1942. A meeting of the OCIAA approved the new proposal.[81]

Logan was asked, as an adviser to the Rockefeller Commission, to review the ACLS proposal. He was quite pleased with the prospects of the ACLS-sponsored conference, but, as he was not wont to forget real or imagined slights (like the cutting of his project by two thirds), he warned Harrison that the conference was no substitute for projects submitted by African Americans.[82] In a meeting of the joint OCIAA–State Department–ACLS committee charged with overseeing Inter-American cultural projects, this conference was justified on the grounds of national defense. "It is an excellent vehicle to counteract Nazi propaganda attacking the United States in connection with alleged mistreatment of negroes [*sic*] . . . [and] significant as an antidote to the Nazi glorification of the superiority of the 'pure races.'" A member of the joint committee from the State Department, Richard Pattee, stated that the conference was an important affirmation "that the Inter-American Cultural Program is not neglecting consideration of negro [*sic*] problems."[83]

Logan felt that his project would dovetail nicely with the ACLS conference. "Rockefeller asked whether my project tied in with the Havana Conference. Yes, my two months of preparatory work should enable me to participate in the conference and, if I attended it, I should meet others working in the field and thus be better prepared to continue my study."[84] The conference would be an excellent forum to broadcast the demands of African Americans in the postwar era, and because he believed that he and other like-minded African Americans would have a say in developing the conference, Logan hoped that it could be a functional equivalent of the Pan-African gathering that he had been promoting since the late 1930s.

In contrast to the general support that he received from Rockefeller and the OCIAA, the State Department and ACLS members of the joint committee showed increasing disfavor to Logan's project. Despite the fact that Logan had over the previous ten years amassed a formidable amount of research on Latin America, Richard Pattee determined that Logan did not have the ability to conduct a historical study of Latin American Negroes, and he opposed authorization of the project. Waldo Leland of the ACLS wanted Logan to confine himself to a survey of the available materials for Negro studies, and the joint committee decided that Howard University ought to foot the bill rather than the OCIAA. Neither Pattee nor Leland apparently considered Logan to be an exceptional scholar. Leland entered into negotiations with Logan, who put on an agreeable face and agreed to limit his study to a history of Negroes in Panama, Colombia, and Venezuela:

> After further consideration of the proposal that you made to me . . . and after consultation with some of my friends I should prefer to combine, as much as possible, your plan with my original project. . . . This project, it seems to me, would embody the best features of my original plan and of your excellent suggestion.[85]

Inwardly, however, Logan fumed. He complained to Charles Thomson of the State Department that "suspicion was growing that all projects sponsored by Negroes were being turned down."[86] He penned a bitter letter to Wallace Harrison demanding to know why his original project was scrapped without his having an opportunity to tailor it to the committee's ideas and why it requested that the new project be funded in whole or in part by Howard.[87] After more negotiations with Leland, however, Logan agreed to a study of the "Negro Contribution to Hemispheric Solidarity, with Special Reference to Cuba, the Dominican Republic and Haiti," which would be funded for $6,800 entirely by the OCIAA.[88] After considerable delay in obtaining a passport, Logan left for Havana on March 10, 1942, for a two-month journey to the three island republics.[89]

The departure point for Logan's investigation was the need to improve the economies of the Caribbean republics, which was the original mandate of the Rockefeller Commission. On an earlier occasion Logan had reminded Rockefeller that he, Rockefeller, had pointed out that democracy in Latin America could be promoted only by raising the standard of living of the masses; to this Logan added that it was among the masses that "most of the Negroes are to be found."[90] From the beginning of his trip he sensed a fear on the part of Cubans, Dominicans, and Haitians that the improved relations they were experiencing with the United States were merely temporary and based upon wartime exigencies. He noticed a "natural hesitation" to launch campaigns for increased production of sugar and rubber, for example, "because of the inevitable post-war regression" and fear that the United States would "use Haiti during the war and then drop her 'like a hot potato.' "[91]

The initial memorandum establishing the OCIAA had stated that the indebtedness of the Latin countries ought not be an obstacle to improved relations, and Logan believed Nelson Rockefeller to be sincere. But the question that dogged him throughout his tour of the Caribbean was: What would be the postwar economic relations between the United States and Latin America? Would the United States again occupy Haiti if it defaulted on a loan? Such an action would be futile and would only earn the United States ill will. If Haiti's rubber plantations, whose development and expansion were encouraged by the United States, could not make a go of it, Haiti absolutely could not repay a loan, "Occupation or no Occupation."[92]

The report that Logan wrote for the Rockefeller Commission contained two principal ideas.[93] The first, he was

> tentatively calling the People's Inter-American Rehabilitation Fund, i.e., contributions whether in the form of gifts or loans by the people of the U.S. and any other rich nation (Brazil, Chile, Argentina, Uruguay, Venezuela, Mexico) for low cost housing, schools, etc. *In other words a kind of Western Hemisphere New Deal largely financed by the people of the U.S.*

Only the U.S. government, using taxpayer dollars, could carry out such a program, which he also called the "Good Neighbor New Deal." Cuba and Haiti were undoubtedly "to a certain extent under the control of American capital and the American government." The United States government, then, ought to recognize this control and use its wealth to raise the living standards in those countries; but in order to safeguard against abuse, "the control should be international." The alternative—private investment in the Latin economies—was simply dollar diplomacy and was bound to fail to raise the standard of living, for Wall Street would invest only in profitable enterprises, and not housing rehabilitation and education. In the long run, of course, the investment in the welfare of Latin America would benefit the United States. North Americans would have to be educated to see that they "would really be making a profitable investment for themselves: some of the money would be spent in the U.S. and ultimately, the peoples of Latin America would be able to buy more American products."[94]

The second recommendation was that people living in the rich American countries, especially the United States, should pay enough for goods produced in poor countries so that workers there could have a decent year-round standard of living. Logan's investigation of the sugar industry in Cuba led him to believe that the sugar companies could not pay higher wages solely out of their profits.

> They probably can pay a little more but at the present price of sugar, I do not see how, out of company profits, enough can be extracted to maintain the workers during the dead season. Cut away all the graft, etc., and there still would not be enough.

He wanted assurances, though, that if the price of such commodities as sugar was raised, "the increase should go to the workers . . . and not to the companies."[95] If North Americans were unwilling to pay this higher price, he told an audience at Antioch College in Ohio in 1944, "we are individual imperialists."[96] On the other hand he was convinced that the three republics would not prosper if the sole U.S. contribution to their economies was promoting large-scale production of sugar and bananas.[97] It was his opinion that this type of expansion in Haiti had rendered that country even more dependent upon the United States than during the occupation. Logan never received a response from the OCIAA to his report, and he suspected that this was due to his critical evaluation of Haiti.[98]

Logan's trip was more than an education in economics. He was a keen observer of race relations and the nexus between race and class. "The class and race pattern is crazy quilt here," he wrote in reference to Cuba.[99] Because of the extent of intermarriage, blacks were excluded from few jobs, and in some occupations whites and blacks got along well. With the exception of a very few hotels that catered to rich clientele and North Americans, blacks could find accommodations practically anywhere. Blacks were excluded from high society, though, he observed; an assiduous search of the society pages of Havana's newspapers turned up features of only one or two black women. But it was some compensation that "in the intellectual world, colored men are accepted individually as equal. . . ."[100]

Toward the end of his journey, Logan reflected that

I had frequently emphasized in my classes the fact that there is no necessary connection between the form of government and the *rights* of the people. But this is the first time, I believe, that I have applied the statement to race relations, i.e., to social and to a certain extent industrial (from race relations point of view) democracy.[101]

Cuba, the Dominican Republic, and Haiti all had dictatorships. They also all suffered from endemic poverty. Yet he felt freer in some respects in these countries than he did in the "half-democratic" United States of his birth. Here—and elsewhere in Latin America—he was excluded from the upper reaches of society, a serious drawback in the mind of a person so status conscious as Logan. But as an intellectual he would have been treated as an equal, and this mattered as much to Logan as acceptance in high society, and perhaps more. In the United States, by contrast, he enjoyed the singular pleasure of socializing with Nelson Rockefeller; this meant a great deal to Logan, but even he could not pretend that the occasional cocktail with Rockefeller constituted social acceptance by the highest echelons of American society. On the other hand, he discovered anew, through his experiences with the ACLS, that he did not enjoy the respect of the white intellectual establishment.

Logan was particularly exercised by the fact that the ACLS was ignoring him in its preparation for its Conference on Negro Studies. The daily work of planning the conference fell to the society's Committee on Negro Studies, which was headed by Melville Herskovits. Logan and other African-American scholars were well aware of Herskovits's and the committee's propensity to substitute their own judgment for that of African Americans in matters vital to blacks. Even L. D. Reddick, the curator of the Schomburg Collection and a member of the Committee on Negro Studies, criticized Herskovits and the ACLS for blocking projects that were under the direction of African Americans.[102] Herskovits's reputation was the reason Logan had the conference's project authorization amended to oblige the organizers to consult with him, especially on the matter of delegates.[103]

But as Logan feared, Herskovits excluded from the Conference on Negro Studies any African American with whom he disagreed; in fact, the U.S. delegation was restricted to members of the committee. Du Bois felt that Herskovits's actions were a step backward. In a meeting with Logan and Waldo Leland and D. H. Daugherty of the ACLS about the composition of the delegation, Du Bois said that in the "old days" at least whites had a token African American to advise them on black affairs; now, Herskovits was packing his committee with his friends and refusing to listen to outside advice.[104]

At bottom, the ACLS considered Logan and Du Bois—and, by extension, African-American academics generally—propagandists and not scholars of African-American studies. Defending Herskovits's designation of the Committee on Negro Studies as the U.S. delegation, Leland informed Du Bois and Logan that the conference was called

> with the intention of establishing bases for a scientific approach to Negro studies and that we had not considered it necessary to represent groups or factions, but only to secure the attendance of scholars whose interest was scientific. . . .

Leland replied to Du Bois's and Logan's criticisms of the composition of the Committee on Negro Studies by telling them that this was an internal affair of the ACLS and consequently none of their business.[105] So egregious was Leland's treatment of Du Bois and Logan that Nelson Rockefeller had to intervene; probably at the instigation of Logan, he asked the ACLS to reconsider its failure to include Du Bois in the delegation.[106]

Logan feared that with Herskovits in charge of the ACLS conference, Latin American studies would develop "along parallel racial lines." In fact, Herskovits, who did so much to discredit theories of biological racism, did little to integrate African-American scholars into the mainstream. The Committee on Negro Studies was his bailiwick, and through it he could confer upon or deny any project on African Americans the legitimacy of the ACLS. As he feared a challenge from African-American scholars, Herskovits kept them a numerical minority on the Committee on Negro Studies and kept them well beyond the committee's locus of power.[107]

In the end, the Conference on Negro Studies was never held. After switching dates and locations a few times, the joint committee let the project die.[108] The net result, then, was that neither Logan's original plan for a conference nor the ACLS's was realized. On one level, it meant merely the postponement of plans for a Pan-African-type meeting. This would not be realized until the Fifth Pan-African Congress in 1945, and its convoking would signal a changing of the guard; for while W. E. B. Du Bois would participate in the meeting, to be held in Manchester, England—Logan would not—the ascendant figures in the Pan-African movement were Africans who were preparing to lead their countries to independence.

On another level, however, Logan's experiences with the Rockefeller Commission and the American Council of Learned Societies added up to a painful lesson. It was not just that his original proposal was whittled down or that his plans for a Pan-African meeting did not materialize. The ACLS in effect signaled to him that he was not an equal member in the intellectual community. This was not the first time Logan had received such messages, of course—the Encyclopedia of the Negro project was still fresh in his memory. But it was one of a rapid series of bad-faith encounters that helped shape the course of his professional career for the next fifteen years.

chapter six

WHAT THE NEGRO WANTS
AND THE "SILENT SOUTH"

ᓂ

(1941–1944)

THE PUBLICATION IN 1944 of *What the Negro Wants* by the University of North Carolina Press has long been an intriguing footnote in the prehistory of the civil rights movement. The controversy surrounding its publication is an outstanding example of racial paternalism and a startling instance of southern liberal hypocrisy. Entering the World War II era, many African-American leaders had preserved a measure of faith in the good will of white southern liberals; by the time *What the Negro Wants* was issued, though, this hope was all but gone, dispatched by the liberals' own mendacity. Furthermore, within this episode one can hear the gathering of Afro-America's collective voice for full equality that would begin to register in the national conscience a decade later. The publication conflict and the book itself deserve more than a passing glance.[1]

What the Negro Wants was a collection of essays by fourteen African-American leaders edited by Rayford Logan, by then a prominent historian at Howard University. It went beyond other well-known books by African Americans on the race question. Robert Russa Moton, in *What the Negro Thinks* (1929), catalogued the grievances of "thinking Negroes" in such spheres of life as public transportation, housing, suffrage, and public policy; and while he decried the debilitating effects of segregation—and punctured the white southerners' dogma that they "know the Negro"—he accepted its existence and did not challenge it as a system.[2] James Weldon

Johnson based his arguments in *Negro Americans, What Now?* (1934) directly on the belief that all Americans should enjoy equal rights, but his book was concerned principally with strategy and only secondarily with political demands.[3] The contributors to *What the Negro Wants* elaborated upon these works; for the first time before a national, interracial audience, prominent African Americans of all political persuasions and from the South as well as the North declared that segregation must end. The debate in the post–World War II era would no longer be about reforming the old system but about constructing a new one.

History has judged William Terry Couch to be a fair-minded, progressive southerner. As director of the University of North Carolina Press he covered the most sensitive issues of the day. Under his leadership the press published books on trade unionism, the use of injunctions in strikes, religious fundamentalism, and lynching and other subjects on African-Americans.[4] He saw himself as a champion of free speech and critical inquiry, and in a region known for its racism and censorship, he published the works of African Americans on a variety of scholarly topics. Daniel Singal, a historian who wrote a detailed biographical essay on Couch, states that "on an intellectual level" he related to the Negro intellectuals with whom he came into contact as his equals.[5] The record of *What the Negro Wants*, however, suggests a different attitude. For despite his self-image as an intellectual egalitarian and the ease with which he posed controversial issues for the white South, like the vast majority of his southern liberal friends he could not fathom the mind and mood of the African-American spokespersons and people. It was one matter to write *about* African Americans and to expose lynching. It was quite another matter, however, to have blacks themselves condemn lynching and call for an end to segregation.[6]

In November 1941 Rayford Logan submitted a manuscript to the UNC Press on the "Negro and the post-war society," which he hoped would fulfill a few purposes. As yet untitled, this manuscript surveyed the conditions imposed on black people around the world by colonialism, offered specific anti-imperialist and democratic solutions, and warned of dire consequences for the colonial powers should they ignore the issues he raised. Logan hoped that the work would establish his reputation as a political theorist of distinction and considerably burnish his reputation as a "race man" and intellectual. By submitting his monograph to the UNC Press, he hoped to expand his influence beyond Afro-America and establish himself among white American opinion makers. Couch was at first enthusiastic and agreed to publish the book, "provided certain minor revisions can be made." But within a month, he cooled noticeably, writing to Logan that "If you should be interested in revising, I think it possible that we might be able to publish for you."[7]

Couch's mind was changed by an unflattering review of the manuscript by Guy B. Johnson, a University of North Carolina sociologist and fellow racial liberal. Johnson thought the subject matter timely, but the organization and tone of the manuscript unsatisfactory. Johnson proposed a new conception of the project. Instead of one author's views, Logan ought to "edit a book which represents the personal creed of 10 or 15 prominent Negroes."[8] Couch passed on the unfavorable review to Logan. But he chose not to inform Logan of Johnson's suggestion of an anthology until March 1943—almost a year later—when he presented the idea as his own.[9] Logan could not know it then, but this "on again, off again," less-than-honest pattern would be a significant characteristic of their partnership in *What the Negro Wants*.

At the end of March Logan readily agreed to edit such a volume. Unaware of Couch's intentions to give him carte blanche to shape the project, Logan asked Couch to help him define the book's character. "Should we," he inquired, "deliberately exclude such men as Richard Wright, Paul Robeson, Langston Hughes, and Max Yergan, whose affiliations are said to be euphemistically extreme left?"[10] Why would Logan suggest that a significant strand of African-American thought be excluded from the proposed symposium? As a Pan-Africanist Logan disagreed with the Marxist-oriented left, but that never prevented him from working with African Americans or whites of that persuasion, even when that was the safe course of action. Logan maintained a close political relationship with Yergan, he enjoyed a cordial social relationship with Robeson, and his friendship ties with Hughes dated to Paris in the 1920s. Logan's eagerness to cooperate with Couch may have stemmed from a desire to see that the symposium would be palatable to the southern liberals and the white mainstream generally that was the target audience.

In fact Couch counseled Logan to *include* left-wing blacks. "[I]t seems to me the book will be most interesting if it represents all the more important views now current among negroes, whether these views are radical or conservative or in between," he wrote Logan. This involved politically delicate decisions, but such was the editor's job, Couch wrote.

He said he wanted to limit his role to that of an adviser while leaving all final choices entirely to Logan. He consistently qualified his suggestions with statements like "this is a matter on which you can use your own judgment," "do what you think is best," and "I mean this merely as a suggestion."[11]

For his part, Logan was busy lining up contributors. In early April he received acceptances from President Willard Townsend of the United Transport Service Employees–CIO, A. Philip Randolph, W. E. B. Du Bois, Sterling Brown, Walter White, the journalist George Schuyler, President F. D. Patterson of Tuskegee, and Langston Hughes. By late June Logan had heard favorably from the remainder of the contributors: Gordon B. Hancock, Mary McLeod Bethune, Charles H. Wesley, Leslie Pinckney Hill, Doxey Wilkerson of the Communist party, and Charles S. Johnson. (Johnson later withdrew after being typically unable to meet several deadlines. Walter White submitted a draft but was unable to revise it, due to an especially heavy schedule; he withdrew in favor of Roy Wilkins, whose submission was substantially similar to White's.)[12]

The honeymoon did not even last until the end of May. Couch had been corresponding with Guy Johnson, who was concerned about the representativeness of the list of contributors. While Logan thought the roster was well balanced, Johnson thought the list too radical.[13] The list, he told Couch, "needs a better balancing toward the *Right*—i.e., (1) conservative 'inter-racial cooperation' type, and if possible someone (2) who is really extreme right." He thought the addition of one or two presidents of Deep South state colleges for Negroes would dilute the list sufficiently.[14] Couch, who had previously been content to let Logan take charge of the volume, now questioned the wisdom of his initial decision. He worried that the book would not represent all views, and in particular that the left-wing point of view would dominate. "[Y]ou should not have two extreme left-wingers unless to balance them you have two extreme right-wingers," he now wrote to the editor. Logan resisted adding more conservatives.[15]

Logan delivered the assembled manuscript to Couch on September 8, and Couch was taken aback at its contents. He and Johnson half-expected the radicals to overshadow the moderates and conservatives, but they had no idea that the conservative African-American leaders would join the left in demanding an end to segregation. One contributor after another, from Gordon Hancock to Doxey Wilkerson, called for complete equality and the discontinuance of Jim Crow. Couch complained that this made the articles redundant, but Logan had earlier anticipated this agreement and wrote to the contributors that "some repetition will inevitably result, but that repetition and perhaps unanimity on certain points will be all the more impressive."[16]

Logan was pleasantly surprised by the shape the book was taking. Du Bois's piece was excellent—"of course." He was amused by Doxey Wilkerson's article because, as a Communist, Wilkerson was "all-out for the war and . . . more enthusiastic about the progress the Negro has made during the war" than any of the authors. Among the conservative contributions, Logan thought that Leslie Pinckney Hill's article was "beautifully written" and rated Patterson's essay "surprisingly courageous."[17]

He was most surprised, however, with the contribution of Gordon B. Hancock, a prominent racial gradualist. He had not expected to like it. The two men had been political enemies since the mid-1920s when both taught at Virginia Union University, and had engaged in several intense debates about the strategy and tactics of the incipient civil rights movement.[18]

Logan invited Hancock to write his article from the perspective of the Durham Conference, which gathered together leading southern African Americans in October 1942 in an effort to ameliorate racial tensions in the South. The idea for the conference originated with the white Texan Jessie Daniel Ames, the prominent feminist, suffragist, and leader of the Commission on Interracial Cooperation. Ames, seeking to redeem the influence of southern white liberals, wrote Hancock, urging him to organize a leadership meeting that would address major problems of race relations short of segregation. The conference's statement, known as the Durham Manifesto, called for equality in pay in industry, a federal antilynching law, hiring of African-American police, and the abolition of the poll tax and the white primary. But it also recognized segregation, chose to downplay the fight against it, and reserved the adjustment of race relations for action by southerners.[19] Logan had "especially asked him to present the point of view of this conference which I 'deplored' in my own contribution."[20] But when he read the article, Logan was impressed. It was, he said, "by no means bad," a comment on a political enemy that from Logan's pen was tantamount to a compliment.[21]

It was significant that Logan thought Hancock was modifying his position. For more than two decades, Hancock had guarded the right wing of the African-American people's movement for equality. During the

1930s Hancock advocated a "Hold-Your-Job" campaign that counseled blacks to go to any length to keep from being laid off, including accepting wage cuts, taking more abuse, and avoiding unions. Hancock was also a staunch interracial cooperationist and admirer of Booker T. Washington, the type Guy Johnson dreamed of having as a contributor.[22] In this essay for Logan, he did not shed his entire previous program, to be sure, but he did move slightly yet significantly to the left. While he did not abandon his interracial cooperationist stance, he cast a jaundiced eye at its present worth. White southern liberals, he wrote, took half-measures only, and consistently capitulated to those whites who favored the continued subjection of the African American.[23] Further, he was less insistent that the South be left alone to adjust racial tensions, and he cautioned that continued segregation meant "the extermination of the Negro."[24]

Mary McLeod Bethune also typified the new conservative position. As a college president, New Deal adviser, and friend of Eleanor Roosevelt, Bethune preferred to work quietly, behind the scenes, and in a conciliatory fashion calculated not to rattle white opinion. As the director of the National Youth Administration's Division of Negro Affairs she acquiesced to the dictum of "separate but equal," and although she gallantly tried to enforce the "equal" part of that corollary, she remained silent about the issue of segregation.[25] Yet her essay in *What the Negro Wants*, "Certain Unalienable Rights," was a strident declaration for equality and a marked departure from her past style.

Opening her essay, Bethune declared that those who rioted in Harlem in June 1943 in response to reports that an African-American soldier was shot by a white policeman were the modern-day equivalents of the participants in the Boston Tea Party. The violence in Harlem, along with the riot in Detroit that same month, were graphic signs that blacks were increasingly unwilling to participate in the defense of the United States so long as it refused to grant them full democratic rights. The rioters were venting their "resentment against the mistreatment of Negroes in uniform, against restriction and oppression and discrimination." While some saw only "a band of hoodlums [that] have challenged law and order to burn and pillage and rob," she saw something far different. "Just as the Colonists at the Boston Tea Party wanted 'out' from under tyranny and oppression . . . colored Americans want 'out.' "[26] Bethune's solution to the vexing problem of race relations included the right to vote, equal employment opportunities, elimination of the color bar in labor unions, and "realistic interracial co-operation"—"not 'one as the hand and separate as the fingers,' but one as the clasped hands of friendly cooperation."[27] She advocated tactics of resolute challenge to every attempt to restrict or limit the African Americans' "full American citizenship."[28]

The conservative position among the African-American leadership had shifted to the left, but that did not mean that it was identical with the center and left. Logan's essay, a wide-ranging piece called "The Negro Wants First-Class Citizenship," discussed the outstanding differences. His central argument was that the race problem was a national problem and that this fact afforded a solution. As far as Logan was concerned, many of the specific demands of the Durham Manifesto were proper, but the conservative assumption that they could be achieved only within a southern framework was a step backward.[29]

Logan also argued with the left. Nationwide protests, like the threatened 1941 March on Washington, were powerful only within definite limits. Logan believed that the African-American leadership could mobilize the masses in numbers large enough to avoid being considered a bluff only on rare occasions. "I definitely favor the March-on-Washington or on other cities only as a rare, dramatic, powerful weapon that should be used only when all other methods have failed," he wrote, thus demarcating himself from those like Randolph who considered the march a staple tactic.[30] Similarly, he had no principled objection to the nonviolent resistance advocated by militant interracial groups like the Fellowship of Reconciliation; his concern was that the protracted process would sap the movement of energy and would not yield a commensurate return.[31]

Logan's method for achieving first-class citizenship resembled the NAACP's in substance: coordinated lobbying activities to pass federal legislation guaranteeing equitable expenditures of federal education funds; unity between the movement for equality and the CIO, with built-in safeguards against discrimination by the labor movement; abolition of the poll tax and the white primary; strict enforcement of the Fourteenth Amendment to reduce the South's strength in Congress in proportion to the number of disfranchised African Americans.[32] What distinguished Logan from the NAACP (aside from factional rivalry) was the tone with which he put forward his program. Logan saw no pressing need to be diplomatic or "responsible"; he often cast his statements in prophetic tones. This became especially clear once *What the Negro Wants* moved beyond the dismantling of legal Jim Crow.

If the contributors' unanimity on the issue of segregation dismayed Couch, some of their treatment of interracial marriage gave him apoplexy. Fear of interracial unions was perhaps the most frequent reason whites gave for the maintenance of segregation and the denial of social equality.[33] With the completion of the manuscript of *What the Negro Wants,* Couch now had "proof" that the real agenda of the African-American leaders was miscegenation.

Of the four authors who addressed the question of interracial liaisons, only Gordon Hancock tried to quiet white fears.[34] Charles H. Wesley, historian and president of Wilberforce University, devoted all of one sentence to the issue, demanding the right of every American to marry the person of his or her choice. Even so, Wesley offered no comfort to fearful whites.[35]

The other two contributors who wrote about intermarriage were not in the business of reassuring the white world. Unwilling to sacrifice the personal rights of African Americans in the quest for political rights, Logan and Du Bois flouted convention and twitted white sensibilities. Logan conceded that "Most white Americans remain . . . opposed to intermarriage and many of them to the abolition of public segregation as a possible first step toward it." But white hysteria about the mongrelization of the race flew in the face of all scientific fact as well as the social preferences of most African Americans and whites. Logan, however, refused to coddle white opinion. If, after African Americans achieved economic, political, and cultural equality as a result of the abolition of public segregation, custom still opposed intermarriage, there would be few mixed marriages. But in a typically cavalier fashion Logan continued: "If, on the other hand, laws and public opinion should change and there should be more mixed marriages—why, we shall all be dead in 2044 and the people will do what they wish."[36]

W. E. B. Du Bois was, from the standpoint of the white southerner, most impertinent of all. In his autobiographical essay on his evolving program for racial equality, Du Bois recalled his time as a student in Germany. The Germans in the early 1900s, he noted, were not color conscious at all; in fact he fit in quite well with the other students, both male and female. The few tense moments occurred when visiting white Americans took offense at his familiar relations with European women; they tried, he said, to introduce Jim Crow in the student circles, but they did not succeed. A German woman, a colleague of Du Bois, wanted to marry him—immediately, he said. He regretted that he had to turn her down; but it would have been unfair to subject her to certain ostracism or worse in America. Logan suspected that Du Bois's remarks, which frankly and unapologetically discussed interracial marriage, touched the rawest part of Couch's psychological makeup. The white South's fear of miscegenation, especially when the white partner was a consenting woman, was pathological, and prompted Couch to determine that the manuscript was not publishable.[37]

Couch's negative appraisal received support from the press's manuscript reviewers. O. J. Coffin was a liberal southerner, and he was disturbed that the book advocated "overnight the reordering of His world." Like Couch, Coffin disbelieved that the authors were speaking for the majority of African Americans. The contributors were "self-elected leaders," whose demands would "come as a distinct shock to the vast majority of whites, South, North, East and West." The southern way of life was threatened by the contributors, who "talk of intermarriage and world congresses of Negroes as nonchalantly as Walrus and Carpenter might discuss cabbages and kings." The press was unwise even to consider publishing the manuscript, for the public would receive it poorly. Coffin returned his ten-dollar reviewer's fee, instructing Couch to give it to some "Negro charity."[38]

Other reviewers were equally negative, but they encouraged Couch to publish *What the Negro Wants*. Foremost among this group of reviewers was Howard Odum. Since 1920 this eminent sociologist had been at the University of North Carolina, establishing and leading the Institution for Research in Social Science and editing the journal *Social Forces*. His constant refrain was that race relations policy be based on knowledge procured through objective, dispassionate observation, yet he derided both the Ku Klux Klan and Walter White and the NAACP for their extremism. The one was just as bad as the other, he believed, staking out the so-called rational middle ground in the race relations debate for the southern liberals. By the late 1930s, though, this dean of race relations sociology was declining in influence, and when Gunnar Myrdal snubbed him during his work on *An American Dilemma*, Odum felt compelled to fight back.

One way he did this was by challenging the authors of *What the Negro*

Wants. Howard Odum thought publication of the book would be a good way to expose the damage he thought the African-American leaders were doing.

> The weakest chapter is Walter White's, which is too weak to publish in any book, but I would like to have it go in that way so that the public can get a real appraisal of Walter White's abilities. I am convinced that he is doing great harm and is likely to do more, but the only way to approach this problem is to let the public make its own appraisal.

Odum was quite pleased with what he gauged were the essays' weaknesses and cautioned Couch against changing them. "Extreme statements, cynical references, misstatement of fact—all of those are a part of the value inherent in the book," he wrote.[39]

N. C. Newbold, the North Carolina superintendent of public instruction and a local leader in the interracial cooperation movement, was equally negative. He felt that *What the Negro Wants* was bound to upset the racial status quo that he had helped form and maintain. Publication in its present form, he believed, would harden southern attitudes toward African Americans. Further, Newbold thought that northern African Americans were overrepresented among the contributors; he worried that this might create an impression among "Southern Negroes that their local leadership is not competent or cannot be trusted to treat the problems involved on a national scale." The book did not reflect a widespread militancy, but it could generate such opinion. Newbold wanted major changes in orientation in the articles, but in the event the authors were unwilling to comply he suggested several specific alterations, including the deletion of all references to intermarriage.[40] Finally, he suggested that Couch write an introduction to the volume detailing the press's, the university's, and the southern majority's position on the contributors' positions.[41]

Couch digested the criticisms of the manuscript and packaged them up for Logan. The essays abounded in errors of grammar and syntax, but these were not the manuscript's chief sins, according to Couch. A significant weakness of the work was that none of the contributors addressed the African-American people's own complicity in their condition.

> I had been hoping that at least two or three of the fifteen authors would raise the question of how far the Negro is responsible for his condition, and deal

with the problem of what Negroes themselves can do, regardless of what white people may do.

Even if blacks were only one half of one percent responsible for their condition and whites were nearly 50 percent responsible—with fate accounting for the balance—this minuscule responsibility indicated culpability on the part of the African-American population. "I cannot," Couch wrote, "escape the view that failure to give any attention to this question is a serious weakness and may lead to failure to achieve an enlarged responsibility."[42] Despite these weaknesses, Couch recommended publication, even if the authors declined to make the requested changes.[43]

But Couch was running out of patience with the project and rued ever having proposed it to Logan. In early November he penned an exasperated letter to Logan etched with a hard line on publication. "It never occurred to me during our negotiations that in response to our request a work of this nature would be written and submitted to us for publication." Publication of the book would have "extremely unfortunate" consequences for southern race relations. He then put his position to Logan in the bluntest terms possible:

> The things Negroes are represented as wanting seem to me far removed from those they ought to want. Most of the things they are represented as wanting can be summarized in the phrase: complete abolition of segregation. If this is what the Negro wants, nothing could be clearer than that what he needs, and needs most urgently, is to revise his wants.[44]

It was useless, he wrote, to cite the Declaration of Independence and the concept of equality as arguments for desegregation. In the first place, the Declaration also spoke of majority rule, Couch wrote, and the fact was that whites were in the majority. "A little thinking on this problem will show, in my opinion, that equality in the sense in which it was written into the Declaration would be destroyed by the application of the definition accepted by most of the authors of the articles in 'What the Negro Wants.' "[45] "Equality," as used in the Declaration of Independence, had a special meaning; it meant that a person was entitled to the resources and training necessary for him or her to realize his or her full potential. Couch implied here, and stated explicitly elsewhere, that since African Americans were culturally and racially inferior to whites, they were entitled to fewer resources than whites.

In a letter to Langston Hughes around this time, Couch elaborated on his concept of equality. Individual African Americans may possess great talent—Couch named Joe Louis and Marian Anderson—and he could certainly not consider himself their equal. Their greater talent entitled them to certain claims on society—presumably the right to keep Couch out of the boxing ring and off the concert stage—to "segregate" him. Couch's presence in these arenas would dilute the caliber of talent. (He did not take note of the fact, as Hughes did, that even people of great talent like Louis and Anderson were forced to bear the indignities of segregation despite their claims on society.) Because African Americans as a race were of inferior caliber to whites, Couch wrote to Hughes, "There seem to me to be areas in which a mechanically applied . . . discrimination is essential."[46]

Couch pleaded with Logan for cooperation. He was still interested in "getting a book worth publishing," and was willing to "spend hours, days, weeks on the problem, and will go to Washington to discuss it with you if you care to have me come."[47]

Perhaps he was not entirely satisfied with the contents of this letter, because Couch set it aside for more than a week. Ten days later, he sent Logan a different letter, one similar in tone, but with significant exceptions.[48] After attacking the theories of racial equality of social scientists like Gunnar Myrdal and Melville Herskovits, Couch expressed feelings of betrayal: "For years I have been . . . telling people the Negro . . . is not interested in social equality." Of more immediate importance to the publishing fate of What the Negro Wants was another change in tone. Replacing the patience of the earlier letter was a take-it-or-leave-it attitude: "I look forward to hearing what you and the contributors think of the criticisms and whether you think the articles can be revised so as to make them publishable." As further indication of Couch's mood, he got the press's board of directors to approve a resolution to publish the book only if it was revised to meet the criticisms made by N. C. Newbold, the interracial cooperation leader.[49]

Couch's offensive seemed to have its desired effect, for Logan noticeably softened. When the barrage began in the middle of October, Logan resisted making changes in the manuscript.[50] But by the middle of November Logan began to bend. He was not convinced by the intellectual force of Couch's arguments, as Couch may have thought, but by other circumstances. Logan had earlier received encouraging words from the Book-of-the-Month Club (BOMC). The editors at the BOMC told Logan that they were contemplating giving the book a favorable review in their monthly newsletter and even making *What the Negro Wants* a selection of the month. But this was impossible, they related to Logan, so long as the book remained in its original form. His chance to make an impact on the white public depended upon his altering the manuscript to conform to white sensibilities.

Logan faced the recurring conflict between standing for principle and achieving respect and recognition in the white world. In his mind and in his experience one option excluded the other, for the white establishment allowed only politically "safe" African Americans to cross over and attain considerable success.[51] But after reviewing his options, Logan assented to Couch. "The enclosed letters," he wrote to Couch, referring to his correspondence with the BOMC, "have finally convinced me that I must depart more and more from my previous position and try to make the best book possible, with your generous assistance."[52] The prospect of a large audience of educated whites was too alluring to pass up. Not many African Americans had been presented with the opportunity of BOMC distribution; it had only been in 1940 that the club offered Richard Wright's *Native Son* as a main selection, and the BOMC in this instance, too, required substantial changes in the manuscript.[53]

Another reason for Logan's capitulation to Couch was his career difficulties at Howard University. Since 1942 Logan had been acting dean of the Graduate School. In his—and President Mordecai Johnson's—opinion, he had served loyally and with distinction, but in April 1943, Johnson hinted that he planned to replace Logan. Charles Thompson, who was the dean of the College of Liberal Arts, the head of the School of Education, and founder of the *Journal of Negro Education,* had done a miserable job as dean. Johnson, according to Logan, felt he could not just let Thompson go, so he decided to "kick him upstairs" by making him dean of the Graduate School and asking Logan to oversee the Evening School.[54]

As 1943 wore on, it became clear to Logan that he would be replaced. By the end of October Logan saw himself as a victim of university politics and contemplated resigning from Howard. On December 17 he met with Johnson, who asked Logan to step down as acting dean and requested that he take charge of a series of special forums for Howard. Logan refused and ended up "in the 'doghouse' at the University." At Howard, Logan wrote, the reward for failure was promotion, while the price of loyalty was dismissal. He again contemplated resigning. Logan felt humiliated, and as 1943 wound down, he reviewed the year in a gloomy manner. He was demoted at the university and was not in good graces with Johnson. "I have very little to show in the way of accomplishments for the year," he wrote.[55] Given his feelings of mistreatment by Howard, Logan must have felt that on a personal level, the BOMC's demands were not so onerous when weighed against the benefits of wide distribution.[56]

For a moment it appeared as if Logan and Couch were headed toward an agreement. Taking the advice of N. C. Newbold, Couch proposed a framework for resolving outstanding differences, and Logan agreed to it. Actually the framework was meant not so much to resolve differences as to convert the contributors' views into views acceptable to southern liberals. Contributors were to rework their articles so that they would make only those demands which could be justified on the basis of "rights and common humanity." Each contributor would refrain from saying things that "might gravely jeopardize the interests of the Negro or seriously expose him to the charge of being unable to justify his wants." Couch had already determined that the demand for an end to segregation could not be justified on the basis of "rights and common humanity." Finally, as Couch proposed (and as Logan accepted), there was no real conflict between the "real interests" of African Americans and those of whites, and "that in the majority of cases where conflict appears it does so because the problem of real interests has not been understood."[57]

Harmony shortly turned to dissonance. Although Logan agreed to alter the manuscript, he could not convince the contributors to do so. He met with W. E. B. Du Bois and Sterling Brown, who refused to budge. Du Bois had told Logan that the UNC Press would not "have the guts to publish it," and that he refused to make "anything but verbal changes here and there" in his piece.[58] Brown called Couch "muddleheaded" and "slightly 'crazy.'" The three of them resolved that Couch should come to Washington to confer with all the contributors.[59] Willard Townsend felt that Couch had "not acted in good faith."[60] At first Couch agreed to meet sometime in mid-December, but, suddenly hardening his position, declined to meet, suggesting consultation by mail.[61] This was enough to end Logan's vacillations. He no longer considered Couch's suggestions an improvement; they would, in fact, "create a great deal of perplexity in their [the contributors'] mind in view of the fact that they were specifically requested to present their ideas of '*What the Negro Wants*.' "[62]

In mid-December matters came to a head. Couch informed Logan that the UNC Press would not publish *What the Negro Wants* without drastic revisions along the lines Couch proposed. Logan should, he said, search for a new publisher, and then he added this parting shot: "Perhaps I ought to add I have no doubt a book worth publishing could be written opposing all the views I have expressed; but this would require more skill and imagination than are apparent in the present manuscript."[63]

Faced with this rebuff from Couch, Logan's sense of virtue finally won out over his desire for fame. Logan had considered that this project, and the UNC Press and Couch generally, would provide him with access to the world of white public opinion. But Couch's invitation to find another publisher made Logan realize that the white establishment would not accommodate him; unless he surrendered to white supremacy, the establishment would reject him. Logan felt that Couch had deserted him: "I went along with him," he wrote, "until he told me to find another publisher."[64] So four days after Couch's rejection, Logan fired off a one-sentence letter that stated, "In reply to your letter of December 14 I have to say that I am consulting my attorneys."[65]

In the face of Logan's unexpected resistance, Couch panicked. To N. C. Newbold, Couch wrote that he could not fathom Logan's change in attitude. He could only wonder why Logan did not respond to more of the hard sell. Someone with evil intentions, he concluded, had Logan's ear: "I am afraid he is asking and accepting advice from someone who would prefer to see trouble rather than to see a good job done."[66]

Couch also drew upon the counsel of three leading southern liberals: Jackson Davis, Mark Ethridge, and Virginius Dabney. Their interactions illustrate the southern liberals' ineptness at interpreting African-American demands. Indeed, they missed almost completely the articulation of these demands by a representative group of African-American intellectuals. Davis, sensing Couch's jitters, urged him to be calm. As a longtime official of the Rockefeller-funded General Education Board, Davis was skilled at squelching the militant demands of African Americans. He passed his strategic view toward the expression of militancy by blacks along to Couch: "I don't think you have to worry about the dynamite that it [the book] may contain. It will be in the nature of a safety valve. . . ."[67]

Mark Ethridge, the publisher and editor of the *Louisville Courier-Journal*, was also a segregationist. Among his more pungent epigrams was a 1942 statement that "There is no power in the world . . . which could now force the Southern white people to the abandonment of the principle of social segregation."[68] He advised Couch that the agitation of "extremist Negroes" was a fever that had to run its course. Until the fever spiked, he noted, African Americans could not assess their situation "with anything touching reason." But things would improve after that, unless, that is, the works of Gunnar Myrdal continued to hold sway. In that case, "it will tend to solidify Negroes in the feeling that the white man owes them a great deal more than he does."[69]

Virginius Dabney was the most perceptive as to the cause of the new militancy among African Americans. He was not surprised by the manuscript, although he thought some of the writing especially bad. But he expected such articles when a man like Logan was given free reign to solicit them.

> Logan is what I should term a radical. . . . Certainly nothing but extremism and denunciation of the whites, especially in the South, could have been anticipated from such contributors as Randolph, White and Schuyler. . . .
> . . . you were under the delusion, when you arranged for this book, that the Negro does not want the abolition of segregation, establishment of complete social equality etc.

Back in 1941 Dabney believed as Couch did, he wrote, but intervening events forced him to reevaluate his position. World War II was the underlying cause of Negroes' radicalization, according to Dabney. "The war and its slogans have roused in the breasts of our colored friends hopes, aspirations and desires which they formerly did not entertain, except in the rarest instances." The fourteen contributors did indeed speak for the African-American people on the issue of segregation. The conservative southern Negro leaders had to play catch-up and criticize segregation, "lest they be considered 'Uncle Toms' or 'Handkerchief Heads.' "[70]

Dabney's insight into the causes of the radicalization of African-American opinion did not mean that he thought that opinion ought to be publicized. Publication of the book, he warned, would do great harm in the South, causing a reaction against "reasonable concessions." Walter White and the NAACP were making extreme demands on white America and causing a great deal of tension. Their inflammatory rhetoric provoked the white southern demagogues and would certainly cause racial violence. Segregation must stay. This was also the thrust of a major article he penned for the January 1943 issue of the *Atlantic Monthly,* entitled "Nearer and Nearer the Precipice."[71]

While Couch was calling upon his fellow southern liberals for advice, he was defending his actions to Logan. His only mistake, he wrote, was to give Logan too much freedom to produce a book. Logan had botched the project by soliciting articles that "repeat each other unnecessarily and at length," and now he had to clean up the mess.[72] To Couch the repetition was redundant; he still did not grasp how widespread was the demand to end segregation.

The momentum had shifted, and the more Logan thought matters over, the more he concluded that he, and not Couch, was right. Most of the contributors were on Logan's side, with Langston Hughes weighing in with the comment that "the southern intellectuals are in a pretty sorry boat. Certainly they are crowding Hitler for elbow room."[73] On January 14, 1944, Logan wrote Couch, threatening to sue him should the press not publish *What the Negro Wants,* and five days later Couch relented. The book would be published, but only with a publisher's introduction disclaiming responsibility for the views expressed in the articles.[74]

The "Publisher's Introduction" was a polished version of Couch's previously stated views on race relations. It opened, though, with a rather curious statement that "the authors of the present book are representing their people faithfully, that the Negro really wants what they say he wants, and that he reasons about democracy, equality, freedom, and human rights just as they do."[75] Apparently Virginius Dabney had convinced Couch that despite "the psychopathic condition the manuscript reveals among Negro intellectuals,"[76] the book did indeed reflect the demands of Afro-America as a whole. Still, Couch continued to insist that this radicalization was not a result of the war, but rather was artificially induced by contemporary anthropological and sociological theory, especially that embodied in Herskovits's scholarship and in Myrdal's *An American Dilemma.*

In his view, the condition of African Americans was caused by their inferiority, but this condition—and race prejudice—could be overcome. What was required was that they recognize their inferiority and make a concerted effort to rise above their "natural" (that is, less than civilized) ways. The "Negro's interest requires that he show qualities of greatness; that he not be so much concerned over the label 'equal,' but that he concentrate all his energies on being not merely equal to, but better than the white man."[77] Failure to achieve greatness was proof that Negroes were capable only of being "natural," not far removed from savagery.

The anthropologists and sociologists who were advocating racial equality were in effect encouraging the dismantling of a superior culture. *An American Dilemma* "was written under gross misapprehensions of what such ideas as equality, freedom, democracy, human rights, have meant, and of what they can be made to mean. I believe the small measure of these gained by western man is in serious danger of destruction" by the ideas in that book. Disingenuously interchanging concepts of "culture" and "race," Couch argued for racial superiority and purity. Whites had the right to protect "their" values against the encroachments of a people who lived in a "natural" state. Absent any indication that African Americans could achieve greatness, it was criminal to remove the barriers between the races. The alternative to segregation was biological integration and the dragging down of the white race. Myrdal and his fellow social scientists were distracting African Americans from acquiring what they really needed—diligent work habits and self-control—in favor of something the majority would never allow them to have—the abolition of segregation.

Couch's statement became the southern liberal's creed. Jackson Davis applauded it, and Virginius Dabney wrote, "It seems to me to be excellent, and to place the whole project in its proper perspective." Mark Ethridge told Couch that "your paper pretty well presents my viewpoint."[78] Gerald Johnson, a North Carolina–born journalist and regular writer for the *New Republic* and columnist for the *Baltimore Evening Sun,* sent word to Couch that he was in favor of letting African Americans say what they wanted, but he did not favor giving it to them. "I like your introductory essay—" he wrote, "nimblest footwork I have seen in a coon's age."[79]

Despite Couch's obsession about revising the Negro people's wants and his pessimism concerning the marketability of the book, *What the Negro Wants* sold well. By its November 4, 1944 publication date the book had gone through three printings totaling 10,000 copies. In the first thirteen months, the book sold 8,872 copies.[80]

Many reviewers received the book enthusiastically. Some northern publications employed southern whites to review *What the Negro Wants.* Paula Snelling, a close collaborator of Lillian Smith's, wrote a lengthy review for the *New York Herald-Tribune*'s book supplement, the *Weekly Book Review.* She found much to boost her spirits. The book would provoke a healthy soul-searching among white Americans, she hoped. But her optimism was tempered by the publisher's introduction, "which gives documentary evidence that the Anglo-Saxon mind here retains its old facility for throwing up verbal smoke screens when painful knowledge presses too close."[81]

The editors of the *New York Times Book Review* asked William Shands Meacham, the chairman of the Virginia State Board of Parole, and a trustee of the Hampton Institute, to review the anthology. Perhaps one quarter of his article was devoted to a condemnation of miscegenation, even though intermarriage was only a minor theme in *What the Negro Wants*. Even the mere discussion of intermarriage "risks poisoning the atmosphere in which countless white Americans of good will would like to eliminate needless differentials." Once he had calmed himself, however, Meacham lent a sympathetic ear to the authors' demands for first-class citizenship. He was reluctant to grant full citizenship rights at once— such things could not be accomplished "by an aggressively race-conscious group or by government fiat"—but he welcomed the book as a refreshing change of pace. "Rationalization and sublimation have been the means by which we have tried to solve the American race problem, and this ably written book published by a Southern press is an outstanding example of the frontal approach."[82]

Not all educated southern white opinion was so kind. H. C. Brearley, the reviewer for *Social Forces*, found little to like in the volume. Did the authors, he asked, speak for African Americans? No, for contrary to the book's claim, "realistically it is a collection of essays . . . by fourteen Negro intellectuals who were requested to say what they think the Negro wants." In his opinion, "Most of the writers make no effort to conceal the antagonism toward the whites that is characteristic of the upper class Negro." In fact, the most attractive essay was the publisher's introduction.[83] Neither could E. B. Reuter, a veteran southern race relations sociologist, believe that the authors spoke for anyone but themselves. But the book had value, he wrote, as a current index of the race problem. Race relations would enter a new phase only when an articulate leadership arose that mobilized the masses and gave expression to their demands. "This book does not do this; but . . . [it does] indicate that a new phase of the Negro-white problem may not be far away."[84] This was a prescient comment for a southern liberal to make in 1945, especially when most of his brethren were interpreting matters so differently.

African-American reviewers hailed *What the Negro Wants* as a masterly statement. If anything, their reviews reinforced the unanimity of African Americans against segregation. J. Saunders Redding, writing for the *New Republic,* warned readers not to underestimate the authority of the contributors because their names were unfamiliar.

> They speak with authority. Ask any expert—and any expert would be any literate Negro. Indeed, the validity of this book is derived from the undisputable fact that the editor might have chosen fourteen other contributors and achieved the same general result.[85]

E. Franklin Frazier informed readers of *The Nation* that "The volume as a whole provides an excellent summary of the intellectual orientation of the majority of articulate and educated Negro leaders in the present crisis."[86] Reviewers at *Opportunity,* the *Journal of Negro History,* the *Crisis,* and the *Journal of Negro Education* all felt that *What the Negro Wants* was one of the most important books to date on race relations.[87] Not incidentally, with the exception of the reviewer for *Opportunity,* all the reviewers took Couch to task for his introduction. The *Chicago Defender* and the Schomburg Collection of the New York Public Library placed Logan on their respective honor rolls for 1944 in recognition of *What the Negro Wants.*[88]

The wide acclaim from the black and northern liberal press was welcome to Logan, but it was overshadowed by his conflict with Couch. Logan learned once again that achieving success in the white world and remaining true to his principles were incompatible goals. He resolved to preserve his integrity as he perceived it, and for the next decade his scholarly efforts, while sound, were uncompromising in their criticism of racism and colonialism and were published by what amounted to vanity presses.[89]

The polemics over the publication of *What the Negro Wants* helped usher in a new configuration of forces in the struggle for civil rights in the postwar era. White southern liberals had previously successfully argued that they knew best how to handle race relations and that the only alternative to their "mild" form of segregation was that of race haters like the Ku Klux Klan. They could parry the attacks by white social scientists who preached racial equality by claiming that they were the scholarly equivalents of outside agitators. In this fashion the southern liberals like W. T. Couch clung to their national leadership on the race problem. The appearance, however, of a broad-based African-American intellectual and political *movement* against segregation seriously undermined the southern race liberals' moral authority. By acknowledging, however reluctantly, that the authors of *What the Negro Wants* did indeed represent the demands of African Americans, white southern race liberals in effect gave up their claim to paternal omniscience on the race problem.

The southern liberals' precarious grip on race relations leadership was further undermined by the growing legitimacy of civil rights among northern white intellectuals.[90] If African Americans had previously felt compelled to align themselves with the less than satisfactory southern race liberals because the only alternative was the Klan, this was no longer the case; they could, in the postwar era, stand up to the apologists of Jim Crow and still be fairly certain of substantial white support.

While the southern liberals admitted they did not know "what the Negro wanted," they were unwilling to engage in good-faith negotiations with African Americans. Even the most enlightened among them refused to come to terms with the system of Jim Crow. Throughout the 1940s, the Southern Conference on Human Welfare tried in vain to reconcile its opposition to the poll tax and its silence on the issue of black disfranchisement. Frank Porter Graham, president of the University of North Carolina, opposed President Truman's Civil Rights Commission report in 1948 because he feared it would defeat measures for voting rights and fair employment practices by raising the issue of social equality. In Georgia, the liberals shrank in the face of a race- and red-baiting campaign for governor. In addition to weakening their own position, the actions of W. T. Couch and his fellow race liberals strengthened the African-American leadership's convictions that segregation must be abolished. Some, like Rayford Logan, became more convinced of the duplicity of the southern liberals.[91]

It would, of course, take some time for the conviction to percolate into direct action against segregation. In practice most African Americans who skirmished across the color line felt they were strong enough to tilt it, not abolish it. Until the end of 1950, the NAACP's carefully crafted legal challenges to inferior educational facilities for African Americans were designed to make the segregated schools truly equal. The association's political calculus indicated that that was the outer limit to which American justice could be pushed. Then in November of that year, Thurgood Marshall went before the U.S. District Court in Charleston, South Carolina, to argue that black schools in Clarendon County were not equal. Judge Julius Waties Waring, a Charleston aristocrat who had been converted to the cause of civil rights, instructed Marshall to recast his case to challenge directly segregation.[92] Even in the early phases of the Montgomery bus boycott of 1955–56 African Americans demanded only truly separate-but-equal seating before insisting on an end to public segregation. What these instances show, however, is not an acceptance of segregation, but a calculation of what the movement could achieve.

The *What the Negro Wants* controversy helped clear the ground for this later phase of civil rights movement. It synthesized African-American opinion on segregation across the political spectrum. It also exposed to African-American spokespersons the ineffectiveness of southern racial liberals and their impotence as political buffers against the Ku Klux Klan and other race haters. Shorn of illusions, African Americans were more ideologically prepared than ever to break through the color bar and wage a sustained assault on the system of segregation.

chapter seven

THE POSTWAR WORLD

Africa and the United Nations

ટ✤

(1945–1960)

E VEN BEFORE IT was certain that the Allies would prosecute successfully the war against Hitler, the question that came to dominate
the minds of African Americans, Africans, and other dependent
peoples was: Who would win the peace? Africans under British rule were
especially clear that in the postwar world, the status quo antebellum
would not suffice. The war had increased Britain's dependence upon its
colonies, over which it increased centralized economic control. This colonial exploitation sparked resistance, including labor unrest in Britain's
Asian and Caribbean possessions in the 1930s. One result was that Britain and France combined economic centralization with political concessions. Island-wide political fermentation led to Britain granting in 1944 a
new constitution to Jamaica, which promised self-government and full
representation.[1]

Africans had their hopes raised when Britain and the United States
issued the Atlantic Charter. Signed on August 12, 1941, and broadcast
around the world, the charter declared that all nations had the right to
self-determination and to choose the form of government under which
they would live. Africans took this to mean that an Allied victory would
end colonialism. In the absence of Winston Churchill, who had not yet
returned from signing the Atlantic Charter, the West African Students
Union in London invited Deputy Prime Minister Clement Attlee to con-

firm this interpretation. He did, saying that "we fight this war not just for ourselves alone, but for all peoples." Seizing upon this statement, the Labour party's newspaper ran the headline: "The Atlantic Charter: *it means dark races, too.*"[2]

Hopes were dashed as quickly as they were raised. Once Churchill returned, he made clear that self-determination referred only to white Europeans who were living under Hitler's occupation, and that the question of the future of those colonial subjects who owed allegiance to the British Crown was altogether separate. The response from the colonial press was swift. George Padmore, journalist and veteran Pan-Africanist, was convinced that Britain was more interested in protecting its positions in Asia than in fighting Japanese fascism in the region. Nmadi Azikiwe, the Nigerian editor of the *West African Pilot* and an independence fighter, wrote to Churchill: "Are we fighting for the security of Europe to enjoy the Four Freedoms whilst West Africans continue to live under pre-war status?"[3] The West African Students Union in April 1942 issued its minimum demand of internal self-government for a period of five years to be followed immediately by independence. While the Africans' furor never reached the intensity generated by Britain's Asian and Caribbean colonial subjects, it nevertheless alarmed the British government. It issued new labor and welfare regulations (although they were subordinate to the efficient and profitable running of the colonial economies) and other measures designed to preempt all but the most radical resistance. The British did not achieve the desired result, however, and discussion of self-rule and independence electrified Africans both at home and abroad.[4]

The swirl of activity among Africans had its counterpart in the United States. In April 1941, W. E. B. Du Bois suggested that Logan, in Du Bois's name, announce the convocation of a Fifth Pan-African Congress as soon after the war as practicable, with the expressed aim of putting before the world's victorious powers "the demands of the peoples of African descent."[5] Logan, whom Du Bois had asked to be his official assistant at the congress, believed that Du Bois was finally accepting his lead.[6] Indeed, Logan had been quite busy preparing the political ground for such a conference. Of paramount importance in matters of preparation was uniting the African-American leadership around a vision of the postwar world *and* getting a hearing for this vision within the U.S. government. This two-track strategy reflected Logan's anxieties about the process of building a postwar world. He worried that African Americans would not articulate fully their own vision of the future, with the result that one would be articulated for them by well-meaning white liberals who were nevertheless essentially ignorant of the African-American people's desires and who could "not know the yearnings that are in our hearts." Logan also feared that unless African Americans were taken seriously by the U.S. government, they would be marginalized in the peace process.[7]

In December 1942, he submitted a confidential "Memorandum on a Proposed New Mandate System" to Dr. Benjamin Gerig, an academic acquaintance and a mid-level functionary in the State Department's Division of Special Research.[8] The first half of the memo was a critique of the old League of Nations mandate system. Almost fifteen years had elapsed since Logan first expressed his doubts about the mandates in his article for the *Journal of Negro History* on "The Operation of the Mandate System in Africa."[9] Those years had confirmed for Logan that the chief evil of the mandate system was the principle of national administration. Such a system was inherently wrong, Logan wrote, and as proof he cited the U.S. government's laissez faire attitude toward the southern states' treatment of African Americans:

> In our own country, in practically every case in which the States have been given the administration of funds provided by the national government, Negroes in the Southern states have not received equitable benefits. Our Federal government has either been powerless or unwilling to remove glaring injustices. In the same way, so long as national administration of the mandated areas prevails, the mandatory will find means of ignoring the ideals of the system and of circumventing the efforts of the supervisory body to assure those ideals.

The ideals of a mandate system—the protection of the rights and interests of dependent peoples and their preparation for independence—could be realized only so long as that system featured international administration.

In the second half of his memorandum, Logan detailed his view of a new mandate system. Its express purpose should be the easing of the transition of dependent peoples to self-government and then to independence. As decolonization was the task at hand, Logan wanted to make sure that the colonial powers did not control the new system; composition of a new mandates commission, therefore, was supremely important. Membership in the international administration should be open to nationals of any country, and at least two-thirds of the administration should be nationals of noncolonial powers. But in anticipation of the emergence of neocolonialism, Logan took care to define "colonial power." He recognized that some Western powers, while not possessing formal colonies, could, through investments in mandated areas, exert more influence in the developing world than poor colonial powers like Portugal.

Logan's proposal guaranteed representation of people of color—and Africans, in particular—in the administration. "At least one Negro should be a member of this new body since most African peoples living in the mandated areas . . . are treated like Negroes," he wrote. Brazil ought to have a permanent seat in the administration because of its own success in resolving racial problems; another permanent seat ought to be awarded to either Haiti or Liberia because of their international standing as independent black republics. The chief requirement for administration membership was, in Logan's schematic, "both knowledge of colonial problems and a constructively sympathetic understanding of Negro peoples." The administration staff should be chosen by competitive exam, without a way of identifying the applicant, "and without the latitude which permits personnel officers in our government regularly to overlook the colored applicant or applicants among the highest three." To train administration officers, Logan proposed the establishment of an International School of Colonial Administration. Finally, the new international administration—Logan also referred to it as the Permanent Mandates Commission (PMC)—ought to be located in Africa.

Perhaps the greatest sin of the League of Nations' mandates system was the restrictions it placed upon the rights of dependent peoples to petition for redress of grievances. As Logan noted in his earlier article on the mandates, the Mandates Commission was empowered to entertain only written complaints. Under Logan's new rules, the PMC was compelled to hear all petitions, even those upon which it chose not to act. Unlike the old PMC, the new one could also hear oral petitions; further, the travel costs associated with the oral petitions would be paid by the commission and not by the complainant.

Logan propagated his position among whites whenever he could. In February 1943 he sent President Roosevelt a copy of his "Operation of the Mandate System in Africa," which had been reprinted in 1942 with an introduction that propounded the ideas in Logan's memorandum to the State Department. Roosevelt's reply was typically noncommittal, but a personal note showed that he both regarded Logan as a serious scholar and recognized the gravity of the issue: "I found it extremely interesting,"

Roosevelt wrote, "but do not believe the time is ripe to take it up in detail. I am keeping it, however, for future reference."[10]

In 1942 Logan joined the Committee on Africa, the War, and Peace Aims, which was organized by the philanthropist Anson Phelps Stokes in 1941. Stokes's long interest in Africa was evidenced by the missionary work the Phelps-Stokes Fund sponsored and his patronage of the Encyclopedia of the Negro. The Committee on Africa, the War, and Peace Aims, like his other endeavors, was composed of whites and African Americans who were interested in both Africa and American race relations.[11] Many of the whites had a history of activism in the interracial cooperation movement: Will W. Alexander, the former director of the Commission on Interracial Cooperation; Jackson Davis, associate director of the General Education Board; Frederick Keppel, former president of the Carnegie Corporation; and Thomas Jesse Jones, educational director of the Phelps-Stokes Fund. The most active African Americans were Ralph Bunche, who was on leave from Howard University and working for the State Department; Charles S. Johnson of Fisk University; and Channing Tobias, the senior secretary in the YMCA's Colored Work Department.[12]

The committee's principal product was a detailed study on *The Atlantic Charter and Africa from an American Standpoint*. Written by Stokes, Ralph Bunche, Charles S. Johnson, Thomas Jesse Jones, Emory Ross, and Channing Tobias, the study opens with the declaration that "the emergence into political consciousness of the non-white peoples of the world is a recent phenomenon of great significance." The old colonialism would have to go—it had no place in a post-Hitler world. The most urgent question, then, was how to manage the nascent political consciousness among people of color, and especially Africans.[13] None of the African countries was ready for self-government (let alone independence), the committee felt, which would require a protracted period of between twenty and sixty years "before the people are qualified through education and experience to make use of it [self-government] wisely and effectively."[14] The committee was hopeful that the colonial powers—and chiefly Britain and Free France—would strive to promote the interests of Africans. The writers of the report felt that on balance the colonial powers had done much to improve life for the Africans; despite the legacy of the slave and liquor trades and the virtual absence of education, health care, and fair wages, the European powers had succeeded in bringing a measure of civilization to their dependencies.[15]

Despite the presence of Logan, W. E. B. Du Bois, and Walter White, the committee had a decidedly paternalistic tinge. Logan's principal disagreement with the committee was over the form of Western trusteeship over Africa. Stokes and the other reporters believed in a system of national mandates like the one operated by the League of Nations, supplemented by some form of international oversight;[16] Logan placed his faith in an international administration. On one point, though, Logan and Du Bois were able to influence the debate over the mandates. During one meeting of the Stokes committee, most participants leaned toward legitimating a modified spoils system in which Italy's African holdings would be transferred to one of the Allies and not be subject to the mandate system. Logan argued that this was "Jesuitical exegesis," and equated it with the Allies' placing Germany's colonies in trusteeship after World War I while exempting their own from such international control. The two evidently argued forcefully enough to overpower the rest of the committee, for the final version of the document called for a system of international inspection for all colonies in Africa.[17]

Logan had no quibble with the committee's estimate of the present ability of Africans to rule themselves. But while he shared this point of view with the white committee members, he was acutely sensitive to their propensity to pretend to know what was best for Africans. While they sincerely abhorred the debilitating effects of racial and colonial oppression, they believed in the cultural superiority of white Europeans and Americans, and they had a collective blind spot for liberal imperialist plans. The committee report took at face value the pronouncements of South African Prime Minister Jan Christiaan Smuts on the future of race relations in his country. Smuts, the principal architect of South African segregation, had declared in a 1942 speech on "The Basis of Trusteeship" that race relations must be taken "out of the heated atmosphere of politics and controversy." He also avoided using the words "inferior" and "superior" when he discussed race relations in South Africa, and this especially lifted the committee's spirits.[18]

But as Logan pointed out in an article on South Africa for the *Crisis*, Smuts wanted to set aside discussions of racial superiority not because he suddenly believed in equality, but because it was a "barren controversy" that "produced nothing except ill-feeling and bitterness."[19] For most of his political career, Smuts supported the color bar, which excluded black Africans from all but the worst jobs, and he opposed equality of pay between black and white workers. He also supported urban residential segregation and the establishment of Bantustans for Africans. His idea of removing race relations from politics meant disfranchising the black population in much the same manner that southern whites solved the race problem in the United States. Thus, white liberals in the United States were fooled by Smuts's rhetoric. He claimed not to want to define race relations in terms of inferior and superior groups, but his advocacy of white trusteeship over black Africa did just that. "One fact is crystal clear," Logan wrote. "Under whatever guise he may present his end policy, good-will, justice or trusteeship, segregation is the fundamental basis."[20]

Logan had correctly concluded that white liberals, no matter how well-meaning they might be, could not be trusted to speak accurately for Africans and African Americans. But as he fought off the imperialist prejudices of these liberals and demanded an international mandates system as the only fair treatment for the dependent peoples in Africa, he also encountered resistance from some Africans who were beginning to demand immediate self-rule and independence. During a Negro History Week celebration at Howard University in 1942, Logan shared the stage with Kwame Nkrumah, " 'an educated native' from the Gold Coast," who was studying in the United States and who in 1955 was to become the prime minister of independent Ghana. Nkrumah "made a fervent plea for the immediate independence of Africa."[21] A Nigerian, whom Logan did not name, also spoke at this program, and made a similar appeal. K. O. Mbadiwe, a Nigerian prince, also told Logan that the majority of his country's tribal leadership had begun to express themselves in favor of independence.[22]

"Very definitely 'No' " was Logan's answer to the question of whether any African country was ready for self-rule. He envisioned instead a situation similar to Haiti in the 1930s: an apprenticeship during which responsibility would steadily devolve from the mandatory to the Africans themselves. The length of the trusteeship would be inversely proportionate to the people's previous administrative experience. For much of Africa this meant a forty-year apprenticeship, he thought, primarily because of the minuscule amount of education available to Africans and the near total neglect of their welfare and economic development since 1927.[23]

But relative unpreparedness for self-government was not the only reason Africa needed a mandate system, said Logan; geopolitical realities also intruded on dreams of African freedom. The United States would not allow Africa to be decolonized if that meant the continent would be opened up to postwar enemies. Winston Churchill had declared that Britain would hold on to its colonies. Africa would be devastated if European capital was withdrawn. Further, Africa had not the means to dislodge the Europeans by force. That is why, when he presented his remarks to the Negro History Week gathering at Howard, "I prefaced my discussion of the Mandate System by saying that I wished it was unnecessary for me to talk about the Mandate System, but that I would 'eat crow' if Africa got her independence at the end of this war."[24]

While his opposition to immediate independence for Africa was based at least in part on an assessment of the balance of forces that was different from Nkrumah's and others', it also reflected a cultural gap between him and the Africans. He certainly didn't believe that Africans were childlike or needed guardians, but he felt that the African advocates of independence and their American supporters (like Leo Hansberry, Logan's Howard colleague and great African historian) tended to "swing the pendulum too far in the opposite direction—in our desire to prove that Africans are not savages we make them demi-gods." Africa's contributions to world civilization did not equip it for independence. "Much had been said about the great kingdoms of Africa, Ghana, Mellestine, Songhay," he said of Howard's Negro History Week forum,

> but the speakers had been talking about a "glorious past." They seem to have forgotten that Songhay had been destroyed in 1591, that there had been five hundred years of slave-trading, and almost 75 years of ruthless exploitation with practically no training in self-government.[25]

A few times Logan was on the receiving end of similar attitudes on the part of Africans about African Americans. The Ethiopian ambassador to the United States, Logan thought, looked down on African Americans and spurned their support. Logan and Leo Hansberry discovered that he was "courteous, but none too cordial." The ambassador, according to Logan, thought that African Americans as a lot were a primitive people, especially as compared to Ethiopians, a people with thousands of years of history. Logan and Hansberry cajoled the minister into adopting a more friendly attitude by threatening to isolate the Ethiopians in the United States. "If they wanted to be friendly, we would be, but . . . if they wanted to remain apart, we would leave them severely alone" was Hansberry's message to the minister. This done, "Hans then had a chance to educate the Minister.

He let the Minister know that we go rather freely to Northern Universities from Harvard on down; that American Negroes have achieved distinction in every walk of life."[26]

Logan's dialogue with the African politicians intensified as the war wound down and the Allies devoted more attention to the configuration of the postwar world. In October 1944, he addressed the National Council of Negro Women on the results of the Dumbarton Oaks Conference, in which the United States, Britain, France, the Soviet Union, and China sketched plans for the United Nations Charter. Logan was aghast at the Dumbarton proposals. They did not proclaim the equality of races. They listed the fundamental objectives of the United Nations as international peace and security while omitting any mention of the attainment of justice. They neglected to mention the colonial problem and even intimated returning to Germany and Italy their former colonies as a basis for peace in Europe.[27]

In the name of AΦA and as the foreign affairs adviser to the Association of Colleges and Secondary Schools for Negroes, the National Baptist Convention, and the *Pittsburgh Courier,* Logan again called upon an ailing President Roosevelt in January 1945 to "give serious consideration to the problem of the dependent areas," and help create an international system that would afford first-class citizenship to the world's people of color.[28] But during an official briefing on government proposals for the postwar world, Henry Morgenthau and Dean Acheson told Logan, W. E. B. Du Bois, Jeanetta Welch Brown of Alpha Kappa Alpha, and Alphaeus Hunton of the Council on African Affairs that colonial questions were excluded from most discussions with the Allies.[29]

Logan turned his attention to preparing for the San Francisco Conference of the United Nations, which convened in May 1945 to draw up the United Nations Charter. W. E. B. Du Bois, Walter White, and Mary McLeod Bethune had been selected for the official U.S. delegation, while Logan had been deputized to cover the conference for the *Courier.* As part of the preparation, Logan worked with Du Bois to organize a meeting "to formulate a program for San Francisco."[30] The meeting, planned by Logan, Du Bois, Alphaeus Hunton, and L. D. Reddick, an African-American member of the ACLS's Committee on Negro Studies and the curator of the New York Public Library's Schomburg Collection, was named the Colonial Conference and met on April 6–7, 1945, at the 135th Street branch of the New York Public Library.

The Colonial Conference was significant as a gauge of the African leaders' commitment to the goal of independence. Kwame Nkrumah spoke passionately at the conference against mandates, for that "implies sell-out to the colonial powers."[31] But, as he had been doing for the previous two years (according to Logan), he was equivocal on the demand for full independence and finally endorsed a conference resolution that read:

> Naturally so momentous a change [decolonization] cannot be immediately achieved but we demand that the United Nations at San Francisco establish an international Colonial Commission. . . . This body shall be empowered to oversee and facilitate the transition of peoples from colonial status to such autonomy as colonial peoples themselves may desire.[32]

In 1942 Logan noted that Nkrumah had "wavered considerably [on independence] and seemed once willing to accept a preparatory stage." After the Colonial Conference, Logan again noted that "Nkrumah, an African, seems to have accepted international trusteeship."[33]

The Harlem meeting was not limited to Africans and African Americans, but drew together prominent anticolonial figures from throughout the Third World. In addition to Logan, Du Bois, and Nkrumah, the conferees also included John Andu from Indonesia, Maung Saw Tun from Burma, Kumar Goshal from India, and Julio Pinto Gandia from Puerto Rico.[34] To be sure, this was not the first time that African Americans had concerned themselves with the struggles of colonial peoples other than Africans. In 1942, for example, the Council on African Affairs sponsored a rally of four thousand people in New York to demand a Free India. Paul Robeson was a true internationalist, and often spoke out against anti-Semitism and for freedom for India, Ireland, and China.[35]

But these were exceptions. James R. Hooker, the biographer of George Padmore, wrote that African nationalists like Padmore, who in the past had extensive contacts with other colonial peoples, increasingly excluded these allies from their thoughts and became "aloof from, even impatient with, non-African considerations."[36] The *Pittsburgh Courier* reported that Africans from the independent states of Ethiopia and Liberia disregarded even the concerns of African Americans.[37] On the American side, leaders like Du Bois were most reluctant to link the fates of Africa and Afro-America with those of the colonial peoples in Asia. When Logan was invited in May 1945 to serve on the NAACP's committee to plan for a postwar Pan-African Congress, he suggested that "rather than Pan-African Congress, the name of the meeting should be the Dependent Peoples' Congress."[38] Du Bois's answer was swift—and negative:

> It would be a fatal blunder for us to surrender our priority to the name *Pan-African Congress*. . . . [Also] while we have a pretty clear right to speak for Africa and cooperate with African peoples, we have no obvious right to organize or conduct propaganda for all dependent peoples. The peoples of Asia would more than likely repudiate such assumptions on our part.[39]

The Fifth Pan-African Congress was convened in Manchester, England, in July 1945, with an exclusively African focus, with only nominal participation of the NAACP, and, because Africans had found their own voice, with Du Bois as its titular head. The Harlem Colonial Conference can be viewed as a tributary to this congress, but only in the sense that it was one of several smaller gatherings in Europe and the United States leading up to it.[40] But the conference's larger thrust and its intellectual legacy—Logan's idea of Afro-Asian solidarity—did not become a material reality until ten years later, with the convocation of the Bandung Conference in Indonesia in 1955.

With the successful conclusion of the Harlem Colonial Conference, Logan made his way by train to San Francisco to report for the *Courier* on the founding of the United Nations. The excursion was a veritable Talented Tenth parade, as Logan was joined by P. L. Prattis, the executive editor of the *Courier;* P. B. Young, publisher of the *Norfolk Journal and Guide;* Walter White; W. E. B. Du Bois; Mary McLeod Bethune; and others who were attending the conference as observers, consultants, or reporters. Certainly the travelers engaged in some strategizing, but the cross-country trek had a celebratory bent. There were late-night bull sessions in the club car. When the train stopped over in Chicago, part of the group moved the socializing to a restaurant near the station, as Prattis (and likely Logan, too) met Windy City resident Horace Cayton, the sociologist, and Willard Townsend of the redcaps' union, and the writer Arna Bontemps, who was then the librarian at Fisk, for a sumptuous dinner at the Stevens Hotel. A few days later, the train rolled into Reno, Nevada, and the more adventurous disembarked, heading for the casinos.[41] By the time they reached the final destination, the conference-goers were relaxed and prepared to engage in serious business.

The journey west was unusual not only for the distinguished passenger list, but also for the absence of Jim Crow restrictions on the train. As a frequent rider of the nation's railroads, Logan often suffered the humiliations that befell African-American travelers on the lines that crisscrossed the South. That he was not as a matter of course subjected to second-class treatment is explained by two conditions. First, his complexion was light enough that ticket vendors, conductors, and stewards either thought he was white or were unsure enough not to challenge him. "I haven't the faintest idea whether he knew that I am colored" is a typical musing of Logan's concerning this racial ambiguity.[42]

A second reason was lack of uniformity in the conventions of segregation on the lines that passed through the South. In some areas of the country, black passengers might eat on the "third call," after whites were served on the first two, while in other areas, blacks and whites might eat simultaneously, but with black passengers forced to dine behind a green curtain. On some lines, dining cars were segregated but club cars and washrooms were not. Logan speculated that because the Southern's crews often came from New York, in practice that road was more flexible in its race policies; the Louisville & Nashville, on the other hand, ran exclusively in the South and so was rigid in its implementation of Jim Crow. On some of the lines, African Americans could purchase a Pullman berth. On others, however, they had to ride day coach. On still others, they were restricted to "Lower 13." (A Pullman car had twelve upper and lower berths and a drawing room at one end; for the price of a berth, black passengers were sometimes allowed to sleep in the common area, which was temporarily labeled "Lower 13" and was used by all travelers during the day.)

The inconsistency in regulations were pregnant with irony. On trips from New York to Washington, Logan might eat in a dining car with an undrawn curtain and hard by a table of whites; when the train continued on to Atlanta, the curtain was drawn and he became invisible to passengers who could see him before. Further, a curtain generally was used only to separate tables that were side by side; no fabric cordoned off tables in front of the Jim Crow section, which was at one end of the car. Consequently, several tables of white diners could still see their black counterparts, leading Logan to observe that "horizontal segregation and oblique segregation had been abolished, but that vertical segregation had to be maintained. In other words, it was not the fact of segregation that was the important thing, but the symbol."[43] Another time, Logan avoided shabby treatment by speaking French to the hostess at the restaurant at Washington's Union Station; despite the fact that he was with another African American, the hostess assumed that they were foreigners, and was especially attentive to Logan's party.[44]

The situations that at times could provoke only bewildered amusement usually aroused in Logan a quiet rage. On a trip between New Orleans and Houston, he took his meal as he gazed out the window upon billboards proclaiming "States' Rights and White Supremacy."[45] He never intentionally passed for white when he journeyed by train, and he always presented himself at the Jim Crow ticket window or waiting area; but he frequently challenged the right of the roads to segregate him. In February 1937, he was thrown off a Memphis-to-Atlanta train when the conductor refused to honor his ticket for a Pullman berth and Logan refused to accept Lower 13; he responded by suing the Pullman Company and winning an out-of-court settlement.[46] Three years later, a ticket agent in Washington, D.C., refused to sell him a Pullman berth for a trip to New Orleans unless he accepted Lower 13; this time, Logan remained firm, successfully bullying the agent and his supervisor into accommodating him.[47] He also created opportunities to flaunt segregation by eating before the third call and entering and exiting train stations by the "whites only" door.[48]

He once told an assembly at Fisk University that segregation made him "regret that I was a historian and not a physicist," for he could have then produced an atomic bomb and coerced the government into dismantling Jim Crow.[49] More usually, though, Logan reached catharsis by recording these affronts in his diary, and over the years he amassed dozens of first-hand accounts. "What goddamned humiliating, degrading tomfoolery," he wrote. There was another reason, too, for committing his experiences to paper. Ever the historian, Logan wanted to make sure that the experiences of African Americans were preserved for the record: "I hope," he wrote after one of countless incidents, "the time will come when a colored man travelling in the United States will not have to record all such details. But in 1947 they are essential to a description of American life."[50]

The train carrying the UN-bound Logan and other African Americans pulled into Oakland's Trans-Bay Terminal, and the passengers were greeted by official escorts; sailors were on hand to help them with their baggage, take them to the ferry to San Francisco, and deposit them at their first-class hotels: the Sir Francis Drake, the Palace, the Bellevue. This trip,

Logan and the others were not worried about Jim Crow in transportation and accommodations. What was of immediate concern, though, was exclusion from the conference table. It was just as he had feared as early as 1941: that African Americans, small nations, and dependent peoples would be locked out of the peace process. The organization of the United Nations and the postwar order was largely determined "behind closed doors by representatives of the so-called great powers—the United States, Russia, Great Britain, China, possibly France."[51] The principal Western powers at San Francisco opposed a new international mandates system. The recently deceased President Roosevelt had been sympathetic to international trusteeship, Logan thought, but the navy was not, for it demanded that the United States annex conquered Japanese Pacific islands. Similarly, Britain wanted to appropriate Italy's former African colonies in order to protect its colonial interests. None of the colonial powers intended to place its existing holdings under international authority.[52]

There was the matter of class, racial, and gender composition of the delegates, too. As Logan wrote in the *Courier:*

> Two-thirds of the people represented at this conference are the darker people of the world. But nine-tenths of the delegates here are white.
>   One-half of the peoples represented at this conference are women. But there are hardly a dozen women among the several hundred delegates.
>   Most of the peoples of the world are workers. But there isn't a pair of overalls among the delegates.[53]

Du Bois's presence at San Francisco as an official U.S. observer meant that African Americans would be in contact with delegates and observers from the anticolonial world; on his initiative the NAACP received mandates to represent an array of African-American protest, professional, and religious organizations. He used this opportunity to cement ties with anticolonial activists, especially from the Indian delegation. But Du Bois was not, and could not be, a passive observer, and his position also entitled him to be a State Department consultant. In this capacity, he and virtually every other representative of a popular organization were shut out. The U.S. delegation listened with polite indifference to his proposals for UN-sponsored decolonization.[54] Neither Du Bois and the NAACP nor any of the other popular organizations represented at San Francisco could bypass the U.S. delegation and get a hearing from the entire conference; the machinery at San Francisco was such that nongovernmental organizations were prevented from influencing conference proceedings. As Logan noted,

> If Negroes, Jews, organized labor and other minority groups have not already made their wishes known, they are going to be little more than kibitzers and there is going to be slight opportunity for them to state their wishes until the decisions of the Conference have been made public and submitted for ratification.[55]

With restricted input from American minorities and popular organizations and the world's small nations and colonial peoples, it was no surprise to Logan that the UN Charter had serious flaws. Between the end of the San Francisco Conference in 1945 and 1948, Logan turned his considerable scholarly and oratorical skills to exposing the shortcomings of the new international organization that was designed to keep world peace.

The charter was, he said, a "tragic joke."[56] The trusteeship arrangements rendered it incapable of ridding the world of war, for under the UN Charter, the placing of dependent territories in trusteeship was left to each colonial power.[57] In July 1945 he wrote a detailed article for the *Pittsburgh Courier* on the ineffectiveness of the UN in preventing war.[58] But his most complete statement on the subject was *The African Mandates in World Politics*, which he published privately with his own money.[59] The Rosenwald Fund deemed it an important enough study to grant Logan a year's fellowship in 1944–45 to enable him to do the research, but the University of North Carolina Press, which was still one of the few presses that published scholarly books on African-American topics, after considerable delay, refused to publish it. Logan, who still smarted from the treatment he had received from the UNC Press over *What the Negro Wants*, was convinced that, with a conservative political climate gathering force in the United States, no major publisher would take his work so long as he offered a radical interpretation of contemporary events.[60]

In 1948, the year Logan published *The African Mandates*, the Second World War was not even five years past, but international tensions were again on the rise; many people thought a third world war was a likely possibility. International attention was again focused on East-West tension in Europe: the Berlin blockade and the dispute over the future of Austria were in the headlines. Strategic thinking, scholarly efforts, and the battle for public opinion converged around drawing lessons about the start of World War II and how to prevent another world war. Conventional wisdom had it that the war was a result of Nazi aggression in Europe. One seminal lesson that the conventional wisdom drew, then, was that world peace depended upon a successful confrontation of the Soviet Union in Europe. Logan did not dispute Hitler's insistence on conquering Europe, but he brought into the open a factor in world politics little regarded by post–World War II strategists and scholars: the struggle among the principal European powers for African colonies. Bringing this aspect to the forefront was made even more important as Italy, with the backing of at least some people in the U.S. government, was agitating the UN to have Eritrea and its other former African colonies returned to it in the form of a mandate.[61]

Logan's thesis was that the recovery of its African colonies had been a major objective of German activity ever since Versailles. All parties in Germany, with the exception of the Communists, wanted to regain the African colonies, which had been turned over to Britain, France, and South Africa. Germans felt that their national honor was at stake; that their "legally" obtained colonies were stripped away "illegally"; that they needed *Lebensraum*. After extensive searches through official documents, semiofficial newspapers and speeches, Logan concluded that the adjustment of the colonial question figured into nearly every German demand for the modification of the Versailles treaty.

British, French, and South African opinion was almost solidly opposed to the return of colonies to Germany. Chief among the stated reasons for this opinion was that Germany mistreated the Africans they had dominated and that their treatment of the Jews further disqualified them from having African colonies. Logan, however, showed that Britain and Germany differed little in their treatment of their colonial subjects; further, neither side in this dispute bothered to take into account the wishes of Africans. Even after Britain and France took over Germany's former colonies in the form of mandates, they tried to integrate them into their existing colonial structures.

The Allied governments tried to portray Germany's insistence on retrieving its colonies as an example of Germany's recalcitrant pride; this was the basis, Logan argued, for some proponents of appeasement to urge that Germany be given African territory, in the form of either colonies or mandates. But Germany's determination was a matter of economics and politics, not merely an expression of national pride. The world war, Logan argued, was not the result of German colonial aspirations only; British and French aspirations played their part as well. So if appeasement was not a successful strategy for peace, neither was confrontation over the issue of colonies. Logan's conclusion was that the only way to remove imperialist competition as a potential cause for world war was to remove imperialism. The United Nations had to promote self-determination and independence, with an internationally administered mandate system as an interim step.

Another principal fault of the United Nations was that its human rights provisions were extraordinarily weak.

> The UN Charter proclaims its intentions of "promoting and encouraging respect for human rights and for the fundamental freedoms for all, without regard to race, sex, language or religion." This is, of course, only a statement of purpose, for no certain means of implementation is anywhere provided. Since practically all the governments represented at San Francisco violate these very principles, one is naturally led to remember the Declaration of Independence in which slave-holders asserted that "all men are created equal. . . ."[62]

Good intentions were negated by the fact that the charter had no enforcement provisions. Further, it had pointedly excluded from the organization's consideration the internal affairs of any member state; sovereignty reigned supreme, and all a Nazi Germany or a colonial power had to do to avoid United Nations scrutiny was claim that alleged violations were internal matters.[63]

Logan's opinion of the UN was reinforced during his three-year appointment, between 1947 and 1950, to the United States National Commission for UNESCO. The Constitution of the United Nations Educational, Scientific and Cultural Organization (UNESCO) proposed that member nations establish national commissions to advise their respective government delegations to the organization's general conferences and to help implement the UNESCO program. Established by an act of Congress in 1947, the U.S. National Commission had one hundred members, including sixty who represented labor, religious, minority, professional, business, and citizens organizations; the balance, made up of local, state, and government officials and public personalities, was appointed by the State Department.[64] Logan represented the American Teachers Association, the organization of African-American educators that was established because blacks in the South were barred from the National Education Association; he was also on the commission's executive committee. During Logan's appointment, the commission was chaired by Milton Eisenhower, Dwight's brother.

Logan defined his role as increasing the representation of African Americans in State Department policy and fighting for the rights of colonial peoples within UNESCO. In April 1946, just before UNESCO's formal formation in London, Logan, along with the educators Norma Boyd and President Martin Jenkins of Morgan State College and Josephine Kyles of the Federal Council of Churches, met with Charles Thomson, a State Department official in charge of U.S. preparations for UNESCO's founding. Logan pushed two points: that one of the five U.S. delegates to the UNESCO conference be a specialist in the area of education in non-self-governing areas and that the State Department sponsor a conference on this issue; that the State Department inform him, as the head of an ad hoc group, of any employment opportunities within the UNESCO Secretariat.[65]

Thomson rejected Logan's proposals. On a five-member delegation, there was no room for a specialist, or "representation for pressure groups." Thomson suggested that the Trusteeship Council of the UN hold Logan's proposed conference. When Logan reminded him that there were as yet no areas under trusteeship, Thomson told Logan that such a conference would, if sponsored by the State Department, rankle the colonial powers. As for UNESCO employment, the State Department was unaware of any African American who was competent to perform UNESCO jobs.[66] (This last response must have stung, for it was clear from the way Logan shaped his proposals that he was offering his services to the State Department.) Logan left the meeting very dissatisfied. It foreshadowed Logan's participation on the commission: while he could garner the support of the other participants in the meeting for his proposals, the State Department was free to reject his ideas, and often did.

This first encounter indicated a wide rift between Logan's appraisal of UNESCO and the State Department's. The State Department was wary of UNESCO on at least two levels. It was uncomfortable with the idea of an advisory body for its UNESCO activities. Many government officials feared that it would act irresponsibly and against the best interests of the United States. The government also discouraged participation in UNESCO's activities by the American people. Similarly, many of the national commission's first members felt that the State Department would try to strong-arm them and use them as a rubber stamp, a view that was reinforced when the government regularly chose to ignore the commission's advice.[67]

Which is not to say that Logan did not win minor victories. At his insistence, the February 1948 commission meeting adopted a statement urging constituent organizations to hold their meetings on UNESCO on a nonsegregated, nondiscriminatory basis; this proposal received the support of the CIO, the National Education Association, the American Council on Education, and the Library of Congress. The State Department's Cultural Relations office showed its approval of the resolution by refusing to book its affairs at the Carlton Hotel in Washington, D.C., which refused to cater integrated parties.[68] Logan also proposed the representation for the United States' non-self-governing territories on the commission, and the adoption of his proposal led to the appointment of Jaime Benitez, the chancellor of the University of Puerto Rico, to the commission.[69]

The United States also opposed an expansive role for UNESCO in the postwar world. Many of the Western European countries desired an organization that would expend a majority of its energies in reconstructing the war-torn European continent. India, on the other hand, argued that in the long run the newly emerging countries in Asia and Africa should be major recipients of economic, scientific, and educational assistance, while the West should come better to understand and appreciate the traditional cultures of the East.[70] Each in its own way was struggling to define a coherent role for UNESCO in shaping world peace.

The United States, though, preferred a loosely defined UNESCO mission and an organization that was more like a clearinghouse than an active agent.[71] The U.S. government had no clear conception of the role of UNESCO in American foreign policy, but it did prefer that its trade and assistance programs be bilateral in form, which it could more completely control. The ideal U.S. aid programs were the Marshall Plan for the reconstruction of Europe and the thwarting of communism, and later, the Point Four program, which reached out to the Third World. In UNESCO's multilateral form, the United States would be only one voice, while underdeveloped areas presumably would have more of a say.[72]

One of UNESCO's most important functions, especially during its first decade, was the promotion of human rights. The U.S. National Commission chose to get involved in this issue, but the government chose to disregard its advisory body's progressive advice. In November 1949, Logan attended a meeting sponsored by the State Department to discuss the United Nations' proposed Draft Covenant on Human Rights. At this meeting, Eleanor Roosevelt "candidly revealed" that the draft covenant excluded provisions contained in the 1948 Universal Declaration of Human Rights that guaranteed social and economic rights. Articles 22–27 stated that social security, the right to join a trade union, equality of pay, and access to housing, medical care, and other necessary social services were human rights. "In answer to my question," Logan reported to Roy Wilkins, "she flatly stated that all the colonial powers oppose the inclusion of these provisions."[73] This meeting turned out to be the opening shot in a ten-month struggle to get the United States to recognize the full range of human rights for minorities and colonial peoples.

At the April 1950 meeting of the commission Logan introduced a resolution that stated the commission's opinion that Articles 22–27 be incorporated into the draft covenant because they "represent rights of man which it [the commission] would wish to have respected." The resolution also challenged the State Department to explain its opposition to this measure; the commission was then to evaluate State's position critically, "and, unless those reasons are overwhelmingly compelling, to go on record as urging the Department to agree to incorporate these items in the Covenant."[74] As he reported to the American Teachers Association, "To my surprise and gratification several members [of the commission] immediately seconded the resolution."[75] He was surprised because his experience on the commission was that other members did not want to deal with issues related to race, and this was one that concerned overwhelmingly people of color, most of whom lived in dependent areas. With the support of the CIO, the resolution passed, with only the representative of the Junior Chamber of Commerce dissenting.[76]

The State Department's reply came in the form of a letter from Edward Barrett, assistant secretary of state for public affairs. The United States would support the inclusion of civil and political rights only. According to Barrett, the Universal Declaration of Human Rights was merely a statement, but the Covenant on Human Rights would be legally binding. The State Department did not think that the American people supported the economic and social rights enumerated in the declaration. Not only that, these rights were not accepted throughout most of the Western world, whereas civil and political rights were. Finally, economic and social rights were the province of the states, not the federal government.[77] This last point was crucial to official thinking, for the federal government was of no mind to infringe upon the rights of the southern states to enforce segregation.

Logan's reply was sharp. He decried Barrett's attempt to convert the issue of human rights into an East-West issue by implying that "outside the Iron Curtain" there was a consensus on civil and political rights. There were plenty of U.S.-backed "dictatorships and quasi-dictatorships" that did not respect these rights, and even the United States "does not have an unblemished record. . . ." Economic and social rights were more commonly recognized in the West than the State Department let on: the Scandinavian and Latin American countries, Canada, Australia, New Zealand, and even the United States had enacted some form of social protective legislation. With this widespread acceptance, Logan wondered why the State Department opposed an international guarantee of these rights. The only conclusion he could draw was that the federal government was working in concert with the American South and the colonial powers, who opposed guaranteeing these rights to their subjects.[78]

This dispute dominated the proceedings of the July meeting of the commission's executive committee. Logan's term on the commission was up, but he was asked to stay on to settle the matter. Sentiment for his position was unusually strong in the executive committee, for the CIO representative, Charles S. Johnson, and Waldo Leland favored including social and economic rights among the protected human rights. The chair of the commission, Milton Eisenhower, stated his opinion that the State Department had not come up with "overwhelmingly compelling" reasons for the exclusion of these rights, but he claimed ignorance of the issue and said he would abstain from any vote. The matter was resolved for good when the State Department members of the commission pushed through a motion that buried Logan's resolution in a committee.[79] In August 1951, the United States prevailed upon UNESCO to adopt a resolution urging the UN General Assembly to exclude economic and social rights from the Covenant on Human Rights.[80]

Two years later, with the debate in the UN still continuing, the United States announced that it would not sign the Draft Covenant on Human Rights, which still contained guarantees for social and economic rights. Despite this refusal, the United States continued to ask that the covenant be amended to ensure that nothing in it would "operate so as to bring within the jurisdiction of the federal authority of a federal State . . . any of the matters referred to in this Covenant which, independently of the

Covenant, would not be within the jurisdiction of the federal authority."
In other words, the United States wanted to include "states' rights" in an
international human rights document. The government also voted in the
UN against expanding human rights for women and protecting racial and
religious minorities from "incitement to hatred."[81]

Logan's stint on the United States National Commission for UNESCO
and his tussle with the State Department occurred during a time when the
African-American leadership was defining its attitude toward American
foreign policy and, more generally, its place in the Cold War. W. E. B. Du
Bois, with whom Logan had been associated since 1921 and whose political physiognomy Logan largely shared, moved rapidly and decisively to
the left. Du Bois had been an admirer of Franklin Roosevelt, but when he
died and Harry Truman ascended to the presidency, Du Bois saw many
former Roosevelt Democrats embracing the incipient Cold War. In late
1946, Du Bois joined forces with the Progressive Citizens of America, the
precursor to Henry Wallace's Progressive party, because of its program of
abolition of segregation, the enactment of federal civil rights legislation,
the elimination of the House Committee on Un-American Activities, and
its opposition to a resurgent militarism and imperialism. Along with Paul
Robeson, Du Bois was the most prominent African American to support
Wallace's run for president in 1948.[82]

In 1947, Du Bois launched, initially with the support of the NAACP, a
petition campaign to bring to the attention of the United Nations the
infringement of the human rights of African Americans. The petition, *An
Appeal to the World: A Statement on the Denial of Human Rights to
Minorities in the Case of Citizens of Negro Descent in the United States of
America and an Appeal to the United Nations for Redress,* was a compact
statement covering the historical and contemporary aspects of the economic, political, social, and legal denial of human rights. Hundreds of
African-American organizations endorsed the petition: the National Negro Congress and the Council on African Affairs, two left-wing organizations, gave their approval, as did the National Baptist Convention, the
National Fraternal Council of Negro Churches, the Urban League, and
the National Association of Colored Women. The CIO supported the
petition, and even the AFL, not known as a particularly staunch ally of
African Americans, agreed to help.[83]

Although the petition attracted international attention, especially from
Third World and socialist countries, its progress toward UN consideration

was cut short by the United States. Eleanor Roosevelt, an NAACP board member, considered it an embarrassment for the United States' racial practices to be discussed in an international forum, and she refused, as a delegate to the UN's Commission on Human Rights, to sponsor such a petition; she also believed it was an affront for any other country to do so.[84] Logan had contributed the document's final chapter, in which he discussed the human rights provisions of the UN Charter. The violation of these rights of African Americans was "well-nigh universal" and was a classic case for UN intervention. But he stated in blunt terms that the United States, South Africa, or any colonial country could easily block consideration of such petitions by the UN on grounds that it was a domestic matter.[85] The United States killed consideration of the petition in November 1947, after the Soviet Union introduced it.

Two other indices of Du Bois's radicalization were his joining Paul Robeson's Council on African Affairs (CAA) and his opposition to the Marshall Plan and Point Four, among the most important U.S. foreign policy initiatives in the postwar era. The CAA was founded in 1937 as a clearinghouse for information on Africa and a lobby for African interests; it was not designed to be a membership organization, and in the 1940s it met only three times annually and had fewer than two dozen members, including Robeson, Max Yergan, and Alphaeus Hunton (a Marxist who had previously taught at Howard University and who would join Du Bois in Ghana in 1961 to assist him on the Encyclopedia Africana). In its early days the CAA kept in close touch with the State Department, with which it regularly had full-day sessions to discuss African affairs. But by 1942 the council had been branded a communist front. Logan joined it in 1944 "in order to show that as a Liberal I would not be frightened by red-baiting."[86]

When Du Bois joined the council in 1948 and became its vice-chairman, it already regularly opposed the United States' foreign policy. The CAA opposed the Marshall Plan as a program for propping up a "weakened imperialist economy of Western Europe . . . increasingly . . . [at the expense] of the colonial peoples, particularly in Africa." When Truman announced his Point Four program in his January 1949 inaugural address, the CAA categorically denounced it, too. Point Four was Truman's "bold new program" to aid the Third World and prevent socialism from gaining a foothold there. As the CAA pointed out, the United States would make investment decisions in consultation with the respective colonial powers and without the input from representatives of the colonial peoples; further, American investment would stabilize the colonial economy and give the United States access to restricted markets, thus making it a major neocolonial power. Certainly Africans wanted development, but it would have to occur on their terms and for their benefit. The precondition for this was self-government.[87]

Logan shared Du Bois's and the CAA's perspective on the human rights abuses of the colonial powers and their opinion on the dim prospects for UN intervention on behalf of colonial peoples; he in fact developed the critique that Du Bois adopted. Logan could be quite strident, even hyperbolic in his warning of the consequences that would befall any country that denied human rights to the black people of the world:

> Is it utterly fantastic to conceive that black men will one day perfect an atomic bomb? No, it is not. I can picture an international conference, not more than twenty-five years from now, in which a black delegate will rise and declare: "Gentlemen: five hundred years is long enough for any people to be held in bondage, degraded, spit upon, exploited, disfranchised, segregated, lynched. Here is the formula for a home-manufactured atomic bomb. Give us liberty or we will give you death."[88]

But Logan could not move into opposition to the United States in foreign affairs in the manner of Du Bois. He supported Point Four, but with reservations. "In the past similar programs had bogged down because of the superior attitude of many Americans toward the people of the country they were supposed to be helping," he wrote to Walter White.[89] But certain measures could be taken to ensure that Point Four would be implemented equitably. Selection of personnel should be made without regard to race, gender, religion, or language, "but with careful regard for ability to work effectively and sympathetically with the peoples of underdeveloped areas." Labor in the colonial areas should be afforded protection equal to that provided to capital, and organized labor in the United States should be encouraged to help develop unions in the dependent areas. Colonial peoples must be involved in decisions concerning aid programs, and, more generally, representatives from the non-self-governing territories should be represented on the specialized agencies of the UN, like UNESCO, the International Labor Organization, and the World Health Organization.[90]

The Council on African Affairs blasted Logan for his position on Point

Four. A feature article in the CAA's newsletter *New Africa* ridiculed Logan's pleas for democratic safeguards in the implementation of Point Four. None of these conditions was in effect in the United States, the article stated, yet Logan pretended they could be obtained in the colonies. The council accused Logan of tipping his hat "to democratic sentiments while actually embracing the United States' imperialistic foreign policy."[91]

If the council was accurate in charging Logan with daydreaming when it said that his conditions for supporting Point Four would remain forever unfulfilled, its ad hominem attack was nonetheless probably motivated by Logan's involvement in two other events. In 1947–48 the council was rent by Cold War politics, as Max Yergan, its executive director, succumbed to right-wing pressure. Since the 1920s, when he was in charge of the YMCA's missionary work in southern Africa, Yergan had dedicated himself to a decolonized Africa. His experiences with South African officials, colonial administrators, and white American philanthropists had convinced Yergan of the efficacy of a left-wing solution to Africa's problems and drew him close to the American Communist Party. In 1947, though, he began to waver in his communist commitment. He accused the Communists of disabling the CAA, and he vowed to clean house.[92]

He went about doing this in February and March 1948 by calling rump meetings of the council, claiming authority to sack several members for their alleged communist leanings, and changing the locks on the council's office doors. While Yergan's conversion may have been genuine, there was more than a hint of financial impropriety and organizational sloppiness on his part. During 1947, for example, he had failed to send to Africa money that was collected for famine relief and to establish a permanent Africa Relief Committee. In May 1948, Robeson and Hunton led a successful counterattack that expelled Yergan from the council. In later years, Yergan became a professional anticommunist and a supporter of rapprochement with the apartheid regime of South Africa.[93]

Surprisingly, Logan was the first to learn of Yergan's change of heart when, in November 1947, Yergan told him that he "had decided to break off all connections (meaning Communists) that hampered the work" of the CAA. Yergan may have guessed that Logan, despite his ties with Du Bois and Robeson, pursued his own course in politics. He may even have thought that he could get Logan's assistance. The conversation was, in fact, a measure of Logan's independent cast. He clearly sensed that Yergan's next moves within the CAA were bound to alter the political landscape for African Americans: "This is probably one of the most important entries that I have made in this Diary," he wrote of his talk with Yergan. He told Yergan that he agreed that Paul Robeson's ties with the Communist party were causing him to close "many doors that would otherwise be open to him," and that these ties were not helpful to the African-American cause. At the same time, he would not be compelled to leave the CAA because of the anticommunist attacks upon it.[94] Nevertheless, when Yergan made his move on the council and lost, Logan, in a token gesture of support, left the organization.[95] Logan was not the only member to leave. Mary McLeod Bethune, Channing Tobias, and Adam Clayton Powell, Jr., also left. Yergan's activity delivered a crippling blow to one of the most effective American organizations interested in Africa; the CAA never recovered, and eventually disbanded in 1955.[96]

Hard feelings were likely compounded when, in October 1948, Logan was hired by Walter White as the NAACP's consultant on UN, African, and colonial affairs, barely one month after White had engineered the ouster of W. E. B. Du Bois as the association's director of special research.[97] Du Bois's support for Henry Wallace and the Progressive party and his endorsement of Paul Robeson's Crusade Against Lynching (which White considered an affront to the NAACP's prestige) irritated White, who at any rate could no longer tolerate what he perceived to be Du Bois's challenges to his personal authority.

White's dispatch of Du Bois may have been personally gratifying, but it left a chink in the NAACP's intellectual armor, especially in international affairs. White was an organizational wizard without equal, but he was deficient in his knowledge of world issues and ineffectual in his ability to influence them. Du Bois had commented on White's ineffectiveness as a consultant to the U.S. delegation to the San Francisco Conference: "I think they put over certain decisions on Walter by reason of his unfamiliarity with the broader implications."[98] White was chosen again to be a consultant to the U.S. delegation to the United Nations General Assembly, which was to meet in Paris in September 1948. He had no idea what to say to the delegation on the issue of trusteeships and human rights, and, because of their strained relations, White could not ask Du Bois for advice. Besides, Du Bois argued that the UN would do nothing concerning trusteeships and he felt that it was a waste of time for White to go to Paris. With no one else to turn to, White began to ask Logan for advice.[99]

White's turn with the U.S. delegation convinced him that even if he could do nicely without Du Bois, he could not do at all without someone *like* Du Bois. He explained his reasons for wanting Logan on board this way: "Dr. Logan, who knows more about the mandate system than almost anyone else, together with other members of the staff can do a great deal towards filling this need [of competent representation at the UN]."[100]

Between 1949 and 1950 Logan authored NAACP positions on trusteeship and other international affairs and represented the association at State Department conferences and meetings of nongovernmental organizations.[101] He was a gadfly at these functions, challenging government officials and other interested parties (even liberal and progressive organizations) over their alleged disregard of African affairs and their procolonial attitude toward trusteeship.[102] His tenure with the association was generally uneventful and punctuated only occasionally by feelings that he was being used. He regularly sent White memoranda on Africa, which White used for his newspaper column without giving attribution. "The question must be faced," Logan wrote in his diary after one of his memos was spun into a newspaper article. "Am I to send in memorandums to the NAACP which Walter will use in his columns? At least, I shall have to keep the record straight, as I have done above."[103]

Logan's divergence from Du Bois and his collaboration with the NAACP, though, did not signal his realignment with the political right, as the CAA unfairly implied. Unlike Walter White, Roy Wilkins, A. Philip Randolph, and other civil rights leaders who rushed in the late 1940s and 1950s to disassociate themselves from Du Bois, Paul Robeson, and the African-American left, Logan refused to add his voice to the chorus of denunciation.[104] In September 1944 he had attended a dinner in honor of Ferdinand Smith, an African-American Communist who was the secretary-treasurer of the Communist-led National Maritime Union. In December 1946 he applauded the performance and speech that Paul Robeson gave to the AΦA convention, and he later attended functions honoring Robeson.[105] These activities—as well as his past associations with Communists—caught the attention of the FBI. When bureau agents questioned Logan in May 1953 concerning these contacts, he refused to repudiate them. Smith, he told the special agent, "was a Negro who had been fighting for the rights of Negro seamen. . . ." Robeson was a fraternity brother, Logan said, and although he did not personally agree with his views, it was important to honor a fellow Alpha.[106]

Logan acquitted himself well during his fifty-minute grilling. When the bureau agents asked him if he had ever signed petitions protesting the House Committee on Un-American Activities, Logan replied that if he hadn't yet, it was entirely possible that he would do so that day. The interviewers then threw at Logan a panoply of names of organizations that he endorsed that were on the attorney general's subversives list. He refused the bait, instead responding that he did not care if all of the organizations to which he affiliated were communist; his own personal litmus test for associating with political activists, he told the agents, was whether or not they advanced the cause of African Americans, not what their ideological proclivities were.[107]

Immediately after the interrogation, he summarized this meeting in a letter that he sent to historians around the country; his recounting from memory is in remarkable accord in its detail with the official FBI record. He had been ordered to appear at the Old Post Office building in downtown Washington, D.C., an imposing edifice. "I am convinced that the FBI chose [this site] . . . as its headquarters because both the exterior and the interior closely resemble a prison," he wrote. "The inquisition has descended upon Howard."[108] Like many of his Howard colleagues, Logan divined that the intent of the witch-hunt was to "intimidate us and to sow suspicion among us." To some degree the FBI realized their goal, for as Logan commented, Howard's male faculty feared even to discuss politics in the men's room, lest some professor/informer be hiding in the stalls.[109] But Logan's courageous stand helped to counter the atmosphere of distrust and, judging by the responses to his letter, was heartily appreciated by his fellow historians.

In 1951 Paul Robeson had been pressing his petition to the UN charging the United States government with genocide against African Americans. During the time that his efforts were attracting the greatest attention from the U.S. government, Logan was in Paris, where he was on a Fulbright scholarship to study France's administration of its colonies; he also represented the NAACP at the United Nations General Assembly. The State Department asked Logan to declare his opposition to the petition, *We Charge Genocide*. Logan demurred. While he claimed that the NAACP was in fact more representative of African Americans than Robeson, he stated that the petition had several convincing points, including pervasive physical assaults on blacks (especially civil rights activists) and the "mental harm" inflicted upon African Americans by discrimination and segregation. He turned the request around by asking the government to investigate the recent killing of the leader of the Florida NAACP and to disclose how much it had done to implement the recommendations contained in the U.S. Civil Rights Commission's study, *To Secure These Rights*. He also praised Robeson both for his singing and acting and for his defense of civil rights.[110]

Logan's differences with W. E. B. Du Bois and the African-American left transcended specific political issues; at bottom they were philosophic and ideological in nature. In the late 1940s Du Bois became more convinced that under capitalism black people would always be kept down. In the United States the decisions concerning elemental rights were made antidemocratically, in the corporate boardrooms, and while Du Bois understood that African Americans had made tremendous strides in their material well-being, he believed that they would never share equally in the country's prosperity.

Du Bois also felt keenly the corrupting influence upon African Americans of the United States' acquisitive ethic. He had always criticized the coldheartedness of white America's preoccupation with the cash nexus, but he held out hope for the humanizing nature of African Americans. Now, though, he felt that African Americans were infected with an alien spirit. "This is the sickness of the whole American civilization, money! The insidious thing is that Negroes are taking white Americans as their pattern, to make a life out of buying and selling and becoming rich, spending for show."[111]

This materialism deeply disturbed Du Bois. From the beginning of his involvement in Pan-Africanism he had believed in the superiority of African Americans over Africans and consequently felt that the former would lead the latter to liberation. "We used to think that because they were educated, and had some chance, American Negroes would lead Africans to progress."[112] But it was not only because they possessed education that Du Bois placed African Americans in the vanguard; he also believed they possessed superior Western culture. That assumption was behind his support for trusteeship, even as late as the 1945 Harlem Colonial Conference. But after seeing the U.S. government's behavior in the first half-decade after the war, he no longer believed in the culture's absolute superiority. So although he appreciated the West's technological superiority and its raw power to create a better material life for its inhabitants, he embraced African culture and hoped that socialism and Africa, with its communal heritage, could show the world the way to a better society.

Rayford Logan had no such crisis of convictions, and he stood pat on his previous opinions on Africa. The CAA called for independence and self-government for Africa in 1949. Logan was convinced that Africa still needed a period of years, perhaps even decades, of tutelage before it was ready for independence.[113] When Logan went on his Fulbright to Paris in 1951, he was enthused about the French government's plan to give limited representation to its African colonies in the National Assembly; it appeared to him that the country was returning to its pre–World War I policy of assimilating Africans into French society.[114] He was disabused of this notion only when he came into contact with African students in Paris who jeered Blaise Diagne—the Senegalese politician who had supported assimilation early in the twentieth century and who for Logan was still a symbol of Pan-Africanism—as the African equivalent of an Uncle Tom.[115]

Derision of the students aside, Logan's favorable disposition toward French policy was consistent with his earlier admiration of the French *mission civilatrice* and the convictions of the majority of the francophone African politicians. Unlike their counterparts who lived under British rule, sub-Saharan Africans under French colonialism did not adopt the goal of independence until the mid- to late 1950s. It was only with the commencement of the Algerian revolution and the defeat of the French forces in Vietnam in 1954, the independence of Morocco and Tunisia in 1956, and the advance of nationalism in British Africa that independence movements really took hold in francophone Africa.[116]

Politically, Pan-Africanism was passing Logan by. In April 1955, newly independent African and Asian countries met in Bandung, Indonesia, to consider a common response to racism and colonialism; it was an occasion that Logan had proposed ten years earlier. Now, however, Logan had mixed feelings about the gathering, wondering whether within the concept of Afro-Asian solidarity lay seeds for a worldwide race war. While he viewed these countries' grievances as legitimate, his main concern was that the United States respond favorably to them in order to check Soviet advances in the Third World.[117] In 1956 he wondered whether Africa was moving too fast toward independence,[118] although he quoted a Nigerian, with a bare hint of sadness, as saying that "Europeans are not going to be able to stop the movement toward self-government in Africa. Africans themselves are not going to be able to stop it." His statement was also a warning to the United States to come to terms with an independent Africa, lest the emerging countries abandon it and turn toward the Soviet Union.[119]

Spiritually and culturally, too, Pan-Africanism sped past Logan. In 1953 Logan toured francophone Africa on a State Department grant to continue his study of French colonial administration; self-government was inevitable, he told the State Department, and he wanted to see how prepared the Africans were.[120] Upon his arrival he realized how out of step with Africa he was:

> My trip to West Africa in the summer of 1953 convinced me that the more I knew about "The Dark Continent" the less likely I would participate in a revival of "Black Nationalism" . . . I am more interested in my Wittingham ancestry than in my African forbearers. . . .
>
> When I landed at Dakar, I felt no great kinship to Africa as did Du Bois when he arrived in Monrovia at the end of 1953 [sic] as Envoy Extraordinary and Minister Plenipotentiary of the United States for the inauguration of the President of Liberia.[121]

Logan visited the colonial legislature in Ivory Coast and was suitably impressed with the parliamentary abilities of the African delegates, which, he concluded, was a result of French influence. In fact, the Africans most qualified to lead the independence movement were products of the *mission civilatrice;* they were assimilated and, Logan believed, even thought of themselves as French.[122]

Perhaps the defining moment of his entire sojourn occurred after a sumptuous dinner given in his honor by the governor of Ivory Coast. (Logan habitually noted in his diary menus of important dinner engagements. In this case he wrote, "scotch and soda preceded an excellent dinner with a white wine, red wine, champagne and coffee."[123] A bit of France in Africa!) During an extended discussion of African politics, in which all present seemed to agree that Gold Coast, which in four years was to become independent Ghana, was moving too quickly, Logan volunteered a bit of his personal history as a Pan-Africanist in Paris:

> The guests were agreeably surprised to learn that I had known Blaise Diagne and that one of my favorite spots in Paris was the Rond-Point corner of Champs Elysees where I frequently stopped and asked myself: "What would Africa be without all this?" (meaning the influence of French civilization).[124]

Superiority of the ways of the West was an article of faith for Rayford Logan. He urged those sympathetic to the cause of the emerging African nations not "to substitute a romantic revision of the past, an uncritical denunciation of the 'evils of colonialism,' . . . for the once widely accepted concept of the inherent inferiority of Negroes. . . ."[125] For all his criticism of Western policy toward Africa and Western treatment of black people, Logan believed deeply that "the best interests of most Africans are consonant with the best interests of the Western World."[126]

On a political level, Logan's views on Africa, U.S. foreign policy, the Cold War, and McCarthyism can best be described as maverick. He had always been unafraid of the opinions of others, as his time at Virginia Union and in Atlanta show; likewise, for all his emphasis on the need to organize African Americans, he often chafed at the restrictions imposed by organizations, as his often embattled tenure as an AΦA official illustrates. The postwar era was no different. He owed allegiance to no organization and so had the luxury of speaking his mind. At the same time, it was the luxury of a man on the margins. His critique of U.S. and, more generally, Western, foreign policy was trenchant. But because the government and policymakers ignored his scholarship and because no African-American organization championed him, he left a rich intellectual legacy without, it appears, having left a visible imprint on historic events.

chapter eight

THE GOLDEN YEARS

Howard University

❧

(1938–1968)

I N MID-APRIL 1938 Howard University offered Rayford Logan an
appointment to its Department of History at an annual salary of four
thousand dollars. After thinking on it for about a week, Logan accepted. He finished out the semester at Atlanta University, where he
headed the history department, sold his household goods, packed his
remaining belongings, and moved with his wife, Ruth, back to Washington, D.C., at the end of June.[1]

The university Logan left was certainly an excellent one. It had an
outstanding roster of scholars: W. E. B. Du Bois and Ira DeA. Reid in
sociology, Mercer Cook in Romance languages, Frank Snowden in classics, and William Dean in economics. But Atlanta lacked important benefits like sabbatical leave, tenure, and a retirement plan.[2] Furthermore John
Hope, the school's great president, had died in 1936. His autocratic
manner was partially offset by his vision and his commitment to both civil
rights and serious scholarship. His successor, Rufus Clement, apparently
lacked Hope's broad scope, and this made following marching orders
intolerable for some faculty; if they had chafed under Hope, at least they
had the satisfaction of knowing where they were marching. Other faculty
apparently were content still to follow, even if this meant walking in
circles. How Logan felt about this situation is best captured in a letter he
received from his good friend Ira Reid, whom he left behind. Reid was

frustrated by the passivity exhibited by most of his colleagues. His "muted but revered coworkers" were like a herd of cattle, and their "one motto seems to be 'where they drive me I will follow.'"[3]

Living in the South, too, had taken its toll on Logan. The red scare in 1934–35 surrounding the Angelo Herndon case had intensified the already rigid caste structure in Atlanta and convinced Logan to stay away from all but a handful of southern whites, like Arthur Raper, the sympathetic white academic and member of the Commission on Interracial Cooperation. He even refused to see the agent for the Metropolitan Life Insurance Company, whose practice was to collect premium payments in person. "Although your particular agent seems to be courteous, . . ." he wrote to the company, "I have a definite policy of avoiding as much as possible any contact with southern white people." His solution, which the company reluctantly accepted, was to have a Metropolitan agent visit his mother's home in Washington to receive payment.[4]

Atlanta's suffocating racial climate limited the social activities available to African Americans. Logan rarely went to the movies or the theater because he could not stomach sitting in the "crow's nest," the segregated balcony. Except for the infrequent teas sponsored by the faculty wives and a monthly salon for "intellectual discussions," the principal diversion for an Atlanta University male faculty member was small-stakes poker.[5] Logan was apparently a center of attention, and he could get quite animated at these stag events. John Hope Franklin, who was in 1938 still a graduate student, remembers visiting Logan in Atlanta just prior to his move to Washington; he was astonished to find Logan, Ira Reid, and William Dean hunched over a phonograph trying to learn Ella Fitzgerald's rendition of "A Tisket, a Tasket." Franklin already knew all the words, "and as Rayford and the others listened admiringly, I sang it along with Ms. Fitzgerald and Chick Webb's orchestra!"[6]

Logan's ten years in the South (five each at Virginia Union and Atlanta, separated by graduate school) were the dues that he thought every African-American teacher should pay. But Logan had had enough. Ruth left no record of how she felt about leaving the Deep South. We have only her husband's recollection of her feelings: "My wife, like many other good wives, went where her husband went and what was good for me was good for her."[7] Logan, however, was ecstatic. He was a recognized scholar now, and his appointment to Howard, the "capstone of Negro education," was a statement that he had arrived.

Soon after Logan joined the Howard faculty, he articulated his views on higher education for African Americans and its relation to opportunity for advancement in the national life. The specific question he addressed in his 1939 commencement speech at Miner Teachers College, the Washington, D.C., segregated public college, was whether African Americans ought to press for admission to the predominantly white southern graduate and professional schools—the Supreme Court had recently affirmed this right—or establish separate schools of their own.

Integration was a noble goal, he told the graduates, but it should not be pursued mechanically. The Supreme Court's 1938 *Gaines* decision would benefit only a minuscule number of African-American college graduates who were able to get into white professional schools.[8] "Integration in this instance would mean the application of principles that would result in an aristocracy of colored graduate students. . . ." Taking his cue from W. E. B. Du Bois, who in 1934 advocated voluntary segregation—separate equality—as a way for African Americans to shelter themselves from the oppression of whites while husbanding their community resources, Logan argued that "segregation would result in a more democratic opportunity for a considerable number" of college graduate students; far more African Americans would be able to attend and graduate from black graduate programs than from white public universities. "Since I believe in democracy of education at all levels, I favor the solution of this problem that will produce the largest number of well-trained graduate students," he said.[9]

Separate graduate programs would create job opportunities for their graduates. One of the impediments to a quality higher education for African Americans was the shortage of trained scholars to populate the black college faculty. Logan argued that while the most gifted African Americans in the border states ought to enroll in the white graduate programs whose costs to duplicate were prohibitive, in the Deep South African Americans should establish separate programs and staff them with trained black faculty.[10] Logan argued this point in his speech:

> As I told a group of students in 1933, a Communist revolution may eventually solve all of our problems, but I want some Negroes to be alive when that revolution comes. Integration may, and I devoutly hope that it will, be the ultimate pattern of American society. But I want us to be integrated as healthy, well-educated, American citizens earning a decent living, rather than, in the words of one observer, as a "race of public reliefers."[11]

Some African Americans objected to this strategy, claiming that because the schools would not have adequate funding, they would be farces.

Nevertheless, Logan defended the building of able institutions of higher learning as a courageous attempt by African Americans to achieve racial liberation by their own efforts:

> Today the colored graduate schools would be a farce, if you insist. But what of tomorrow? Are we building for today or for future generations? Suppose that Myrtilla Miner had been discouraged . . . because her idea of education for herself and for free colored girls was a farce? When on December 3, 1851, she opened a normal school in a small apartment with six colored girls, her normal school was a farce. But that farce is the grandparent of Miner Teachers College. Miner Teachers College is what it is today because of what Miner Normal School was not in 1851 and in 1853.[12]

Logan delivered this speech at the end of his first year of teaching at Howard. The first flush of pride of teaching at Afro-America's premier institution of higher learning had not yet faded. Not only was he happy to be back in the city of his youth and to be rescued from his years of southern exile, he was still enamored of Howard University and especially the promise of Negro education.

In fact, Howard University was in many respects an exception to the mediocrity of African-American higher education. Its financial condition and physical plant were far and away superior to every other African-American institution. In 1928, Mordecai Johnson, who had been installed as Howard's first African-American president two years previously, succeeded in securing a law that authorized an annual appropriation from Congress. Even during the Depression, which hit Howard hard, the university was able to stabilize faculty and staff salaries, develop a rudimentary building plan, and streamline and improve its schools of law, medicine, and dentistry.[13]

By contrast, Marie Wood, a colleague of Logan's at an Alabama college, wrote to Logan of the conditions she faced in her school:

> But honestly and truly, Dr. Logan, I am not lying when I tell you that the showers have not been cleaned since school opened. The toilets are still filthy. . . . I have not had a bath or shower since I have been here because I feel dirtier when I leave the shower than I did before entering.[14]

Howard's relative wealth (and the principles of Mordecai Johnson) also allowed it to avoid other ills of the benighted black colleges like dilapidated faculty housing, tasteless faculty meals of dubious nutritional value, official profiteering on textbook concessions, and the "president's 'borrowing' money from a new, untenured faculty member and not repaying it."[15]

Howard was also atypical in that it fostered a critical atmosphere among its faculty. Indeed, the core of Howard's faculty in the 1930s and 1940s not only was the best of any African-American college, it also rivaled some of the best white universities'. Alain Locke (philosophy), Ralph Bunche (political science), Eric Williams (social sciences), Abram Harris (economics), E. Franklin Frazier (sociology), Sterling Brown (English), Charles H. Wesley and John Hope Franklin (history), and E. E. Just (biology) were some of the top scholars in their respective fields. William Hastie and Charles Hamilton Houston in the law school were training a sizable cadre of civil rights lawyers who would figure prominently in the legal challenges to segregation into the 1950s. Charles Thompson of the College of Education founded the *Journal of Negro Education,* which focused on the public policy of segregation. Until its founding in 1932, policy research was the exclusive preserve of white academics. According to the historian Michael R. Winston, "For many years the *Journal* was the best single source of information about the status of segregated schools and shifts in the legal strategies adopted to destroy segregation. . . ." Because African-American scholars were generally ignored by the predominantly white academic journals of their day, the *Journal of Negro Education* published articles that were strictly speaking outside the discipline of education and provided an outlet for Logan, Du Bois, Bunche, Sterling Brown, and many others.[16]

Howard University successfully sidestepped the extreme penury visited upon its less fortunate cousins, but it could not avoid altogether the debilitating effects of segregation and the resultant negative traditions of the African-American college. President Mordecai Johnson was widely regarded as something of a dictator, and he made many enemies among the faculty, alumni, and trustees. By the time Logan arrived in 1938, Johnson had already warred with the venerable Kelly Miller, who was a major figure in the country's black establishment and dean of Howard's College of Liberal Arts; the university secretary-treasurer Emmett J. Scott, who had previously been Booker T. Washington's personal secretary; and with various trustees and the alumni association.

Miller and Scott were prominent persons in their own right; each had strong views on how the university should be run, and neither was used to being ordered around. Johnson accused Scott of overreaching his official functions and tried unsuccessfully to have him removed from the board of trustees. The General Alumni Association tried to have Johnson removed from office; it charged him with favoritism in awarding university contracts and with trying to stifle their input into charting the school's direction; it further claimed that Johnson's contentiousness and hunger for power were directly responsible for the university losing the services of solid professors like the linguist Lorenzo Turner and the distinguished educator Dwight O. W. Holmes, the former dean of the Graduate School, who left to become president of Morgan State College. The faculty disliked Johnson because he insisted that they follow his moral prescriptions and because he liked to flaunt his control over them in the area of salaries. For example, E. E. Just had a $2,500 grant from the Rosenwald Fund that was for his scientific work independent of Howard; Johnson tried to get this grant counted as part of Just's salary as a way to reduce the university's expenses.[17]

Yet Mordecai Johnson was no P. T. Wimbush, the fictional black college president in J. Saunders Redding's *Stranger and Alone*. The charges leveled against Johnson for manipulation and megalomania are too numerous to dismiss, but a more accurate characterization of him would be "enlightened despot." Mordecai Johnson had a vision of building Howard into a top-rank university, not a good university for African Americans only. His plan for excellence collided with both those who chafed at his monopolization of power and those administrators and faculty who were comfortably ensconced in mediocrity. He ousted the dean of the College of Dentistry when he refused to cooperate in a plan that would have benefited the entire school because it required him to surrender some of his authority.[18] His 1930 clash with James Cobb, the vice-dean of Howard's law school, coincided with the hiring of Charles Houston. Johnson wanted a law school that would produce not merely competent African-American lawyers but a legal cadre that could direct a protracted battle for legal equality and against segregation. Under Houston, the law school became exactly that kind of institution.[19]

Mordecai Johnson also distinguished himself in his forthright attitude toward contemporary social issues. In the early years of the Depression he said he believed the Soviet Union was doing a better job of ridding itself of poverty than was the United States. He denounced the persecution of Communists in the United States: he was no Communist, he said, but the way to meet the challenge posed by them was by the articulation "on our own soil" of a social vision "no less splendid [than communism] and which can arouse the wholehearted allegiance of our citizens."[20] Strong statements like this, plus a vigorous defense against government encroachment on academic freedom and considerable oratorical skill, earned Johnson the respect and loyalty of the faculty, which otherwise might have mutinied against his despotic side.[21]

Johnson maintained his courage even during the McCarthy era. When, in 1953, as in 1942, Howard University became a target for an FBI investigation, he publicly denounced the witch-hunt.[22] In 1958, he invited W. E. B. Du Bois to speak at Howard. When the American Legion issued unspecified public threats against the university, Johnson's advisers—including Logan—suggested that he explain that neither he nor Howard subscribed to Du Bois's radicalism, but that a university's job was to educate, even if that meant presenting unpopular ideas. Johnson brushed aside such advice and refused to be baited by the Legion. He conspicuously took a seat in the front of the auditorium, while Logan sat on the podium and introduced Du Bois.[23]

But back in 1938, when Logan first came to Howard, Logan would not have been accorded that honor, much less have been in a position to advise the president of the university. Faculty reaction to Logan's appointment was tepid, and Harold Lewis, a historian of Europe and a colleague of Logan's in the Howard history department, acknowledged a detectable level of hostility toward him upon his arrival. Among the most wary of Logan were Ralph Bunche, E. Franklin Frazier, and Abram Harris, three of Howard's most accomplished professors.[24]

One reason for Bunche's, Harris's, and Frazier's lack of enthusiasm was political disagreements with Logan. In the late 1930s and early 1940s, the three were often joined by Eric Williams in what Logan sometimes called a Marxist clique. If this was not an entirely accurate description, it was nevertheless true that this group emphasized the role of class in society, and Ralph Bunche was particularly outspoken in his critique both of American class society and African-American racial advancement organizations. Logan believed that race was the principal determinant in American and world society. The "triumvirate," as some called them, apparently did not want another bourgeois nationalist to grace Howard's faculty.[25]

One arena where these differences were debated was the annual conference sponsored by the Division of Social Sciences. These multiday meetings were an opportunity for Howard professors and other interested scholars to explore historical and contemporary topics like the Negro in the Americas (1940), the prospects for a federation of independent Caribbean islands (1943), trust and non-self-governing territories (1947), academic freedom and McCarthyism (1953), and "The New Negro Thirty Years Afterward" (1955), which was a retrospective look at Alain Locke's contribution to the Harlem Renaissance.[26] At the 1941 conference, which reprised the previous year's, Logan's differences with Bunche came out clearly. Over the two days, the debate focused on the relative importance of race and economics in history and politics. Bunche was still something of a radical, and he refused to inject the issue of race into discussions of social justice.[27] Nationalism had no real power to improve the conditions of people's lives, he felt, and during one session he asked "whether independence for the Caribbean islands would mean improvement in the standard of living when one considers Haiti and the Dominican Republic." Clearly, Bunche thought, Logan placed too much emphasis on race. Logan's reply was equally to the point. He said that

> under white domination, Negroes were in misery and poverty under colonialism, [but] that under Negro domination, they *might* be in misery and poverty but would be independent, that there would thus be a reduction in the area in which white was a badge of supremacy.[28]

Antipathy toward Bunche was also fueled by a growing feeling among some leading African-American intellectuals that, despite his rhetoric, he was turning into an Uncle Tom. As a government expert during the war on dependent areas affairs, Bunche developed policy within the constraints of the United States' overall foreign policy objectives. By the mid-1940s, this meant that the United States would not challenge Britain's and France's colonial empires and that individual countries and not an international authority would administer trust territories after the war. On the issue of mandates, Bunche wrote a position paper in 1945 that justified the return to Italy of its former African colonies of Eritrea, Libya, and Somaliland in the form of a UN trusteeship.[29]

Whether or not Bunche was merely following instructions from superiors, his actions troubled other African-American intellectuals who saw a severe disjunction between Bunche's words and deeds. W. E. B. Du Bois told Logan just before a meeting of the Encyclopedia of the Negro project that he believed that "Ralph Bunche is getting to be a white folks' 'nigger.'"[30] Arthur P. Davis, Logan's old friend and colleague from the

English department who was not an active participant in Howard's political life, commented on Bunche's ability to hide his service to the establishment behind militant rhetoric. He said that "there were 'bandanna-handkerchief-headed Negroes, and silk-handkerchief-headed Negroes, but Ralph is a cellophane-handkerchief-headed Negro—you have to get off at a certain angle to see him.' "[31]

If faculty spats were partly political in nature, they also had elements of personal rivalry.[32] Harold Lewis recalled that Logan was never invited to the gatherings of the left-wing faculty that Lewis had attended in the late 1930s and early 1940s. Michael R. Winston related that Logan thought Bunche, Frazier, and Harris thought that he, Logan, was an intellectual lightweight.[33] Logan, himself a prickly person, alluded to the jealousy that seemed to pervade Howard's faculty in a discussion about his friend Charles Wesley, who brought him to Howard: "My own opinion of Wesley," Logan wrote in his diary in 1941, "is that he was first of all big enough to bring into the department a potential rival."[34] "He has been the least jealous of those with whom I have had to compete in educational circles," he wrote of Wesley five years later.[35] Logan was lucky to have a friend like Wesley, for the competition at Howard was intense, and often fierce, compounded as it was by the racist nature of American society and the world of higher education. John Hope Franklin observed in 1948 that

> the world of scholarship in America is a mirror of the state of race relations generally. . . . The Negro scholar is in a position not unlike that of Ralph Ellison's Invisible Man; he is a "fantasy," as James Baldwin puts it, "in the mind of the republic." . . .
>
> The world of the Negro scholar is indescribably lonely, and he must, somehow, pursue truth down that lonely path while, at the same time, making certain that his conclusions are sanctioned by universal standards developed and maintained by those who frequently do not even recognize him.[36]

Academic apartheid placed the African-American scholars at Howard and elsewhere in a severe bind until the 1950s. Confined to so-called Negro disciplines (Negro history, Negro sociology, Negro literature) and otherwise ignored by the academy, scholars like Logan produced outstanding scholarship. Logan, like others, knew that race was the sole reason for their lack of recognition, yet they emulated the institutions and associations that excluded them. It wasn't until the 1960s that Sterling Brown read his poetry at Howard because of "a reluctance on the part of some conservative faculty members to appreciate a professor who knew the blues, jazz, and barrel house songs and felt as equally at home with Leadbelly as he did with Ralph Bunche."[37] With little chance for recognition outside the confines of the African-American analogues to the predominantly white professional associations, Howard University evolved several methods for apportioning status to its faculty.

Faculty and administration squabbles were legion and involved an array of seemingly petty issues. John Hope Franklin recalled faculty meetings that ended up in storms of recrimination and accusation because conflicting schedules made it impossible to satisfy everyone in setting dates for future meetings or other activities; a professor, for example, would accuse others of purposely sabotaging his or her work if they scheduled functions when he or she was unable to attend. The victims of stunted careers vented their frustrations on each other.[38] The ubiquitous politicking often supplanted scholarship as the yardstick of accomplishment.

Logan maneuvered well in this milieu. After he became head of the history department upon Charles Wesley's departure for the presidency of Wilberforce University in 1942, he had several confrontations with some of his colleagues concerning the allocation of office supplies, who would get a telephone line in his or her office and how quickly, and whose correspondence would be typed and in what order. Logan could be brutal toward others. Borrowing a page from Mordecai Johnson, Logan exercised his prerogative to determine who would get to teach summer school (and earn dearly needed cash) to reward his friends and punish his rivals and colleagues with whom he did not get on well.[39]

A more insidious measure of merit was the attention that African-American Howard professors received from white academics. In January 1940 Dr. Mary Wilhemine Williams of Goucher College in Baltimore invited Logan, on behalf of the American Historical Association (AHA), to present a paper at the association's annual convention in New York City the following December. The association had never had a panel entirely devoted to Negro history, and since 1909, when Du Bois last addressed the AHA, Monroe Work had been the only African American to appear on the program.[40] If Logan could not give the paper, Williams wrote, he should recommend someone equally competent: "I think that it is very important that the person who presents a paper at New York should be a Negro whose training is not at all open to question, as well as that his paper should be high class."[41]

Logan eagerly accepted the offer and recommended that the panel also include Charles Wesley and W. E. B. Du Bois. Williams agreed. Logan would present a paper on the colonization movement, which took final shape as his *Phylon* article "Some New Interpretations of the Colonization Movement."[42] He, too, was concerned about the quality of the African American who would join him on the podium. "I naturally want us to be represented in such a way that the invitation, as you say, will remain open for the future," Logan wrote to Williams. To Wesley, he was a bit more blunt: "I think that you will agree with me that, quite modestly, we can not be too careful in the selection of some one to represent us." As the program jelled, Logan was even more explicit. "May I add that I feel that it might not be advisable to have too many of us on the first program," he once again wrote to Williams.[43] She apparently agreed, for she told Logan that only those "Negro historians, of whom white historians think well," would be allowed to appear on AHA panels.[44]

The program in December, according to Logan, went splendidly.[45] Du Bois chaired the panel, which included Wesley and Logan and one white presenter ("to prevent any suggestion of race segregation in historical scholarship," said Williams).[46] About one hundred people were in the audience, including six African Americans. "Dr. Du Bois, in opening, said: 'For the first time in the fifty-five years of the Association, an entire session is being devoted to the Negro. This indicates slow but steady progress." Mordecai Johnson later congratulated Logan on his participation in the AHA meeting. "It is this sort of solid work which will gradually gain for Howard University the kind of substantial esteem which we seek," he wrote.[47] Despite the "steady progress" and the anticipated esteem, Logan utilized his participation in the AHA program not to expand the opportunities for African-American historians, but to limit them to the very few whom he deemed qualified.[48]

Logan was on the receiving end of this slavish deference to white academia in 1947 when Mordecai Johnson and the Howard trustees established a new salary scale. In October of that year Charles Thompson, the dean of the Graduate School, informed Logan that Johnson had created a new category of professor—the "super-duper" level—which paid six thousand dollars annually. He further informed Logan that only three professors were to be promoted to this plateau: E. Franklin Frazier, Alain Locke, and Sterling Brown. Furious, Logan went to J. St. Clair Price, the dean of the College of Liberal Arts, and demanded an explanation.

Price told Logan that the rationale behind super-duper professors was to reward those who had taught at white universities. It all started with Frazier, who had apparently been offered an appointment at New York University at a salary of six thousand dollars. Mordecai Johnson was compelled to match the offer. Locke had also taught at white schools during the summer, as had Brown, who had also been offered, and had refused, a position at Vassar in 1945; both these men were elevated to the top rank, too.[49]

Logan's visceral reaction was to resign—but he did not because, he thought, that would have pleased his faculty nemeses.[50] Instead, he detailed his influence among whites—academics and ordinary citizens alike—in a letter to Dean Price.[51] Logan told Price that the African-American sociologist Dr. Ira DeA. Reid, who the previous year had been a visiting professor at New York University, wanted to know whether Logan would be interested in succeeding him in that position. (Logan was not interested because of his commitment to certain research projects at Howard.) "Of course," Logan wrote, "there is no certainty that I would have been appointed, but I doubt that Dr. Reid would have made the inquiry unless he believed that I should have been." He also mentioned his summer 1947 speaking tour on behalf of the American Friends Service Committee. "You will, therefore, be interested to know that I lectured to audiences totalling several thousand, practically all of whom were white," on campuses of several major white universities.

Now that he was the aggrieved party, Logan began to see the injustice of judging Howard professors solely on their contacts with white schools. He claimed that his *Diplomatic Relations of the United States with Haiti, 1776–1891* was "the most scholarly book written by any professor at Howard University." He then listed more than a dozen of his former master's students who had gone on to successful academic careers, either taking the doctorate at prestigious northern universities or teaching in southern black colleges, or both. "Not only do all these students state that they have been most influenced by me, but [nearly] all of them . . . owe their jobs to me." Logan's complaints had an effect: he was awarded a promotion and a higher salary.

He took a personal interest in his students. Not only did he help them get jobs, he also helped some with their personal problems. William Willis, Jr., who went on to become an anthropologist and the first African-American professor at Southern Methodist University, suffered from severe homesickness during his first two years at Howard. His mother wrote to Logan and asked him to help her son, because she knew that Logan took an interest in him.[52] Another student unburdened herself in a letter to Logan. "Don't think I'm crazy for telling you all this," she concluded, "but as you perhaps know by now, you are my only dependable confidant in Washington. I had to get it out or bust!"[53]

In matters of the educational experience at Howard, Logan put aside the philistinism and elitism that characterized his faculty and administrative politicking. He was committed to providing his students with an education that would at once be broad-minded and prepare students for careers in which they could serve both their race and the United States. But by the late 1940s, Logan's faith was shaken in the ability of Howard—indeed all of African-American higher education—to deliver on this promise.

One reason for his disillusionment was the chronic warfare with Mordecai Johnson and the Howard administration. The administration was selfish and willing to sacrifice the quality of education in order to maintain its own level of comfort, he thought. In 1949, when the university faced budget difficulties, the administration threatened to cut faculty salaries.[54] While Howard did not lower salaries, it did dismiss thirty teachers that year, and Mordecai Johnson laid off nineteen more in 1950. Simultaneously, administrators received hefty pay raises and had their staffs augmented with new secretarial and clerical help. Logan was also critical of Johnson's neglect of the university's College of Liberal Arts in his determination to bolster the medical school.[55]

Logan was therefore astonished when Mordecai Johnson proposed—in the midst of draconian faculty cuts—to institute graduate programs leading to the doctorate. Johnson apparently felt that the only way that Howard would be recognized as a great university was for it to grant the Ph.D. In February 1950 he established a Committee on the Ph.D. Degree, which was composed of select members of the Graduate Council. Logan, who was on this committee, believed that such a program would end in one of two debacles. Either it would further damage the quality of the existing undergraduate and master's programs by diverting critical resources from them, or it would gain, and deservedly so, a reputation as a lightweight program. In all likelihood, both would befall any department that offered the Ph.D. before it could adequately support a solid undergraduate and master's curriculum.[56]

Johnson acquiesced and the matter was put to rest until 1954. In May of that year, the Supreme Court, in *Brown* v. *Board of Education of Topeka,* outlawed school segregation and declared dead the separate-but-equal doctrine. Johnson's dilemma of keeping budget cuts from permanently scarring the university was compounded by the *Brown* decision. He now had to scramble "to prepare Howard University to meet the situation resulting from the Supreme Court decisions. . . ."[57] But for some time Logan and others on the history faculty believed that the quality of the graduate students had declined and that the university cared little. John Hope Franklin captured this sentiment best in a letter to Logan:

> It is my impression that the graduate students this year are almost uniformly poor. The history dept. enrollment is so low that I shall offer my Civil War and Reconst. at 5:30 next quarter in the effort to catch some of the many people who drift to other institutions because of the scant offerings at Howard next quarter.[58]

In July 1954 Johnson decided—over the strenuous objections of Logan, E. Franklin Frazier, and others—to institute a Ph.D. program at Howard as a way of coping with desegregation, but the river of faculty resentment ran so deep that it took Johnson until January 25, 1955, to put down the rebellion and get the board of trustees to approve his plan. Among the faculty, Logan reported his ally Frazier as commenting, "all those interested in scholarship voted with us." The debate was acrimonious, and at times intensely personal. Logan accused Johnson of having "less interest in building up an educational institution than he has in demonstrating his ability to outwit any and all opposition." Johnson told a meeting that Logan's and Frazier's opposition to the Ph.D. program was "both non-intelligent and not honorable." Frazier then stormed out of the meeting; Logan retorted by claiming that Johnson's assertions were "neither intelligent nor honorable" and then resigning from the Committee on the Ph.D. "I do not permit anyone, not even the President of the University, to impugn my honor," he wrote in his letter of resignation.[59]

In February 1955, shortly after the conclusion of the Ph.D. bloodletting, Logan suffered a mild heart attack. His physician felt that this last protracted encounter with Mordecai Johnson was a major contributor to the attack. Referring to Mordecai Johnson, Logan recorded in his diary that "the son of a bitch would be perfectly capable of gloating if I were to die of a heart attack which could be attributed in part to his insulting attack on me." He also recorded the names of others whom Johnson had allegedly persecuted into ill health.[60]

As he lay in hospital Logan made some important decisions. Should he die, he forbade his funeral to be held in the Rankin Memorial Chapel on the Howard campus; he also wanted to prevent President Johnson from taking any part in his funeral. He further decided that his diaries, which contained strident criticism and opinion of Howard, would not be deposited at the university; instead they would go to the Library of Congress, beyond the reach of Johnson and the Howard administration.[61]

But the heart attack put him in a reflective mood, too. The struggle over the Ph.D. had taken its toll. Logan could still fight, but he could never be the firebrand he once was.

> I am sorry that "Papa" (Ruth's favorite name for me) had to sit on the side lines. Now that I am virtually *hors de combat*, I am inclined to rate more highly my younger days at Virginia Union and Atlanta when, like Sir Galahad, I sallied forth to slay the dragons. I made mistakes, was impulsive, and all that sort of thing. But I rather wish that I were young in this fight at Howard.[62]

Yet Logan's health was not the only casualty. So was his belief in African-American education. Howard University was now condemned forever to being a second-rate institution. The desegregation of higher education now made it possible for the best African-American students to attend the best public universities in the country. The only students who would enroll at Howard were ones of inferior caliber, he thought. By the same token, "it is likely that more of our best scholars will, in the future leave permanently or temporarily to teach at other [i.e., white] institutions and that they will be replaced by less mature and less capable teachers and scholars. . . . The burden upon those who remain becomes heavier," he told a Princeton University conference in 1956.[63]

In 1962, the board of trustees approved the Department of History to offer a Ph.D. program,[64] and in 1964, the department awarded its first Ph.D. The candidate, according to one of the members of the Ph.D. committee, was thoroughly unprepared. His comprehensive exam was unsatisfactory, his dissertation "abysmal." When the committee member made known his intentions not to pass the candidate, Logan called him aside and told him "not to cross me." Logan wanted to grant the degree. To the member's criticism that the candidate was unqualified, Logan heatedly replied that "this is not the Ph.D. of the type you get from Amherst and Harvard. This is a black Ph.D."[65] Logan's cynicism and cravenness can be measured by the fact that he almost never used "black" to describe Negroes, and when he did employ this term, he did so in a mocking fashion.[66]

With the elimination of most legal barriers that prevented African Americans from attending prestigious public universities, Logan could not imagine that any talented African American would choose a Howard graduate education. Frustrated by the caliber of the graduate program—and by the fact that he was stuck in it rather than teaching at a prestigious white university—Logan finally had decided that graduate education for the doctorate at an African-American college *would* forever be a farce.

The demands of teaching, the distraction of university politics, and participation in race politics may have prevented Logan from concentrating more of his time and intellectual energy upon his scholarly researches.[67] Still Logan managed to write, in addition to at least a dozen scholarly articles, a prodigious number of monographs between 1938 and 1960. In 1941 he revised his dissertation, which the University of North Carolina Press published. *What the Negro Wants* was issued in 1944. In 1945 he published *The Negro and the Post-War World: A Primer* and researched, wrote, and published by himself *The Senate and the Versailles Mandate System,* which was a preliminary volume to his 1948 *The African Mandates in World Politics.* The year 1957 saw the publication of *The Negro in the United States,* a slender textbook that included primary documents and covered African-American history from the arrival of the first Africans in North America to the Cold War.[68]

In addition to this scholarship, Logan also became the director of the Association for the Study of Negro Life and History and editor of the *Journal of Negro History* in May 1950, following the death of Carter G. Woodson, the association's founder, on April 3. The new position was something of a new departure for Logan, for he and Woodson had parted ways in 1936 when he went to work on Du Bois's Encyclopedia of the Negro project; rather suddenly, mention of his name had disappeared from ASNLH publications, including the *Negro History Bulletin,* the association's monthly magazine designed to popularize the teaching of black history in the public schools. The two did not reconcile until the mid-1940s.[69]

Logan apparently was not the first choice to succeed Woodson. Luther

Porter Jackson, the venerable historian from Virginia State College, was first choice.[70] During his scholarly career, Jackson had done pioneering research on Negroes in Virginia, had raised funds for the ASNLH, and was prominent in a variety of civil rights activities in his state, especially voter registration and the NAACP-led teacher-salary equalization campaigns.[71] But just nine days after Woodson's death, Jackson, too, suddenly died. (April 1950 was especially cruel to the cause of black equality, with death also claiming Charles H. Drew and Charles H. Houston.)

Several leading members of the ASNLH believed that a professional historian should succeed Woodson as director, and Mary McLeod Bethune, the organization's president—Woodson always insisted that the ASNLH prominently include lay people in its leadership—tapped Logan.[72] It must not have been an easy choice, for the candidates also included Charles H. Wesley and John Hope Franklin. It is not readily apparent why Wesley was not selected, but Franklin made it known that he would decline.[73] Perhaps Franklin sensed the controversy that was bound to explode when it came time to select an heir to the Woodson dynasty.[74]

His eighteen-month stewardship was, like many of his other endeavors, tempestuous yet productive. As Logan tried to advance the scholarly and educational agenda of the ASNLH, he found that eddies kept knocking him about. Woodson's associates who were not professional historians regarded Logan's return to the association with ambivalence. William Brewer, who worked for the segregated schools in Washington, D.C., and Louis Mehlinger, a District of Columbia attorney, were longtime officials of the ASNLH. While they initially welcomed him as a man of integrity, they also jealously guarded their turf and thought of Logan as an interloper.

Part of the friction concerned who was qualified to continue the Woodson legacy and what exactly it was. For Brewer, whom Logan characterized as a failed man bitter with the results of his life,[75] Woodson alone was at the apex of black history. Woodson was not only a pioneer, according to an essay by Brewer intended for the *Negro History Bulletin,* but a crusader for the glory of black achievement and against the corruption of that history by white philanthropists like Anson Phelps Stokes and projects like the Encyclopedia of the Negro. Unlike most other African-American historians in the field, Woodson maintained historical sweep and successfully avoided the ghettoization of the discipline.[76]

Logan and his professional colleagues, including John Hope Franklin and Lorenzo Greene, the distinguished black historian and a protégé of Woodson, disagreed with this interpretation. Echoing Logan's assessment, Franklin believed that Woodson, perhaps because he was a pioneer in the field, tended to treat historical evidence bearing upon black history un-critically, and said that "I can name, without disparaging Dr. Woodson, more than a half dozen Negro scholars in the field of history" who were more deft in their analysis. Brewer's emphasis on Woodson's conflict with Stokes and the Encyclopedia of the Negro overshadowed what in Frank-lin's opinion was Woodson's singular accomplishment: the establishment of an organization that popularized black history and bridged the gap between the scholar and the general public.[77] Brewer's view of Woodson and the ASNLH's history, while perhaps personally satisfying, would hobble the association in its two-fold job of popularizing Negro history and getting it accepted by the entire scholarly community. Greene con-curred and explained the disjunction between Brewer and the new asso-ciation director: "Brewer, because of his deep admiration for Woodson, probably feels that he is the true interpreter of the latter's philosophy," he wrote to Logan. "I sympathize with your position."[78]

The new director believed in the late founder's mandate that the ASNLH should uncover and promote blacks' contributions to world civilization. But he also felt that the study of Negro history ought not be defined exclusively in these terms. To Logan, anything that touched the lives of African Americans fell within the purview of Negro history. Under his editorship, the *Negro History Bulletin* followed the world politics of human rights, reported on the United Nations and Africa and the struggle against colonialism throughout the Third World; the *Bulletin* also became an outlet for "works in progress," as Logan's graduate students published abstracts of their researches on such topics as the development of vicious anti-Negro stereotypes in the northern popular press around the turn of the century.[79]

The *Journal of Negro History* was at its apex under Logan's direction due to a confluence of circumstances. There was the legacy of Woodson himself, who had insisted on a high quality of scholarship. A second condition was Logan's editorial skills: he had integrity, and he was metic-ulous, demanding, disciplined, and on time. A third factor was a renewed interest in the study of the African-American past, especially among white scholars. (There was a relative decline of interest on the part of black historians. Of the seven issues Logan edited, well over half of the research articles were written by whites; in some numbers—the ones for October 1950 and April 1951, for instance—all of the principal contributors were white.) The whites who began to study black history were infected with the optimism of the New Deal and were motivated by issues of social justice; the character of World War II as a struggle against ideologies of racial superiority was also a stimulus. The white historians were firmly integrationist—a stand consonant with Logan and his professional peers in the ASNLH—and they struggled to make visible the black past and place it in the context of American history. A fourth consideration was that in the first two years of the 1950s, as in the preceding decades, these historians perceived that mainstream scholarly publications were not interested in sustained researches in African-American history, so the *JNH* accrued the riches.[80]

Logan's expansive conception of the ASNLH's scholarly and educational tasks could not be effectively implemented within the framework propounded by Woodson's associates, and despite the high quality of the *NHB* and the *JNH*, the tensions between Logan and Brewer and Mehlinger continued to mount. But unfortunately, while the bedrock of the disagreement concerned principle, the battle itself looked like bickering.

When Logan assumed his new position, he immediately moved to cement his leadership. Knowing that Woodson had in the past run finances of the ASNLH in an informal manner, Logan ordered an outside audit, to be conducted by H. Councill Trenholm, an accountant, fellow fraternity brother, and president of Alabama State College; Trenholm discovered several fiscal irregularities. Logan then proposed that the ASNLH Constitution be amended to create the post of business manager, a move opposed by Brewer and Mehlinger, who was the association's secretary-treasurer. The three again tangled over who would control the Associated Publishers, which was owned by Woodson and which issued ASNLH monographs and actually was financially healthy. Woodson had willed a 95 percent interest in the publishers to the ASNLH, although it was to continue to be run by an independent board of directors; Logan, as the director of the new majority stockholder, struggled to keep control.[81]

The skirmishing continued at a low level through 1950, intensifying in mid-1950. That summer, Logan was awarded the Fulbright scholarship for the academic year 1951–52 to study in Paris the French colonial administration in Africa. He proposed to take a leave of absence from the ASNLH and to promote Williston Lofton, his colleague in the Howard history department, or John Hope Franklin to the position of acting director; he proposed that Adelaide James, one of his graduate students and a longtime administrator in the ASNLH, be given a responsible position in the *JNH* and *NHB*.[82]

His actions infuriated Mehlinger, who felt that Logan purposely kept the association board ignorant of his plans; he then proposed that Logan be removed from his post and replaced by Brewer.[83] Logan then resigned, only to be talked out of it by Charles Wesley; he would stick, he said, to his original plan of taking only a temporary leave.[84] But when the association's annual meeting refused to take his recommendations, and Brewer and Mehlinger apparently conspired to isolate Lofton and James in the organization and to block the adoption of the new position of business manager, Logan, who could not attend because he was in Paris, resigned his office—this time for good: "I hereby resign . . . ," he wrote to Charles Wesley about Brewer and Mehlinger. "It is impossible for me to be associated longer with a man who is a proved common liar and another who is notoriously mad."[85]

Logan did not reclaim his positions as association director and *JNH* editor when he returned to the United States, and he never again served the ASNLH in an official capacity. But he was persuaded to maintain ties with the organization by Lorenzo Greene. He and other professional historians had hoped in vain that what had started out as a dispute over Brewer's article on Woodson could be contained.[86] The conflict had mushroomed, though, and threatened to split the association. Greene asked Logan to be magnanimous and set aside his differences.[87] The reconciliation lasted until July 1955.

That summer a review of Logan's *The Negro in American Life and Thought: The Nadir, 1877–1901* appeared in the *JNH*. Written by a George Grimke from Augusta, Georgia, it was scathing, with a veiled accusation that Logan plagiarized C. Vann Woodward's *Reunion and Reaction*.[88] As he could find no trace of George Grimke in Augusta, Logan suspected, as did Charles Wesley (who had succeeded Mrs. Bethune as association president), that it was a pseudonym of William Brewer, who had replaced Logan as editor of the *JNH*. Logan pleaded with Wesley to force Brewer to own up to his deed and make the *Journal* print a retraction. He even asked Howard Long, a fraternity brother and one of his oldest friends who now served as an administrator under Wesley at Wilberforce University, to intercede. Wesley refused both requests, saying, according to Long, that Brewer had academic freedom and he could not force Brewer to reveal Grimke's true identity or to print a rejoinder from Logan.[89] The unfortunate result of this entire affair is that Logan boycotted the ASNLH for more than two decades, returning only in his last years, and broke off a longstanding friendship with Charles Wesley.[90]

The *JNH* review notwithstanding, *The Negro in American Life and Thought* was Logan's most celebrated work.[91] Logan began the project in 1947,[92] planning to write a comprehensive history of the decline of the status of African Americans as mirrored in presidential politics, public policy, judicial decisions, the growing intolerance of white mass organizations, and white popular culture. Logan assigned students in his 1947 graduate seminar the job of researching various aspects of this vast subject; these seminar papers became the foundations for master's theses, which Logan used as "the raw material for more complete analyses of the newspapers and magazines."[93]

Like nearly all of his intellectual productions, *The Nadir* was ensconced in controversy. He finished writing the book in late 1952 and submitted it to the University of North Carolina Press. This choice of publisher was most puzzling, despite the press's reputation as the premier house for books on blacks and race relations. The *What the Negro Wants* episode had left an indelible mark on Logan. He had accused the press of bad faith in its handling of *The African Mandates in World Politics* and gone so far as to publish it privately in an offset edition rather than seek another publisher. This time Lambert Davis, the new director of the UNC Press, rejected the manuscript. He liked the book—it was "generally satisfactory," he wrote Logan. But the press was compelled to decline the monograph because "even though you have asked for no commitment beyond this volume, there would be at least a strong moral commitment on the part of the Press, in publishing this volume, to carry on." A single work on race relations would not be enough, and rather than issuing Logan's work by itself, the press chose not to publish any work at all on this subject. If by chance the press received a subvention for an entire series, then it would again consider Logan's work. Davis closed his letter with a most baffling statement: "I am returning it [the manuscript] in the hope that it will come back here."[94]

Logan finally did find a publisher. The Dial Press, a British concern, accepted *The Nadir* and published it in 1954. But it printed only 3,000 copies, which Logan had to subsidize with a payment of $5,400.[95] No sales or royalty records are extant, but it must have done well, for it went into a second edition in 1965. For the two years ending June 30, 1967, the book sold more than 7,500 copies; it went through five printings as late as 1970 before it went out of print.[96]

The Nadir helped redirect the discourse on post-Reconstruction and late-nineteenth- and early-twentieth-century African-American historiography. August Meier and Elliott Rudwick, in *Black History and the Historical Profession, 1915–1980,* classed Logan's book with another influential work on race relations, C. Vann Woodward's *Strange Career of Jim Crow,* which was published in 1955.[97] In 1954 the nascent revisionist school of Reconstruction history had not yet discredited the dominant Dunning school, which preached that the end of Reconstruction brought a welcome end to Negro domination in the South and its consequent governmental corruption.[98] Kenneth Stampp's *The Era of Reconstruction* landed a body blow on this school, with its rediscovery of that era's progressive legacy; but it was not published until 1965. C. Vann Woodward had published his *Origins of the New South, 1877–1913* in 1951.[99] This landmark work exposed the Achilles heel of race in American politics and subjected to reanalysis the unfulfilled democratic promise of populism and some of the so-called excesses of Negro rule; Woodward also detailed the virtual exclusion of African Americans from the reform movements after populism's defeat. Yet few of the white historians sympathetic to the story of African Americans wrote about their degradation in American life after the Compromise of 1877.

Logan's work was outstanding on three counts. First, it provided a narrative of the disfranchisement of African Americans and the abdication of four presidents—Hayes, Cleveland, Harrison, and McKinley—on the issue of civil rights. Second, *The Nadir* demonstrated the viciousness with which the American press and popular culture attacked the humanity of African Americans; this attack was an essential part of the climate of violence against blacks and the ideological preparation for their disfranchisement and segregation. On both counts, Logan's research base was encyclopedic, and his presentation was such that *The Nadir* is still a most useful reference work.

The descent into the nadir was a combination of economics, politics, and race, Logan demonstrated. He traced the economic roots of the nadir to the sharecropping system and agricultural overproduction of the 1890s and the exclusion of African Americans from organized labor.[100] He tracked in comprehensive detail the byzantine course of Supreme Court decisions that inexorably led to *Plessy* v. *Ferguson*.[101] His detailed survey of a dozen northern newspapers exposed the eagerness with which the North made up its mind to prevent the question of racial justice from intruding on its attempts to reconcile with the South.[102]

The elimination of African Americans from the national political discourse after 1877 was no simple matter. It also was not only a matter of politics. Before it could be fully accomplished, African Americans had to be dehumanized. On the level of popular culture, the stereotyped lazy, lying, and shiftless African American was the source of much of the national humor during the nadir. These stereotypes merged with a renewed interest in and glorification of the "Lost Cause" and a concurrent nostalgia for the plantation slave and vilification of the antebellum free Negro.

The humor, as Logan pointed out, had a menacing edge, too. The northern press criminalized African Americans. In the span of two weeks in 1895, one typical newspaper ran articles with the following headlines: "Held Up by Masked Negroes"; "She Killed Her Lover—Minnie Hall, a Negress"; "Drunken Farmer Killed by a Negro"; "Death of a Man Shot by a Dissolute Negress"; and "Negro's Horse Stealing Methods." The press also ran a plethora of stories encouraging lynchings and charging African-American men with the rape of white women.[103] Whether through the use of racist humor or the popularization of threatening stereotypes, the northern press reinforced the prevalent Social Darwinist views on the inherent inferiority of African Americans and legitimized their forced subordination in American life.[104]

Logan's conception of examining the political and cultural reactions against African Americans has been adopted by subsequent historians, although the historian of today is obliged to make use of primary material beyond newspapers and magazines. Gilbert Osofsky, for example, tracked the progressive demonization of African Americans in late-nineteenth- and early-twentieth-century Harlem to help explain the formation of a ghetto and the climate of violence against blacks in New York City. Constance McLaughlin Green did likewise in her portrait of Washington, D.C. The phrase "the nadir" has entered the historical vocabulary to describe the status of African Americans between the end of Reconstruction and World War I.[105]

The Nadir attains distinction on a third count as well. When the book was published in 1954, the postwar civil rights movement was on the verge of completing the important phase of the legal struggle for equality; after the Supreme Court's *Brown* decision on school desegregation in 1954, legal action would rapidly be superseded by mass action and civil disobedience. When Logan inquired into the origins of the movement he discovered a continuum that stretched back to the last decades of the nineteenth century. He saw it in the formation of the Talented Tenth that began in earnest in the 1880s and accelerated in the 1890s. He brought attention to the founding of an extensive African-American press and the appearance of race-conscious historians like George Washington Williams and Carter Woodson. In the enlarged edition of this work, published in 1965 as *The Betrayal of the Negro: From Rutherford B. Hayes to Woodrow Wilson,* he expanded his argument on the "roots of recovery" to include events that occurred after 1901: the formation of the Niagara Movement, the NAACP, and the African-American fraternities and sororities.[106]

No doubt this framework is partly autobiographical; Logan was a member of the generation that was an integral part of the "roots of recovery" at the turn of the century. Nevertheless, Logan's assigning credit for the postwar civil rights movement to a much earlier generation set up a paradigm that has yielded significant researches and continues to offer a useful investigative framework. James McPherson, in his book about the struggle for racial equality during the nadir, argued that a core of progressive whites and blacks laid the foundation for the twentieth-century biracial civil rights movement in the face of some of the most virulent racism the United States ever experienced. Paula Giddings narrated an important, but overlooked story of the centrality of nineteenth- and early-twentieth-century African-American women to the "roots of recovery." Willard Gatewood, Jr.'s book on the black bourgeoisie between 1880 and 1920 profiles a class that was often in the vanguard of the civil rights movement's prehistory. *The Nadir* broke important historiographical ground for later historians who were agitated by questions about the African Americans' twentieth-century quest for equality.[107]

A completely different scholarly experience awaited Logan when he was commissioned in 1962 by James Nabrit (who in 1960 succeeded Mordecai Johnson as president of Howard) to coauthor with Sterling Brown the centennial history of Howard University. The book was scheduled to appear in time for the 1967 centennial celebrations, but a succession of several crises in Logan's life delayed its publication until 1969. For

Logan, making a deadline was a point of honor, and the book's absence from the celebrations was not only noticeable, it was the cause of personal embarrassment. Said Logan in retrospect, "The writing and publication of the history . . . constituted in many respects the most prolonged painful experience in my life."[108]

The first trauma Logan encountered was working with Sterling Brown. The two had been great friends as far back as high school; Rayford and Ruth Logan shared an apartment with Sterling and Daisy Brown in Boston when the two husbands were in graduate school at Harvard. The two men got along well—when they were relaxing. But they had antithetical work styles. Where Brown was voluble and informal, Logan was taciturn and reserved. This difference in work habits was compounded by Brown's bout with mental illness in the early 1960s; he was subject to mood swings and had difficulty completing tasks that he had devised for the project. By mid-1965 the two men were hardly speaking to each other.[109] Much to Logan's regret (but with his consent), Brown was removed from the project in July 1965.[110] Logan was exasperated by Brown's conduct, but he was perhaps even more upset by the rupture of a longstanding friendship.

Another personal tragedy struck Logan during the course of this project. In May 1964, Logan's wife, Ruth, who suffered from diabetes, had one of her legs amputated. Ruth was essentially all the family that Logan had. Early in his adult life he had determined an agenda in his life that included career advancement and civil rights advocacy. He left little time for socialization outside of this context, and this meant that Ruth was excluded from a substantial part of his life. But despite her seemingly auxiliary standing in his life, Ruth was devoted to her husband. She had an interest in music and performed recitals at Howard, but she far preferred to keep an elegant house and engage her husband in small talk of their life's minutiae.[111] She refused to complain to Logan of her deteriorating condition, and once, soon after her operation, she mournfully told him, "Papa, I am sorry that this had to happen to you."[112]

On the morning of June 30, 1966, Logan discovered Ruth in an enfeebled state in her bedroom; later that day, she died at the old Freedmen's Hospital in Washington, D.C., which has been supplanted by the Howard University Hospital. His loss was considerable. Ruth had been a lifelong companion, if an invisible one. If he had sacrificed friendships in the pursuit of scholarship and recognition, she had sacrificed even more for his comfort. His sense of distress is evident in the memorial he placed in the newspapers each anniversary of her death: "Cheerful and courageous to the end, You worried more about me than about yourself."[113]

Logan continued to work throughout these personal losses. While Sterling Brown had been responsible for interviewing distinguished Howard graduates (a job which was woefully incomplete), Logan had obtained access to the minutes of the meetings of the board of trustees and its various committees. As a matter of policy, these documents are confidential, and only Logan (and not his research assistant) was allowed to look at them. Logan's plan was to produce an institutional history derived almost entirely from these confidential documents but placed in the context of contemporary events. Each of the twelve chapters of *Howard University: The First Hundred Years* is introduced by a short essay on pertinent aspects of American history, but the lion's share is devoted to a taxonomic description of Howard's growth and development.

Despite its criticisms of J. Stanley Durkee, who immediately preceded Mordecai Johnson as president, and of the early years of Johnson's administration, the centennial history is at its core an uncontroversial narrative. Logan apparently made the decision early in the project that, as this was the official history, he would not include his recollections of the bitter fights at Howard. Furthermore, as a technically excellent practitioner of the historical craft, Logan was conservative when it came to evidence. He occasionally made use of his diaries, but he was thoroughly skeptical of oral testimony and other nontraditional sources of evidence unless they were verified by written documentation.[114] So although he mentioned the debate over the establishment of the Ph.D. program, he drew his documentation entirely from trustee minutes; absent is the acrimonious dispute over the direction of education at Howard.

Barely three months after Ruth's death and seven chapters into the book, though, the trustees decided that they had the right to approve what Logan had written. G. Frederick Stanton, secretary of the university, wrote to Logan that the trustees "hope that you will understand that their interest relates to their office with respect to the legal and public relations of the University, and to the fact that their minutes are privileged."[115]

Logan was furious. In a letter to President Nabrit, Logan reminded him that the university counsel, George E. C. Haynes, had agreed to review the manuscript for possible libel, especially of Mordecai Johnson and his administrators. He had expected that his work would be treated as a scholarly exercise, not some public relations gambit. Accusing the trustees of duplicity, he doubted whether they would even be able to read the manuscript with the requisite care and skill needed to detect libel, or whether they could even reach consensus. With anger building inside him, he wrote, "I refuse to be a party to such outrageous censorship and, therefore, I resign . . . as HISTORIAN OF THE CENTENNIAL HISTORY OF HOWARD UNIVERSITY."[116] The trustees accepted his resignation.[117]

Logan also turned to John Hope Franklin, who was now at Brooklyn College, for advice. Over the years, the two men had developed a close professional relationship. Nearly twenty years Franklin's senior, Logan the accomplished scholar needed no counsel on historical matters. But he was a member of that generation of black academics that for the most part did not benefit from the slight crack that appeared in the edifice of white academia after World War II: the prestigious white institutions were, in the 1950s, not prepared to designate him a distinguished professor, and he was too far along to be hired as an up-and-coming scholar. Furthermore, Logan and his peers reached scholarly maturity at a time when building networks in organizations like the AHA had little career purpose for black scholars; consequently, his extracurricular energies were expended within the restricted universe of Howard University, and he trod clumsily over issues related to professional advancement.

As a younger scholar, John Hope Franklin was better positioned to take advantage of white academia's open door, despite the fact that it was opened "grudgingly and . . . so slight[ly] that it was still almost impossible to enter."[118] As he recollects, when he came to Howard he was focused on the practice of history and certain that he could make an impact upon the historical profession, and he successfully avoided dissipating his energy in the campus's internecine struggles.[119] Further, he dedicated himself to interacting with his black and white colleagues around the country in ways that were not readily available to black academics of earlier generations, and part of the professional payoff was that he was elected to lead the AHA, the Organization of American Historians, and the Southern Historical Association, three of the profession's major professional organizations in the United States. Where Logan found insuperable obstacles, Franklin, largely because of generational differences, found slight fissures through which to pass. Logan was a proud man, but he knew his limitations, and at significant junctures in the later stages of his career, when he tried to burnish his professional reputation, he sought out the opinions of

Franklin on professional matters.[120] It was almost as if Logan knew that his younger colleague would be a tempered counterweight to his own prickly disposition.

Logan was convinced that his argument with the university over the centennial history was the reason that a promotion that he had previously expected was being held up. Franklin was outraged at what he believed was censorship of Logan's manuscript, but unlike the hypersensitive Logan, he saw no conspiracy.[121] Logan continued to fume, even after Franklin informed him that it was the norm for authorized histories of colleges to be approved by the trustees. His advice, which Logan did not take, was to calm down and cease letting this tempest distract him from his other work.[122]

Logan had blown up a misunderstanding into a major incident.[123] But he felt that his honor and integrity were impugned. In accepting his resignation, Stanton Wormley had intimated that the trustees were concerned by the fact that the history would not be ready for the centennial celebrations and that perhaps another person could work with more haste. The trustees, however, could find no one else to do the work, and in March 1967, President Nabrit acceded to Logan's demand for an uncensored manuscript and reinstated him to the project.

Logan's travails were not yet over. As he neared the end of the project, the student movement that rocked campuses around the country also rocked Howard. It was not as if Logan opposed student activism. In his history of Howard, he wrote approvingly of Patricia Roberts Harris—who later became the first black woman to head a cabinet department when she became Jimmy Carter's secretary of housing and urban development—and her participation in protests during the early 1940s against a drugstore chain for its employment discrimination; he also admired the Howard students who marched to end segregation in Washington's suburbs, spent their summers working for voting rights in the Deep South, or performed community service in the neighborhood surrounding the Howard campus.[124] These students acted in the best traditions of the interwar civil rights movement, and their actions at least indirectly paid honor to Logan's past work.

By the mid-1960s, however, the student movement at Howard had moved past the attainment of formal legal equality and had begun to address issues like Black Power and the disproportionate toll the Vietnam War was taking on African Americans. Logan, of course, had long opposed the concept of Black Power and its *Négritude* and Garveyite antecedents; that the lingua franca of *Négritude* was French was a strong indication to Logan of the Western influences on the African diaspora and a potent argument against claims of a pure and inherently superior black culture and spirit. He also frowned upon the conclusions drawn by some African-American students who opposed the war: namely, that blacks ought not fight in it. This was an alien idea to Logan, who had struggled mightily for the integration of the armed forces, especially in World War II.

His growing unease turned to opposition in March 1967, when a group of students shouted down General Lewis B. Hershey, the director of the Selective Service, when he tried to speak on campus on the operation of the draft system. When the students were disciplined by the university, the punishment itself became an issue of contention as student leaders demanded amnesty for the protesters. A series of incidents followed in May, including the disruption of a university disciplinary hearing and a successful one-day boycott of classes.[125] The student activists had exceeded Logan's conception of the bounds of respectability. He opposed what he perceived as the students' excesses and wrongheadedness, and he took their revolt personally, as if they were deliberately belittling everything for which he stood.[126] He was not alone in his feelings, for although Sterling Brown became the faculty sponsor to the Nonviolent Action Group (the Howard unit of the Student Nonviolent Coordinating Committee), most faculty members believed that the activists had gone too far.[127]

The unrest at Howard violated Logan's sensibilities and distracted him from the completion of the centennial history manuscript. But it also illustrated how remote Logan had become from the course of the civil rights movement. In the 1930s and 1940s Logan had fire in the belly. But in 1968, as he made the final revisions on *Howard University: The First Hundred Years,* and as the Black Power movement raged around him, Logan could only lament to his editor that he was having some difficulty meeting deadlines "because of anticipation that students might occupy and hold the Administration Building in which my offices are located. . . ."[128] His mournfulness was an apt punctuation mark not only to a flawed project, but to an active relationship to a civil rights movement that he had worked so diligently to build several decades before.

conclusion

"HORS DE COMBAT"

⅌

(1963–1982)

I N MARCH 1963, Rayford Logan became the second African-American member of the Cosmos Club, previously an exclusive preserve in Washington, D.C., of high-powered white intellectuals and politicians. Less than two years before, Carl Rowan, the highly regarded African-American journalist, had been rejected for membership on account of his skin color. Several of the more open-minded members objected to this flagrant practice of the color bar as incompatible with the liberal professions of the organization, and in December 1962 they elected John Hope Franklin, a man of impeccable qualifications, for membership.[1]

Logan was ecstatic. During World War II he had met his friend Raymond Leslie Buell, who was a member, at the club, but the two then headed to Union Station, which had the only integrated restaurant in the city. After the war, he had eaten at the Cosmos Club as a guest of Waldo Leland of the American Council of Learned Societies when the two served on the U.S. National Commission for UNESCO. But for the longest time it was beyond his ken that he would actually be allowed to join.[2] Membership in an until-recently racially exclusive club was a sign to Logan that he had at last received recognition by the white establishment, something he had coveted for his entire professional career. Election to the Cosmos Club was, along with the awarding of an honorary doctorate by Williams College three years later, among the highlights of his career. It was proof to him "that it is possible for a Negro of equal opportunity, education and employment to compete on equal terms with white scholars." Ever the elitist, he allowed that he, "along with . . . one or two others," had validated this assertion.[3]

His entry into the rarefied surroundings of the white intellectual elite coincided with an increasingly pronounced disaffection with the civil rights movement. The 1963 March on Washington "revealed the capacity of large numbers of Negroes to demonstrate with quiet dignity," he wrote to a high school student who asked Logan for his views on the civil rights movement.[4] But subsequent actions were rather harmful, principally because they raised in an unwarranted fashion the expectations of African Americans. Logan announced his opposition to a plan by a group of African Americans to tie up traffic at the New York World's Fair in 1964 because it was too radical.[5] He assigned primary credit for the progress of civil rights to the Supreme Court and criticized James Farmer of the Congress on Racial Equality and Martin Luther King, Jr., "for leading 'some Negroes to think they are going to get their rights now.'" Farmer's and King's rhetoric, he felt, fueled the street riots that erupted in Harlem and other cities on the East Coast.[6] While he acknowledged the positive effects of the sit-ins and street demonstrations on the passage of the 1964 Civil Rights Act, he cast doubt on "the effectiveness on the local level of 'taking to the streets,'" and he accused those who raised the slogan "Freedom Now!" of engaging in demagogy.[7] Whatever personal quirkiness he displayed here, Logan's position on militant action and rhetoric was consonant with that of other members of his generation. They had in various ways struggled for full legal equality, and they felt vindicated by such landmarks as the *Brown* decision and the Civil Rights Act of 1964. The younger radicals, he felt, lacked historical perspective and were in danger of squandering the hard-won gains of thirty years of struggle.

Beginning in the late 1960s, and in an increasingly vituperative timbre, Logan began the campaign for which, unfortunately, he is best remembered: he labored to excise the word "black" from the racial dictionary. "Black," in his opinion, was a separatist term, while its college campus advocates and the proponents of black studies programs were charlatans.[8] The originators of the appellation acted in the tradition of Marcus Garvey and drew color distinctions among African Americans.

His behavior approached the eccentric, as he boycotted organizations, projects, and people who insisted upon describing in his presence American Negroes as blacks. He resigned from AΦA, the fraternity that he had strained to lead into significant civil rights activity, when it began to call itself a black fraternity. He was an adviser to the Frederick Douglass Papers project, but left it over the same linguistic tiff.[9] In the early 1970s, friends occasionally teased him by calling him "old black Rayford," but they stopped when, in his rage, he would storm out of the room and terminate for a time his relations with the offenders. This is one reason why he became more isolated and alone in the years after his wife died. While his friends and acquaintances were not interested in offending him, neither were they keen on watching their every word when they were around him; eventually they decided that the best solution was to stay away.[10]

The most bizarre incident of this nature concerned a planned third edition of *The American Negro: Old World Background and New World Experience,* which he wrote with Irving Cohen, a high school teacher in the New York City public schools.[11] Originally published in 1967, it was adopted for use by the New York City schools and sold quite well. By the end of 1968, Logan made over two thousand dollars in royalties on sales of almost thirty-five thousand copies. Houghton Mifflin, the publisher, issued a second edition in 1970, which also sold well over the next two years.[12] In 1973, Richard DeBruin, the editor in chief of Houghton Mifflin's social studies department, informed Logan that his company wanted to publish a third, updated edition. Perhaps DeBruin had heard of Logan's prickliness about racial language, for he approached the topic gingerly: "The book needs to have a more contemporary look, in illustration program, design, and perhaps a new title."[13] Sensing danger in this seemingly harmless letter, Logan wrote a guarded response. He was pleased about a new edition, but "I am concerned about your desire for a new title. I hope that you do not have in mind changing it to *The Black American.* . . . I believe that Houghton and Mifflin . . . would like to hold the line against capitulating to this mania."[14]

Thus began a year-long tussle in which Logan fought a rear-guard action against the changing racial terminology and impugned the integrity of his coauthor and his publisher. Houghton Mifflin claimed that according to both its salespeople and Irving Cohen's classroom experience, students and teachers alike were put off by the title. "We are, therefore, rather reluctantly going to use a new title for the revision," DeBruin told Logan.[15] Logan was infuriated: "The sheer effrontery of your letter . . . astounds me. . . . You and Mr. Cohen clearly want to use the word black in place of Negro in order to gain a few dollars." Perhaps Logan's reaction was conditioned by his experiences three decades earlier with the University of North Carolina Press, which had tried to bully him. In any event, he objected to what he perceived as Houghton Mifflin's dictatorial style: "Count me out. This is 1973, not 1863."[16]

Logan finally closed the door to the new edition in early 1974 with an acid letter to Houghton Mifflin. Accusing the publishing house of intellectual bankruptcy, he wrote, "I still do not understand why you are so craven. . . . I am convinced that HM will not want to be known in 1975 and to posterity as the last man in the last rank of the intellectual adversaries of the Blackologists. The small and special constituency of Mr. Irving S. Cohen should not make HM hold to this inglorious position." This issue as Logan saw it was one of principle: "[D] not expect me to commit the crime of violating my intellectual integrity by agreeing to the total elimination of 'Negro.'" He closed the letter with a derisive "Pleasant dreams," followed by his signature.[17]

It would be easy to dismiss Logan's behavior as either the eccentricities of a cranky old man or a creeping conservatism. While there are certainly elements of each in the last fifteen years of his life, such an evaluation is simplistic and therefore wide of the mark. Until the end of his life he insisted that he stood by W. E. B. Du Bois's 1906 statement that

> we will not be satisfied to take one jot or tittle less than our manhood rights. We claim for ourselves every single right that belongs to a free born American, political, civil and social, and until we get these rights we will never cease to protest and assail the ears of America.

He also declared his partisanship for Paul Robeson's 1958 opinion that "our country will never be truly great and good until you and all the rest of our young people are permitted to flower in complete fulfillment and bring your gifts to the highest levels of our nation's life."[18]

Logan was not the only African American of his generation to join the semantic debate.[19] Richard B. Moore (1893–1976) was a Caribbean Marxist activist who had lived in Harlem since 1909. In 1960, Moore rejected "Negro" to denote African Americans. "Negro" was the term of inferiority that Europeans imposed on enslaved Africans. Yet he also rejected "black" as a "loose, racist, color" designation that had "no basic, obvious or unmistakable linkage with land, history, and culture." Moore favored Afro-American, which Logan thought acceptable, but barely so.

In 1972, Moore succeeded in getting the ASNLH to change its name to the Association for the Study of Afro-American Life and History.[20] Logan and Moore came to opposite conclusions about "Negro," but in their mutual opposition to "black" each promoted a nonracial vocabulary that emphasized the historical and cultural roots of African Americans.

Part of Logan's animadversion to changing the racial taxonomy was his hostility to separatism. His brief flirtation with separatism, as evidenced in his speech to the graduates of Miner Teachers College, came during the 1930s, when the prospects were dim for racial tolerance and understanding; still, his advocacy of separate equality was conditioned by his belief in the ultimate inclusion of African Americans in the national life. Logan spent most of his life from adolescence on struggling to be accepted by the white world. During his expatriation in France he had come to respect what he believed was France's greater tolerance of black people, and he never gave up hope that white America would one day adopt this attitude. His regard for the West was so high that it was inconceivable to him that African Americans should desire to separate themselves from it. He scorned "black" because in his view it glorifies "*Négritude* and disdains the European origins of Negroes."[21]

By the 1930s Logan favored the designation "Negro" over "colored." The latter term, according to him, was used to draw both a class and a color line among African Americans. Mary Church Terrell, the light-skinned aristocrat of color, he once told Michael Winston, called herself colored as a way to distinguish herself from the (mostly dark-skinned) masses. When Mrs. Terrell once corrected Logan's speech by telling him that he was "colored," and not "Negro," Logan then tilted toward using "Negro," for this designation included all classes and tones of African Americans.[22] This episode may be apocryphal, but it indicates Logan's concerns during the 1930s for promoting racial unity.

Other African Americans of his generation were uncomfortable with the appellation "black"—Sterling Brown called the insistence on new terminology "the flicker and not the flame"—but few made it a line of demarcation in the way Logan did.[23] (John Hope Franklin refused to change the racial terminology even in the sixth edition of *From Slavery to Freedom* [1988]—the work bears the subtitle "A History of Negro Americans"—but in other writings he uses "black" as well as Negro.) Yet Logan worked out a tortured logic defending the use of Negro over black. He claimed that black was exclusionary, for he and so many other mulattoes were not dark. Those who favored the change denied that black was color-exclusive and claimed that it should be understood as a generic term, not a literal one. Advocates of change were searching for a new catholic term to describe their race, just as Logan had done in the 1930s. Yet Logan denied them this prerogative. In several essays, most of them shrill in tone, he ignored Du Bois's and his own occasional past use of "black," and "colored," and denied that there was historical basis for the use of black. While there was some basis for "Afro-American," it was used less often than "Negro."[24]

This is the central point in Logan's polemics. The Black Power activists and the civil rights movement in general were, according to Logan, ignorant of their past and therefore had forgotten the pioneering role of Logan and his generation. The civil rights movement had moved into the streets and chanted "Freedom Now!" but it had no concept of the history of the struggle for racial equality and the progress made since the nadir; eschewing judicial and legislative remedies, the movement appreciated neither the achievement of legal equality nor the importance of legal methods for achieving it. "It is clear that I have serious doubts about the educational value of these activist movements," he said.[25] In one of his jeremiads—this one before a 1974 Negro History Week audience at Morehouse College in Atlanta—he reminded the movement of the indispensability of his generation:

> It is impossible accurately to assess the importance of these early movements in the election of Negroes to the Atlanta City Council, [and] the Georgia State Legislature. . . . May I suggest, however, that the Black Revolutionists and Black Nationalists did not start the Black Revolution that led to the Civil Rights Acts of 1957 and the 1960s, especially the Voting Rights Act of 1965[?][26]

The more Logan tried to ensure that he and his generation would be memorialized for their formative work in the civil rights movement, the more he was regarded as a relic. William Willis, one of Logan's students from the 1940s who in the late 1960s became the first African-American faculty member at Southern Methodist University in Texas, implored Logan to soften his position. The only alternative, he told Logan, was alienation from future generations of activists.

> You were a militant against White racism decades before they were born. . . .
> I do not want them in their ignorance and in their zeal to classify you into a

category that you do not belong. Also, I believe that it will be good for them to know that they do not stand alone, separated by an impassable gulf from all members of an older generation. . . . It seems to me that the best way to convey this is the establishment of the lineal descent that exists in important ways—but not *in toto*—between them and Douglass, Du Bois, and Logan.[27]

Logan continued categorically to reject this sound advice.[28] Yet he could no more police the language of black nationalists and African Americans in general than he could command the respect of the white intellectual establishment or compel Walter White to follow his lead in previous decades. Logan was unrepentant, even as his health deteriorated and it was sufficiently clear that his admonitions were not only falling on deaf ears but were causing him to be seen as a caricature of himself.

In his determination to illuminate the contributions of his generation to the advancement of African Americans, Logan inadvertently obscured his own. Coming of age in the nadir of American race relations, Rayford Logan was one of a cohort of African Americans that consciously decided to put its considerable talents in service to its race. Trained since adolescence to be a "race man," he had striven to be a tribune for African Americans. As a Pan-Africanist in the 1920s, he helped articulate a program for racial equality in America and the protection and development of Africans. In the 1930s he pioneered the civil rights tactics of voter registration drives and citizenship schools, while in the 1940s he led activity that chipped away at racial exclusion in the U.S. military.

Throughout his civil rights career, Logan was a diligent second-tier leader. He labored in the shadow of Du Bois in the Pan-Africanist movement. He tried to bring AΦA, the foremost black fraternity, into the struggle for equality. AΦA was to be the base from which he could exercise authority in the movement, but the resistance by a significant portion of the fraternity to change in AΦA's traditional posture thwarted Logan's plans. Consequently, his prescient criticisms of the NAACP's legalism and conservatism in the 1930s and 1940s remained just that— criticism. He wanted to be a major figure in the civil rights movement, but he instead became a prophet, damning America's racism and revealing the flaws in the NAACP's program for racial advancement.

By definition, prophets are not only without honor in their homes, they are also marginal people. More often than not, Logan was unable to capitalize on his solid local or regional civil rights work and develop a sustained national recognition and influence. His personal papers, and especially his diaries, frequently fulminate at one or another prominent activist for monopolizing the limelight or trying to steal the credit for some particularly sharp idea or for preventing him from advancing within the civil rights establishment. From what is known about Walter White, for example—repeatedly on the receiving end of Logan's wrath—it is difficult to dismiss Logan's outbursts as the ranting of a jealous, second-rate activist. It is tempting, however, to conclude that Logan was comfortable as an outsider and on the fringe of power, and there is some justification for this view. He was not the sort who could easily be contained by organizational discipline. There must have been some security in knowing that however incisive were his criticisms, he would bear no responsibility for implementing alternative plans. Protestations notwithstanding, his self-appointed role as movement gadfly was a balm for the wounds he suffered by being denied a permanent seat at the leadership summit.

But his absence from the acme of power is also a commentary on the relationship between black leadership of the front rank and subordinate ranks. The civil rights movement in the localities often exhibited remarkable independence from the central leadership. Logan's voting rights work was duplicated in many other areas of the South by organizations that were dedicated to this activity but whose membership roster overlapped that of the NAACP local branch; the NAACP often chose not to become officially involved. Similarly, local NAACP chapters became involved in the issue of black participation in the national defense in a manner that went against the wishes of the national leadership.

What likely distinguished Logan from the majority of the local leaders was his long apprenticeship for race leadership, his academic training, and his broad intellectual sweep of the national and international dimensions of issues of race. Such qualities, even when placed alongside his well-known irascibility and crossness, ought to have commended him to some place of distinction in the movement establishment.

But the confounding of his aspirations may suggest that the top leadership was reluctant to coopt the most talented of the second-tier activists, especially if their thinking and actions were heterodox. Even when Walter White listened to Logan, as he did on post–World War II international affairs, he did not give him credit for his ideas, instead appropriating them as his own. In 1951, A. Philip Randolph, about whom he was most enthusiastic, asked Logan on behalf of the Committee of Negro Leaders to

write a memorandum for a protest campaign aimed at government discrimination against blacks in the State Department; this committee also
included Walter White and Clarence Mitchell of the NAACP; Lester
Granger of the Urban League; Channing Tobias, who at that time was the
director of the Phelps-Stokes Fund; and Mary McLeod Bethune. Logan
was the obvious choice for this job, because in late 1950 he had written on
this subject for the *Pittsburgh Courier*. Although Logan's articles earned
him a citation in 1951 from the Capitol Press Club for distinguished
public service, when it came time to present the findings to the secretary of
state, Logan's name was excluded from the list of conferees, which included only the movement luminaries. He was added to the roster of
participants only when he threatened to withdraw his services.[29] To be
sure, Logan bore these slights poorly and saw them as personal affronts,
but his abrasiveness alone cannot explain the front-rank leadership's
reluctance to enlarge itself. This pattern of exclusion was not unique to
Logan, as in the 1950s and 1960s the NAACP was suspicious of Martin
Luther King and could not absorb the most forthright and active of the
movement's leaders.

Rayford Logan did not fit in. A gifted intellect, he clearly had the talent
to be recognized as a top scholar. But he was also African-American, and
in the minds of white America, and more important, in the mind of white
academia, this negated all his assets. He grew up believing that he was
special—different from other African Americans—and each snub by the
white establishment would cause paroxysms against it for its racism. Yet
time and again he sought its approval.

"It must have been a most unrewarding experience for the Negro
scholar to answer those who said that he was inferior by declaring: 'I am
indeed *not inferior*.' "[30] So wrote John Hope Franklin. For Logan, the
world of Negro scholarship was both exhilarating and confining. Logan
was a trailblazer in the field of Negro history, one of a handful of African-
American scholars who embraced it in the 1920s and early 1930s. At
Atlanta and Howard Universities, Logan rubbed shoulders with the finest
African-American scholars—some of the best scholars of any race—of his
day.

But along with the thrill of carving out a new discipline, Logan also
inherited an obligation to fight racism. Virtually all of his scholarship was
dedicated to sorting out the United States' tangled history of race relations. His numerous polemics and political writings reinforced the direc-

tion of his life's work. Was this a distraction? Did this necessary racial advocacy prevent Logan from making an indelible mark on the world of scholarship, as he wished? There is no way to know this for certain, of course. His scholarship on race is a considerable deposit in the treasury of American intellectual history, and Logan could be justly proud of his contributions to the advancement of African Americans. But for the longest time the academy did not see it this way; to it, Logan was a Negro scholar laboring in Negro studies. It was easy to categorize him and shunt him off to the margins. Logan fought this to the end, but with mixed success.

For more than the last ten years of his life he and Michael R. Winston labored to produce the *Dictionary of American Negro Biography*, which was published in 1982.[31] Logan deliberately chose this name both to emphasize "Negro" and emphatically to declare that African Americans were an integral part of the national history. With more than seven hundred entries, many of them written by Logan, the *Dictionary* fills an egregious gap in the historical record and will certainly long be regarded as an important reference work. It is, on a smaller scale, a close cousin of the "Encyclopedia of the Negro," which Du Bois conceived half a century earlier. As such, the *Dictionary of American Negro Biography* stands as a monument to the tradition of historical scholarship founded by Du Bois and Carter Woodson and of which Logan was one of the foremost practitioners.[32]

In 1969 Logan endowed the Rayford W. Logan Lecture Series, which presented distinguished historians of the African and African-American experience. In one of his last significant acts before he died on November 4, 1982, he made out his will in August 1977. As he reviewed his life after nearly eighty years, he must have been proud of his achievements. He wanted to be known to posterity for three, in particular: his coauthorship of both Executive Order 8802 and the section of the Burke-Wadsworth Selective Service bill, and his 1940 meeting with President Roosevelt that resulted in more African-American soldiers and officers called to active military duty. As he had no children, he generously bequeathed half of the residuals of his estate to Williams College (in memory of his friend Roger William Riis) and half to Howard University; each received nearly eighty thousand dollars. The only restriction on the use of these gifts was that no person could deliver a Logan lecture who had ever referred to African Americans as blacks and that no part of the bequests could support any program or person designated as "black." Black studies, black student organizations, and students who professed faith in the Black Muslims were all excluded from Logan's largesse; so, too, were Holy Rollers and members of Sun Myung Moon's Unification Church.[33] The proviso made news in the African-American press and is now regarded as Logan's outstanding characteristic by all who knew him and many who knew of him.

But since his death its implementation has been ignored at least as often as it has been observed. The lecture series showcases distinguished scholars who include "black" in their vocabulary; it is not known how Howard and Williams are spending their gifts. When he died, the obituary in *The New York Times,* paper of record, was headlined: "Dr. Rayford Logan, Professor Who Wrote Books on Blacks."[34]

NOTES

❧

1. Growing Up in the Nadir

1. Arthur P. Davis, interview by author, October 2, 1989, Washington, D.C., tape recording in author's possession; Dorothy Porter Wesley, interview by author, June 14, 1990, Washington, D.C., tape recording in author's possession.

2. Rayford W. Logan, untitled autobiographical manuscript, vol. 1, chap. 1, pp. 1–2, Rayford W. Logan Papers, Installation Two, box 15, unprocessed manuscript, Moorland-Spingarn Research Center, Howard University, Washington, D.C. Hereafter cited as RL(H)-II; the first installation will be cited as RL(H)-I. Logan first wrote the autobiography in 1948, revising it between 1970 and 1978; portions of the original draft are in RL(H). Unless otherwise stated, citations are from the 1970–78 draft. The autobiography went under several names, including "The Autobiography of a Second Class Citizen" and "Within and Without the Veil."

3. Ibid., vol. 1, chap. 2, p. 1, RL(H)-II, box 15.

4. Luther Porter Jackson, *Free Negro Labor and Property Holding in Virginia, 1830–1860* (New York and London: D. Appleton-Century Co., 1942; reprint, New York: Atheneum, 1969), x, 61–63.

5. Rayford W. Logan Diary, September 6, 1941, Rayford W. Logan Papers, unprocessed manuscript, Library of Congress, Washington, D.C. Hereafter cited as Logan diary. Other material from this collection hereinafter cited as RL(LC).

6. Logan autobiography, vol. 1, chap. 1, pp. 2–3, RL(H)-II, box 15.

7. Ibid., pp. 3–5. Information from Powell Gibson, who was the principal of the segregated high school in the nearby town of Winchester, Virginia, is contained in a letter from Powell Gibson to RWL, December 1, 1948, quoted in the Logan autobiography.

8. Logan autobiography (1948 draft), RL(H)-II, doc. box. 16, "Autobiography."

9. On the Supreme Court decisions see Rayford W. Logan, *The Betrayal of the*

Negro: From Rutherford B. Hayes to Woodrow Wilson, new enl. ed. (London: Collier Books, 1965), chap. 6. On the history and implementation of the Fourteenth Amendment, see Eric Foner, *Reconstruction: America's Unfinished Revolution, 1863–1877* (New York: Harper & Row, 1988), 253–61.

10. Arnold Rampersad, *The Life of Langston Hughes,* vol. 1, *1902–1941: I, Too, Sing America* (New York: Oxford University Press, 1986), 100.

11. Jessie Fauset to Langston Hughes, October 23, 1925, quoted in Rampersad, *Langston Hughes,* 1:115.

12. Quoted in Willard B. Gatewood, Jr., "Aristocrats of Color: South and North, the Black Elite 1880–1920," *Journal of Southern History* 54 (February 1988): 15–16.

13. Rampersad, *Langston Hughes,* 1:99–101; Langston Hughes, *The Big Sea* (New York: Alfred A. Knopf, 1940), 207.

14. Constance McLaughlin Green, *The Secret City: A History of Race Relations in the Nation's Capital* (Princeton, N.J.: Princeton University Press, 1967), 144–48; August M. Meier, *Negro Thought in America, 1880–1915: Racial Ideologies in the Age of Booker T. Washington* (Ann Arbor: University of Michigan Press, 1963), 135–36.

15. Rampersad, *Langston Hughes,* 1:99.

16. Jean Toomer, cited in Cynthia Earl Kerman and Richard Eldridge, *The Lives of Jean Toomer: A Hunger for Wholeness* (Baton Rouge: Louisiana State University Press, 1987), 47.

17. Logan autobiography, vol. 1, chap. 2, pp. 2–3, RL(H)-II, box 15.

18. Gatewood, "Aristocrats of Color," 3–20; David L. Lewis, *The District of Columbia: A Bicentennial History* (New York: W. W. Norton, 1976), 72–73.

19. Steven Mintz, "A Historical Ethnography of Black Washington, D.C.," *Records of the Columbia Historical Society of Washington, D.C.* 52 (1989): 239–40.

20. Ibid., 238–40. For a discussion of the living arrangements of the African-American family across place and time, see Herbert G. Gutman, *The Black Family in Slavery and Freedom* (New York: Vintage, 1976), esp. 432–60, 521–26.

21. Logan autobiography, vol. 1, chap. 2, p. 1, RL(H)-II, box 15.

22. Ibid., chap. 3, pp. 11–12.

23. Ibid., chap. 2, p. 1; Rayford W. Logan, "Growing Up in Washington: A Lucky Generation," *Records of the Columbia Historical Society of Washington, D.C.* 50 (1980): 505.

24. Alrutheus Ambush Taylor, *The Negro in the Reconstruction of Virginia* (Washington, D.C.: The Association for the Study of Negro Life and History, 1926), 160, 190–91.

25. Rayford W. Logan, "Walter H. Brooks," in *Dictionary of American Negro Biography,* ed. Rayford W. Logan and Michael R. Winston (New York: W. W. Norton, 1982), 62–64.

26. Mintz, "Ethnography of Black Washington," 236; Paul A. Groves, "The Development of a Black Residential Community in Southwest Washington: 1860–

1897," *Records of the Columbia Historical Society of Washington, D.C.* 49 (1973–74): 267–73.

27. G. R. F. Key, interview by author, December 7, 1989, Washington, D.C., tape recording in author's possession.

28. Logan autobiography, vol. 1, chap. 2, p. 14, RL(H)-II, box 15.

29. Ibid. On Joe Gans and his bout with Battling Nelson, see Rayford W. Logan, "Joe Gans," *Dictionary of American Negro Biography,* 251.

30. Logan autobiography, vol. 1, chap. 2, p. 14, RL(H)-II, box 15.

31. Logan, "Growing Up in Washington: A Lucky Generation," 506.

32. Logan autobiography, vol. 1, chap. 2, pp. 4, 5, 9, RL(H)-II, box 15. On the migration of African Americans to Washington, see Mintz, "Ethnography of Black Washington," 237, and Green, *Secret City,* 200. There is a paucity of substantial material on color distinctions among African Americans, but see Gatewood, "Aristocrats of Color," and *Aristocrats of Color: The Black Elite, 1880–1920* (Bloomington: Indiana University Press, 1990); W. Lloyd Warner, Buford H. Junker, and Walter A. Adams, *Color and Human Nature* (Washington, D.C.: American Council on Education, 1941); Joel Williamson, *New People: Miscegenation and Mulattoes in the United States* (New York: The Free Press, 1980; reprint, New York: New York University Press, 1984); St. Clair Drake and Horace R. Cayton, *Black Metropolis: A Study of Negro Life in a Northern City,* 2 vols., rev. ed. (New York: Harcourt, Brace & World, 1970). Leo Spitzer, *Lives in Between: Assimilation and Marginality in Austria, Brazil, West Africa 1780–1945* (London: Cambridge University Press, 1989) addresses this question among Afro-Brazilians.

33. Discrimination based on skin color and other physical traits is present in other minority groups, too. Where some African Americans speak of "good" (i.e., straight) hair or "fine" features (e.g., Caucasian nose or lips), some Jews speak approvingly of an infant's or young child's "gentile nose," the nose being the most prominent feature distinguishing Jews from white gentiles. According to Michael R. Marrus, *The Politics of Assimilation: A Study of the French Jewish Community at the Time of the Dreyfuss Affair* (Oxford: Oxford University Press, 1971), chaps. 2 and 5, French Jews sought to assimilate by identifying their Jewishness with the French Republic; they developed theories that the French Revolution had created conditions whereby they could shed the backward and servile characteristics of the Jewish race, thereby merging with the French race.

34. Drake and Cayton, *Black Metropolis,* 2:495–96.

35. Ibid., 2:496–98.

36. Ibid., 2:498–99, 509.

37. Ibid., 2:498–502.

38. Warner, Junker, and Adams, *Color and Human Nature,* 160–92.

39. Drake and Cayton, *Black Metropolis,* 2:500.

40. Ibid., 512.

41. Logan autobiography, vol. 1, chap. 1, p. 6, RL(H)-II, box 15.

42. M. G. Walcott to Arthur Logan, February 2, 1927, RL(H)-II, box 18, "Arthur C. Logan, Jr."

43. Frederic C. Walcott to RWL, January 10, 1930, and January 5, 1936 [incorrectly dated 1935], RWL to Walcott, January 10, 1936, RL(H)-II, box 17, "Frederic C. Walcott"; Walcott to Arthur C. Logan, Jr., November 15, 1928, and August 12, 1932, RL(H)-II, box 18, "Arthur C. Logan, Jr."; RWL to Walcott, July 26, 1941, RL(H)-II, box 18, "Post-War World Proposal, Abortive."

44. James Lincoln Collier, *Duke Ellington* (New York: Oxford University Press, 1987), chap. 1, esp. 8–11.

45. Ibid., 41–42, 132–33, 164–66.

46. Logan autobiography (1948 draft), RL(H)-II, doc. box 16. Here and elsewhere, Logan overstates his father's monthly income by five dollars.

47. Logan autobiography, vol. 1, chap. 2, p. 15, RL(H)-II, box 15.

48. G. R. F. Key, interview by author.

49. For personal accounts of several prominent individuals who grew up in turn-of-the-century segregated Washington, see Sterling Brown, Montague Cobb, and Mae Miller Sullivan, "Reminiscences of Growing Up in Segregated Washington," a panel discussion that formed part of the symposium "In the Shadow of the Capitol," held at the Folger Shakespeare Library, Washington, D.C., April 9–10, 1981, copy of tape-recorded sessions in RL(H)-II, box 10.

50. Green, *Secret City,* 154.

51. Roi Ottley, cited in Gatewood, "Aristocrats of Color," 10; Drake and Cayton, *Black Metropolis,* 2:515.

52. For the history of M Street High School, see Mary C. Terrell, "History of the High School for Negroes in Washington," *Journal of Negro History* 2 (1917): 253–56; Henry S. Robinson, "The M Street High School, 1891–1916," *Records of the Columbia Historical Society of Washington, D.C.* 51 (1984): 119–43; Jervis Anderson, "A Very Special Monument: The Dunbar High School on First Street," *The New Yorker,* March 20, 1978, 93ff.; Mary Gibson Hundley, *The Dunbar Story* (New York: Vantage Press, 1965); Louise Daniel Hutchinson, *Anna J. Cooper: A Voice from the South* (Washington, D.C.: Smithsonian Institution Press, 1981), chaps. 3 and 4; Leona C. Gabel, *From Slavery to the Sorbonne and Beyond: The Life & Writings of Anna J. Cooper* (Northampton, Mass.: Department of History of Smith College, 1982), chaps. 4 and 6.

53. Edmund Drago, *Initiative, Paternalism and Race Relations: Charleston's Avery Normal Institute* (Athens, Ga.: University of Georgia Press, 1990) is a book-length treatment of the history of this companion school to M Street.

54. G. R. F. Key, interview by author.

55. Green, *Secret City,* 168.

56. Hutchinson, *Anna J. Cooper,* 57–58; Robinson, "M Street High School," 141.

57. Kenneth R. Manning, *Black Apollo of Science: The Life of Ernest Everett Just* (New York: Oxford University Press, 1983), 18, 27. See 18–37 for a discussion of Just's life at Kimball and Dartmouth.

58. Gabel, *From Slavery to the Sorbonne,* 49.

59. On Neval Thomas, see the Schomburg Clipping File on microfiche, fiche no. 5,248.

60. Logan autobiography, vol. 1, chap. 3, pp. 10–11, RL(H)-II, box 15.

61. Ibid., pp. 9, 17–18.

62. G. R. F. Key, interview by author.

63. Campbell C. Johnson, "Autobiography of Campbell C. Johnson," typescript, Campbell C. Johnson Papers, box 57-1, folder 1, Moorland-Spingarn Research Center, Howard University. See also Charlotte S. Price, "Campbell Carrington Johnson," *Dictionary of American Negro Biography,* 345–47.

64. RWL, valedictory address, M Street High School, Washington, D.C., June 1913, RL(H)-II, box 5.

65. Logan diary, September 18, 1945.

66. Michael R. Winston, interview by author, December 6, 1989, Washington, D.C., tape recording in author's possession.

67. David L. Reid, "The Black Man at Williams: From Freak to Afro-American" (student paper, 1969), Special Collections, Sawyer Library, Williams College, Williamstown, Massachusetts.

68. Leverett Wilson Spring, *A History of Williams College* (Boston: Houghton Mifflin, 1917), 279.

69. Ibid., 354; Reid, "The Black Man at Williams."

70. Reid, "The Black Man at Williams."

71. David Klugh to RWL, January 20, 1937; RWL to Klugh, January 24, 1937, RL(H)-I, box 9a, "Correspondence."

72. Logan autobiography, vol. 1, chap. 5, p. 3, RL(H)-II, box 15.

73. Sterling A. Brown, "A Son's Return: 'Oh Didn't He Ramble,'" in *Perspectives: A Williams Anthology,* ed. Frederick Rudolph (Williamstown, Mass.: Williams College, 1983), 320–21.

74. Logan autobiography, vol. 1, chap. 5, p. 2, RL(H)-II, box 15; N. H. Wilson to author, March 21, 1990, in author's possession. Wilson was a classmate of Logan's at Williams.

75. Logan autobiography, vol. 1, chap. 5, pp. 1, 5, RL(H)-II, box 15.

76. RWL to Klugh, January 24, 1937, RL(H)-I, box 9a, "Correspondence."

77. Brown, "A Son's Return," 321–23.

78. For the experience Logan's high school classmate Eugene Davidson had at Harvard, see Eugene Davidson, interview by unknown person, June 28, 1968, transcript, Civil Rights Documentation Project, Manuscript Division, Moorland-Spingarn Research Center, Howard University.

79. Logan autobiography, vol. 1, chap. 4, p. 3; chap. 5, p. 7, RL(H)-II, box 15.

80. Ibid., chap. 5, p. 7.

81. Handwritten drafts of both speeches are in RL(H)-I, box 15.

82. On Garvey's opinion of the Ku Klux Klan and other white supremacists, see Tony Martin, *Race First: The Ideological and Organizational Struggles of Marcus Garvey and the Universal Negro Improvement Association,* Contributions in Afro-American and African Studies, no. 19 (Westport, Conn.: Greenwood Press, 1976), chap. 12.

83. Rayford Logan's cumulative transcript, Williams College Archives, copy in author's possession.

84. Cited in Reid, "The Black Man at Williams"; Logan autobiography, vol. 1, chap. 5, p. 7, RL(H)-II, box 15.

85. Logan autobiography, vol. 1, chap. 5, p. 13, RL(H)-II, box 15.

86. For a discussion of the "mulatto escape hatch," see Carl N. Degler, *Neither Black nor White: Slavery and Race Relations in Brazil and the United States* (New York: Macmillan, 1971; reprint, Madison: University of Wisconsin Press, 1986), 223–32.

2. Mr. Wilson's War and Mr. Logan's War

1. W. E. Burghardt Du Bois, "The African Roots of War," *Atlantic Monthly* 115 (May 1915): 707–14.

2. "Resolutions of the Washington Conference," *Crisis* 14 (June 1917): 59–60.

3. G. R. F. Key, interview by author, December 7, 1989, Washington, D.C., tape recording in author's possession.

4. Arthur E. Barbeau and Florette Henri, *The Unknown Soldiers: Black American Troops in World War I* (Philadelphia: Temple University Press, 1974), 56–69; W. E. Burghardt Du Bois, "An Essay Toward a History of the Black Man in the Great War," *Crisis* 18 (June 1919): 67–69.

5. Henri and Barbeau, *Unknown Soldiers*, 19–20, 77.

6. Du Bois, "An Essay Toward a History," 73–74.

7. Bulletin No. 35, the military's order denying African-American soldiers the right to go public places to which they were entitled to go, is published in Emmett J. Scott, *The American Negro in the World War* (Chicago: Homewood, 1919), reprinted as Emmett J. Scott, *Scott's Official History of the American Negro in the World War* (New York: Arno Press and *The New York Times*, 1969), 97–98.

8. For accounts of two of the most flagrant uses of force to intimidate black soldiers in Houston and Spartanburg, South Carolina, see Barbeau and Henri, *Unknown Soldiers*, 26–31, 72–74, and Scott, *American Negro in the World War*, 79–80.

9. Logan autobiography, vol. 1, chap. 6, p. 3, RL(H)-II, box 15.

10. Ibid., p. 7.

11. Barbeau and Henri, *Unknown Soldiers*, 40–41; Logan autobiography, vol. 1, chap. 6, p. 9, RL(H)-II, box 15.

12. Barbeau and Henri, *Unknown Soldiers*, 165–66.

13. Ibid., 167–70; quote is on 167.

14. Ibid., 166–67.

15. Commanding Officer, 372d Infantry to The Commanding General, American E[xpeditionary]. F[orce]., August 24, 1918, "Documents of the War," compiled by W. E. B. Du Bois, *Crisis* 18 (May 1919): 18.

16. Barbeau and Henri, *Unknown Soldiers*, chap. 8.

17. Logan autobiography, vol. 1, chap. 6, pp. 10–11, RL(H)-II, box 15.

18. Ibid., pp. 22–24.

19. Veterans Administration, file no. XC-01-577-512, Logan, Rayford Whittingham, Veterans Administration Regional Office, Atlanta, Georgia, copy in author's possession.

20. Logan diary, June 13, 1943.

21. Logan autobiography, vol. 1, chap. 6, pp. 25, 30, RL(H)-II, box 15.

22. French Military Mission Stationed with the American Army, "Secret Information Concerning Black American Troops," August 7, 1918, in "Documents of the War," 16–17.

23. Ibid., 17.

24. "The Colored Americans in France," *Crisis* 17 (February 1919): 167–68. For other anecdotes of the interaction between the French population and African-American soldiers, see Michel Fabre, *La Rive Noire: De Harlem à la Seine* (Paris: Lieu Commun, 1985), chap. 2, passim.

25. Rayford W. Logan, "The Confessions of an Unwilling Nordic," in *The Negro Caravan,* ed. Sterling Brown (New York: The Dryden Press, 1941), 1043–50. Quotes appear on 1050. This essay originally appeared in 1927 in *The World Tomorrow.*

26. Logan autobiography, vol. 1, chap. 6, pp. 11–12, 13–16, 29. RL(H)-II, box 15.

27. Ibid., pp. 31–35; Logan diary, June 13, July 30, 31, 1943.

28. On the red summer of 1919, see Arthur I. Waskow, *From Race Riot to Sit-In, 1919 and the 1960s: A Study in the Connections between Conflict and Violence* (Garden City, N.Y.: Doubleday, 1967); David Levering Lewis, *When Harlem Was in Vogue* (New York: Vintage, 1982), 17–20, 22–23, 24; and August Meier and Elliott Rudwick, *From Plantation to Ghetto,* 3d ed. (New York: Hill and Wang, 1976), 239–42.

29. Logan autobiography, vol. 1, chap. 6, p. 1, RL(H)-II, box 15.

30. Fabre, *Rive Noire,* 58.

31. James Weldon Johnson, *Along This Way* (New York: Penguin, 1933; reprint, New York: Penguin, 1990), 209–11; J. A. Rogers, "The American Negro in Europe," *American Mercury* 20 (May 1930): 1–10.

32. Arnold Rampersad, *The Life of Langston Hughes,* vol. 1, *1902–1941: I, Too, Sing America* (New York: Oxford University Press, 1986), 83–92; Phyllis Rose, *Jazz Cleopatra: Josephine Baker and Her Times* (New York: Doubleday, 1989), 64, 68–69.

33. Rampersad, *Langston Hughes,* 1:83; Rose, *Jazz Cleopatra,* 69–72; Logan autobiography, vol. 1, chap. 7, p. 8, RL(H)-II, box 5.

34. Fabre, *Rive Noire,* 59–62; Rogers, "American Negro in Europe," 3–5.

35. Logan, "Confessions of an Unwilling Nordic," 1048.

36. Ibid., 1048–49.

37. Report, Washington Field Office [to Director, FBI], March 30, 1953, Bureau File 101-1579-17, contains some of Logan's travel itinerary as recorded by the State Department, while Logan autobiography, vol. 1, chap. 7, pp. 4–7, RL(H)-II, box 5, contains other information.

38. Logan autobiography, vol. 1, chap. 7, pp. 4–7, RL(H)-II, box 5.

39. Logan, "Confessions of an Unwilling Nordic," 1050.

40. W. E. B. Du Bois, *The World and Africa*, new enl. ed. (New York: International Publishers, 1965), 7.

41. Quoted in Imanuel Geiss, *The Pan-African Movement*, trans. Ann Keep (New York: Africana Publishing Co., 1974), 190.

42. Ibid., 190–92.

43. Ibid., 5–6.

44. Ibid., 172.

45. Ibid., 236; Du Bois, *The World and Africa*, 11–12.

46. Geiss, *Pan-African Movement*, 234–40.

47. Roster of members of the Permanent Bureau of the First Pan-African Congress, [February 1919], the Papers of W. E. B. Du Bois, reel 8, frame 80. Hereinafter cited as Du Bois Papers.

48. A good discussion of assimilation is contained in Leo Spitzer, *Lives in Between: Assimilation and Marginality in Austria, Brazil, West Africa, 1780–1945* (New York: Cambridge University Press, 1989), chap. 1.

49. Assimilation was the general policy applied by the European powers toward Africa until the late nineteenth century, although France continued it into the twentieth. This began to change under the influence of the ideas of scientific racism. Perceived cultural inferiority became linked with racial inferiority, and the Europeans began to fear that assimilation would lead to the dilution of European superiority. The idea of eventual, gradual extension of rights was abandoned, as was a policy of enfranchising those colonial subjects who strived for westernization. For Senegal, this shift in policy meant a reorganization of colonial rule. In 1920 this shift was completed when the *Conseil General* was transformed into the *Conseil Colonial*. The French stress on developing the leadership of the *evolués* was replaced by one that emphasized the leadership of tribal chiefs. The French now opposed both the extension of the rights of French citizens to Africans and the idea that Africans could eventually become French. Thus, Diagne's insistence that he was French was his insistence that Africans under French colonial rule were entitled to all rights under French law, and he feared that criticism of France, especially from African Americans, would further endanger the attainment of these rights. See John Gaffar LaGuerre, Ph.D., *Enemies of Empire* (St. Augustine, Trinidad and Tobago: University of the West Indies, 1984), 1–33.

50. See Spitzer, *Lives in Between*, 145, for a discussion on the personal transformations experienced by those who deeply believed in assimilation and were then marginalized.

51. RWL to Jessie Fauset, July 1, 1920, Du Bois Papers, reel 9.

52. Blaise Diagne to W. E. B. Du Bois, November 11, 1920, Du Bois Papers, reel 9.

53. On Marcus Garvey, see Tony Martin, *Race First: The Ideological and Organizational Struggles of Marcus Garvey and the Universal Negro Improvement Association* (Westport, Conn.: Greenwood Press, 1976); and Edmund D. Cronon, *Black Moses* (Madison: University of Wisconsin Press, 1955).

54. Ida Gibbs Hunt to Du Bois, June 7, 1921, Du Bois Papers, reel 9.

55. RWL to Du Bois, August 22, 1921, RWL to Du Bois, [between August 23 and August 26, 1921], Du Bois Papers, reel 9.

56. Logan autobiography, vol. 1, chap. 7, p. 16, RL(H)-II, box 5; Michael R. Winston, *History of Howard University Department of History, 1913–1973* (Washington, D.C.: Department of History, Howard University, 1973), 82.

57. Logan autobiography, vol. 1, chap. 7, p. 16, RL(H)-II, box 5; RWL to Du Bois, August 22, 1921, RWL to Du Bois, [between August 23 and August 26, 1921], RWL to Du Bois, August 26, 1921, Du Bois Papers, reel 9; Geiss, *Pan-African Movement*, 245–48.

58. Jessie Fauset, "Impressions of the Second Pan-African Congress," *Crisis* 23 (November 1921): 12.

59. W. E. B. Du Bois, "To the World (Manifesto of the Second Pan-African Congress)," *Crisis* 23 (November 1921): 5–10.

60. Fauset, "Impressions," 14.

61. *African World* (London), September 10, 1921, copy in Du Bois Papers, reel 10; Logan autobiography, vol. 1, chap. 7, p. 15, RL(H)-II, box 5; Fauset, "Impressions," 14–15.

62. *West African* (London), monthly supplement, [September 1921], copy in Du Bois Papers, reel 10; *Le Petit Parisiene*, September 5, 1921, copy in Du Bois Papers, reel 10.

63. *West African* (London), monthly supplement, [September 1921]; Fauset, "Impressions," 14–15; *Le Petit Parisiene*, September 5, 6, 1921, copy in Du Bois Papers, reel 10; *Figaro* (Paris), September 5, 1921, copy in Du Bois Papers, reel 10.

64. Cited in Winston, *History of the Howard University Department of History*, 83.

65. Geiss, *Pan-African Movement*, 248–49.

66. Isaac Beton to Du Bois, February 4, 1922, Du Bois Papers, reel 11.

67. Logan autobiography, vol. 1, chap. 7, p. 18, RL(H)-II, box 5.

68. Du Bois to Beton, March 1923, Du Bois Papers, reel 11.

69. Beton to Du Bois, February 4, May 29, 1922, Du Bois to Beton, March 1922, Du Bois Papers, reel 11.

70. Beton to Addie W. Hunton, August 2, 1923, Beton to Du Bois, August 3, 1923, Du Bois to Beton and Jose de Magalhaes, August 13, 1923, Du Bois Papers, reel 12; Du Bois to RWL, August 24, 1923, Du Bois Papers, reel 11.

71. RWL to Du Bois, September 6, 1923, Du Bois Papers, reel 11.

72. Ida Gibbs Hunt to Du Bois, September 11, 1923, Du Bois to Hunt, September 27, 1923, Du Bois Papers, reel 11.

73. RWL to Du Bois, September 6, 1923, Du Bois Papers, reel 11.

74. RWL to Fauset, September 19, 1923, Du Bois Papers, reel 11; see also Ida Gibbs Hunt to Du Bois, September 11–13, 1923, Du Bois Papers, reel 11.

75. Du Bois to RWL, August 24, September 20, 1923, Du Bois Papers, reel 11.

76. RWL to Fauset, September 19, 1923, RWL to Du Bois, September 26, 1923, Du Bois Papers, reel 11.

77. RWL to Du Bois, October 4, 1923, Du Bois Papers, reel 11; Minutes of the meeting of the Permanent Bureau of the Pan-African Association, October 5, 1923, handwritten copy, Du Bois Papers, reel 12.

78. "The Third Pan-African Congress," *Crisis* 27 (January 1924): 120–22.

79. Logan autobiography, vol. 1, chap. 7, pp. 18–20, RL(H)-II, box 5.

80. Minutes of a meeting held on January 15, 1925, at the Salem A. M. E. Parish House in Harlem to plan the speaking tour are in RL(H)-I, box 15, "Diagne."

81. Du Bois to Diagne, October 22, 1924, RWL to Du Bois, November 16, 1924, Du Bois Papers, reel 13; Du Bois to Gertrude A. Curtis, February 16, 1925, Curtis to Du Bois, February 17, 1925, Du Bois Papers, reel 15.

82. Logan autobiography (1948 draft), RL(H)-II, doc. box 16.

83. Ibid., Logan autobiography, vol. 1, chap. 7, pp. 20–21, RL(H)-II, box 5.

84. Logan autobiography, vol. 1, chap. 7, pp. 20, 23, RL(H)-II, box 5.

85. Ibid., pp. 26, 23–24, 27.

3. Professor and Politician

1. Andrew Buni, *The Negro in Virginia Politics, 1902–1965* (Charlottesville: University Press of Virginia, 1967), 16–19. On the disfranchisement movement in the South, see C. Vann Woodward, *Origins of the New South,* 2d ed. (Baton Rouge: Louisiana State University Press, 1971), chap. 12, and esp. 341–43 for the movement in Virginia.

2. Buni, *Negro in Virginia Politics,* 78.

3. Ibid., 81–89; Henry Lewis Suggs, *P. B. Young, Newspaperman: Race, Politics, and Journalism in the New South, 1910–1962* (Charlottesville: University Press of Virginia, 1988), 49–52. On John Mitchell, Jr.'s career, see Ann Alexander, "John R. Mitchell, Jr.," in *Dictionary of American Negro Biography,* ed. Rayford W. Logan and Michael R. Winston (New York: W. W. Norton, 1982), 444–45.

4. Buni, *Negro in Virginia Politics,* 72.

5. Charles E. Wynes, "The Evolution of Jim Crow Laws in Twentieth Century Virginia," *Phylon* 28 (Winter 1967): 419; Buni, *Negro in Virginia Politics,* 101–102; Suggs, *P. B. Young,* 59–61.

6. Wynes, "Evolution of Jim Crow," 419–20. For other segregation laws, see, for example, the *Richmond Planet,* June 7, 1924, October 31, 1925.

7. T. Arnold Hill, "Richmond—Louisville—Cincinnati," *Opportunity* 9 (July 1931): 218; Charles W. Sheerin, "In Defense of Richmond," *Opportunity* 9 (September 1931): 282; Josephus Simpson, " 'The Best Negroes in the World,' " *Opportunity* 9 (September 1931): 283; Thomas L. Dabney, "Local Leadership Among Virginia Negroes," *Southern Workman* 59 (January 1930): 31–35.

8. Raymond Gavins, *The Perils and Prospects of Southern Black Leadership: Gordon Blaine Hancock, 1884–1970* (Durham: Duke University Press, 1977), 48–49.

9. Richard Kluger, *Simple Justice* (New York: Vintage, 1977), 459.

10. *Chicago Defender,* July 10, 1943, 20; *Baltimore Afro-American,* November 7, 1925, 1, notes that the NAACP lent at least verbal support to the campaign.

11. Simpson, " 'The Best Negroes,' " 283.

12. Dabney, "Local Leadership Among Virginia Negroes"; Simpson, " 'The Best Negroes.' "

13. Josephus Simpson, "Are Colored People in Virginia a Helpless Minority?" *Opportunity* 12 (December 1934): 374.

14. Rayford W. Logan, interview by *Amistad* magazine, [June 1970], transcript, RL(H)-II, doc. box 6, "Amistad."

15. Raymond Wolters, *The New Negro on Campus: Black College Rebellions in the 1920s* (Princeton: Princeton University Press, 1975), 197.

16. Marie Wood to RWL, [October 30, 1938], RL(H)-II, box 24, "Correspondence."

17. J. Saunders Redding, *Stranger and Alone* (New York: Harcourt, Brace, 1950; reprint, Boston: Northeastern University Press, 1989).

18. Ibid., 119–20.

19. Kenneth R. Manning, *Black Apollo of Science: The Life of Ernest Everett Just* (New York: Oxford University Press, 1983), chap. 4. For the GEB's attitude toward science programs at other black colleges, see George R. Twiss to Wallace Buttrick, August 10, 1922, GEB Records, series 1.2, box 270, folder 2792, Rockefeller Archive Center, Pocantico Hills, N.Y.; GEB Records, series 1.1, box 44, folder 394 documents the unsuccessful efforts of Georgia State College between 1926 and 1931 to establish a science program; Mary McLeod Bethune's futile struggle for GEB help for Bethune-Cookman College between 1905 and 1930 is documented in excruciating detail in GEB Records, series 1.1, box 33, folders 303–4; Rockefeller's gifts to Duke University for science programs are documented in GEB Records, series 1.1, box 110, folders 995–99.

20. John H. Stanfield, *Philanthropy and Jim Crow in American Social Science,* Contributions in Afro-American and African Studies, no. 82 (Westport, Conn.: Greenwood Press, 1985), 192. Stanfield's book is a detailed study of the manipulation of African-American colleges, particularly by the General Education Board and the Julius Rosenwald Fund.

21. Gavins, *Perils and Prospects,* 79–81.

22. Rayford W. Logan, "Mammy Hall," *Virginia Union Bulletin* 29 (February 1929): 5–6; Logan, interview by *Amistad* magazine.

23. Logan autobiography, vol. 1, chap. 8, pp. 2–4, RL(H)-II, box 5; Arthur P. Davis, interview by author, October 2, 1989, Washington, D.C., tape recording in author's possession.

24. Hylan Lewis, interview by author, November 30, 1989, New York City, tape recording in author's possession; Arthur P. Davis, interview by author, October 2, 1989, Washington, D.C., tape recording in author's possession. The following articles, culled from the irregular publications of VUU, illustrate the potency of the debate: Rayford W. Logan, "The Fourth Pan-African Congress,"

Union Hartshorn Bulletin 28 (November 1927): 14–16; Gordon B. Hancock, "A By-Product of Our Advancement," *Virginia Union Bulletin* 29 (January 1929): 3–5; Logan, "Mammy Hall"; Mary Elisabeth Johnson, "Race Consciousness or Race Pride," *Virginia Union Bulletin* 29 (February 1929): 7–8; Rosebud Lauretta Cooper, [Class of 1929], "Social Life at Virginia Union University," *Virginia Union Bulletin* 29 (February 1929): 8–11; Dorothy M. Johns, [Class of 1930], "As Seen by a Student," *Virginia Union Bulletin* 29 (February 1929): 11–12; Arthur P. Davis, "Art: Our One Talent," *Virginia Union Bulletin* 30 (November 1929): 4–6; Hancock, " 'Getting By' and Getting Caught," *Virginia Union Bulletin* 30 (November 1929): 7–8; "This Season and Last in Negro Literature," *Virginia Union Bulletin* 30 (November 1929): 11–12.

25. Arthur P. Davis, "A New Teacher's Impression of Union," *Virginia Union Bulletin* 30 (November 1929): 8–10.

26. Gordon B. Hancock, untitled statement, *The Panther,* Yearbook of Virginia Union University (1928), 138.

27. On the "Hold-Your-Job" campaign and related efforts by Hancock, see Gavins, *Perils and Prospects,* 59–70.

28. Hancock, untitled statement.

29. Gavins, *Perils and Prospects,* 61.

30. Gordon B. Hancock, " 'Getting By' and Getting Caught," 7.

31. Gavins, *Perils and Prospects,* 60–61.

32. Hylan Lewis, interview by author.

33. Ibid.; a synopsis of the Logan-Hancock face-off can be found in Gavins, *Perils and Prospects,* 32–33.

34. Rayford W. Logan, "Nat Turner: Fiend or Martyr?" *Opportunity* 9 (November 1931): 337–39.

35. Rayford W. Logan, "The Hiatus—A Great Negro Middle Class," *Southern Workman* 58 (December 1929): 531–35.

36. Ibid.

37. Logan, interview by *Amistad* magazine; Gavins, *Perils and Prospects,* 33.

38. *Virginia Union University Catalogue,* 1925–26, 1926–27, 1927–28, 1928–29.

39. R. W. Logan, "Negro History Week," *Virginia Union Bulletin* 29 (January 1929): 8–9.

40. *The Panther* (1928), 133; Oliver W. Epps to RWL, September 14, 1979, RL(H)-II, box 21, "Correspondence." Logan taught Epps at Virginia Union in 1929, and Epps wrote Logan to thank him and to recall some of the fundamental lessons he learned in class.

41. *Baltimore Afro-American,* January 23, February 6, 1932; Rayford W. Logan, "Hancock Not Best Spokesman on Negro Racial Problems," letter to editor, *Richmond News Leader,* October 6, 1931.

42. Hylan Lewis, interview by author; Thomas L. Dabney to Ruth Logan, February 1, 1932, RL(H)-II, box 16, "Correspondence"; Ruth Logan to RWL, January 22, 1932, RL(LC), "Letters 1931–1932."

43. Elizabeth Daly, telephone interview by author, July 10, 1990, notes in author's possession; Ulric Haynes, Jr., telephone interview by author, July 13, 1990, notes in author's possession. Haynes was married to Daly's daughter and also had a professional relationship with Logan later in his life. The date and place of Ruth Logan's birth are drawn from her passport, dated July 26, 1951, which is located in RL(H)-I, box 9, "Personal Papers."

44. Gordon Hancock to RWL, August 8, 1966, RL(H)-II, doc. box 2, "Correspondence."

45. Luther P. Jackson to RWL, February 21, 1941, RL(H)-II, box 7, "Speaking Engagements"; Helen Lake, telephone interview by author, June 16, 1990, notes in author's possession. Lake was Ruth's maid of honor.

46. Helen Lake, telephone interview by author; Ruth Robinson to RWL, July 21, 1926, RL(LC), "Letters 1926 (April–August and undated)"; Ruth Robinson to RWL, September 28, December 2, 1926, RL(LC), "Letters, 1926 (September–December)."

47. Ruth Robinson to RWL, July 29, 1926, RL(LC), "Letters, 1926 (April–August and undated)."

48. Logan diary, June 19, 1941.

49. Dorothy Porter Wesley, interview by author, June 14, 1990, Washington, D.C., tape recording in author's possession; Ulric Haynes, telephone interview by author.

50. Hollie I. West, "Out of the Shadow of Segregation," *The Washington Post,* February 27, 1977, H1ff.

51. Frederic C. Walcott to RWL, January 10, 1930, RL(H)-II, box 17, "Frederic C. Walcott." Walcott was Logan's father's employer and a Republican senator from Connecticut; he was a good friend of the Riis family and also a strong recommender of Logan.

52. RWL to William H. Doughty, Jr., March 20, 1937, RL(H)-II, box 24, "Correspondence"; James Phinney Baxter III to Bill Riis, February 2, 1946, RL(H)-I, box 15, "James Phinney Baxter."

53. See chap. 5.

54. Edward Michelson, telephone interview by author June 12, 1990, notes in author's possession; see also letters from Riis to RWL in RL(LC). Michelson worked for Riis in the 1930s.

55. Rayford W. Logan file, Office of the Registrar, Williams College, Williamstown, Massachusetts; Rayford W. Logan, "Education in Haiti," *Journal of Negro History* 15 (1930): 401–60.

56. Rayford W. Logan, "The Haze in Haiti," *The Nation* 124 (1927): 281–83; Rayford W. Logan, "The New Haiti," *Opportunity* 5 (April 1927): 101–3.

57. For the U.S. occupation of Haiti, see Robert Debs Heinl, Jr., and Nancy Gordon Heinl, *Written in Blood: The Story of the Haitian People, 1492–1971* (Boston: Houghton Mifflin, 1978), 406–515.

58. Rayford W. Logan, "Haiti: The Native Point of View," *Southern Workman* 58 (January 1929): 36–40.

59. Ibid.

60. Rayford W. Logan, "The Operation of the Mandate System in Africa," *Journal of Negro History* 13 (October 1928): 423–77.

61. Enshrined by Article XXII of the Versailles treaty, the mandate system was a compromise between advocates of direct annexation—in the spirit of "to the victors go the spoils"—and those who favored international administration of colonial territories. In fact, the compromise, which produced high-sounding but extremely obscure verbiage (the authority of the PMC was never articulated), worked in favor of those imperialists who wanted exclusive, unimpeded control over their respective mandates.

62. Raymond Leslie Buell to RWL, March 13, 1935, April 11, 1935, May 9, 1935, May 21, 1935, Francis Dwight Buell [wife of Raymond Leslie Buell] to RWL, August 5, 1935, RL(H)-II, box 19, "Raymond Leslie Buell." On the history of American loans to Liberia, which benefited American banks but did little to relieve Liberia's financial distress, see Raymond Leslie Buell, *The Native Problem in Africa* (Cambridge, Mass.: Bureau of International Research of Harvard University and Radcliffe College, 1928; reprint, London: Frank Cass & Co., 1965), 2:795–818. The Firestone concession is covered on 2:818–36, while U.S. government support for Firestone is summarized on 2:837–54.

63. Logan, "The Operation of the Mandate System," 431–32.

64. Rayford W. Logan, "Abyssinia Breaks into the Movies," *Southern Workman* 58 (August 1929): 339–44.

65. Rayford W. Logan, "The International Status of the Negro," *Journal of Negro History* 18 (1933): 33–38.

66. Rayford W. Logan, "A 'More Definite Policy' in Haiti," *Southern Workman* 59 (March 1930): 132–35; Rayford W. Logan, "West or South Africa in East Africa?" *Southern Workman* 58 (November 1929): 483–89; Rayford W. Logan, "The Eleko Case," *Southern Workman* 60 (November 1931): 480–82; Logan, "The Operation of the Mandate System," 459; Buell, *Native Problem,* 1:463–64.

67. Buell, *Native Problem,* 2:77–96.

68. Logan, "The International Status of the Negro," 34; Kenneth James King, *Pan-Africanism and Education: A Study of Race Philanthropy and Education in the Southern States of America and East Africa* (Oxford: Clarendon Press, 1971), 75–76.

69. Logan autobiography, vol. 2, chap. 3, pp. 2–3, RL(H)-II, box 5.

70. Wilson Jeremiah Moses, *The Golden Age of Black Nationalism, 1850–1925* (Hamden, Conn.: Archon Books, 1978), chap. 8; Harold R. Isaacs, "Pan-Africanism as 'Romantic Racism,'" in *W. E. B. Du Bois: A Profile,* ed. Rayford W. Logan (New York: Hill and Wang, 1971), 210–38; Imanuel Geiss, *The Pan-African Movement: A History of Pan-Africanism in America, Europe and Africa,* trans. Ann Keep (New York: Africana Publishing Co., 1974), 258–62.

71. Moses, *Golden Age,* 258.

72. Logan, "West or South Africa in East Africa?" 488; idem, "The Operation of the Mandate System," 476: "It is perhaps fitting that the American Negro

should be allowed the last word in making recommendations for the improvement of the [Permanent Mandate] Commission's work."

73. William Loeb, Jr., "Summer Sewing Circle: The Decline of Williamstown [A Somewhat Jaundiced View of the Williamstown Institute of Politics] [1930]," in *Perspectives: A Williams Anthology,* ed. Frederick Rudolph (Williamstown, Mass.: Williams College, 1983), 253–65; Alain Locke to Rayford Logan, November 23, 1928, Alain Locke to Paul Kellog, [written after November 21, 1928], RL(H)-II, box 24, "Correspondence"; Paul U. Kellog to Alain Locke, November 21, 1928, Paul Kellog to Miss Ogden, November 20, 1928, Alain Locke Papers, unprocessed manuscript, Moorland-Spingarn Research Center, Howard University, Washington, D.C. I thank Esme Bhan of the MSRC for bringing to my attention the letters in the Locke Papers.

74. Rayford W. Logan, interview by August Meier, March 3, 1981, transcript, copy in author's possession; Patricia W. Romero, "Carter G. Woodson: A Biography" (Ph.D. diss., Ohio State University, 1971), 92. I sincerely thank Professor Meier for granting me access to this interview, which is deposited at the Schomburg Center for Research in Black Culture, New York.

75. Logan autobiography, vol. 1, chap. 9, p. 2, RL(H)-II, box 5; August Meier and Elliott Rudwick, *Black History and the Historical Profession, 1915–1980* (Urbana: University of Illinois Press, 1986), 90. No copy of this lecture has been uncovered. The autobiography strongly implies that this lecture was delivered to his class at the Ford Hall Forum.

76. Logan, interview by Meier.

77. Rayford W. Logan, *The Diplomatic Relations of the United States with Haiti, 1776–1891* (Chapel Hill: University of North Carolina Press, 1941).

78. Kate Hanke [for Lewis Hanke] to author, August 27, 1990; Lewis Hanke, the distinguished Latin Americanist and former president of the American Historical Association, was a Harvard classmate of Logan's. For two books that evince Logan's impact on the fields of Caribbean studies and diplomatic history, see Alfred N. Hunt, *Haiti's Influence on Antebellum America: Slumbering Volcano in the Caribbean* (Baton Rouge: Louisiana State University Press, 1988), esp. chaps. 3 and 4; and Heinl and Heinl, *Written in Blood: The Story of the Haitian People, 1492–1971.*

79. Ruth Logan to RWL, January 18, 1932, RL(LC), "Letters, 1931–1932."

80. RWL, speech delivered to the current events forum of the Salem M. E. Church, [1932]," RL(H)-I, box 15, "West Africa Trip, 1953." Only a portion of the speech is extant. I have been unable to identify further the Salem M. E. Church, but it is possible that it was the one located in Harlem, under the pastorate of Frederic Cullen.

81. Sharon Hartman Strom, "Florence Luscomb: For Suffrage, Labor, and Peace," in *Moving the Mountain: Women Working for Social Change,* ed. Ellen Cantorow (Old Westbury, N.Y.: Feminist Press, 1980), 4, 6, 26.

82. RWL to Sharon Strom, October 17, 1973, RL(H)-II, box 12, "Correspondence"; Logan autobiography, vol. 1, chap. 9, p. 6, RL(H)-II, box 5.

83. Logan autobiography, vol. 1, chap. 9, pp. 5–6, RL(H)-II, box 5; RWL to Strom.

84. Lewis Hanke to RWL, August 14, 1970, RL(H)-II, box 19, "Lewis Hanke"; Kate Hanke to author.

85. Logan autobiography, vol. 1, chap. 9, p. 8, RL(H)-II, box 5; Kate Hanke to author.

86. William H. Dean to RWL, October 13, 1938, RL(H)-I, box 15, "William Dean."

87. Rayford W. Logan, "William H. Dean," in *Dictionary of American Negro Biography,* ed. Rayford W. Logan and Michael R. Winston (New York: W. W. Norton, 1982).

88. Ruth Logan to RWL, December 11, 1931, RL(LC), "Letters, 1931–1932"; Richard Hurst Hill to RWL, February 6, 1932, RL(H)-II, box 16, "Correspondence."

89. E. P. Davis to RWL, July 5, 1932, RL(H)-II, box 24, "Correspondence."

90. Ruth Logan to RWL, January 20, 1932, RL(LC), "Letters, 1931–1932."

4. *"Bad Negro with a Ph.D."*

1. Patricia W. Romero, "Carter G. Woodson: A Biography" (Ph.D. diss., Ohio State University, 1971), 88–92; quote is on 92. On the hostile public opinion against African Americans and scientific racism, see Dr. Rayford W. Logan, *The Betrayal of the Negro: From Rutherford B. Hayes to Woodrow Wilson* (London: Collier Books, 1965), chap. 18; George M. Frederickson, *The Black Image in the White Mind* (New York: Harper & Row, 1971), chaps. 8 and 9; C. Vann Woodward, *The Strange Career of Jim Crow,* 3d rev. ed. (New York: Oxford University Press, 1974), chap. 3.

2. On Logan, Wesley, Taylor, Greene, Porter, and Savage, see August Meier and Elliott Rudwick, *Black History and the Historical Profession, 1915–1980* (Urbana: University of Illinois Press, 1986), 73–95.

3. John Hope Franklin, "On the Evolution of Scholarship in Afro-American History," in *The State of Afro-American History: Past, Present, and Future,* ed. Darlene Clark Hine (Baton Rouge: Louisiana State University Press, 1986), 14–15. For Logan's own evaluation of the *Journal of Negro History,* see Rayford W. Logan, "An Evaluation of the First Twenty Volumes of *The Journal of Negro History,*" *Journal of Negro History* 20 (1935): 397–405.

4. Meier and Rudwick, *Black History,* 91.

5. On Woodson's approach to black history and the differences in emphasis between Woodson and other scholars since the 1940s, see ibid., 119.

6. Rayford W. Logan, "Magloire Pélage," *Opportunity* 18 (January 1940): 14–15.

7. Rayford W. Logan, "Estevanico, Negro Discoverer of the Southwest: A Critical Reexamination," *Phylon* 1 (1940): 305–14.

8. Meier and Rudwick, *Black History,* 91; Carter G. Woodson, *The African Background Outlined, or Handbook for the Study of the Negro* (Washington, D.C.: Association for the Study of Negro Life and History, 1936; reprint, New York: Negro Universities Press, 1968).

9. Woodson, *African Background Outlined,* 21–22, 27 *n.* 19, 47 *n.* 3, 183.

10. Ibid., 24.

11. Romero, "Carter G. Woodson," 103–4.

12. Meier and Rudwick, *Black History,* 35, 43, 50–51.

13. On Thomas Jesse Jones, see Kenneth James King, *Pan Africanism and Education: A Study of Race Philanthropy and Education in the Southern States of America and East Africa* (Oxford: Clarendon Press, 1971), chap. 3, passim; on the substance of the issues in dispute between Jones and Woodson, see 62–63, 81–84. See also Meier and Rudwick, *Black History,* 43.

14. John H. Stanfield, *Philanthropy and Jim Crow in American Social Science,* Contributions in Afro-American and African Studies, no. 82 (Westport, Conn.: Greenwood Press, 1985), 77–81. On the stultifying effects of this policy, see John Hope Franklin, "The Dilemma of the American Negro Scholar," in John Hope Franklin, *Race and History: Selected Essays, 1938–1988* (Baton Rouge: Louisiana State University Press, 1989), 295–308.

15. Carter G. Woodson to Jackson Davis, April 21, 1932, Carter G. Woodson Papers, box 118-1, folder 1, Moorland-Spingarn Research Center, Howard University, Washington, D.C.

16. W. E. B. Du Bois to RWL, September 10, 1934; RWL to Du Bois, October 10, 1935, the Papers of W. E. B. Du Bois, reel 44.

17. "Memorandum on the 'Encyclopedia of the Negro,'" January 9, 1932, W. E. B. Du Bois and Guy B. Johnson, *Encyclopedia of the Negro: Preparatory Volume with Reference Lists and Reports* (New York: The Phelps-Stokes Fund, Inc., 1945), 191–93; RWL, "William Edward Burghardt Du Bois," address given at Howard University, June 5, 1968, RL(H)-I, box 15, "Du Bois—DANB"; Anson Phelps Stokes to Du Bois, April 21, 1938, Phelps-Stokes Fund Papers, Schomburg Center for Research in Black Culture, New York Public Library, New York City. More specific citation of material in the Phelps-Stokes Fund Papers is impossible, for as of December 1990, the collection was being reprocessed.

18. Du Bois to James H. Dillard, November 30, 1931, Du Bois Papers, reel 34; Du Bois to Anson Phelps Stokes, December 9, 1931, Du Bois Papers, reel 35.

19. Stokes to Jackson Davis, March 31, 1932, Phelps-Stokes Fund Papers.

20. Jackson Davis to Stokes, April 19, 1932, Phelps-Stokes Fund Papers.

21. Carter Woodson to Benjamin Brawley, November 27, 1931, Du Bois Papers, reel 34; Woodson to the Promoters of the "Negro Encyclopaedia," October 22, 1932, Phelps-Stokes Fund Papers.

22. Romero, "Carter G. Woodson," 202.

23. Patricia W. Romero, Woodson's biographer, concluded that the matter "cannot be answered satisfactorily." The idea probably occurred to him in the 1920s, and he had on hand certain elements of an encyclopedia, including lists of

topics and some biographical sketches. Ibid., 199–201. In his profile of Woodson, Logan stated that Woodson in fact developed the idea of an encyclopedia first. Rayford W. Logan, "Phylon Profile VI: Carter G. Woodson," *Phylon* 6 (1945): 315–21. He remembered that one of his tasks as Woodson's assistant was to help prepare the encyclopedia, which was to be drawn from material extant in the *Journal of Negro History*. Rayford W. Logan, interview by August Meier, March 3, 1981, Washington, D.C., copy of notes in author's possession.

24. Du Bois to Woodson, January 29, 1932, Woodson to Du Bois, February 11, 1932, Du Bois Papers, reel 37; Woodson to John Hope, February 9, 1934, quoted in Stokes to Woodson, February 12, 1934, Phelps-Stokes Fund Papers.

25. Carter G. Woodson, "Remember 1917," June 17, 1936, Woodson Papers, folder 19. This item was a press release to the *Baltimore Afro-American*.

26. On Robert Park and Booker T. Washington, see Fred H. Matthews, *Quest for an American Sociology: Robert E. Park and the Chicago School* (Montreal: McGill-Queens University Press, 1977), chap. 3.

27. Du Bois to Stokes, November 1, 1937, Du Bois Papers, reel 47.

28. Anson Phelps Stokes to Thomas Jesse Jones, April 25, 1935, Du Bois Papers, reel 44; "Preliminary Memorandum on the 'Encyclopedia of the Negro' Project," January 11, 1932, Du Bois Papers, reel 42; Stokes to Jackson Davis, February 12, March 4, 1938, Du Bois to Stokes, memo, February 25, 1938, Phelps-Stokes Fund Papers. On the American Council of Learned Societies, see Robert L. Harris, Jr., "Segregation and Scholarship: The American Council of Learned Societies' Committee on Negro Studies, 1941–1950," *Journal of Black Studies* 12 (1982): 315–31.

29. Du Bois to RWL, April 6, 1936, RWL to Du Bois, April 8, 1936, Du Bois Papers, reel 46.

30. Du Bois to Anson Phelps Stokes, November 11, 1935, Du Bois Papers, reel 44; Du Bois to RWL, October 16, 1936, Stokes to Du Bois, March 21, 1936, RWL to Stokes, December 14, 1936, Du Bois Papers, reel 46; Professor Rayford W. Logan, "Bibliography of Bibliographies Dealing Directly or Indirectly with the Negro," *Encyclopedia of the Negro*, 183–90. Logan's Latin American network continued to meet informally into the 1940s.

31. RWL to Du Bois, October 3, 1936, "Opinion on an Encyclopaedia of the Negro, 1935–1936," Du Bois Papers, reel 46.

32. RWL to Woodson, November 13, 1935, Woodson to Clarence Bacote, January 14, 1936, Woodson to RWL, April 7, 1936, Rufus Clement to Woodson, October 20, 1937, RL(H)-I, box 15, "ASNLH"; Logan, "Phylon Profile," 318; Woodson, "An Open Letter to the *Afro-American* on the Negro Encyclopedia," June 3, 1936, Woodson Papers, folder 15.

33. Meier and Rudwick, *Black History,* 92. The authors quote letters from Woodson to Alrutheus A. Taylor, December 23, 1936, and from RWL to Taylor, December 14, 1936, in the A. A. Taylor Papers, Fisk University, Nashville, Tennessee. As of June 1992, however, these papers remain unprocessed and are closed to scholars.

34. Ralph J. Bunche, "A Critical Analysis of the Tactics and Programs of Minority Groups," *Journal of Negro Education* 4 (1935): 308–20; the citation appears on 316.

35. See RWL to Du Bois, October 3, 1936.

36. RWL to Du Bois, March 6, 1939, Du Bois Papers, reel 50.

37. On Herskovits's career, see Walter Jackson, "Melville Herskovits and the Search for Afro-American Culture," in *Malinowski, Rivers, Benedict and Others: Essays in Culture and Personality,* ed. George W. Stocking, Jr. (Madison: University of Wisconsin Press, 1986), 93–126.

38. Melville Herskovits to Elsie Clews Parsons, June 8, August 23, 1936, Parsons to Herskovits, June 11, 1936, Melville J. Herskovits (1895–1963) Papers 1906–63, box 18, folder 3, Africana Manuscripts, Northwestern University Archives, Evanston, Illinois.

39. RWL, "William Edward Burghardt Du Bois."

40. Logan diary, February 14, 1951. Logan had this conversation with Herskovits over lunch in Evanston and wrote it down the following day. Herskovits's negative response to the GEB was not the last time he tried to stop funding for the project. In 1940 he replied in a similar fashion to a Library of Congress inquiry about whether it should provide a smaller grant to the Encyclopedia of the Negro. Herskovits to Madison Bentley, February 8, 1940, Herskovits Papers, box 7, folder 19.

41. See, for example, "J. D. interview with Walter White," January 18, 1939, General Education Board Records, series 1.2, box 260, folder 2688, Rockefeller Archive Center, Pocantico Hills, New York.

42. Jackson Davis to Stokes, April 3, 1937, Du Bois Papers, reel 47.

43. Davis to Stokes, April 7, 1938, Phelps-Stokes Fund Papers. In a letter to Benjamin Brawley, Stokes explained the GEB's reasoning. Even with all the built-in controls, the philanthropy was "not sufficiently convinced that the Encyclopaedia could be removed entirely from propaganda and made absolutely scientific and objective to be willing at this time to grant the money." Stokes to Brawley, April 13, 1938, Phelps-Stokes Fund Papers.

44. Stokes to Davis, November 10, 1938, Phelps-Stokes Fund Papers. The Carnegie Corporation's unfavorable disposition to the Encyclopedia project was evident as early as a year before its final decision. See Frederick Keppel to Stokes, December 20, 1937, Du Bois Papers, reel 47.

45. Stanfield, *Philanthropy and Jim Crow,* 195.

46. RWL, "William Edward Burghardt Du Bois."

47. RWL to Mordecai Johnson, March 31, 1948, RL(H)-II, box 18, "Mordecai Johnson."

48. Frederic C. Walcott to RWL, January 10, 1930, RL(H)-II, box 17, "Frederic C. Walcott."

49. *Baltimore Afro-American,* July 7, 14, 21, 1934.

50. RWL to John Hope, July 31, 1934, RL(H)-II, box 19, "John Hope."

51. *Baltimore Afro-American,* August 11, 1934.

52. Ibid., and August 25, 1934.

53. On Hughes's essay and visit to Haiti, see Arnold Rampersad, *The Life of Langston Hughes*, vol. 1, *1902–1941: I, Too, Sing America* (New York: Oxford University Press, 1986), 204–9.

54. *Baltimore Afro-American*, August 18, September 8, 1934. On the end of the occupation and its credits and debits, see Robert Debs Heinl and Nancy Gordon Heinl, *Written in Blood: The Story of the Haitian People, 1492–1971* (Boston: Houghton Mifflin, 1978), 506–14.

55. *Baltimore Afro-American*, August 18, 1934. Although this sounds quixotic, he later drafted a proposal on the post–World War II Western Hemispheric economy for Nelson Rockefeller that was in part based on this embryonic idea. See chap. 5 below.

56. RWL to John Hope, January 10, 1936, RL(H)-II, box 19, "John Hope." Logan finally achieved his goal of increased participation by the African-American scholarly community in U.S–Latin American relations when he went to Howard University in 1938 and established a close relationship between the university and the Library of Congress's Hispanic Foundation, which was headed by his old friend Lewis Hanke. See RWL to Mordecai Johnson, November 13, 29, 1939, RL(H)-II, box 18, "Mordecai Johnson."

57. Raymond Leslie Buell to RWL, April 3, 11, 1935, RL(H)-II, box 19, "Raymond Leslie Buell."

58. Charles H. Wesley, *The History of Alpha Phi Alpha*, fourteenth printing (Chicago: The Foundation Publishers, 1981), is the standard account of the fraternity.

59. Ibid., 172–76.

60. RWL, "The Negro and the National Recovery Program," speech to the Alpha Phi Alpha Annual Convention, St. Louis, Mo., December 31, 1933, RL(H)-II, doc. box 15, "Writings."

61. "The Negro and the New Deal," *Sphinx* 20 (May 1935): 2–39; "New Deal vs. the Negro," *Sphinx* 22 (December 1936): 33–43; "New Deal Report," *Sphinx* 23 (February 1937): 10–13, 33–34.

62. Wesley, *History of Alpha Phi Alpha*, 219.

63. John B. Kirby, *Black Americans in the Roosevelt Era* (Knoxville: University of Tennessee Press, 1980), 155–58. For a list of member organizations and evidence of Wesley's participation in the JCNR, see *Senate Misc. Docs.* no. 217, 74th Cong., 2d sess., (Serial 10016), 37–38.

64. Kirby, *Black Americans in the Roosevelt Era*, 177–78.

65. Arthur C. Logan to RWL, August 8, 1936, RL(H)-I, box 9, "New Deal Investigation"; capitalization in original.

66. *Memphis World*, January 7, 1941, clipping in RL(H)-I, box 15, "Colored Reserve Officers."

67. Arthur C. Logan to RWL, January 12, 1935, Lawrence A. Oxley to RWL, February 18, 1935, Arthur C. Logan to Joseph H. B. Evans, September 1, 1936, RL(H)-I, box 9, "New Deal Investigation."

68. Robert L. Fairchild to RWL, January 11, 1937, RL(H)-I, box 9, "New Deal Investigation."

69. B. T. McGraw to RWL, January 27, 1941, RL(H)-I, box 9a, "Alpha Phi Alpha—Correspondence."

70. On the "Go-to-High School, Go-to-College" campaign, see Wesley, *History of Alpha Phi Alpha,* 204–5.

71. RWL, "The Negro and the National Recovery Program"; RWL to Alpha Phi Alpha chapters, March 27, 1934, RL(H)-II, box 11, "Alpha Phi Alpha."

72. RWL, speech to a meeting of the Federation of Parent-Teachers Associations, Cardozo High School, Washington, D.C., March 15, 1939, RL(H)-II, doc. box 13, "Writings."

73. RWL to Charles Wesley, February 22, 1934, RL(H)-II, box 11, "Alpha Phi Alpha."

74. Report attached to letter from Rose Cosby to William Pickens, May 30, 1934, NAACP Papers, Group I, Series G, Box 44, "Atlanta, GA, May–July 1934," Library of Congress, Washington, D.C., hereinafter cited as NAACP(LC). On Lugenia Burns Hope's role in the citizenship school, see Jacqueline Anne Rouse, *Lugenia Burns Hope: Black Southern Reformer* (Athens: University of Georgia Press, 1989), 119–20.

75. Rayford W. Logan, interview by *Amistad* magazine, [June 1970], transcript, RL(H)-II, doc. box 6, "Amistad."

76. RWL to Charles Wesley, February 22, 1934; RWL to Walter White, September 29, 1934, Walter White to RWL, October 3, 1934, RL(H)-I, box 15, "Walter White."

77. RWL to AΦA Chapters, March 27, 1934, RL(H)-II, box 11, "Alpha Phi Alpha."

78. Benjamin J. Davis to RWL, May 14, 1938, RWL to Benjamin J. Davis, June 7, 1938, RL(H)-II, doc. box 16, "Correspondence."

79. RWL, "The Quest for Democracy," report to the Second All-Southern Negro Youth Conference, April 1, 1938, RL(H)-II, doc. box 15, "Writings"; *Atlanta Daily World,* April 4, 1938, RL(H)-II, box 21, "Addresses." At the Southern Negro Youth Conference, two years before the NAACP initiated *Smith* v. *Allwright,* Logan called for a legal challenge to the white primary. On *Smith* v. *Allwright,* see Richard Kluger, *Simple Justice* (New York: Vintage: 1977), 234–37.

80. E. Franklin Frazier, *Black Bourgeoisie* (New York: The Free Press, 1957), chap. 4, esp. 94–95.

81. See, for example, R. W. Lights to RWL, November 7, 1934, RL(H)-I, box 7, "Correspondence"; RWL to William H. Gray, Jr., September 12, 1939, Gray to RWL, November 22, 1939, B. A. Jones to RWL, March 13, 1940, Roscoe C. Giles to RWL, January 22, 31, 1941, B. T. McGraw to RWL, January 27, 1941, Vertner W. Tandy to RWL, January 7, 1941, C. Arthur Jackson to RWL, May 5, 1941, RL(H)-I, box 9a, "Alpha Phi Alpha—Correspondence." The letter from Tandy, a founding member of the fraternity, comments on the hazing.

82. *Pittsburgh Courier,* May 4, 1935, *Nashville Globe and Independent,* [April or May] 1935, *Kansas City Star,* [1935], *Chicago Defender,* May 11, 1935, *Atlanta Daily World,* May 5, 1935, *Baltimore Afro-American,* May 25, 1935. These clippings—and several others from unidentified newspapers—are all in RL(H)-II, box 11, "Alpha Phi Alpha." See also George Peterson, Jr., to RWL, August 1, 1937, C. A. Cowan to Mack C. Spears, December 20, 1935, RL(H)-II, box 11, "Alpha Phi Alpha"; H. James Greene to RWL, August 21, 1937, RL(H)-I, box 7, "Correspondence."

83. Charles Wesley to RWL, January 10, 21, 24, 1936, RWL to Wesley, January 15, 1936, RL(H)-II, box 11, "Alpha Phi Alpha"; Thurgood Marshall to RWL, January 17, 1936, RL(H)-II, box 18, "Thurgood Marshall."

84. C. A. Cowan to Mack C. Spears, December 20, 1935, RL(H)-II, box 11, "Alpha Phi Alpha"; *Norfolk Journal and Guide,* May 11, 1935.

85. RWL to Dr. L. Lloyd Burrell, Jr., January 21, 1945, RL(H)-II, doc. box 13, "Correspondence."

86. See chap. 5 below.

87. There is an urgent need for hard research into the role of the black fraternities in the social and political movements of the 1930s and 1940s.

88. Logan was elected to the executive committee in March 1936; see Dorcia Steele to NAACP Headquarters, July 1, 1936, NAACP(LC) I,G,44, "Atlanta, GA, January–March 1936." Some of the other twenty members elected to the committee were the Reverend M. L. King (father of Martin Luther King, Jr.), Lugenia Hope, A. T. Walden, Eugene Martin (brother-in-law of Walter White), and Forrester Washington, the director of the Atlanta University School of Social Work, who was elected branch president.

89. Charles H. Martin, *The Angelo Herndon Case and Southern Justice* (Baton Rouge: Louisiana State University Press, 1976), 30–31, 98–99.

90. Ibid., 32–34.

91. Josephine Dibble Murphy to Walter White, July 30, 1934, NAACP(LC), I,G,44, "Atlanta, GA, May–July 1934"; *Atlanta Daily World,* July 29, 1934.

92. Josephine Dibble Murphy to Walter White, July 30, 1934, May 31, 1934, NAACP(LC), I,G,44, "Atlanta, GA, May–July 1934"; Eugene Martin to Walter White, March 11, 1936, NAACP(LC), I,G,44, "Atlanta, GA, January–March 1936"; Rouse, *Lugenia Burns Hope,* 153–54 *n.* 54.

93. Martin, *Angelo Herndon Case,* 85.

94. Walter White to A. T. Walden, January 24, 1933, Daisy Lampkin to Roy Wilkins, February 4, 1933, NAACP(LC), I,G,44.

95. Dan T. Carter, *Scottsboro: A Tragedy of the American South,* rev. ed. (Baton Rouge: Louisiana State University Press, 1979), 62–63, 85–86.

96. RWL, "The Growth of Liberal and Radical Thought Among Negroes," address to the NAACP Convention, June 30, 1933, Chicago, RL(H)-II, box 7, "Correspondence."

97. Martin, *Angelo Herndon Case,* 121–28; Logan autobiography, vol. 1, chap. 10, pp. 20–22, RL(H)-II, box 5.

98. RWL to Florence Luscomb, February 9, 1935, Florence Luscomb Papers,

Schlesinger Library, Radcliffe College, Cambridge, Massachusetts; Logan auto-biography, vol. 1, chap. 10, pp. 20–22, RL(H)-II, box 5.

99. RWL to Raymond Leslie Buell, May 15, 1935, Buell to RWL, May 21, 1935, RL(H)-II, box 19, "Raymond Leslie Buell"; *Atlanta Constitution,* May 7, 1935.

100. Logan, interview by *Amistad* magazine.

101. RWL to Raymond Leslie Buell, May 25, 1935, RL(H)-II, box 19, "Raymond Leslie Buell"; Logan autobiography, vol. 1, chap. 10, p. 22, RL(H)-II, box 5.

102. Nannie H. Burroughs to RWL, November 4, 1939, RL(H)-II, box 24, "Correspondence."

103. *Chicago Defender,* July 10, 1943.

104. B. Joyce Ross, *J. E. Spingarn and the Rise of the NAACP, 1911–1939* (New York: Atheneum, 1972), 174, 170–73.

105. On the Amenia Conference and Abram Harris, see ibid., 161, 162, 180–85, 220, and Harvard Sitkoff, *A New Deal for Blacks: The Emergence of Civil Rights as a National Issue* (New York: Oxford University Press, 1978), 250–51. E. Franklin Frazier and Ralph Bunche were also at Amenia. Logan was invited—only thirty-three people were asked to participate—but illness prevented him from attending. RWL to Joel E. Spingarn, May 2, August 12, 1933, Joel E. Spingarn Papers, box 94-7, folder 285, Moorland-Spingarn Research Center, Howard University, Washington, D.C.

106. On Ralph Bunche's radical phase, see Charles P. Henry, "Civil Rights and National Security: The Case of Ralph Bunche," in *Ralph Bunche: The Man and His Times,* ed. Benjamin Rivlin (New York: Holmes & Meier, 1990), 50–66. See also John B. Kirby, "Race, Class, and Politics: Ralph Bunche and Black Protest," in *Ralph Bunche: The Man and His Times,* 28–49; a discussion of Bunche and the NNC is on 35–38. On the NNC, see Mark Naison, *Communists in Harlem during the Depression* (Chicago and Urbana: University of Illinois Press, 1983; reprint, New York: Grove Press, 1984), 178–80; quote is on 180. See also Sitkoff, *New Deal for Blacks,* 258–60, and Kirby, *Black Americans in the Roosevelt Era,* 164–70.

107. A synopsis of the NNC's national and local activity is in Sitkoff, *New Deal for Blacks,* 259–60.

108. RWL, "The Negro and the National Recovery Program."

109. Ibid.

5. *"The White Man's Distress Is the Black Man's Gain"*

1. Logan's time at Howard is discussed in chap. 8.

2. David Levering Lewis, "The Origins and Causes of the Civil Rights Movement," *The Civil Rights Movement in America,* ed. Charles W. Eagles (Jackson: University Press of Mississippi, 1986), 3–18.

3. Harvard Sitkoff, *A New Deal for Blacks: The Emergence of Civil Rights as a*

National Issue (New York: Oxford University Press, 1978), 298–99; Walter White to RWL, July 18, 1935, RL(H)-I, box 15, "Walter White"; John Hope Franklin and Alfred A. Moss, Jr., *From Slavery to Freedom: A History of Negro Americans,* 6th ed. (New York: Knopf, 1988), 406.

4. Rayford W. Logan, "Negro Studies War Some More for New Angle," *Norfolk Journal and Guide,* June 28, 1935. This article appeared with modified titles in newspapers across the country throughout the summer and fall of 1935.

5. Ulysses Lee, *The Employment of Negro Troops,* United States Army in World War II, Special Studies (Washington, D.C.: Office of the Chief of Military History, United States Army, 1966), 51, 52–53, 55–65; *Pittsburgh Courier,* May 4, June 8, December 13, 1940; Logan diary, June 1, 1940.

6. "Objectives of the Committee on Participation of Negroes in the National Defense Program," NAACP(LC) II,A,333, "LABOR, Discrimination in National Defense Industries, General 1940–41."

7. List of state affiliates to the CPNNDP, RL(H)-I, box 2, "CPNNDP"; Charles W. Anderson, Jr., to RWL, April 3, 1941, RL(H)-I, box 9a, "Alpha Phi Alpha—Correspondence"; B. T. Holmes to RWL, April 11, 1941, RL(H)-I, box 2, "CPNNDP."

8. Senate Committee on Appropriations, *Military Establishment Appropriation Bill for 1941: Hearings Before the Subcommittee on Appropriations,* 76th Cong., 3d sess., 14 May 1940, 365–71, 371–73.

9. House Committee on Military Affairs, *Selective Compulsory Military Training and Service: Hearings Before the Committee on Military Affairs,* 76th Cong., 3d sess., 14 August 1940, 585–89.

10. *Pittsburgh Courier,* September 7, 1940; Logan diary, August 31, 1940. Charles Houston's position is complicated. In his testimony before the Senate subcommittee hearings on Burke-Wadsworth, Houston represented exclusively the CPNNDP. By August, though, Houston again backed the NAACP position. It is not clear why Houston changed his position.

11. Logan diary, September 4, 6, 14, 1940; Lee, *Employment of Negro Troops,* 72.

12. Ibid., September 26, 1940.

13. Walter White, *A Man Called White* (New York: Viking, 1948), 186.

14. Ibid., 187.

15. Logan diary, October 12, 1940; Roy Wilkins and Thurgood Marshall to Walter White, October 19, 1940, NAACP(LC) II,A,416, "March on Washington, General, 1940–41"; *Pittsburgh Courier,* October 19, 1940. The *Pittsburgh Courier,* October 26, 1940, reported that Eugene Kinckle Jones of the Urban League distanced his organization from White by stating that it did not take part in the White House meeting.

16. RWL, speech to a rally organized by the CPNNDP, [Cincinnati], [March 9, 1941], RL(H)-I, box 15, "Colored Reserve Officers."

17. Roy Wilkins to Walter White, September 16, 1940, NAACP(LC), II,A,441, "National Defense, General, 1940–41."

18. Roger William Riis to Lowell Mellett, October 10, 1940, RL(H)-I, box 15, "Colored Reserve Officers."

19. Logan diary, October 25, 1940; RWL to Bill Riis, October 25, 1940, Franklin D. Roosevelt to RWL, November 7, 1940, cited in full in RWL, speech to Alpha Phi Alpha Annual Convention, December 22, 1940, RL(H)-I, box 15, "Colored Reserve Officers." In this speech, Logan made much of the fact that he, Patterson, and Long were loyal to and active in AΦA: "I shall have time to mention only one other achievement of Alpha men. This is of such historic significance that I have included the letter to me from President Roosevelt which proves that three Alpha men succeeded, after others had failed, in obtaining assurances that colored Reserve officers would be assigned to not only National Guard units but also to the newly created units."

20. For evidence of the NAACP rank and file's views, see Roy Wilkins to Walter White, December 5, 1940, NAACP(LC), II,A,442, "National Defense, Participation of Negroes in, Conference, 1940–41."

21. Report of the Findings Committee of Military and Naval Defense [of the Hampton Conference on the Participation of the Negro in National Defense], November 25–26, 1940, Roy Wilkins to Walter White, December 5, 1940, NAACP(LC), II,A,442, "National Defense, Participation of Negroes in, Conference, 1940–41"; *Pittsburgh Courier*, December 6, 1940. William Dean, Logan's close friend and son-in-law of Channing Tobias, wrote to Logan that "I see by the newspapers that you were *the* Conference at Hampton." Dean to RWL, November 29, 1940, RL(H)-I, box 15, "William Dean."

22. Logan diary, January 26, June 25, 27, 1941. For other elements of Logan's plans on the legislative front, see Logan diary, January 13, March 19, 25, 1941; *Pittsburgh Courier*, January 25, February 8, 22, 1941; Louis Lautier to Walter White, January 15, 1941, NAACP(LC), II,A,333, "LABOR, Discrimination in National Defense Industries, General 1940–41."

23. On White's efforts to get Senate backing for Senate Resolution 75, see Jeanetta Welch to White, April 23, 1941, White to Welch, April 24, 1941, White to Welch, telegram, April 24, 1941, Welch to Charles F. Clark, June 20, 1941, Welch to White, June 20, 1941, White to Welch, July 14, 1941, White to Welch, July 29, 1941, NAACP(LC), II,A,524, "Senate Resolution #75—Alpha Kappa Alpha"; White to Stephen Spingarn, July 15, 1941, Stephen Spingarn to White, July 16, 1941, NAACP(LC), II,A,525, "Senate Resolution #75, Correspondence, General 1941." For a comparison of Logan's and White's plans for hearings and lobbying strategy, see Logan diary, January 26, March 19, March 25, 1941; Walter White to William Hastie, December 27, 1940, Walter White to the Executives, memo, December 19, 1940, "Tentative List of Witnesses for Proposed Senate Investigation of the Treatment of the Negro in the National Defense Program—Submitted by the National Association for the Advancement of Colored People to the Senate Committee on Education and Labor," March 27, 1941, NAACP(LC), II,A,525, "Senate Resolution #75, Correspondence, General 1941."

24. Walter White to A. Philip Randolph, April 24, 1941, NAACP(LC),

II,A,525, "Senate Resolution #75, Correspondence, General 1941." See also White, *A Man Called White,* 189.

25. On Logan's dispute with White and White's efforts to cancel the Truman committee hearings, see RWL to William G. Nunn [managing editor of the *Pittsburgh Courier*], July 4, 1941, Nunn to RWL, July 10, 1941, RWL to Nunn, July 12, 1941, RWL to Nunn, August 3, 1941, RWL to Harry Truman, [written after July 9, 1941], RWL to Henry J. Richardson, Jr., July 17, 1941, RL(H)-I, box 2, "CPNNDP"; Charles P. Clark to RWL, August 16, 1941, RL(H)-II, box 24, "Correspondence"; Logan diary, June 28, July 11, 1941; Stephen Spingarn to Walter White, July 16, 1941, NAACP(LC), II,A,525, "Senate Resolution #75, Correspondence, General 1941." On White's uncompromising position, see Walter White to Stephen Spingarn, July 15, 1941, NAACP(LC), II,A,525, "Senate Resolution #75, Correspondence, General 1941." The *Kansas City Call,* July 18, 1941, criticized White for his unbending stand, as did the *Pittsburgh Courier,* July 5, 1941, which carried also a bitter attack upon White by Logan. White's reply appeared in the *Courier,* July 12, 1941.

John H. Bracey, Jr., and August Meier believe that it was Logan who sabotaged the NAACP's efforts to get Senate hearings on discrimination. John H. Bracey, Jr., and August Meier, "Allies or Adversaries?: The NAACP, A. Philip Randolph and the 1941 March on Washington," *Georgia Historical Quarterly* 75 (1991): 1–17. But Logan's support for the NAACP's call for a congressional investigation, White's success in delaying indefinitely the convocation of the Truman committee hearings (even though they were supported by African-American luminaries like Mary McLeod Bethune, the sociologist Ira Reid, Robert Weaver, Rev. R. W. Brooks, and John P. Davis), and White's own aversion to participating in anything he did not control suggest otherwise. I want to thank Professors Bracey and Meier for graciously sharing their article with me before it was published; references to this article are to the unpublished typescript.

26. Logan diary, June 28, 1941.

27. *Pittsburgh Courier,* July 5, 12, 19, 1941.

28. On Vann's war with the NAACP and A. Philip Randolph and how this dovetailed with his efforts to build the *Courier*'s circulation, see Andrew Buni, *Robert L. Vann of the PITTSBURGH COURIER: Politics and Black Journalism* (Pittsburgh: University of Pittsburgh Press, 1974), chap. 7, esp. 146–71.

29. Walter White to Stephen Spingarn, July 15, 1941, Spingarn to White, July 16, 1941, NAACP(LC), II,A,525, "Senate Resolution #75, Correspondence, General 1941."

30. Logan diary, December 13, 1941.

31. Information on Ted Berry was drawn from G. James Fleming and Christian E. Burckel, eds., *Who's Who in Colored America,* 7th ed. (Yonkers-on-Hudson: Christian E. Burckel & Assoc., 1950), 588; Iris Cloyd, ed., *Who's Who Among Black Americans,* 6th ed. (Detroit: Gale Research, 1990), 95.

32. Ted Berry to Walter White, February 24, 1941, White to Berry, February 3, 1941, NAACP(LC), II,A,333, "LABOR, Discrimination in National Defense In-

dustries, General 1940–41." For other evidence of White's noncooperation, see Louis Lautier to Walter White, July 1, 1940, Lautier to White, July 18, 1940, Roy Wilkins to Lautier, July 28, 1940, Lautier to White, January 15, 1940, White to Lautier, January 25, 1940, NAACP(LC), II,A,333, "LABOR, Discrimination in National Defense Industries, General 1940–41."

33. Logan diary, October 22, 1940; Arthur C. Logan to RWL, January 12, 1935, RL(H)-I, box 9, "New Deal Investigation."

34. William H. Hastie to the Secretary [Walter White], memo, January 4, 1941, NAACP(LC), II,A,525, "Senate Resolution #75, Correspondence, General 1940–41"; Logan diary, January 26, 1941.

35. *Pittsburgh Courier,* February 22, 1941.

36. Logan diary, October 22, 1940.

37. Ibid., August 13, 1942.

38. RWL to Col. George J. B. Fisher, August 14, 1942, RL(H)-I, box 15, "From 1942 Diary."

39. Logan diary, June 24, 1941.

40. A. Philip Randolph to RWL, April 24, 1941, RL(H)-I, box 15, "March on Washington."

41. The manifesto, which appeared in black newspapers across the country, was published in the *Pittsburgh Courier,* January 25, 1941.

42. Mark Naison, *Communists in Harlem During the Depression* (Urbana: University of Illinois Press, 1983; reprint, New York: Grove Press, 1984), 310–12, points out that Randolph appropriated the Communist party's protest tactics and was in a position to implement them far more thoroughly than it was. Randolph billed it as a "Negro march" in large part to exclude the Communists.

The best general account of the March on Washington is Herbert Garfinkel, *When Negroes March: The March on Washington Movement in the Organizational Politics for FEPC* (Glencoe, Ill.: The Free Press, 1959). On the NAACP's role in the MOWM, Garfinkel has been supplanted by Bracey and Meier, who conclude that the NAACP, far from being an unwilling participant, eagerly embraced the march after their own program failed, but then backed away from its tactics after the movement won Executive Order 8802.

43. A. Philip Randolph to Walter White, March 18, 1941, cited in Bracey and Meier, "Allies or Adversaries?"

44. *Pittsburgh Courier,* January 4, April 19, May 3, 1941; Bracey and Meier, "Allies or Adversaries?"

45. On the *Courier'*s opposition to the MOWM, see Ira Lewis to Phil Randolph, June 9, 1941, NAACP(LC), II,A,416, "March on Washington, General 1940–41"; *Pittsburgh Courier,* June 14, 1941.

46. Minutes of subcommittee meeting on "March to Washington" held in NAACP Office, April 10, 1941, NAACP(LC), II,A,416, "March on Washington, General 1940–41"; Lester Granger to RWL, April 14, 1941, RL(H)-I, box 15, "March on Washington."

47. Walter White to the Executives [of the NAACP], memo, December 19,

1940, White to William Hastie, December 27, 1940, NAACP(LC), II,A,525, "Senate Resolution #75, Correspondence, General 1941"; Logan diary, April 30, March 25, 1941; Bracey and Meier, "Allies or Adversaries?"

48. Eugene Davidson, "The Birth of Executive Order 8802," Eugene Davidson Papers, box 91-2, Folder 43, Moorland-Spingarn Research Center, Howard University, Washington, D.C. Davidson was the assistant director of the MOWM as well as the marshal of the march.

49. The account of this meeting is based on Logan diary, June 24, 1941, and Eugene Davidson, "The Birth of Executive Order 8802." These are the only two accounts by participants in the final negotiations. Logan wrote his right after the conclusion of the talks; the date of Davidson's essay is unknown. Significantly, they are similar in almost every detail.

50. Garfinkel, *When Negroes March*, 53–60, details the blustery statements by Walter White, who said the NAACP's membership alone would guarantee one hundred thousand participants in the march. But Garfinkel argues that there is no certain way to determine whether the march would have been a success, because it certainly tapped a vein of sentiment in the African-American community. Bracey and Meier state that the MOWM's victory was "probably based more on bluff than power. . . ."

51. RWL, speech to the American Teachers Association, [before August 4, 1941], RL(H)-I, box 2, "CPNNDP."

52. Ibid.

53. [RWL, "The History of the Committee on Participation of Negroes in the National Defense Program," September 1941], RL(H)-I, box 2, "CPNNDP."

54. Logan diary, March 19, May 11, 1941, February 22, 1942.

55. RWL, speech to a rally organized by the CPNNDP, [Cincinnati], [March 9, 1941], RL(H)-I, box 15, "Colored Reserve Officers."

56. Rayford W. Logan, "The Crisis of Democracy in the Western Hemisphere," *Journal of Negro Education* 10 (1941): 344–52. The quote is on 351–52.

57. RWL, speech to a rally organized by the CPNNDP, [March 9, 1941].

58. RWL, speech to the American Teachers Association, [before August 4, 1941]. The soft spots of the opponents of civil rights are recounted ably in Sitkoff, *New Deal for Blacks*, chap. 12.

59. RWL, speech to a rally organized by the CPNNDP, [March 9, 1941].

60. Louis Lautier to Walter White, January 15, 1941, NAACP(LC), II,A,333, "LABOR, Discrimination in National Defense Industries, General 1940–41," expresses Logan's position, which he developed in a 1944 essay, "The Negro Wants First-Class Citizenship," in *What the Negro Wants*, ed. Rayford W. Logan (Chapel Hill: University of North Carolina Press, 1944; reprint, New York: Agathon Press, 1969), 1–30. For more on *What the Negro Wants*, see chap. 6.

Logan would not compromise on this issue. In 1941, some unions tried to find a middle ground between exclusion and integration. The International Association of Machinists proposed the establishment of a separate national union for African Americans. Logan rejected this out of hand. Logan diary, July 11, 1941.

61. Rayford W. Logan, *The Negro and the Post-War World: A Primer* (Washington, D.C.: The Minorities Publishers, 1945), 87. Logan said that his stump speech on "the white man's distress" was coolly received in Detroit because, he thought, his criticism of organized labor went against the grain of many African Americans in that union stronghold. Logan diary, January 13, 1941.

Logan answered the criticism—leveled by unions and others—that giving government power to compel unions to break down the color bar also gave it the right to interfere in labor's affairs at will and even to uphold the right of unions to discriminate by recognizing this possibility but pointing out "that our proposing compulsion would not *give* the government this right." Logan diary, February 22, 1941.

62. Logan diary, December 6, 1942.

63. RWL, address to a meeting of the National Council of Negro Women, [Washington, D.C.], October 17, 1941, RL(H)-II, box 18, "Post-War World Proposal, Abortive."

64. RWL, address to Alpha Phi Alpha Annual Convention, December 1941, RL(H)-I, box 15, "Colored Reserve Officers."

65. "Conference on Education and Post-War Reconstruction," May [1942], American Council of Learned Societies Papers, series B, box 89, "Post-War Planning Memoranda," Manuscript Division, Library of Congress, Washington, D.C. Hereafter cited as ACLS(LC). The entire run of ACLS proposals on postwar planning are in ACLS(LC), B,89.

66. RWL to Raymond Leslie Buell, April 8, 1941, RWL to Buell, August 4, 1941, RL(H)-II, box 19, "Raymond Leslie Buell"; Logan diary, February 22, 1942.

67. Logan diary, March 16, 1940.

68. Ibid., April 14, 1944; see also RWL to Du Bois, April 14, 1944, Du Bois Papers, reel 56.

69. Logan diary, June 28, 1941.

70. Ibid., June 23, 1946, January 20, 1941, July 18, December 14, 1942. The passage is quoted from December 14, 1942.

71. [Donald W. Rowland], *History of the Office of the Coordinator of Inter-American Affairs* (Washington, D.C.: Government Printing Office, 1947), 3–4. On Rockefeller's interest in Latin America and the origins of the OCIAA, see Claude Curtis Erb, "Nelson Rockefeller and United States–Latin American Relations, 1940–1945 (Ph.D. diss., Clark University, 1980), chap. 1; Joe Alex Morris, *Nelson Rockefeller: A Biography* (New York: Harper & Brothers, 1960), 106–7, 115–17.

72. Morris, *Nelson Rockefeller,* 129; [Rowland], *History of the Office,* 5, 6–9.

73. Mary Winslow to Nelson Rockefeller, memo, April 7, 1941, Records of the Office of the Coordinator of Inter-American Affairs, Record Group 229, box 411, "Negroes," National Archives, Washington, D.C.; hereinafter cited as R.G. 229, followed by the box number and folder. Winslow conducted the search for an African-American representative for Rockefeller.

74. Mary McLeod Bethune to Nelson Rockefeller, July 14, 1941, Mary Winslow to Nelson Rockefeller, memo, May 14, 1941, memo, July 8, 1941, memo, July 24, 1941, Howard Thurman to Mary C. Winslow, June 16, 1941, R.G. 229, box 411, "Negroes." Other nominees included Mercer Cook, a professor of Romance languages at Atlanta University who later served in various UNESCO posts; William Hastie; Charles S. Johnson; L. D. Reddick; Valaurez Spratlin, professor of Romance languages at Howard; Charles H. Houston; E. E. Just, the Howard University biologist; Eugene Kinckle Jones and Lester Granger of the Urban League; and Channing Tobias. List of nominees for Negro Affairs Advisor, May 14, 1941, R.G. 222, box 411, "Negroes."

75. Nelson Rockefeller, memo, August 5, 1941, R.G. 229, box 411, "Negroes."

76. RWL to Nelson Rockefeller, August 5, 1941, R.G. 229, box 411, "Negroes."

77. Logan diary, August 5, 1941.

78. Ibid., August 22, 1941.

79. Ibid., October 30, 1941.

80. Ibid., October 17, 1943.

81. Ibid., September 3, 13, October 18, 30, 1941.

82. RWL to Wallace Harrison, October 20, 1941, R.G. 229, box 411, "Inter-American Conference on Negro Studies."

83. Minutes of the Joint Committee Meeting on Cultural Relations, October 10, 1941, ACLS(LC), B,96, "State Department Joint Committee on Cultural Relations—I, 1941."

84. Logan diary, October 30, 1941.

85. Minutes of the Joint Committee on Cultural Affairs, October 31, November 10, 18, 1941, ACLS(LC), B,96, "State Department Joint Committee on Cultural Relations—I, 1941"; Waldo Leland to John W. Clark [Director of the Social Science and Education Division, OCIAA], February 13, 1942, R.G. 229, box 411, "Inter-American Conference on Negro Studies"; RWL to Waldo G. Leland, November 14, 1941, ACLS(LC), B,98, "Logan—Caribbean Negro History."

86. Logan diary, November 3, 1941.

87. RWL to Wallace K. Harrison, November 5, 1941, RL(H)-II, box 18, "Nelson Rockefeller."

88. Minutes of the Joint Committee on Cultural Relations, November 26, 1941, ACLS(LC), B,96, "State Department Joint Committee on Cultural Relations—I, 1941"; project authorization, October 23, 1941, R.G. 229, box 527, "Negro Contribution to Hemispheric Solidarity."

89. RWL to Waldo G. Leland, March 7, 1942, ACLS(LC), B,98, "Logan—Caribbean Negro History."

90. Logan diary, October 30, 1941.

91. Ibid., March 20, 1942, May 19, 1944.

92. Ibid., April 6, 1942. For Logan's professed belief in Rockefeller's sincerity, see also Logan diary, March 1, 1942.

93. A copy of Logan's report, "The Contributions of Negroes in the Dominican Republic, Haiti and Cuba to Hemispheric Solidarity as Conditioned by the Agrarian Problems in Each," is in RL(H)-I, box 14. Its major conclusions are drawn from the diary that he kept regularly during his trip.

94. Logan diary, March 30, April 5, 1942. For the first formulation of this idea, see Logan diary, March 20, 1942. Logan also recorded his opinion about private capital in Logan diary, August 22, 1941.

95. Logan diary, March 30, 1942.

96. *Dayton* (Ohio) *Journal,* July 10, 1944; Logan diary, July 14, 1944.

97. Logan, "Contributions of Negroes in the Dominican Republic, Haiti and Cuba," no pagination.

98. Logan diary, May 19, 1944.

99. Ibid., March 17, 1942.

100. Ibid., March 23, 1942. See also March 11, 12, 14, 20, 1942.

101. Ibid., April 21, 1942.

102. Ibid., November 3, 10, 1941.

103. RWL to Wallace K. Harrison, October 20, 1941, D. H. Daugherty [Secretary of the Committee on Negro Studies of the ACLS] to John M. Clark [Director of the Cultural Relations Division of the OCIAA], January 13, 1942, Clark to Waldo Leland, February 7, 1942, Leland to Clark, February 13, 1942, R.G. 229, box 411, "Inter-American Conference on Negro Studies"; Logan diary, October 30, 1941, January 13, 1942.

104. Logan diary, January 13, 1942.

105. Waldo Leland to John M. Clark, February 13, 1942.

106. Nelson Rockefeller to Waldo Leland, March 6, 1942, R.G. 229, box 411, "Inter-American Conference on Negro Studies."

107. Logan diary, December 22, 1941; Robert L. Harris, Jr., "Segregation and Scholarship: The American Council of Learned Societies' Committees on Negro Studies, 1941–1950," *Journal of Black Studies* 12 (1982): 315–31.

108. Waldo Leland to John Clark, March 21, 1942, Nelson Rockefeller to Leland, May 11, 1942, R.G. 229, box 411, "Inter-American Conference on Negro Studies."

6. What the Negro Wants *and the* "Silent South"

1. Daniel Joseph Singal, *The War Within* (Chapel Hill: University of North Carolina Press, 1982), 296–301, treats this controversy with Logan as evidence of the extreme difficulty an otherwise fair-minded southern liberal had in dealing with African Americans and the race question. David W. Southern, *Gunnar Myrdal and Black White Relations* (Baton Rouge: Louisiana State University Press, 1987), 83–84, and Morton Sosna, *In Search of the Silent South* (New York: Columbia University Press, 1977), 111, focus on Couch's role in the controversy,

but they are far less charitable than Singal and conclude that Couch's disposition in the controversy reveals the Achilles heel of southern liberalism—its refusal to abandon segregation. Richard M. Dalfiume, "The 'Forgotten Years' of the Negro Revolution," _Journal of American History_ 55 (1968): 90–106, merely notes that the publication of _What the Negro Wants_ showed that African Americans wanted to scuttle Jim Crow. For a searching look at southern liberalism and the race question during and after World War II, see Harry S. Ashmore, _Hearts and Minds: A Personal Chronicle of Race in America_ (Cabin John, Md.: Seven Locks Press, 1988). John T. Kneebone, _Southern Liberal Journalists and the Race Issue, 1920–1944_ (Chapel Hill: University of North Carolina Press, 1985), provides an unvarnished but sympathetic view.

2. Robert Russa Moton, _What the Negro Thinks_ (Garden City, N.Y.: Doubleday, 1929).

3. James Weldon Johnson, _Negro Americans, What Now?_ (New York: Viking, 1934).

4. William Terry Couch, "A University Press in the South," _Southwest Review_ 19 (1934): 195–204.

5. Singal, _The War Within_, 299.

6. When the prominent southern liberal journalist Virginius Dabney argued that rape had little to do with lynching—an explosive opinion in the South—he relied upon an argument by the Southern Commission for the Study of Lynching, a predominantly white group, even though the NAACP—and Ida B. Wells-Barnett before it—had earlier thoroughly documented this position. See Kneebone, _Southern Liberal Journalists_, 77–84, for the ambivalence with which southern liberals approached the issue of lynching.

7. RWL to Dr. W. T. Couch, July 24, 1941, Couch to RWL, July 28, 1941, RWL to Couch, November 28, 1941, Couch to RWL, January 15, 1942, Couch to RWL, February 5, 1942, University of North Carolina Press Records, Sub-Group 4, Series 1, "Logan, R. W. (ed.) What the Negro Wants," Southern Historical Collection, Library of the University of North Carolina at Chapel Hill. Hereinafter cited as UNC Press Records. A copy of the original manuscript that Logan submitted to the UNC Press is in RL(H)-II, doc. box 16. A considerably altered version of this manuscript appeared as Rayford W. Logan, _The Negro and the Post-War World: A Primer_ (Washington: Minorities Publishers, 1945).

8. Johnson to Couch, January 22, 1942, UNC Press Records.

9. Couch to RWL, March 26, 1943, UNC Press Records.

10. RWL to Couch, March 29, 1943, UNC Press Records.

11. Couch to RWL, March 31, 1943, UNC Press Records.

12. RWL to Couch, April 12, 26, 1943; RWL to contributors, July 5, 1943, UNC Press Records.

13. Logan's list cut across the political spectrum: five conservatives (Bethune, Patterson, Hancock, Hill, and Charles S. Johnson); five radicals (Wilkerson, Du Bois, Schuyler, Randolph, and Hughes); and five centrists (Logan, Wesley, Townsend, White, and Brown). This particular refraction of the political spectrum is

Logan's and refers to the state of affairs in 1943. Political alignments were quite fluid then; within a matter of a few years, for example, George Schuyler moved to the extreme right.

14. Guy B. Johnson to Couch, [May 1943], Couch to Johnson, May 18, 1943, UNC Press Records. J. Saunders Redding, *Stranger and Alone* (New York: Harcourt Brace Jovanovich, 1950; reprint, Boston: Northeastern University Press, 1989), developed a fictional yet essentially truthful portrait of Jim Crow institutions of higher education in the Deep South. The novel's two protagonists, Shelton Howden, an African-American educator, and his mentor, President Winbush of fictional Arcadia State College for Negroes, lord it over their minions of "darkies"; at the same time they are vulnerable to the whims of their patrons, the white state education officials, whose outlook they have adopted. At their core Howden and Winbush are cynical and have no principles. They are not "race men," and they do not believe in the struggle for the race; they believe only in the personal struggle for advancement. Another view of the Negro college presidential autocracy, and specifically of the conflict between Mordecai Johnson and E. E. Just at Howard University, is contained in Kenneth R. Manning, *Black Apollo of Science: The Life of Ernest Everett Just* (New York: Oxford University Press, 1983), chap. 6.

15. Couch to RWL, April 29, May 10, 1943, RWL to Couch, May 22, 1943, UNC Press Records.

16. RWL to contributors, July 5, 1943, UNC Press Records.

17. Logan diary, August 17, 1943.

18. For Logan's time at Virginia Union University and his conflicts with Gordon Hancock, see chap. 3.

19. Sosna, *In Search of the Silent South*, 117–19; Raymond Gavins, *The Perils and Prospects of Southern Black Leadership: Gordon Blaine Hancock, 1884–1970* (Durham, N.C.: Duke University Press, 1977), 120–28. Kneebone, *Southern Liberal Journalists*, 202–8, argues that the authors of the Durham Manifesto actually opposed segregation and helped to lead southern liberals to inject more "equality" into their separate-but-equal world. But, Kneebone continues, the manifesto's cautious language obscured its significance. On Jessie Daniel Ames's role in the Durham Conference and subsequent southern efforts to improve race relations, see Jacqueline Dowd Hall, *Revolt Against Chivalry: Jessie Daniel Ames and the Women's Campaign Against Lynching* (New York: Columbia University Press, 1979), 258–61.

20. Logan diary, August 14, 1943.

21. Ibid., August 17, 1943.

22. Gavins, *Perils and Prospects*, 59–71, 86.

23. Gordon B. Hancock, "Race Relations in the United States: A Summary," in *What the Negro Wants*, ed. Rayford W. Logan (Chapel Hill: University of North Carolina Press, 1944; reprint, New York: Agathon Press, 1969), 226, 228.

24. Ibid., 223, 247.

25. For the New Deal career of Mary McLeod Bethune, see B. Joyce Ross, "Mary McLeod Bethune and the National Youth Administration: A Case Study of

Power Relationships in the Black Cabinet of Franklin D. Roosevelt," in *Black Leaders of the Twentieth Century,* ed. John Hope Franklin and August Meier (Urbana: University of Illinois Press, 1982), 191–219. For a more comprehensive view of Mrs. Bethune's strategy and activity in the Black Cabinet and the women's club movement, see Paula Giddings, *When and Where I Enter: The Impact of Black Women on Race and Sex in America* (New York: Bantam, 1985), 199–230.

26. Mary McLeod Bethune, "Certain Unalienable Rights," in *What the Negro Wants,* 248–50.

27. Ibid., 253–55.

28. Ibid., 256.

29. Rayford W. Logan, "The Negro Wants First-Class Citizenship," in *What the Negro Wants,* 18.

30. Ibid., 16. Logan delineated his position as the March on Washington Movement's negotiations with the Roosevelt administration over what eventually became Executive Order 8802 proceeded; Logan was a participant in the final negotiations over the wording of the order. See Logan diary, June 24, 1941. The difficulty of sustaining the March on Washington mass movement is explored in Herbert Garfinkel, *When Negroes March: The March on Washington Movement in the Organizational Politics for the FEPC* (Glencoe, Ill.: The Free Press, 1959), especially chaps. 4–6. Jervis Anderson, *A. Philip Randolph, A Biographical Portrait* (New York: Harcourt Brace Jovanovich, 1973), 262–65, states that the glue that held the March on Washington Movement together was the promise of a march. Consequently, Randolph determined that he had no choice but to "continue dangling his threat." Although he withdrew the threat in April 1942, he shifted tactics only slightly when he called instead for local mass meetings and rallies. Randolph also felt obliged to continue the mass pressure because the only alternative was the conservative, legalistic tactics of the NAACP. For a different view of the March on Washington Movement, see John H. Bracey, Jr., and August Meier, "Allies or Adversaries? The NAACP, A. Philip Randolph and the 1941 March on Washington," *Georgia Historical Quarterly* 75 (1991): 1–17.

31. Logan, "The Negro Wants First-Class Citizenship," 16–17.

32. On Logan's considerable lobbying activities, see Logan diary, April 30, 1941, April 7, 1943; for a more comprehensive statement of his position on organized labor, see Logan diary, July 26, 1941.

33. Joel Williamson, *A Rage for Order* (New York: Oxford University Press, 1986), 82–85, 88–89, 188–90, and passim, has an extended discussion of the southern white male's pathological fear of miscegenation. See also Neil R. McMillen, *Dark Journey: Black Mississippians in the Age of Jim Crow* (Urbana: University of Illinois Press, 1990), 14–19. W. T. Couch, a paragon of racial liberalism, was quite agitated by intermarriage. He stated his willingness to use violence to prevent it in a letter to the black sociologist Oliver C. Cox, who was trying to get the UNC Press to publish his manuscript. "If I have to make a choice, I am of course more interested in the welfare of white people than I am of Negroes. If I am faced with choosing between mob violence and the destiny indicated above

["biological integration"], I have to choose violence." Couch to Oliver C. Cox, April 5, 1944, UNC Press Records.

34. Hancock, "Race Relations in the United States," 232–33.

35. Charles H. Wesley, "The Negro Has Always Wanted the Four Freedoms," in *What the Negro Wants,* 109–10.

36. Logan, "The Negro Wants First-Class Citizenship," 27–28.

37. W. E. Burghardt Du Bois, "My Evolving Program for Negro Freedom," in *What the Negro Wants,* 42; Logan, Introduction to the reprint of *What the Negro Wants,* no pagination.

38. O. J. Coffin to Couch, October 10, 1943, Couch to Coffin, October 11, 1943, UNC Press Records.

39. Howard Odum to Couch, September 17, 1943, UNC Press Records.

40. N. C. Newbold to Couch, October 20, 1943, UNC Press Records.

41. Ibid., October 21, 1943.

42. Couch to RWL, October 8, 1943, UNC Press Records.

43. Ibid., October 21, 1943.

44. Ibid., November 9, 1943.

45. Ibid.

46. Couch to Langston Hughes, December 27, 1943, Hughes to Couch, February 5, 1944, UNC Press Records.

47. Couch to RWL, November 9, 1943, UNC Press Records.

48. Ibid., November 17, 1943.

49. Couch to Newbold, November 12, 1943, UNC Press Records.

50. RWL to Couch, October 18, 1943, UNC Press Records.

51. See, for example, Logan diary, April 12, 1947, and May 6, 1950.

52. RWL to Couch, November 17, 1943, UNC Press Records.

53. Arnold Rampersad, notes to *Early Works* by Richard Wright (New York: Library of America, 1991), 911–13.

54. Logan diary, April 29, 1943.

55. Ibid., December 17, 23, 24, 31, 1943.

56. Ibid.

57. Couch to RWL, November 12, 1943, UNC Press Records. For the origins of this framework, see Newbold to Couch, October 20, 1943, UNC Press Records.

58. W. E. B. Du Bois to RWL, December 9, 1943, RL(H)-I, box 15, "W. T. Couch."

59. Logan diary, December 24, 1943; RWL to Couch, November 27, 1943, UNC Press Records.

60. Logan diary, December 24, 1943.

61. Couch to RWL, November 29, 1943, Couch to RWL, telegram, November 30, 1943, UNC Press Records.

62. RWL to Couch, December 6, 1943, UNC Press Records.

63. Couch to RWL, December 14, 1943, UNC Press Records.

64. Logan diary, December 24, 1943.

65. RWL to Couch, December 18, 1943, UNC Press Records.

66. Couch to Newbold, December 22, 1943, UNC Press Records. See also Couch to Virginius Dabney, December 20, 1943, UNC Press Records, for more on Couch's surprise at Logan's actions.

67. Jackson Davis to Couch, February 11, 1944, UNC Press Records.

68. Quoted in Gavins, *Perils and Prospects,* 133–34.

69. Mark Ethridge to Couch, April 11, 1944, UNC Press Records.

70. Virginius Dabney to Couch, January 10, 1944, UNC Press Records.

71. Virginius Dabney, "Nearer and Nearer the Precipice," *Atlantic Monthly,* January 1943, 90–106.

72. Couch to RWL, December 22, 1943, UNC Press Records.

73. Langston Hughes to RWL, December 21, 1943, RL(H)-I, box 15, "W. T. Couch."

74. RWL to Couch, January 14, 1944, Couch to RWL, January 19, 1944, UNC Press Records.

75. William Terry Couch, Publisher's Introduction, *What the Negro Wants,* no pagination.

76. Couch to Dabney, January 14, 1944, UNC Press Records.

77. Couch, Publisher's Introduction.

78. Jackson Davis to Couch, February 11, 1944, Virginius Dabney to Couch, February 25, 1944, Mark Ethridge to Couch, April 11, 1944, UNC Press Records.

79. Gerald Johnson to Couch, October 9, 1944, UNC Press Records.

80. Couch to RWL, October 12, 1944, UNC Press Records; royalty statement, July 1, 1946, RL(H)-II, box 18, "Royalties Paid."

81. Paula Snelling, "To Be Counted as Human Beings," *Weekly Book Review,* November 12, 1944, 3.

82. William Shands Meacham, "The Negro's Future in America," *New York Times Book Review,* November 5, 1944, 28.

83. H. C. Brearley, review of *What the Negro Wants,* in *Social Forces* 23 (1945): 469–70.

84. E. B. Reuter, review of *What the Negro Wants,* in *American Journal of Sociology* 50 (1945): 317–18.

85. J. Saunders Redding, "Fourteen Negro Voices," *The New Republic,* November 20, 1944, 665–66.

86. E. Franklin Frazier, "Wanted: Equality," *The Nation,* December 23, 1944, 776.

87. *Opportunity* 23 (1945): 158; *Journal of Negro History* 30 (1945): 90–92; *Crisis,* December 1944, 395; *Journal of Negro Education* 14 (1945): 67–68.

88. *Chicago Defender* to RWL, telegram, [1945], L. D. Reddick to RWL, February 19, 1945, RL(H)-II, box 19, "Citations."

89. The Book-of-the-Month Club finally offered *What the Negro Wants* in its January 1945 *News;* its lukewarm recommendation—and its failure to make the book a main or alternate selection—may have been the consequence of Logan's refusal to compromise.

90. Walter A. Jackson, *Gunnar Myrdal and America's Conscience: Social Engi-*

neering and Racial Liberalism, 1938–1987 (Chapel Hill: University of North Carolina Press, 1990), 273–79.

91. For evidence of Couch's own personal capitulation, see Margaret Duckett to Couch, November 6, 1944, and Arthur G. Powell to Couch, December 31, 1944, UNC Press Records; on the capitulation of southern racial liberalism, see Sosna, *In Search of the Silent South,* chap. 8.

92. Richard Kluger, *Simple Justice* (New York: Vintage Books, 1977), 295–305.

7. The Postwar World

1. David Killingray and Richard Rathbone, Introduction, *Africa and the Second World War,* ed. David Killingray and Richard Rathbone (New York: St. Martin's Press, 1986), 4–6.

2. Both Attlee and the newspaper headline cited in P. Olisanwuche Esedebe, *Pan Africanism: The Idea and Movement, 1776–1963* (Washington, D.C.: Howard University Press, 1982), 145; James R. Hooker, *Black Revolutionary: George Padmore's Path from Communism to Pan-Africanism* (New York, Washington, D.C., London: Frederick A. Praeger, 1967), 63.

3. Cited in Hooker, *Black Revolutionary,* 63.

4. Killingray and Rathbone, *Africa and the Second World War,* 5; Hooker, *Black Revolutionary,* 64–69; Esedebe, *Pan Africanism,* 148–52; on African students abroad, see Imanuel Geiss, *The Pan-African Movement: A History of Pan-Africanism in America, Europe and Africa,* trans. Ann Keep (New York: Africana Publishing Co., 1974), 297–304, 374–81.

5. W. E. B. Du Bois to RWL, April 19, 1941, Du Bois Papers, reel 52.

6. Logan diary, April 21, 1941.

7. RWL, speech to a meeting of the Committee for the Participation of Negroes in the National Defense Program, [Cincinnati], [March 9, 1941], RL(H)-I, box 15, "Colored Reserve Officers."

8. RWL to Dr. Benjamin Gerig, "Memorandum on a Proposed New Mandate System," December 9, [1942], RL(H)-I, box 2, "Mandate System." The year on this memorandum is given incorrectly as 1941; Logan diary, December 2, 1942, verifies that the correct year is 1942. Unless otherwise noted, this paragraph and the four that follow are based upon this memorandum. On Benjamin Gerig, see Lawrence S. Finkelstein, "Bunche and the Colonial World: From Trusteeship to Decolonization," in *Ralph Bunche: The Man and His Times,* ed. Benjamin Rivlin (New York: Holmes & Meier, 1990), 109–31 passim.

9. Rayford W. Logan, "The Operation of the Mandate System in Africa," *Journal of Negro History* 13 (October 1928): 423–77. For a discussion of this article, see chap. 3 above.

10. Franklin D. Roosevelt to RWL, March 1, 1943, RL(H)-II, box 18, "Presidents Eisenhower and Johnson."

11. Committee on Africa, the War, and Peace Aims, *The Atlantic Charter and Africa from an American Standpoint* (New York: n.p., 1942), vii.

12. See ibid., 151–53, for a list of committee members. For Jackson Davis and the General Education Board, see chaps. 4 and 6 above; for Anson Phelps Stokes, the Carnegie Corporation, and the Encyclopedia of the Negro project, see chap. 4 above.

13. *The Atlantic Charter and Africa*, 1–2; the quote is on 1.

14. Ibid., 38 *n*, 3; quote is on 3.

15. Ibid., 13–17, 22–23, 85.

16. Ibid., 9, 54–58.

17. Logan diary, May 26, 1942; *The Atlantic Charter and Africa*, 56–57.

18. *The Atlantic Charter and Africa*, 54–55; quote from Smuts's speech is on 54.

19. Jan Christiaan Smuts, "The Basis of Trusteeship," cited in Rayford W. Logan, "Smuts Speaks of Africa, 1917–1942," *Crisis* 50 (September 1943): 264–67, 278–79; quote is on 279.

20. Logan, "Smuts Speaks of Africa," 279. On Smuts's pivotal role in establishing apartheid in South Africa, see John W. Cell, *The Highest State of White Supremacy: The Origins of Segregation in South Africa and the American South* (Cambridge: Cambridge University Press, 1982), 68–72, 224–25.

21. Logan diary, February 11, 1942.

22. Ibid., May 11, 1943.

23. Ibid., December 2, February 11, 1942.

24. Ibid., February 11, 1942.

25. Ibid.

26. Ibid., December 24, 1943. For other anecdotal evidence on the gap between Africans and African Americans, see Arnold Rampersad, *The Life of Langston Hughes*, vol. 1, *1902–1941: I, Too, Sing America* (New York: Oxford University Press, 1986), 73–80. See also Rayford W. Logan, "The American Negro's View of Africa," *Africa Seen by American Negroes* (n.p.: Presence Africaine, [1958]), 217–27.

27. RWL, address to the National Council of Negro Women, Washington, D.C., October 13, 1944, RL(H)-II, doc. box 15, "Writings."

28. RWL to Franklin Roosevelt, January 21, 1945, RL(H)-II, doc. box 2, "Correspondence." On Logan's appointment as adviser to the *Pittsburgh Courier*, see Logan diary, February 27, 1945.

29. Logan diary, March 1, 1945.

30. Ibid., February 27, 1945.

31. Cited in Gerald Horne, *Black and Red: W. E. B. Du Bois and the Afro-American Response to the Cold War, 1944–1963* (Albany: State University of New York Press, 1986), 30; see also the account of the meeting in the *Pittsburgh Courier*, April 14, 1945.

32. Resolutions of the Colonial Conference, April 6, 1945, RL(H)-II, doc. box 15, "Writings."

33. Logan diary, February 11, 1942, April 11, 1945.

34. *Pittsburgh Courier,* April 14, 1945; Resolutions of the Colonial Conference.

35. Dorothy Hunton, *Alphaeus Hunton: The Unsung Valiant* ([New York]: n.p., 1986), 57; Martin Bauml Duberman, *Paul Robeson* (New York: Alfred A. Knopf, 1988), 178, 235, 243, and passim.

36. Hooker, *Black Revolutionary,* 90–91; quote is on 90.

37. *Pittsburgh Courier,* May 12, 1945.

38. Walter White to RWL, June 4, 1945, RL(H)-I, box 15, "Walter White"; RWL to Walter White and W. E. B. Du Bois, June 30, 1945, Du Bois Papers, reel 57. White, in his letter to RWL, named the other members of the NAACP committee: Dr. Louis T. Wright, Ralph Bunche, Elmer A. Carter, Russell W. Davenport, Bill Hastie, Arthur Spingarn, Channing Tobias, and W. E. B. Du Bois.

39. W. E. B. Du Bois to RWL, July 3, 1945, Du Bois Papers, reel 57.

40. Geiss, *Pan-African Movement,* 382–84, 387–98. Geiss treats only the Pan-African aspects of the Harlem Conference, ignoring the "Bandung" aspects. For Du Bois's account of the Fifth Pan-African Congress, see W. E. Burghardt Du Bois, *The World and Africa,* new enl. ed. (New York: International Publishers, 1965), 242–45, 306.

41. P. L. Prattis, "Conference Confetti!" *Pittsburgh Courier,* May 5, 1945. Curiously, Logan did not keep a private record of his trip to San Francisco, although he is frequently mentioned by Prattis as a participant in the revelry; the record of the socializing that took place among the blacks present at the conference is in Prattis's "Conference Confetti!" column, a regular feature in the *Courier* during May and June 1945.

42. Logan diary, November 2, 1940.

43. Logan autobiography, vol. 1, chap. 11, p. 41, RL(H)-II, box 5.

44. Logan diary, September 30, 1943.

45. Ibid., June 12, 1944.

46. RWL to James Cobb, November 10, 1937, January 4, March 31, 1938, Cobb to RWL, March 29, 1938, RL(H)-II, box 24, "Correspondence."

47. Logan diary, April 16, 1940.

48. Ibid., December 3, 1941, June 12, 1944.

49. Ibid., December 8, 1945.

50. Ibid., June 23, 1947.

51. P. L. Prattis and Dr. Rayford W. Logan, "Race Equality at Conference," *Pittsburgh Courier,* May 5, 1945.

52. *Pittsburgh Courier,* April 28, 1945.

53. Dr. Rayford W. Logan, "The 'Little Man' Just Isn't Here," *Pittsburgh Courier,* May 5, 1945.

54. Horne, *Black and Red,* 35–37.

55. *Pittsburgh Courier,* May 5, 1945.

56. Ibid., June 16, 1945.

57. A particularly trenchant criticism of the UN's trusteeship system is in

Rayford W. Logan, "The System of International Trusteeship," *Journal of Negro Education* 15 (1946): 285–99.

58. *Pittsburgh Courier,* July 21, 1945.

59. Rayford W. Logan, *The African Mandates in World Politics* (Washington, D.C.: Public Affairs Press, 1948).

60. Vandi V. Haywood to RWL, April 19, 1944, Rosenwald Fund Papers, Fisk University, Nashville, Tennessee; Logan diary, September 9, 1948.

61. On the power politics surrounding the proposed return of Italy's colonies, see Logan, "The System of International Trusteeship," 290–91.

62. *Pittsburgh Courier,* July 21, 1945.

63. Rayford W. Logan, "The Charter of the United Nations and Its Provisions for Human Rights and the Rights of Minorities and Decisions Already Taken Under This Charter," in *An Appeal to the World: A Statement on the Denial of Human Rights to Minorities in the Case of Citizens of Negro Descent in the United States of America and an Appeal to the United Nations for Redress,* ed. W. E. Burghardt Du Bois (New York: NAACP, 1947), 91.

64. Walter H. C. Laves and Charles A. Thomson, *UNESCO: Purpose, Progress, Prospects* (Bloomington: Indiana University Press, 1957), 320; a list of organizations that were eligible to nominate members to the national commission is on 447–50.

65. Logan diary, April 30, 1946.

66. Ibid. On the employment of African Americans in the UNESCO Secretariat, see also Logan diary, February 23, 1946.

67. Laves and Thomson, *UNESCO: Purpose, Progress, Prospects,* 322–23, 330, 321.

68. Logan diary, February 18, 17, 1948.

69. Ibid., April 18, 1948, May 15, 1950.

70. Laves and Thomson, *UNESCO: Purpose, Progress, Prospects,* 336–37.

71. On the struggle over guiding principles for UNESCO, see James P. Sewell, *UNESCO and World Politics* (Princeton, N.J.: Princeton University Press, 1975), 106–19.

72. Laves and Thomson, *UNESCO: Purpose, Progress, Prospects,* 330.

73. RWL to Roy Wilkins, November 12, 1949, NAACP(LC), II,A,404, "Rayford Logan, 1948–49." The Universal Declaration of Human Rights is reprinted in Laves and Thomson, *UNESCO: Purpose, Progress, Prospects,* 432–36.

74. "Resolutions Relating to the Draft Covenant on Human Rights," adopted by the United States National Commission for UNESCO, April 15, 1950, RL(H)-II, box 21, "Writings."

75. RWL to American Teachers Association [and the NAACP], April 15, 1950, RL(H)-II, box 12, "Reviews of Books by RWL."

76. Logan diary, February 12, April 15, 1950.

77. Edward W. Barrett to Members of the U.S. National Commission for UNESCO, June 19, 1950, RL(H)-II, box 21, "Writings."

78. RWL to [UNESCO Relations Staff], August 13, 1950, RL(H)-II, box 21,

"Writings." The addressee of this letter was supplied by a separate handwritten draft entitled "Separate section on the Draft Covenants," RL(H)-II, box 21, "Writings," which appears to have been written in the 1970s and seems to be a fragment of Logan's autobiography.

79. Logan diary, July 22, August 26, 1950.

80. *Washington Post,* August 30, 1951.

81. Mary Lord, *New U.S. Action for Human Rights,* Department of State Publication 5195, International Organization and Conference Series III, 96 (Washington, D.C.: Department of State, Division of Publications, 1953), 215–22. Lord represented the United States on the UN Human Rights Commission.

82. Horne, *Black and Red,* 84–86. On Paul Robeson and the Progressive party, see Duberman, *Paul Robeson,* chap. 16.

83. Horne, *Black and Red,* 76–77.

84. Ibid., 79–82.

85. Rayford W. Logan, "The Charter of the United Nations and its Provisions," 85–94. Quote is on 91.

86. Duberman, *Paul Robeson,* 257–58; Logan diary, November 16, 1947.

87. *New Africa,* July–August 1949, 1, 3–4. *New Africa* was the monthly newsletter of the Council on African Affairs. "Bold new program" was Truman's phrase.

88. Rayford W. Logan, *The Negro and the Post-War World, a Primer* (Washington, D.C.: Minorities Publishers, 1945), 88. The manuscript had been rejected earlier by the University of North Carolina Press. Logan could not find another publisher and so decided to publish it himself; the Minorities Publishers' address was the same as that of Logan's home.

89. RWL to Walter White, March 21, 1949, NAACP(LC), II,A,404, "Rayford Logan, 1948–49."

90. RWL to Roy Wilkins, June 9, 1949, RL(H)-I, box 15, "Walter White"; RWL to Walter White, March 29, 1949; RWL, "Draft of Resolutions on International Affairs, 1950," RWL to Roy Wilkins, January 2, 1950, NAACP(LC), II,A,404, "Rayford Logan II, 1950–51"; Rayford W. Logan, "Bold New Program or Old Imperialism[?]," *New Times and Ethiopian News,* June 11, 1949.

91. *New Africa,* July–August 1949.

92. Logan diary, November 16, 1947.

93. Duberman, *Paul Robeson,* 330–33; Horne, *Black and Red,* 115–19.

94. Logan diary, November 16, 1947.

95. Report, SAC, Washington, D.C., to Director, FBI, May 13, 1953, Rayford Whittingham Logan, Bureau File 101-1579-20.

96. Duberman, *Paul Robeson,* 333. If Yergan recorded his views of his split with the CAA and his conversion to anticommunism, they are likely tucked away in his personal papers, which are deposited at Howard University's Moorland-Spingarn Research Center but which, in 1992, are still closed to scholars.

97. Walter White to NAACP Budget Committee, October 26, 1948, NAACP(LC), II,A,404, "Rayford Logan, 1948–49."

98. Cited in Horne, *Black and Red,* 37.

99. Logan diary, September 5, 10, 1948.

100. Walter White to NAACP Budget Committee, October 26, 1948.

101. For a partial log of affairs at which Logan represented the NAACP, see RWL to Walter White, March 21, 1949, RWL to Roy Wilkins, September 20, November 12, 1949, NAACP(LC), II,A,404, "Rayford Logan, 1948–49"; "Activities of Dr. Rayford W. Logan on Point Four," March 27, 1950, NAACP(LC), II,A,404, "Rayford Logan II, 1950–51"; see also Logan diary, January 30, June 4, 1949, February 5, 12, 1950. For instances of Logan's handiwork on NAACP positions, see RWL, "Negroes Ask Plebiscite for Former Italian Colonies," September 9, 1948, RWL to Walter White, telegram, March 30, 1949, Walter White to Dean Acheson, telegram, [after March 30, 1949], RWL to White, May 30, 1949, Walter White to Roy Wilkins and the Board of Directors, memo, June 6, 1949, Ralph Bunche to Walter White, June 17, 1949, NAACP(LC), II,A,404, "Rayford Logan, 1948–49"; RWL, draft resolutions on international affairs for 1950 NAACP Convention, NAACP(LC), II,A,404, "Rayford Logan II, 1950–51."

102. RWL to Roy Wilkins, January 2, 1950, NAACP(LC), II,A,404, "Rayford Logan II, 1950–51."

103. Logan diary, January 30, 1949.

104. On the anticommunist backlash among the African-American leadership, see Duberman, *Paul Robeson,* 342–44, 347, and Horne, *Black and Red,* chap. 10.

105. Logan diary, September 18, 1944, January 9, 1947.

106. Report, SAC, Washington, D.C., to Director, FBI, May 13, 1953, Rayford Whittingham Logan, Bureau File 101-1579-20.

107. Report, SAC, Washington, D.C., to Director, FBI, May 13, 1953, Rayford Whittingham Logan, Bureau File 101-1579-20.

108. RWL to Merle Curti, A. M. Schlesinger, and others, May 27, 1953, RL(H)-I, box 17, "FBI Interrogation." Judging from the replies he received— Curti's was dated May 26, 1953, while Schlesinger's was penned on May 21—it is reasonable to assume that Logan misdated his. See Merle Curti to RWl, May 26, 1953, A. M. Schlesinger to RWL, May 21, 1953, RL(H)-I, box 15, unmarked file (with a handwritten index on its front).

109. Logan autobiography, vol. 2, chap. 2, pp. 26–27, RL(H)-II, box 5. Logan appears to have taken the anecdote about McCarthyism and Howard's men's rooms from his diary.

110. RWL to Walter White, November 19, December 28, 1951, NAACP(LC), II,A,404, "Rayford Logan II, box 1950–51"; Logan autobiography, vol. 2, chap. 1, pp. 15–16, 30, 31–32, 50, RL(H)-II, box 5.

111. W. E. B. Du Bois, cited in Harold R. Isaacs, "Pan-Africanism as 'Romantic Racism,'" in *W. E. B. Du Bois: A Profile,* ed. Rayford W. Logan (New York: Hill & Wang, 1971), 245.

112. Ibid., 246.

113. Logan diary, June 4, 1949; Logan autobiography, vol. 2, chap. 3, p. 29, RL(H)-II, box 5.

114. For a discussion of the French *mission civilatrice* and the policy of assimilation, see chap. 2 above.

115. RWL, handwritten autobiographical account of his Fulbright year in France, n.d., RL(H)-II, doc. box 13, "Miscellaneous Correspondence to be Selected for Memoirs."

116. See Joseph E. Harris, *Africans and Their History*, rev. ed. (New York: Penguin, 1987), 222–26, and chap. 14, passim, for a comparison of independence movements in British and French Africa. A useful summary of the independence drives in the 1950s is Gwendolen M. Carter, *Independence for Africa* (New York: Frederick A. Praeger, 1960). I thank Professors Joseph Harris and Elliot Skinner for helping me to sort out the politics of decolonization.

117. *Schenectady* (N.Y.) *Gazette,* January 11, 1955; RWL, "Criteria for New Self-Governing Countries: Historical Background and General Problems," inaugural speech to Howard University Forum Series for 1955, February 28, 1955, RL(H)-II, box 10, "Race as a Factor in World Politics."

118. *Washington Star,* March 21, 1956.

119. RWL, "Criteria for New Self-Governing Countries: Historical Background and General Problems." Logan identified the African official as a Mr. Fafunwa, an assistant Nigerian liaison officer in Washington, D.C.; but in a 1958 speech, entitled "The Impending Crisis in Africa," RL(H)-II, doc. box 13, "Correspondence," Logan credits Prime Minister Olympio of French Togoland for the quote.

120. RWL to Ruth Sloan, December 4, 1952, RL(H)-II, box 7, "Correspondence."

121. Logan autobiography, vol. 2, chap. 3, pp. 1–2, RL(H)-II, box 5.

122. RWL, "The Influence of French Ideas and Policies on the Brazzaville Bloc," speech to the Society for French Historical Studies, Princeton University, Princeton, N.J., April 14, 1961, RL(H)-II, doc. box 15, "Writings."

123. Cited in Logan autobiography, vol. 2, chap. 3, p. 32.

124. Ibid.

125. RWL, "The Influence of French Ideas and Policies on the Brazzaville Bloc."

126. RWL, undated, untitled manuscript [after 1958], RL(H)-II, doc. box 3, "Speeches."

8. *The Golden Years*

1. Charles H. Wesley to RWL, April 16, 1938, RWL to Wesley, April 27, 1938, RL(H)-I, box 15, "Charles Wesley"; inventory of household items and bill of sale of household items, June 4, 1938, RL(H)-I, box 9, "Finance." Wesley was at that time the head of the Department of History and the acting dean of the College of Liberal Arts.

2. Rayford W. Logan, interview by *Amistad* magazine, [June 1970], transcript,

RL(H)-II, doc. box 6, "Amistad"; Michael R. Winston, "Through the Back Door: Academic Racism and the Negro Scholar in Historical Perspective," *Daedalus* 100 (1971): 695–96.

3. Ira Reid to RWL, October 6, 1938, RL(H)-II, doc. box 13, "Correspondence." On Atlanta University see Clarence Bacote, *The Story of Atlanta University* (Atlanta: Atlanta University, 1969). An excellent biography of John Hope is Ridgley Torrence, *The Story of John Hope* (New York: Macmillan, 1948; reprint, New York: Arno Press, 1969).

4. RWL to Metropolitan Life Insurance Company, February 1, 1936, RL(H)-II, box 24, "Correspondence."

5. Logan, interview by *Amistad* magazine.

6. Ira Reid to RWL, October 6, 1938; John Hope Franklin, "Rayford Wittingham Logan, 1897–1982," [November 10, 1982], copy in author's possession. I want to thank Professor Franklin for sending me the eulogy he delivered at Logan's funeral and for being generous with his time and considerable knowledge about Logan.

7. Logan, interview by *Amistad* magazine.

8. *Missouri ex. rel. Gaines* v. *Canada* voided the southern states' practice of providing African-American students with out-of-state scholarships and required these states either to integrate their professional and graduate programs or to establish separate and equal ones for African Americans. See Richard Kluger, *Simple Justice* (New York: Vintage, 1977), 202–4, 213; and Harvard Sitkoff, *A New Deal for Blacks: The Emergence of Civil Rights as a National Issue* (New York: Oxford University Press, 1978), 239–41.

9. RWL, commencement address at Miner Teachers College, Washington, D.C., June 22, 1939, RL(H)-II, box 21, "Addresses."

10. For a discussion of the African-American middle class's stake in segregated society, see two essays by E. Franklin Frazier: "Human, All Too Human: The Negro's Vested Interest in Segregation," and "The Negro Middle Class and Desegregation," both in *E. Franklin Frazier on Race Relations: Selected Writings,* edited and with an introduction by G. Franklin Edwards (Chicago: University of Chicago Press, 1968), 283–91 and 292–309, respectively.

11. RWL, commencement address at Miner Teachers College.

12. Ibid.

13. Rayford W. Logan, *Howard University: The First Hundred Years, 1867–1967* (New York: New York University Press, 1969), 258–70.

14. Marie Wood to RWL, Sunday the 30th [November 30, 1941, November 30, 1947, or October 30, 1949], RL(H)-II, box 24, "Correspondence."

15. Logan autobiography, vol. 1, chap. 8, pp. 2–5, RL(H)-II, box 5; Christopher Jencks and David Riesman, "The American Negro College," *Harvard Educational Review* 37 (1967): 23.

16. Winston, "Through the Back Door," 697–98. For the views of four scholars on what comprised the "typical" fare of African-American higher education, see Jencks and Riesman, "The American Negro College"; Kenneth R. Manning,

Black Apollo of Science: The Life of Ernest Everett Just (New York: Oxford University Press, 1983), chap. 4; E. Franklin Frazier, "The Failure of the Negro Intellectual," *E. Franklin Frazier on Race Relations*, 271; and E. Franklin Frazier, *Black Bourgeoisie* (New York: The Free Press, 1957), chap 6.

17. Logan, *Howard University*, 284–92, 333–46; Manning, *Black Apollo of Science*, 213. Anecdotal information on Johnson's insistence on a morally upright faculty is in Logan diary, September 15, 1942.

18. Logan, *Howard University*, 285–88. Logan's observations on Mordecai Johnson's institution-building activities are particularly important because for much of his time at Howard, Logan opposed Johnson.

19. Kluger, *Simple Justice*, 125–31.

20. Logan, *Howard University*, 293, 295. The quote, from a speech Johnson made on June 4, 1933, appears on 295.

21. Logan, who was highly critical of Johnson and tangled with him several times, concurred in the veracity of this statement and provided his own anecdotal proof: "Ran into Dean [Chauncey] Cooper [of the College of Pharmacy] on the campus yesterday. He told me of an amusing experience. He had met Pres. Johnson on his way to his office. Cooper: 'How are you, Mr. President?' Pres. J.: 'For a man of my years and wickedness, very well.' Cooper had then gone into [Secretary of the University G. Frederick] Stanton's office. Cooper: 'How are you, Mr. Stanton?' S.: 'For a man of my years and wickedness, very well.' Nearly every member of the faculty tries to imitate President Johnson's oratorical, somewhat (at times) pompous tones. But Pres. J. can be relaxed and one of the most witty and felicitous persons I know." Logan diary, January 23, 1944.

22. Mordecai Johnson, "Address of Dr. Mordecai W. Johnson," *Academic Freedom in the United States: Papers Contributed to the Fifteenth Annual Spring Conference of the Division of Social Sciences, March 11, 12, 13, and 14, 1953*, ed. Gustav Auzenne, Jr. (Washington, D.C.: Howard University Press, 1953), 117–42. For Logan's reactions to the FBI investigation, see Logan diary, February 22, 1942; RWL to Arthur M. Schlesinger, Howard K. Beale, and others, May 27, 1953, RL(H)-I, box 17, "FBI Interrogation"; Logan autobiography, vol. 2, chap. 2, pp. 23, 26–27, RL(H)-II, box 5; and chap. 7 above.

23. RWL, remarks at Mordecai W. Johnson, Sr., Honor Day, Hamline United Methodist Church, Washington, D.C., May 6, 1973, RL(H)-II, box 18, "New York Times Book Review."

24. Harold Lewis, interview by author, December 7, 1989, Washington, D.C., tape recording in author's possession.

25. Anthony M. Platt, *E. Franklin Frazier Reconsidered* (New Brunswick, N.J.: Rutgers University Press, 1991) is an excellent biography, although it barely touches the Howard milieu. On Ralph Bunche's radicalism, see John B. Kirby, "Race, Class and Politics: Ralph Bunche and Black Protest," in *Ralph Bunche: The Man and His Times*, ed. Benjamin Rivlin (New York: Holmes and Meier, 1990), 28–49.

26. Logan, *Howard University*, 439–40. For some of the conferences' lectures

and reports of some of the proceedings, see *The Negro in the Americas: Public Lectures of the Division of the Social Sciences of the Graduate School, Howard University,* ed. Charles H. Wesley (Washington, D.C.: The Graduate School, Howard University, 1940), *Trust and Non-Self-Governing Territories: Papers and Proceedings of the Tenth Annual Conference of the Division of the Social Sciences, the Graduate School, Howard University, April 8 and 9, 1947,* ed. Merze Tate (Washington, D.C.: Howard University Press, 1948), *Academic Freedom in the United States: Papers Contributed to the Fifteenth Annual Spring Conference of the Division of Social Sciences, March 11, 12, 13, and 14, 1953,* ed. Gustav Auzenne, Jr. (Washington, D.C.: Howard University Press, 1953), *The New Negro Thirty Years Afterward: Papers Contributed to the Sixteenth Annual Spring Conference of the Division of Social Sciences, April 20, 21, and 22, 1955,* ed. Rayford W. Logan, Eugene C. Holmes, and G. Franklin Edwards (Washington, D.C.: Howard University Press, 1955).

27. Raymond Leslie Buell's 1935 observation of Ralph Bunche still held true in 1941: "[Bunche] says he is completely an anti-racialist and apparently does not even favor talking about it. His idea is that we should work for an improved social system which will benefit white and black alike." Buell to RWL, May 9, 1935, RL(H)-II, box 19, "Raymond Leslie Buell."

28. Logan diary, May 20, 1941. At the 1940 conference, Eric Williams argued for independence for the British West Indies as the only way to eradicate the social and economic distress in which their population found itself. See Eric Williams, "The Negro in the British West Indies," in *The Negro in the Americas,* 7–19.

29. On Bunche's involvement in African affairs for the U.S. government, see Martin Kilson, "Ralph Bunche's Analytical Perspective on African Development," in Rivlin, *Ralph Bunche,* 83–95, Lawrence S. Finkelstein, "Bunche and the Colonial World: From Trusteeship to Decolonization," in Rivlin, *Ralph Bunche,* 109–31.

30. Logan diary, September 9, 1941.

31. Ibid., April 12, 1947.

32. Logan certainly personalized these disputes. At one time he lumped Melville Herskovits, the African anthropologist at Northwestern University who was a bitter professional rival, together with E. Franklin Frazier and accused them of bad-mouthing others for the purpose of boosting their own reputations. Yet Frazier and Herskovits had clear differences with each other over the survival of Africanisms in the New World and were known not to like each other. See Logan diary, September 8, 1941.

33. Harold Lewis, interview by author; Michael R. Winston, interview by author, December 6, 1989, Washington, D.C., tape recording in author's possession.

Evidence for this view of Howard is anecdotal and mixed. John Hope Franklin states that he was not aware of any ostracism when he first came to Howard; but that may have been because he was fully focused on the work of research and teaching and did not concern himself with faculty rivalries. He arrived in September 1947 as a full professor, yet even his colleagues whom he superseded in rank were warm or, at the least, cordial. He did, however, identify a "cool, dignified reserve" on the part of faculty and students, who were not especially friendly and rarely spoke to one another as they walked across campus. John Hope Franklin, telephone interview by author, April 20, 1991, notes in author's possession.

34. Logan diary, July 24, 1941.

35. Ibid., July 27, 1946.

36. John Hope Franklin, "The Dilemma of the American Negro Scholar," in John Hope Franklin, *Race and History: Selected Essays, 1938–1988* (Baton Rouge: Louisiana State University Press, 1989), 303–4.

37. Joanne V. Gabbin, *Sterling A. Brown: Building the Black Aesthetic Tradition*, Contributions in Afro-American and African Studies, no. 86 (Westport, Conn.: Greenwood Press, 1985), 58.

38. John Hope Franklin, interview by author, October 3, 1989, Durham, North Carolina, tape recording in author's possession.

39. See, for example, Logan diary, June 19, 1950; Harold Lewis, interview by author; RWL to Charles H. Thompson, April 7, 1948, RL(H)-II, doc. box 2, "Correspondence"; Ruth Logan to RWL, October 14, 1951, RL(H)-II, box 12, "Letters from Ruth to Me"; RWL to Mordecai Johnson, August 7, 1954, RL(H)-II, box 18, "Mordecai Johnson"; Logan autobiography, vol. 2, chap. 4, pp. 64–67, RL(H)-II, box 5; John Hope Franklin, interview by author, October 3, 1989; and John Hope Franklin, interview by unknown person, 1972, tape recording, Civil Rights Documentation Project, Howard University, Washington, D.C.

40. August Meier and Elliott Rudwick, *Black History and the Historical Profession, 1915–1980* (Urbana: University of Illinois Press, 1986), 98.

41. Dr. Mary Wilhemine Williams to RWL, January 1, 1940, RL(H)-II, doc. box 2, "Correspondence."

42. RWL to Williams, January 3, 1940, RL(H)-II, doc. box 2, "Correspondence"; Williams to RWL, January 24, 1940, RWL to Williams, January 25, 1940, RL(H)-II, doc. box 13, "Correspondence"; Rayford W. Logan, "Some New Interpretations of the Colonization Movement," *Phylon* 4 (1943): 328–34.

43. RWL to Williams, January 3, 1940, RWL to Charles H. Wesley, January 5, 1940, RL(H)-II, doc. box 2, "Correspondence"; RWL to Williams, January 25, 1940, RL(H)-II, doc. box 13, "Correspondence."

44. Williams to RWL, February 1, 1940, RL(H)-II, doc. box 13, "Correspondence."

45. Logan's account of the AHA conference is in Logan diary, January 13, 1941. Unless otherwise noted, quotes in this paragraph are from this source.

46. Williams to RWL, February 1, 1940.

47. Mordecai Johnson to RWL, January 27, 1941, RL(H)-II, box 18, "Mordecai Johnson."

48. Meier and Rudwick, *Black History,* 152, state that between 1946 and 1961, Logan and John Hope Franklin were the only African Americans to address the AHA.

49. Logan diary, November 26, 1947. An account of the postwar salary increases, minus the acrimony, is in Logan, *Howard University,* 364–67.

50. Logan diary, November 16, 1947. Logan's threats to resign—from university committees, official positions, and Howard itself—when he believed his opinions weren't given sufficient weight or when he felt slighted are a prominent feature of his behavior at Howard. He contemplated resigning at the end of 1943 over a particularly nasty dispute with Mordecai Johnson; see chap. 6 above. In 1948, he resigned from the Definitive Review Committee, which was established to codify the requirements for tenure, because he was outvoted. President Johnson, who often did not respond to faculty complaints, did respond to Logan's threats: he reversed the committee's position and invited Logan to rejoin. RWL to Mordecai Johnson, February 10, 1948, Johnson to RWL, February 12, 1948, RL(H)-II, box 18, "Mordecai Johnson." (An account of the committee's activities, minus Logan's resignation, is in Logan, *Howard University,* 384–90.)

Included in this pattern of behavior was his litigiousness. Again in 1948, Logan threatened to sue Charles Thompson because Thompson would not release three hundred dollars in the Graduate School's surplus budget to print up the proceedings of the 1947 Social Sciences conference. Thompson apparently thought that President Johnson would not approve the request, and Logan accused Thompson of "thinking primarily of your 'batting average' rather than of doing the best you can to meet a given situation." Logan's threats again motivated President Johnson to act; he implored Logan not to go to court, telling him that the issue could be settled "within the University family." The money was released and the proceedings published. See RWL to Charles H. Thompson, April 7, 1948, RL(H)-II, doc. box 2, "Correspondence"; Mordecai Johnson to RWL, April 27, 1948, RL(H)-II, box 18, "Mordecai Johnson."

51. RWL to J. St. Clair Price, October 10, 1947, RL(LC), unfiled. This paragraph and the next are based upon this letter.

52. Mrs. W. S. Willis to RWL, March 5, 1940, January 13, 1941, RL(H)-I, box 7, "Correspondence."

53. Maurita to RWL, April 23, 1940, RL(H)-II, doc. box 13, "Correspondence."

54. John Hope Franklin to RWL, June 21, 1949, RL(H)-I, box 15, "John Hope Franklin."

55. RWL to Mordecai Johnson, April 19, 1950, [April 24, 1950], Alain Locke to RWL, RL(H)-II, box 16, "Special Committee, 1950." Logan was writing on behalf of members of the Faculty Reduction Committee, some of whose members were Alain Locke, Sterling Brown, Arthur P. Davis, and Eugene C. Holmes. On Johnson's strategy to improve the medical school, see Logan, *Howard University,* 370–72, 423–28.

56. Minutes of the Committee on the Ph.D. Degree, February 2, 1950, Resolutions of the Committee on the Ph.D. Degree, February 2, 1950, RL(H)-I, box 17, "Ph.D. Committee."

57. Logan autobiography, vol. 2, chap. 4, pp. 26–27, RL(H)-II, box 5.

58. John Hope Franklin to RWL, December 4, 1951, RL(H)-I, box 15, "John Hope Franklin." Logan delivered this indictment of Howard: "[Howard's] role at the present time is 'to provide superior programs on the undergraduate and graduate [i.e., master's] levels.' The University is unable generally to perform this function on either the undergraduate or graduate level. It is unable to do so, among other reasons, because the vast majority of students are inferior as a result of poor training, lack of ability, etc. . . . ." RWL, "Revised Statement Submitted by Professor Rayford W. Logan in Support of His 'Overriding Considerations,'" [1954], RL(H)-I, box 9, "Deposited 7/8/83."

59. Logan autobiography, vol. 2, chap. 4, pp. 26–49 passim, RL(H)-II, box 5. For Logan's letter of resignation, see RWL to William Stuart Nelson, December 15, 1954, RL(H)-I, box 17, "Ph.D. Committee." Other relevant documents concerning the struggle of the Ph.D. program are RWL, "Statement Read to the Faculty of the College of Liberal Arts," April 19, 1954, RL(H)-II, box 7, "Ph.D. Program"; [RWL for the] Division of Social Sciences to Charles H. Thompson, December 21, 1954, RL(H)-I, box 17, "Ph.D. Committee."

60. Cited in Logan autobiography, vol. 2, chap. 4, p. 77, RL(H)-II, box 5.

61. Ibid., p. 75.

62. Ibid., p. 79.

63. RWL, "The American Professor—Teacher and Scholar," paper read at the Conference on Higher Learning in the United States, Princeton University, June 16, 1956, RL(H)-II, box 21, "Writings—Speeches." See also RWL, "American Negroes and the Changing Character of Education," [1964], RL(H)-II, doc. box 15, "Writings."

64. Stanton L. Wormley, Acting Dean, to RWL, May 9, 1962, RL(H)-II, doc. box 13, "Correspondence."

65. The committee member declined to be identified.

66. For more on Logan's semantics, see Conclusion below.

67. Hylan Lewis, interview by author, November 30, 1989, New York City, tape recording in author's possession.

68. Rayford W. Logan, *The Senate and the Versailles Mandate System* (Washington, D.C.: Minorities Publishers, 1945); Rayford W. Logan, *The Negro in the United States: A Brief History,* (New York: Van Nostrand Reinhold, 1957).

The address of the Minorities Publishers was 1519 Jackson Street, N.E., Washington, D.C., which was also Logan's home address. See chap. 3 above for a discussion of Logan's dissertation, chap. 6 above for *What the Negro Wants,* and chap. 7 above for *The African Mandates in World Politics.* For a discussion of Logan's most important articles, see chaps. 3, 4, and 7 above.

69. Rayford W. Logan, "Phylon Profile VI: Carter G. Woodson," *Phylon* 6 (1945): 315–21; Logan diary, November 1, 1942.

70. Logan diary, May 6, 1950; Rayford W. Logan, "Report of the Director," *Journal of Negro History* 35 (1950): 359.

71. On Luther Porter Jackson, see Meier and Rudwick, *Black History,* 85–89.

72. Mary McLeod Bethune to RWL, May 11, 1950, RL(H)-I, box 15, "ASNLH."

73. Logan diary, May 6, 12, 1950. The part that Wesley played in the selection of Woodson's successor is likely documented in his papers, which were not available to the author.

74. See, for example, John Hope Franklin to RWL, [July 1950], RL(H)-I, box 15, "ASNLH."

75. Logan diary, July 2, 1950.

76. William Brewer, untitled typescript commemorating Carter G. Woodson, copy in RL(H)-I, box 15, "ASNLH." The article never appeared in print. For Brewer's published deification of Woodson, see W. M. Brewer, "Annual Report," *Journal of Negro History* 37 (1952): 359–67.

77. John Hope Franklin to RWL, [July 1950], RL(H)-I, box 15, "ASNLH." See also John Hope Franklin, "The Place of Carter G. Woodson in American Historiography," *Negro History Bulletin* 13 (May 1950): 174–76.

78. Lorenzo Greene to RWL, July 6, 1950, RL(H)-I, box 15, "ASNLH."

79. See, for example, *Negro History Bulletin* 14 (October 1950) for extensive coverage of the Universal Declaration of Human Rights, (April 1951) for articles on the United Nations and education in trust territories, and (June 1951) for student articles on the portrayal of Negroes in the popular press.

80. Meier and Rudwick, *Black History,* 126, 136–37. Meier and Rudwick came to the conclusion during their research that the editors of the mainline historical journals were actually far more open to scholarship on African Americans than the historians had ever imagined. August Meier to author, July 7, 1992, letter in author's possession; I want to thank Professor Meier for sharing his thoughts with me on this issue.

81. RWL to H. Councill Trenholm, August 30, 1951, RL(H)-II, box 7, "Correspondence"; Logan diary, September 3, November 2, 4, 1950. The new constitution, which was adopted at the October 1951 annual meeting, did not provide for the post of business manager; it vested all fiduciary responsibilities in the secretary-treasurer. See "Proceedings of the Annual Meeting of the Association," *Journal of Negro History* 37 (1952): 1–10.

82. RWL to Louis Mehlinger, June 30, 1951, RL(H)-I, box 15, "ASNLH."

83. Louis Mehlinger to the ASNLH Executive Committee, July 2, 1951, Mehlinger to RWL, July 5, 1951, Adelaide James to RWL, July 3, 1951, RL(H)-I, box 15, "ASNLH"; John Hope Franklin to RWL, August 23, 1951, RL(LC), "Loose Material from National Diary—1950."

84. RWL to Mehlinger, July 10, 1951, RWL to Charles Wesley, August 14, 1951, RL(H)-I, box 15, "ASNLH."

85. Williston Lofton to RWL, November 15, 1951, Adelaide James to Charles Wesley, January 7, 1952, RWL to Charles Wesley, December 18, 1951, RL(H)-I, box 15, "ASNLH."

86. John Hope Franklin to RWL, [July 1950], Lorenzo Greene to RWL, July 6, 1950.

87. Lorenzo Greene to RWL, August 29, 1952, RL(H)-I, box 15, "ASNLH."

88. George W. Grimke, review of *The Negro in American Life and Thought: The Nadir, 1877–1901,* by Rayford W. Logan, in *Journal of Negro History* 40 (1955): 281–84.

89. Howard Long to RWL, June 16, 1956, RL(H)-I, box 15, "George W. Grimke."

90. Michael R. Winston, interview by author.

91. Rayford W. Logan, *The Negro in American Life and Thought: The Nadir, 1877–1901* (London: Dial Press, 1954). This book was reissued with four new chapters as Rayford W. Logan, *The Betrayal of the Negro: From Rutherford B. Hayes to Woodrow Wilson,* new, enl. edition (London: Collier Books, 1965), from which come all further references, even when the book is cited in the text as *The Nadir.*

92. RWL to J. St. Clair Price, October 10, 1947; Elvena B. Tillman, telephone interview with author, April 25, 1991, notes in author's possession.

93. Logan, Preface to original edition, *The Betrayal of the Negro,* 9.

Logan utilized the researches of some two dozen of his graduate students. See the following M.A. theses done at Howard, which for the most part highlighted the vicious anti-African-American stereotypes of the post-Reconstruction era: Leinster H. Moseley, "The Negro as Portrayed in the New York *Globe,* New York *Freeman,* and New York *Age,* 1883–1892"; Pearle Mintz Oxendine, "An Evaluation of Negro Historians During the Period of the Road to Reunion"; Genevieve Swann Brown, "An Analytical and Statistical Study of Higher Education Among Negroes During the Period 1877–1900"; Adelaide F. James, "Legislative Proposals Dealing with the Negro in the Senate, Fifty-first Congress"; Hattie M. Rice, "The Negro as Portrayed in the Boston *Evening Transcript,* 1901–1907"; John Moore, "The Negro as Portrayed in the Indianapolis *Journal,* 1900–1902"; Thelma O. Venable, "Decision of State Courts Involving the Rights of Negroes, 1877–1900"; Beatrice H. Grevenberg, "A Study of the American Federation of Labor, 1881–1900"; Emma L. Fields, "The Women's Club Movement in the United States, 1877–1900"; Mary Frances Cowan, "The Negro in the American Drama, 1877–1900"; Elvena S. Bage, "Social Darwinism in the United States and its Racial Implications"; David W. Bishop, "The Attitude of the Interstate Commerce Commission Towards Discrimination on Public Carriers, 1887–1910"; Merland M. Turner, "The Negro as Portrayed in *Harper's New Monthly Magazine,* 1877–1901"; Mary E. Waters, "The Negro as Portrayed in the *Atlantic Monthly,* 1877–1900"; Betty R. Jordan, "The Negro as Portrayed in the *North American Review,* 1877–1900"; Queen C. Green, "The Negro as Portrayed in *Scribner's Monthly* and *Century,* 1877–1901"; Purvis M. Carter, "The Astigmatism of the Social Gospel, 1877–1901"; Wilhelmina I. Barnett, "The American Negro, 1878–1900, as Portrayed in the San Francisco *Examiner*"; Shirly M. Smith, "The Negro, 1877–1898, as Portrayed in the Cincinnati *Enquirer*"; Kathryn M. Leigh, "The American Negro, 1877–1900, as Portrayed in the New York *Times*"; Ercell I. Watson, "The American Negro, 1890–1899, as Portrayed in the

Chicago *Tribune* and the House of Representatives"; Jacqueline L. Jones, "The American Negro, 1877–1900, as Portrayed in the Boston Evening *Transcript*"; Romaine F. Scott, "The Negro in American History, 1877–1900, as Portrayed in the Washington *Evening Star*"; Dorothy H. Cunningham, "An Analysis of the *A.M.E. Church Review*, 1884–1900"; Mark D. Brown, "The Negro in the United States Army, 1866–1898."

94. Lambert Davis to RWL, March 27, 1953, RL(H)-I, box 15, "Former Students."

95. Logan autobiography, vol. 2, chap. 4, pp. 8–10, RL(H)-II, box 5.

96. Collier Books to RWL, [July 1967], RL(H)-II, box 18, "Royalties Paid."

97. Meier and Rudwick, *Black History*, 151.

98. For a succinct overview of Reconstruction historiography, see Eric Foner, "Reconstruction Revisited," *Reviews in American History* 10 (1982): 82–100. See also John Hope Franklin, "Whither Reconstruction History?" in John Hope Franklin, *Race and History: Selected Essays, 1938–1988;* this essay originally appeared in the *Journal of Negro History* in 1948.

99. C. Vann Woodward, *The Origins of the New South, 1877–1913,* [2nd ed.], (Baton Rouge: Louisiana State University Press, 1971).

100. Logan, *Betrayal of the Negro,* chaps. 7 and 8.

101. Ibid., chap. 6.

102. Ibid., chaps. 10 and 11.

103. Ibid., 220–21, 221–27.

104. On the declining place of African Americans in the national mind, see ibid., chaps. 12 and 13.

105. Gilbert Osofsky, *Harlem: The Making of a Ghetto, Negro New York, 1890–1930* (New York: Harper & Row, 1968); Constance McLaughlin Green, *The Secret City: A History of Race Relations in the Nation's Capital* (Princeton, N.J.: Princeton University Press, 1967); William H. Harris, *The Harder We Run: Black Workers Since the Civil War* (New York: Oxford University Press, 1982).

106. Logan, *Betrayal of the Negro,* chaps. 15–17, passim.

107. James McPherson, *The Abolitionist Legacy: From Reconstruction to the NAACP* (Princeton, N.J.: Princeton University Press, 1975); Sitkoff, *New Deal for Blacks;* Paula Giddings, *When and Where I Enter: The Impact of Black Women on Race and Sex in America* (New York: Bantam, 1985); Willard B. Gatewood, Jr., *Aristocrats of Color: The Black Elite, 1880–1920* (Bloomington: Indiana University Press, 1990). Richard M. Dalfiume, "The 'Forgotten Years' of the Negro Revolution," *Journal of American History* 55 (1968): 90–106 identifies important antecedents of the post–World War II civil rights movement. Eric Foner, *Reconstruction: America's Unfinished Revolution, 1863–1877* (New York: Harper & Row, 1988), Epilogue, identifies several continuers of the struggle for equal rights after the defeat of Reconstruction who provide a link to the NAACP.

108. RWL, handwritten account of the writing of *Howard University: The First Hundred Years,* RL(H)-II, box 19, "Censorship, Howard University."

109. Michael R. Winston, interview by author, December 6, 1989, Washington, D.C., tape recording in author's possession.

110. Stanton L. Wormley to Sterling Brown, July 22, 1965, RL(H)-II, box 19, "Censorship, Howard University."

111. Michael R. Winston, interview by author; Dorothy Porter Wesley, interview by author, June 14, 1990, Washington, D.C., tape recording in possession of author.

112. RWL, handwritten account of the writing of *Howard University.*

113. Ibid.

114. I wish to thank Michael R. Winston for pointing out Logan's evidentiary biases. Adelaide Ward, a student of Logan's in the 1940s, confirmed this point; in his graduate class in historiography, he insisted that students buttress their arguments with verifiable, written documentation. Adelaide Ward, telephone interview by author, May 3, 1991, notes in author's possession.

115. G. Frederick Stanton to RWL, September 26, 1966, RL(H)-II, box 19, "Censorship, Howard University."

116. RWL to James Nabrit, September 30, 1966, RWL to Stanton Wormley, November 7, 1966, RL(H)-II, box 19, "Censorship, Howard University." The quote is from RWL to Nabrit.

117. Stanton Wormley to RWL, October 24, 1966, RL(H)-II, box 19, "Censorship, Howard University."

118. Franklin, "The Dilemma of the American Negro Scholar," 303.

119. Franklin, interview by author, October 3, 1989, April 20, 1991.

120. Logan asked Franklin for guidance, for example, during his earlier tussles with the University of North Carolina Press over *The African Mandates in World Politics* and *The Negro in American Life and Thought.* See Logan diary, September 5, 1948; John Hope Franklin to RWL, April 30, 1953, RL(H)-I, box 15, "Former Students."

121. John Hope Franklin to RWL, October 26, 1966, RL(H)-I, box 15, "John Hope Franklin."

122. Ibid., February 15, 1967, RL(H)-II, box 19, "Censorship, Howard University."

123. Stanton Wormley to RWL, October 24, 1966; Winston, interview by author.

124. Logan, *Howard University,* 563–64.

125. Ibid., 509–11.

126. See Henry Lake and Helen Lake to RWL, July 30, 1967, Diana Lake to RWL, March 15, 1968, RL(H)-II, box 18, "Mrs. Henry Byron Lake."

127. Logan, *Howard University,* 510; Gabbin, *Sterling A. Brown,* 59–60.

128. RWL to Chris Kentera, October 24, 1968, RL(H)-II, box 18, "NYU Press."

Conclusion

1. John Hope Franklin, interview by author, October 3, 1989, Durham, North Carolina, tape recording in author's possession. Logan was sponsored for mem-

bership by his old friend and colleague Lewis Hanke; see Lewis Hanke to RWL, August 14, 1962, RWL to Hanke, August 21, 1962, RL(H)-II, box 19, "Lewis Hanke."

2. RWL to Philip M. Highfall, Jr., January 16, 1981, RL(H)-II, box 24, "Correspondence"; Ulric Haynes, Jr., telephone interview with author, July 13, 1990, notes in author's possession.

3. Rayford W. Logan, interview by *Amistad* magazine, [June 1970], transcript, RL(H)-II, doc. box 6, "Amistad."

4. RWL to Lois Schultz, October 27, 1964, RL(H)-II, doc. box 2, "Correspondence."

5. Edgar Ansel Mowrer, "World's Fair Stall-In Called Impractical Protest by Logan," article for the Bell-McClure [News] Syndicate, April 22, 1964, RL(H)-II, doc. box 2, "Correspondence."

6. "Moderation Needed in Drive for Rights, Professor Says," *Washington Star,* August 14, 1964, 3x.

7. RWL, "A Decade of Tragedy and Hope," address to Gamma chapter, Phi Beta Kappa, Washington, D.C., May 24, 1965, RL(H)-II, doc. box 15, "Writings." As early as 1956, Logan had expressed misgivings about slogans that he believed raised the expectations of African Americans to unreasonable heights. See RWL to Samuel T. Kelly, March 29, 1956, RL(H)-II, doc. box 6, "African Studies Program."

8. RWL, *Amistad* interview.

9. RWL to Dr. John W. Blassingame, June 9, 1979, copy in author's possession. "My intellectual integrity prevents me from being a party to what, in simple truth, are damn lies," he wrote in his letter of resignation of the editors' decision to call Douglass a black man.

10. Arthur P. Davis, interview by author, October 2, 1989, Washington, D.C., tape recording in possession of author; Michael R. Winston, interview by author, December 6, 1989, Washington, D.C., tape recording in possession of author.

11. Rayford W. Logan and Irving S. Cohen, *The American Negro: Old World Background and New World Experience* (Boston: Houghton Mifflin, 1967).

12. Houghton Mifflin to RWL, royalty statements, March 31, 1969, September 30, 1970, September 30, 1971, September 30, 1972, RL(H)-II, box 18, "Royalties Paid."

13. Richard W. DeBruin to RWL, May 18, 1973, RL(H)-II, box 19, "Houghton Mifflin."

14. RWL to Richard W. DeBruin, June 9, 1973, RL(H)-II, box 19, "Houghton Mifflin."

15. Richard W. DeBruin to RWL, July 12, 1973, RL(H)-II, box 19, "Houghton Mifflin."

16. RWL to Richard W. DeBruin, July 23, 1973, RL(H)-II, box 19, "Houghton Mifflin."

17. RWL to Richard W. DeBruin, February 11, 1974, RL(H)-II, box 19,

"Houghton Mifflin." "Blackologists" and "Blackoisie" were special terms of derision that Logan reserved for black nationalists and even those who he thought compromised with them.

18. Both quotes cited in RWL, "Prophets of Doom and Heralds of Victory," remarks to the Tenth Annual Rayford W. Logan Lecture, April 18, 1974, Howard University, RL(H)-I, box 17, "Annual Rayford W. Logan Lectures."

19. In fact, the debate was joined as early as the first decades of the nineteenth century. See Sterling Stuckey, *Slave Culture* (New York: Oxford University Press, 1987), chap. 4.

20. Joyce Moore Turner, "Richard B. Moore and His Works," in *Richard B. Moore: Caribbean Militant in Harlem, Collect Writings 1920–1972*, ed. W. Burghardt Turner and Joyce Moore Turner, with a Biography by Joyce Moore Turner and an Introduction by Franklin W. Knight (Bloomington: Indiana University Press, 1988), 72; Richard B. Moore, "The Name 'Negro'—Its Origin and Evil Use," (1960), in *Richard B. Moore: Caribbean Militant in Harlem*.

Moore joined the Socialist party in 1918, because he was attracted to A. Philip Randolph's and Chandler Owen's class analysis of the "Negro Question." In 1919 he helped to found the African Blood Brotherhood, which was an alternative to Marcus Garvey's Universal Negro Improvement Association. Many members of the Brotherhood joined the Communist party, and by 1925, Moore was a Party leader in Harlem. In 1942 he was expelled from the Party for nationalism; instead of turning anticommunist, Moore closed that chapter of his life and embarked down the Pan-Africanist road blazed by George Padmore, another ex-Communist. Joyce Moore Turner, 27, 35, 51, 67–69.

21. RWL, "The Development of African-American Historical Tradition," paper delivered to a Faculty-Student Colloquium, Howard University, September 23, 1973, RL(H)-II, box 7, "Correspondence."

22. Michael R. Winston, interview by author.

23. Sterling Brown, cited in Joanne V. Gabbin, *Sterling A. Brown: Building the Black Aesthetic Tradition*, Contributions in Afro-American and African Studies, no. 86 (Westport, Conn.: Greenwood Press, 1985), 59; John Hope Franklin, interview by author, October 3, 1989; Arthur P. Davis, interview by author; Michael R. Winston, interview by author.

24. See, for example, Logan autobiography, vol. 1, chap. 1, RL(H)-II, box 15; RWL, "The Big Lie," [1977], RL(H)-II, box 4, "Writings"; RWL, "Blacks, Blackologists and the Blackoisie," RL(H)-II, box 19, "Blackologists."

25. RWL, "American Negroes and the Changing Character of Education," [1964], RL(H)-II, doc. box 15, "Writings."

26. RWL, "Miracle in Atlanta," Negro History Week address at Morehouse College, Atlanta, Georgia, February 13, 1974, RL(H)-II, box 21, "Writings-Speeches." See also Logan, interview by *Amistad* magazine; and Logan, interview by [Vincent Browne], June 1967, transcript, Civil Rights Document Project, Moorland-Spingarn Research Center, Howard University, Washington, D.C.

27. William Willis, Jr., to RWL, January 13, 1969, RL(H)-II, box 16, "William

Willis, Jr." See also Willis to RWL, March 27, 1969, RL(H)-II, box 16, "William Willis, Jr."

28. Michael R. Winston, who was Logan's close associate and is his literary executor, related a similar experience. Winston, interview by author.

29. On Logan and the Committee of Negro Leaders, see RWL to A. Philip Randolph, April 5, 1951, RWL, memo on behalf of the Committee of Negro Leaders for presentation to Secretary of State, April 13, 1951, RL(H)-II, box 17, "State Department"; Logan diary, April 8, 14, 15, 1951. On the Capitol Press Club award, see, Oscar Haynes to RWL, April 30, 1951, RL(H)-II, box 11, "Correspondence." The Capitol Press Club was an interracial organization devoted to raising standards in journalism and other fields of mass communication. Its members came from major papers, the news services, and the Negro press, as well as the information and public relations professions.

30. John Hope Franklin, "The Dilemma of the American Negro Scholar," in John Hope Franklin, *Race and History: Selected Essays, 1938–1988* (Baton Rouge: Louisiana State University Press, 1989), 295–308; quote is on 299.

31. Rayford W. Logan and Michael R. Winston, eds., *Dictionary of American Negro Biography* (New York: W. W. Norton, 1982).

32. More cannot be said of the genesis and development of the *Dictionary of American Negro Biography,* as the documents concerning it in the Logan Papers at Howard University were closed to the author.

33. Rayford W. Logan case file, administrative no. A002144-82, Superior Court of the District of Columbia, Probate Division, Washington, D.C. The case file contains a copy of Logan's will and material relating to the disposal of his estate.

34. *The New York Times,* November 6, 1982, 15.

SELECTED BIBLIOGRAPHY

༚

Primary Sources

Personal Papers

Eugene Davidson Papers, Moorland-Spingarn Research Center, Howard University, Washington, D.C.

W. E. B. Du Bois Papers, University of Massachusetts, Amherst, on microfilm.
Indispensable for understanding Logan's role in the Pan-Africanist movement, 1919–1945, and for comprehending the Encyclopedia of the Negro project.

Campbell C. Johnson Papers, Moorland-Spingarn Research Center, Howard University, Washington, D.C.

Rayford W. Logan, Federal Bureau of Investigation Files, Bufiles 101-1579 and 161-1369, Washington, D.C., copy in author's possession.
Obtained under the Freedom of Information–Privacy Acts, much of the material is excised. Investigated in 1942 and 1953, the files contain records of his interviews with FBI agents and heavily censored background checks. The files provide the flavor of Logan's resistance to the FBI and McCarthyism.

Rayford W. Logan Papers, unprocessed manuscript, Manuscript Division, Library of Congress, Washington, D.C.
This collection includes Logan's diaries, which he kept on nearly a daily basis between 1940 and 1982. As of 1992, only the years 1940–51 are open to scholars. In 1993, the years 1951–60 will become available. Diaries for the years 1961–70 will be opened in 1998, and the balance will be available in 2003.

The diaries open so far are an invaluable source for Logan's political positions; his activity in the Alpha Phi Alpha fraternity and the Committee for the Participation of Negroes in the National Defense Program (CPNNDP); his differences with the NAACP; the ubiquitous politicking at Howard; and social commentary about the Talented Tenth's life behind the wall of segregation.

Also in this collection are letters between Logan and his wife, Ruth, and between Logan and Bill Riis, his closest white friend.

Rayford W. Logan Papers, unprocessed manuscript, Moorland-Spingarn Research
Center, Howard University, Washington, D.C.
*This collection of thirty-five storage boxes has never before been open to
scholars. It includes two separate drafts of his autobiography: a one-volume
draft written in the mid-1940s and a revised and expanded two-volume draft
written in the 1970s. There are also holographs of such significant events in
Logan's life as his Fulbright year in Paris and the ordeal surrounding the writing
of* Howard University: The First Hundred Years.
    *These papers contain a detailed run of Logan's speeches on civil rights and
historical issues from the 1930s to the late 1970s; voluminous correspondence
concerning the Alpha Phi Alpha fraternity, voter registration, citizenship
schools, and the CPNNDP; correspondence with friends and colleagues; correspondence, speeches, and memoranda concerning Howard University and the
development of African-American higher education; and early drafts of books
and articles.*

Papers of Organizations

American Council of Learned Societies Papers, Manuscript Division, Library of
Congress, Washington, D.C.
Contains documents relating to Logan's activity with the Rockefeller Commission.
Records of the General Education Board, Rockefeller Archive Center, Pocantico
Hills, New York.
*Extensive documentation of the role of white philanthropy in the development
of African-American higher education.*
NAACP Papers, Manuscript Division, Library of Congress, Washington, D.C.
Records of the Office of the Coordinator of Inter-American Affairs, Record Group
229, National Archives, Washington, D.C.
*Important for understanding Logan's tenure with the Rockefeller Commission,
the politics of race in the formulation of the United States' Latin American
policy during World War II, and the attitude of the white intellectual commu-
nity toward issues of race in the post–World War II world.*
Phelps-Stokes Fund Papers, Schomburg Center for Research in Black Culture,
New York Public Library, New York, New York.
Contains important documentation of the Encyclopedia of the Negro project.
University of North Carolina Press Records, Southern Historical Collection, Li-
brary of the University of North Carolina at Chapel Hill.
Extensive documentation of the What the Negro Wants *dispute.*

Interviews Conducted by Author

Daly, Elizabeth. By telephone, July 10, 1990. Notes in author's possession.
Davis, Arthur P. October 2, 1989, Washington, D.C. Tape recording in author's
possession.

Franklin, John Hope. October 3, 1989, Durham, North Carolina. Tape recording in author's possession.

Franklin, John Hope. By telephone, April 20, 1991. Notes in author's possession.

Hanke, Kate [for Lewis Hanke]. Letter to author, answering interview questions, August 27, 1990.

Haynes, Ulric, Jr. By telephone, July 13, 1990. Notes in author's possession.

Key, G. R. F. December 7, 1989, Washington, D.C. Tape recording in author's possession.

Lake, Helen. By telephone, June 16, 1990. Notes in author's possession.

Lewis, Harold. December 7, 1989, Washington, D.C. Tape recording in author's possession.

Lewis, Hylan. November 30, 1989, New York, New York. Tape recording in author's possession.

Michelson, Edward. By telephone, June 12, 1990. Notes in author's possession.

Tillman, Elvena B. By telephone, April 25, 1991. Notes in author's possession.

Ward, Adelaide. By telephone, May 3, 1991. Notes in author's possession.

Wesley, Dorothy Porter. June 14, 1990, Washington, D.C. Tape recording in author's possession.

Winston, Michael R. December 6, 1989, Washington, D.C. Tape recording in author's possession.

Interviews Conducted by Others

Davidson, Eugene. Interview by unknown person, June 28, 1968. Transcript. Civil Rights Documentation Project, Manuscript Division, Moorland-Spingarn Research Center, Howard University, Washington, D.C.

Logan, Rayford W. Interview by [Vincent Browne], June 1967. Transcript. Civil Rights Documentation Project, Manuscript Division, Moorland-Spingarn Research Center, Howard University, Washington, D.C.

Logan, Rayford W. Interview by August Meier, March 3, 1981, Washington, D.C. Interview notes. August Meier Papers, Schomburg Center for Research in Black Culture, New York Public Library, New York, New York.
This collection is not open to the public. I want to thank Professor Meier for making a copy of his interview notes available to me.

Contemporary Published Accounts

Auzenne, Gustav, Jr., ed. *Academic Freedom in the United States: Papers Contributed to the Fifteenth Annual Spring Conference of the Division of Social Sciences, March 11, 12, 13, and 14, 1953.* Washington, D.C.: Howard University Press, 1953.

Bunche, Ralph J. "A Critical Analysis of the Tactics and Programs of Minority Groups." *Journal of Negro Education* 4 (1935): 308–20.

"The Colored Americans in France." *Crisis* 17 (February 1919): 167–68.

Committee on Africa, the War, and Peace Aims. *The Atlantic Charter and Africa from an American Standpoint.* New York: n.p., 1942.

Cooper, Rosebud Lauretta. "Social Life at Virginia Union University." *Virginia Union Bulletin* 29 (February 1929): 8–11.

Couch, William Terry. "A University Press in the South." *Southwest Review* 19 (1934): 195–204.

Dabney, Thomas L. "Local Leadership among Virginia Negroes." *Southern Workman* 59 (January 1930): 31–35.

Dabney, Virginius. "Nearer and Nearer the Precipice." *Atlantic Monthly,* January 1943, 90–106.

Davis, Arthur P. "A New Teacher's Impression of Union." *Virginia Union Bulletin* 30 (November 1929): 8–10.

Du Bois, W. E. Burghardt. "The African Roots of War." *Atlantic Monthly,* May 1915, 707–14.

———. "An Essay toward a History of the Black Man in the Great War." *Crisis* 18 (June 1919): 63–87.

———. "To the World (Manifesto of the Second Pan-African Congress)." *Crisis* 23 (November 1921): 5–10.

———, ed. *An Appeal to the World: A Statement on the Denial of Human Rights to Minorities in the Case of Citizens of Negro Descent in the United States of America and an Appeal to the United Nations for Redress.* New York: NAACP, 1947.

———, comp. "Documents of the War." *Crisis* 18 (May 1919): 16–21.

Fauset, Jessie. "Impressions of the Second Pan-African Congress." *Crisis* 23 (November 1921): 12–18.

Hancock, Gordon B. "A By-Product of Our Advancement." *Virginia Union Bulletin* 29 (January 1929): 3–5.

———. " 'Getting By' and Getting Caught." *Virginia Union Bulletin* 30 (November 1929): 7–8.

Hill, T. Arnold. "Richmond—Louisville—Cincinnati." *Opportunity* 9 (July 1931): 218.

Johnson, James Weldon. *Negro Americans, What Now?* New York: Viking, 1934.

Loeb, William, Jr. "Summer Sewing Circle: The Decline of Williamstown [A Somewhat Jaundiced View of the Williamstown Institute of Politics] [1930]." In *Perspectives: A Williams Anthology,* edited by Frederick Rudolph, 253–65. Williamstown, Mass.: Williams College, 1983.

Meacham, William Shands. "The Negro's Future in America." *New York Times Book Review,* November 5, 1944, 28.

Moton, Robert Russa. *What the Negro Thinks.* Garden City, N.Y.: Doubleday, 1929.

"Resolutions of the Washington Conference." *Crisis* 14 (June 1917): 59–60.

Rogers, J. A. "The American Negro in Europe." *American Mercury* 20 (May 1930): 1–10.

Scott, Emmett J. *The American Negro in the World War.* Chicago: Homewood, 1919; reprinted as *Scott's Official History of the American Negro in the World War.* New York: Arno Press and *The New York Times,* 1969.

Sheerin, Charles W. "In Defense of Richmond." *Opportunity* 9 (September 1931): 282.

Simpson, Josephus. "Are Colored People in Virginia a Helpless Minority?" *Opportunity* 12 (December 1934): 374.

———. " 'The Best Negroes in the World.' " *Opportunity* 9 (September 1931): 283.

Snelling, Paula. "To Be Counted as Human Beings." *Weekly Book Review,* November 12, 1944, 3.

Tate, Merze, ed. *Trust and Non-Self-Governing Territories: Papers and Proceedings of the Tenth Annual Conference of the Division of the Social Sciences, the Graduate School, Howard University, April 8 and 9, 1947.* Washington, D.C.: Howard University Press, 1948.

Terrell, Mary C. "History of the High School for Negroes in Washington." *Journal of Negro History* 2 (1917): 253–56.

"The Third Pan-African Congress." *Crisis* 27 (January 1924): 120–22.

Reminiscences

Ashmore, Harry S. *Hearts and Minds.* New York: McGraw-Hill, 1982.

Brown, Sterling A. "A Son's Return: 'Oh Didn't He Ramble.' " In *Perspectives: A Williams Anthology,* edited by Frederick Rudolph. Williamstown, Mass.: Williams College, 1983.

Hughes, Langston. *The Big Sea.* New York: Knopf, 1940.

Hunton, Dorothy. Alphaeus Hunton: The Unsung Valiant. [New York]: n.p., 1986.

Johnson, James Weldon. *Along This Way.* New York: Penguin, 1933; reprinted, New York: Penguin, 1990.

White, Walter. *A Man Called White.* New York: Viking, 1948.

Newspapers and Magazines

Atlanta Daily World
Baltimore Afro-American
Crisis
Negro History Bulletin
New Africa
Pittsburgh Courier

Selected Works by Rayford W. Logan

Books

The African Mandates in World Politics. Washington, D.C.: Public Affairs Press, 1948.

Betrayal of the Negro: From Rutherford B. Hayes to Woodrow Wilson. New, enl. ed. London: Collier Books, 1965.

The Diplomatic Relations of the United States with Haiti, 1776–1891. Chapel Hill: University of North Carolina Press, 1941.

Howard University: The First Hundred Years, 1867–1967. New York: New York University Press, 1969.

The Negro and the Post-War World: A Primer. Washington, D.C.: Minorities Publishers, 1945.

The Negro in American Life and Thought: The Nadir, 1877–1901. London: Dial Press, 1954.

The Negro in the United States: A Brief History. New York: Van Nostrand Reinhold, 1957.

The Senate and the Versailles Mandate System. Washington, D.C.: Minorities Publishers, 1945.

With Irving S. Cohen. *The American Negro: Old World Background and New World Experience.* Boston: Houghton Mifflin, 1967.

Ed. *The Attitude of the Southern White Press toward Negro Suffrage, 1932–1940.* Washington, D.C.: The Foundation Publishers, 1940.

Ed. *What the Negro Wants.* Chapel Hill: University of North Carolina Press, 1944.

With Eugene C. Holmes and G. Franklin Edwards, eds. *The New Negro Thirty Years Afterward: Papers Contributed to the Sixteenth Annual Spring Conference of the Division of Social Sciences, April 20, 21, and 22, 1955.* Washington, D.C.: Howard University Press, 1955.

With Michael R. Winston, eds. *Dictionary of American Negro Biography.* New York: W. W. Norton, 1982.

Articles in the Baltimore Afro-American

Series on Haiti. July 28, August 4, 11, 18, 25, September 8, 1934.

Articles in the Journal of Negro Education

"Educational Segregation in the North." 2 (1933): 65–67.

"The Crisis of Democracy in the Western Hemisphere." 10 (1941): 344–52.

"The System of International Trusteeship." 15 (1946): 285–99.

Articles in the Journal of Negro History

"The Operation of the Mandate System in Africa." 13 (1928): 423–77.

"Education in Haiti." 15 (1930): 401–60.

"The International Status of the Negro." 18 (1933): 33–38.

"An Evaluation of the First Twenty Volumes of *The Journal of Negro History.*" 20 (1935): 397–405.

Articles in Opportunity

"The New Haiti." 5 (April 1927): 101–3.
"Nat Turner: Fiend or Martyr?" 9 (November 1931): 337–39.
"Magloire Pélage." 18 (January 1940): 14–15.

Articles in Phylon

"Estevanico, Negro Discoverer of the Southwest: A Critical Reexamination." 1
(1940): 305–14.
"Notes on R. R. Wright's 'Negro Companions of the Spanish Explorers.'" 2
(1941): 334–36.
"Some New Interpretations of the Colonization Movement." 4 (1943): 328–
34.
"Phylon Profile VI: Carter G. Woodson." 6 (1945): 315–21.
"Liberia in the Family of Nations." 7 (1946): 5–11.

Articles in the Pittsburgh Courier

Series on the founding of the United Nations and an analysis of the UN Charter.
April 28, May 5, 12, 19, 26, June 2, 9, 16, 1945.
"Charter Will Not Prevent Wars." July 21, 1945.
"The United Nations in Retrospect." Six-part series, June 25, July 2, 9, 16, 23, 30,
1955.
With P. L. Prattis. "Race Equality at Conference." May 5, 1945.

Articles in the Southern Workman

"Haiti: The Native Point of View." 58 (January 1929): 36–40.
"Abyssinia Breaks into the Movies." 58 (August 1929): 339–44.
"West or South Africa in East Africa?" 58 (November 1929): 483–89.
"The Hiatus—A Great Negro Middle Class." 58 (December 1929): 531–35.
"A 'More Definite Policy' in Haiti." 59 (March 1930): 132–35.
"The Eleko Case." 60 (November 1931): 480–82.
"Liberia's Dilemma." 62 (September 1933): 357–62.

Articles in Sphinx

"The Negro and the New Deal." 20 (May 1935): 2–39.
"New Deal vs. the Negro." 22 (December 1936): 33–43.
"New Deal Report." 23 (February 1937): 10–13, 33–34.

Articles in the Virginia Union Bulletin

"Negro History Week." 29 (January 1929): 8–9.
"Mammy Hall." 29 (February 1929): 5–6.

Articles in Other Newspapers, Journals, Magazines, and Books

"The Haze in Haiti." *The Nation,* March 16, 1927, 281–83.
"Negro Studies War Some More for New Angle." *Norfolk Journal and Guide,* June 28, 1935.
"Confessions of an Unwilling Nordic." In *The Negro Caravan,* edited by Sterling Brown, 1043–50. New York: The Dryden Press, 1941.
"Smuts Speaks of Africa, 1917–1942." *Crisis* 50 (September 1943): 264–67, 278–79.
"The American Negro's View of Africa." In *Africa Seen by American Negroes,* edited by John A. Davis, 217–27. N.p.: Presence Africaine, [1958].
"Historical Aspects of Pan-Africanism, 1900–1945." In American Society of African Culture, *Pan-Africanism Reconsidered,* 37–52. Berkeley: University of California Press, 1962.
"Growing Up in Washington: A Lucky Generation." *Records of the Columbia Historical Society of Washington, D.C.* 50 (1980): 500–507.

Secondary Sources

Published Books and Articles

Anderson, Jervis. *A. Philip Randolph, A Biographical Portrait.* New York: Harcourt Brace Jovanovich, 1973.
———. "A Very Special Monument: The Dunbar High School on First Street." *The New Yorker,* March 20, 1978: 93ff.
Barbeau, Arthur E., and Florette Henri. *The Unknown Soldiers: Black American Troops in World War I.* Philadelphia: Temple University Press, 1974.
Bracey, John H., Jr., and August Meier. "Allies or Adversaries?: The NAACP, A. Philip Randolph and the 1941 March on Washington." *Georgia Historical Quarterly* 75 (1991): 1–17.
Buell, Raymond Leslie. *The Native Problem in Africa.* 2 vols. Cambridge: Bureau of International Research of Harvard University and Radcliffe College, 1928; reprint, London: Frank Cass & Co., 1965.
Buni, Andrew. *The Negro in Virginia Politics, 1902–1965.* Charlottesville: University Press of Virginia, 1967.
———. *Robert L. Vann of the PITTSBURGH COURIER: Politics and Black Journalism.* Pittsburgh: University of Pittsburgh Press, 1974.

Carter, Dan T. *Scottsboro: A Tragedy of the American South.* Rev. ed. Baton Rouge: Louisiana State University Press, 1979.

Carter, Gwendolen M. *Independence for Africa.* New York: Frederick A. Praeger, 1960.

Cell, John W. *The Highest State of White Supremacy: The Origins of Segregation in South Africa and the American South.* Cambridge: Cambridge University Press, 1982.

Collier, James Lincoln. *Duke Ellington.* New York: Oxford University Press, 1987.

Contee, Clarence G. "The Emergence of Du Bois as an African Nationalist." *Journal of Negro History* 54 (1969): 48–63.

Cronon, Edmund D. *Black Moses.* Madison: University of Wisconsin Press, 1955.

Dalfiume, Richard M. "The 'Forgotten Years' of the Negro Revolution." *Journal of American History* 55 (1968): 90–106.

Degler, Carl N. *Neither Black nor White: Slavery and Race Relations in Brazil and the United States.* New York: Macmillan, 1971; reprint, Madison: University of Wisconsin Press, 1986.

Drago, Edmund. *Initiative, Paternalism and Race Relations: Charleston's Avery Normal Institute.* Athens: University of Georgia Press, 1990.

Drake, St. Clair, and Horace R. Cayton. *Black Metropolis: A Study of Negro Life in a Northern City.* 2 vols. Rev. ed. New York: Harcourt, Brace & World, 1970.

Duberman, Martin Bauml. *Paul Robeson.* New York: Knopf, 1988.

Du Bois, W. E. B. *The World and Africa.* New enl. ed. New York: International Publishers, 1965.

———, and Guy B. Johnson. *Encyclopedia of the Negro: Preparatory Volume with Reference Lists and Reports.* New York: Phelps-Stokes Fund, Inc., 1945.

Esedebe, P. Olisanwuche. *Pan-Africanism: The Idea and Movement, 1776–1963.* Washington, D.C.: Howard University Press, 1982.

Fabre, Michel. *La Rive Noire: De Harlem à la Seine.* Paris: Lieu Commun, 1985.

Franklin, John Hope. *Race and History: Selected Essays, 1938–1988.* Baton Rouge: Louisiana State University Press, 1989.

———. "The Place of Carter G. Woodson in American Historiography." *Negro History Bulletin* 13 (May 1950): 174–76.

Frazier, E. Franklin. *Black Bourgeoisie.* New York: The Free Press, 1957.

———. *E. Franklin Frazier on Race Relations: Selected Writings.* Edited and with an Introduction by G. Franklin Edwards. Chicago: University of Chicago Press, 1968.

Frederickson, George M. *The Black Image in the White Mind.* New York: Harper & Row, 1971.

Gabbin, Joanne V. *Sterling A. Brown: Building the Black Aesthetic Tradition.* Contributions in Afro-American and African Studies, no. 86. Westport, Conn.: Greenwood Press, 1985.

Gabel, Leona C. *From Slavery to the Sorbonne and Beyond: The Life & Writings of Anna J. Cooper.* Northampton, Mass.: Department of History of Smith College, 1982.

Garfinkle, Herbert. *When Negroes March: The March on Washington Movement in the Organizational Politics for FEPC.* Glencoe, Ill.: The Free Press, 1959.

Gatewood, Willard B., Jr. *Aristocrats of Color: The Black Elite, 1880–1920.* Bloomington: Indiana University Press, 1990.

———. "Aristocrats of Color: South and North, the Black Elite, 1880–1920." *Journal of Southern History* 54 (1988): 3–20.

Gavins, Raymond. *The Perils and Prospects of Southern Black Leadership: Gordon Blaine Hancock, 1884–1970.* Durham, N.C.: Duke University Press, 1977.

Geiss, Imanuel. *The Pan-African Movement.* Translated by Ann Keep. New York: Africana Publishing Co., 1974.

Giddings, Paula. *When and Where I Enter: The Impact of Black Women on Race and Sex in America.* New York: Bantam, 1985.

Green, Constance McLaughlin. *The Secret City: A History of Race Relations in the Nation's Capital.* Princeton, N.J.: Princeton University Press, 1967.

Groves, Paul A. "The Development of a Black Residential Community in Southwest Washington, 1860–1897." *Records of the Columbia Historical Society of Washington, D.C.* 49 (1973–1974): 267–73.

Gutman, Herbert G. *The Black Family in Slavery and Freedom.* New York: Vintage, 1976.

Hall, Jacqueline Dowd. *Revolt against Chivalry: Jessie Daniel Ames and the Women's Campaign against Lynching.* New York: Columbia University Press, 1979.

Harris, Joseph H. *Africans and Their History.* Rev. ed. New York: Penguin, 1987.

Harris, Robert L., Jr. "Segregation and Scholarship: The American Council of Learned Societies' Committee on Negro Studies, 1941–1950." *Journal of Black Studies* 12 (1982): 315–31.

Heinl, Robert Debs, Jr., and Nancy Gordon Heinl. *Written in Blood: The Story of the Haitian People, 1492–1971.* Boston: Houghton Mifflin, 1978.

Hooker, James R. *Black Revolutionary: George Padmore's Path from Communism to Pan-Africanism.* New York: Frederick A. Praeger, 1967.

Horne, Gerald. *Black and Red: W. E. B. Du Bois and the Afro-American Response to the Cold War, 1944–1963.* Albany: State University of New York Press, 1986.

Hundley, Mary Gibson. *The Dunbar Story.* New York: Vantage Press, 1965.

Hunt, Alfred N. *Haiti's Influence on Antebellum America: Slumbering Volcano in the Caribbean.* Baton Rouge: Louisiana State University Press, 1988.

Hutchinson, Louise Daniel. *Anna J. Cooper: A Voice from the South.* Washington, D.C.: Smithsonian Institution Press, 1981.

Isaacs, Harold R. *The New World of Negro Americans.* New York: Viking, 1964.

———. "Pan Africanism as 'Romantic Racism.'" In *W. E. B. Du Bois: A Profile,* edited by Rayford W. Logan, 210–48. New York: Hill and Wang, 1971.

Jackson, Luther Porter. *Free Negro Labor and Property Holding in Virginia, 1830–1860.* New York and London: D. Appleton–Century Co., 1942; reprint, New York: Atheneum, 1969.

Jackson, Walter A. *Gunnar Myrdal and America's Conscience: Social Engineering and Racial Liberalism, 1938–1987.* Chapel Hill: University of North Carolina Press, 1990.

———. "Melville Herskovits and the Search for Afro-American Culture." In *Malinowski, Rivers, Benedict and Others: Essays in Culture and Personality,* edited by George W. Stocking, Jr., 93–126. Madison: University of Wisconsin Press, 1986.

Jencks, Christopher, and David Riesman. "The American Negro College." *Harvard Educational Review* 37 (1967): 3–60.

Kerman, Cynthia Earl, and Richard Eldridge. *The Lives of Jean Toomer: A Hunger for Wholeness.* Baton Rouge: Louisiana State University Press, 1987.

Killingray, David, and Richard Rathbone, eds. *Africa and the Second World War.* New York: St. Martin's Press, 1986.

King, Kenneth James. *Pan-Africanism and Education: A Study of Race Philanthropy and Education in the Southern States of America and East Africa.* Oxford: Clarendon Press, 1971.

Kirby, John B. *Black Americans in the Roosevelt Era.* Knoxville: University of Tennessee Press, 1980.

Kluger, Richard. *Simple Justice.* New York: Vintage, 1977.

Kneebone, John T. *Southern Liberal Journalists and the Race Issue, 1920–1944.* Chapel Hill: University of North Carolina Press, 1985.

LaGuerre, John Gaffar, Ph.D. *Enemies of Empire.* St. Augustine, Trinidad and Tobago: University of the West Indies, 1984.

Laves, Walter H. C., and Charles A. Thomson. *UNESCO: Purpose, Progress, Prospects.* Bloomington: Indiana University Press, 1957.

Lee, Ulysses. *The Employment of Negro Troops.* United States Army in World War II, Special Studies. Washington, D.C.: Office of the Chief of Military History, United States Army, 1966.

Lewis, David L. *The District of Columbia: A Bicentennial History.* New York: W. W. Norton, 1976.

———. *When Harlem Was in Vogue.* New York: Vintage, 1982.

———. "The Origins and Causes of the Civil Rights Movement." In *The Civil Rights Movement in America,* edited by Charles W. Eagles, 3–18. Jackson: University Press of Mississippi, 1986.

Manning, Kenneth R. *Black Apollo of Science: The Life of Ernest Everett Just.* New York: Oxford University Press, 1983.

Marrus, Michael R. *The Politics of Assimilation: A Study of the French Jewish Community at the Time of the Dreyfuss Affair.* Oxford: Oxford University Press, 1971.

Martin, Charles H. *The Angelo Herndon Case and Southern Justice.* Baton Rouge: Louisiana State University Press, 1976.

Martin, Tony. *Race First: The Ideological and Organizational Struggles of Marcus Garvey and the Universal Negro Improvement Association.* Contributions in Afro-American and African Studies, no. 19. Westport, Conn.: Greenwood Press, 1976.

Matthews, Fred H. *Quest for an American Sociology: Robert E. Park and the Chicago School.* Montreal: McGill-Queens University Press, 1977.

McMillen, Neil R. *Dark Journey: Black Mississippians in the Age of Jim Crow.* Urbana: University of Illinois Press, 1990.

Meier, August M. *Negro Thought in America, 1880–1915: Racial Ideologies in the Age of Booker T. Washington.* Ann Arbor: University of Michigan Press, 1963.

————, and Elliott Rudwick. *Black History and the Historical Profession, 1915– 1980.* Urbana: University of Illinois Press, 1986.

————. *From Plantation to Ghetto.* 3d ed. New York: Hill and Wang, 1976.

Mintz, Steven. "A Historical Ethnography of Black Washington, D.C." *Records of the Columbia Historical Society of Washington, D.C.* 52 (1989): 235–53.

Morris, Joe Alex. *Nelson Rockefeller: A Biography.* New York: Harper & Brothers, 1960.

Moses, Wilson Jeremiah. *The Golden Age of Black Nationalism, 1850–1925.* Hamden, Conn.: Archon Books, 1978.

Naison, Mark. *Communists in Harlem during the Depression.* Urbana: University of Illinois Press, 1983; reprint, New York: Grove Press, 1984.

Platt, Anthony M. *E. Franklin Frazier Reconsidered.* New Brunswick, N.J.: Rutgers University Press, 1991.

Rampersad, Arnold. *The Life of Langston Hughes.* Vol. 1, *1902–1941: I, Too, Sing America.* New York: Oxford University Press, 1986.

————. Notes to *Early Works,* by Richard Wright. New York: Library of America, 1991.

Redding, J. Saunders. *Stranger and Alone.* New York: Harcourt, Brace, 1950; reprint, Boston: Northeastern University Press, 1989.

Rivlin, Benjamin, ed. *Ralph Bunche: The Man and His Times.* New York: Holmes & Meier, 1990.

Robinson, Henry S. "The M Street High School, 1891–1916." *Records of the Columbia Historical Society of Washington, D.C.* 51 (1984): 119–43.

Rose, Phyllis. *Jazz Cleopatra: Josephine Baker and Her Times.* New York: Doubleday, 1989.

Ross, B. Joyce. *J. E. Spingarn and the Rise of the NAACP, 1911–1939.* New York: Atheneum, 1972.

————. "Mary McLeod Bethune and the National Youth Administration: A Case Study of Power Relationships in the Black Cabinet of Franklin D. Roosevelt." In *Black Leaders of the Twentieth Century,* edited by John Hope Franklin and August Meier, 191–219. Urbana: University of Illinois Press, 1982.

Rouse, Jacqueline Anne. *Lugenia Burns Hope: Black Southern Reformer.* Athens: University of Georgia Press, 1989.

[Rowland, Donald W.]. *History of the Office of the Coordinator of Inter-American Affairs.* Washington, D.C.: Government Printing Office, 1947.

Sewell, James P. *UNESCO and World Politics.* Princeton, N.J.: Princeton University Press, 1975.

Singal, Daniel Joseph. *The War Within*. Chapel Hill: University of North Carolina Press, 1982.

Sitkoff, Harvard. *A New Deal for Blacks: The Emergence of Civil Rights as a National Issue*. New York: Oxford University Press, 1978.

Sosna, Morton. *In Search of the Silent South*. New York: Columbia University Press, 1977.

Southern, David W. *Gunnar Myrdal and Black-White Relations*. Baton Rouge: Louisiana State University Press, 1987.

Spitzer, Leo. *Lives in Between: Assimilation and Marginality in Austria, Brazil, West Africa 1780–1945*. London: Cambridge University Press, 1989.

Spring, Leverett Wilson. *A History of Williams College*. Boston: Houghton Mifflin, 1917.

Stanfield, John H. *Philanthropy and Jim Crow in American Social Science*. Contributions in Afro-American and African Studies, no. 82. Westport, Conn.: Greenwood Press, 1985.

Strom, Sharon Hartman. "Florence Luscomb: For Suffrage, Labor and Peace." In *Moving the Mountain: Women Working for Social Change*, edited by Ellen Cantorow, 2–51. Old Westbury, N.Y.: Feminist Press, 1980.

Suggs, Henry Lewis. *P. B. Young, Newspaperman: Race, Politics, and Journalism in the New South, 1910–1962*. Charlottesville: University Press of Virginia.

Taylor, Alrutheus Ambush. *The Negro in the Reconstruction of Virginia*. Washington, D.C.: The Association for the Study of Negro Life and History, 1926.

Torrence, Ridgley. *The Story of John Hope*. New York: Macmillan, 1948; reprint, New York: Arno Press, 1969.

Turner, W. Burghardt, and Joyce Moore Turner, eds. *Richard B. Moore: Caribbean Militant in Harlem, Collected Writings 1920–1972*. Bloomington: Indiana University Press, 1988.

Warner, W. Lloyd, Buford H. Junker, and Walter A. Adams. *Color and Human Nature*. Washington, D.C.: American Council on Education, 1941.

Waskow, Arthur I. *From Race Riot to Sit-In, 1919 and the 1960s: A Study in the Connections between Conflict and Violence*. Garden City, N.Y.: Doubleday, 1967.

Wesley, Charles H. *The History of Alpha Phi Alpha*. 14th printing. Chicago: The Foundation Publishers, 1981.

——, ed. *The Negro in the Americas: Public Lectures of the Division of the Social Sciences of the Graduate School, Howard University*. Washington, D.C.: The Graduate School, Howard University, 1940.

West, Hollie I. "Out of the Shadow of Segregation." *Washington Post*, February 27, 1977, H1ff.

Williamson, Joel. *New People: Miscegenation and Mulattoes in the United States*. New York: The Free Press, 1980; reprint, New York: New York University Press, 1984.

——. *A Rage for Order*. New York: Oxford University Press, 1986.

Winston, Michael R. *History of Howard University Department of History,*

1913–1973. Washington, D.C.: Department of History, Howard University, 1973.

———. "Through the Back Door: Academic Racism and the Negro Scholar in Historical Perspective." *Daedalus* 100 (1971): 678–719.

Wolters, Raymond. *The New Negro on Campus: Black College Rebellions in the 1920s*. Princeton, N.J.: Princeton University Press, 1975.

Woodson, Carter G. *The African Background Outlined, or Handbook for the Study of the Negro*. Washington, D.C.: Association for the Study of Negro Life and History, 1936; reprint, New York: Negro Universities Press, 1968.

Woodward, C. Vann. *Origins of the New South*. 2d ed. Baton Rouge: Louisiana State University Press, 1971.

———. *The Strange Career of Jim Crow*. 3d rev. ed. New York: Oxford University Press, 1974.

Wynes, Charles E. "The Evolution of Jim Crow Laws in Twentieth Century Virginia." *Phylon* 28 (1967): 416–25.

Dissertations and Unpublished Papers

Erb, Claude Curtis. "Nelson Rockefeller and United States–Latin American Relations, 1940–45." Ph.D. diss., Clark University, 1980.

Goggin, Jacqueline Anne. "Carter G. Woodson and the Movement to Promote Black History." Ph.D. diss., University of Rochester, 1983.

Reid, David L. "The Black Man at Williams: From Freak to Afro-American." Unpublished student term paper, 1969. Special Collections, Sawyer Library, Williams College, Williamstown, Mass.

Romero, Patricia W. "Carter G. Woodson: A Biography." Ph.D. diss., Ohio State University, 1971.

INDEX